C000165200

TRESPASSERS FORGIVEN

Charles H. Godden led a long and interesting career in the Colonial Office and HM Diplomatic Service, beginning in 1950 following his military service in the Second World War. During that time he served abroad in Belize (formerly British Honduras) twice. He was also Secretary to a United Nations Mission to the High Commission Territories of Southern Africa, Private Secretary to FCO Ministers of State and held positions in Finland, Jamaica, Haiti and Anguilla, from which territory he retired as Governor in 1984. He was made CBE in 1981.

TRESPASSERS FORGIVEN

Memoirs of Imperial Service in an Age of Independence

C.H. GODDEN

The Radcliffe Press

LONDON • NEW YORK

Published in 2009 by The Radcliffe Press
6 Salem Road, London W2 4BU

Distributed in the United States and Canada Exclusively by
Palgrave Macmillan
175 Fifth Avenue, New York NY 10010

ISBN 978 1 84511 780 1

A full CIP record is available from the Library of Congress

Library of Congress Catalog card: available

Printed and bound in Great Britain by CPI Antony Rowe,
Chippenham
Copy-edited and typeset by Oxford Publishing Services, Oxford

DEDICATED, WITH LOVE, TO THE MEMORY
OF FLORENCE WHO ALSO SERVED;
FOR JAN AND SUE, WHO SHARED THE EXPERIENCE,
AND LAURA AND JAMES – SUCCESSORS

Contents

Illustrations

Sketches

Acronyms and Abbreviations

ADC	aide-de-camp
BHBS	British Honduras Broadcasting Service
CBE	Commander of the Order of the British Empire
CID	Criminal Investigation Department
CMG	Commander of the Order of St Michael and St George
COS	Chief of Staff
CS	chief secretary
CJ	chief justice
EST	Eastern Standard Time
FCO	Foreign and Commonwealth Office
FM	first minister
HMS	Her Majesty's Ship
HQ	headquarters
KCMG	Knight Commander of St Michael and St George
MBE	Member of the Order of the British Empire
MC	Military Cross
MFA	Ministry of Foreign Affiars
MILO	Military Intelligence Liaison Officer
MLG	minister for local government
MV	Master Vessel
NAAFI	Navy, Army & Air Force Institutes (a store for service members
NIP	National Independence Party
OAS	Organization of African States
OBE	Officer of the Order of the British Empire
ODECA	Organización de Estados Centroamericanos/ Organization of Central American States
PUP	People's United Party

PWD	Public Works Department
RAF	Royal Air Force
RAMS	Royal Army Medical Services
RASC	Royal Army Service Corps
RD	Reserve (Officers') Decoration
RNR	Royal Navy Reserve
SJC	St John's College
SS	steamship
TB	tuberculosis
UCWI	University College of the West Indies
USAF	United States Air Force
USS	United States Ship

Acknowledgements

FOR THIS BOOK I owe my inspiration and encouragement to Florence to whom I am eternally indebted. On the many occasions when we reminisced about our days in 'BH' (British Honduras: now Belize) she would urge me to write down some of those experiences for Laura and James so that, some day, they might learn to their surprise that the two old fogies whom they recognized as their maternal grandparents had been around a bit and had led interesting and colourful lives. In due course, with Florence jogging my memory, I produced a first draft.

Subsequently, a family friend, Pat Reading (who with her late husband Don was a contemporary of ours during our service in BH) was good enough to read my efforts and to venture a few constructive comments and advice. In particular, she suggested that since I was in a key position to witness events from the inside, as it were, many of the significant ones that influenced or otherwise affected our lives in the early 1960s (for example Hurricane Hattie, the Guatemalan incursion, and the visit of HRH the Duke of Edinburgh) might be of interest to local and expatriate contemporaries who were not privy to the information available in official circles and on which decisions were taken. Perhaps, too, she added, an even wider and more modern audience might be intrigued by this brief glimpse of a bygone colonial age in and around Central America with its history, personalities and anecdotes. This led to an expanded draft and ultimately to these pages.

Others helped directly or indirectly to shape the historical sections. I therefore take this opportunity to thank the librarians at the Foreign and Commonwealth Office for making available to me the first and second volumes of the *Burdon Archives* and relevant colonial calendars. Similarly, I wish to express my thanks also to the librarian at Sussex University for allowing me access to Peter

Ashdown's impressive and deeply researched Ph.D. on political developments in British Honduras in the late nineteenth century, which added considerably to my knowledge of Governor Goldsworthy (Chapter 9). In particular, I am especially grateful to all the authors, past and present, listed in the Bibliography. Rereading their works served to refresh my memory, remind me of events I had seemingly forgotten or provided fresh insights into the history of the colony and region.

Special thanks are due to my family, Jan, Sue and Alan, not only for their support and encouragement but for facilitating the writing of this book by introducing me to the word processor and then teaching me some of its basic functions. Also to Linda Clingo who carried on the tutelage to a more advanced level and then, hey presto, performed what to me was the conjuring trick of transferring the book's typescript into a slim three-inch square of plastic to meet the requirements of the publisher to whom it was sent. The wonders of the modern world never cease to amaze me and probably many more of my generation.

I also take this opportunity to thank Lester Crook, my commissioning editor, for his advice and encouragement in getting this project started; Liz Friend-Smith and Victoria Nemeth for dealing so efficiently with its various aspects; and my copy-editor Selina Cohen, of Oxford Publishing Services, whose diligence, eagle eye and high standard of professionalism have made an effective contribution to the smooth realization of this project.

Finally I wish to record my thanks to my mentors in the practical field of colonial administration, the late Sir Peter Stallard, KCMG, MBE, and the late Michael Porcher, CMG, OBE, to whom I owe a lasting debt of gratitude.

Extract from Aldous Huxley's *Beyond the Mexique Bay* (1934)

I F THE WORLD had any ends British Honduras would certainly be one of them. It is not on the way from anywhere to anywhere else. It has no strategic value. It is all but uninhabited, and when Prohibition is abolished, the last of its profitable enterprises – the re-export of alcohol by rum runners, who use Belize as their base of operations – will have gone the way of its commerce in logwood, mahogany and chicle. Why then do we bother to keep this strange little fragment of the Empire? Certainly not from motives of self interest. Hardly one Englishman in fifty thousand derives any profits from the Britishness of British Honduras. But *le coeur a ses raisons*. Of these mere force of habit is the strongest. British Honduras goes on being British because it has been British. But this, of course, is not the whole story. We have been educated to personify the country in which we live. A collection of incredibly diverse people living on an island in the North Sea is transformed by a simple conjuring trick into a young woman in classical fancy dress – a young woman with opinions that have to be respected and a will that we must help her to assert; with a virginity which is our duty to defend and a reputation, which we may never allow to be questioned, for strength, virtue, beauty and a more than papal infallibility. To the overwhelming majority of British voters, taken individually, it is probably a matter of indifference whether British Honduras remains within the Empire or without. But the non-existent lady in fancy dress would be mortally offended that the place should be painted anything but red on the map. Red therefore it remains. The evidence of things not seen is too much for us.

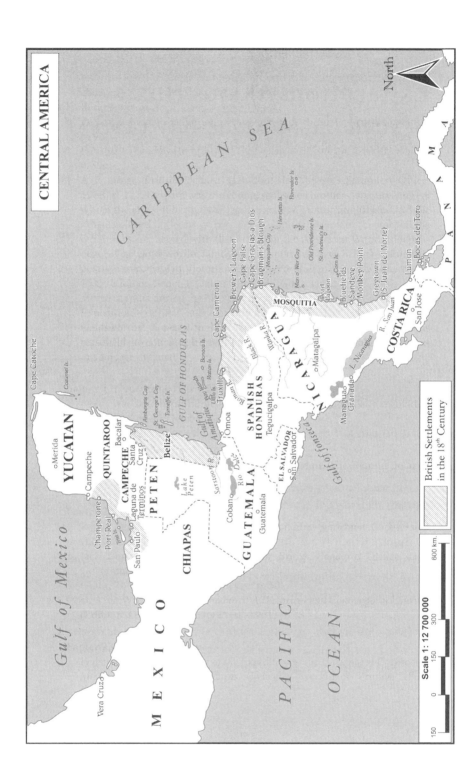

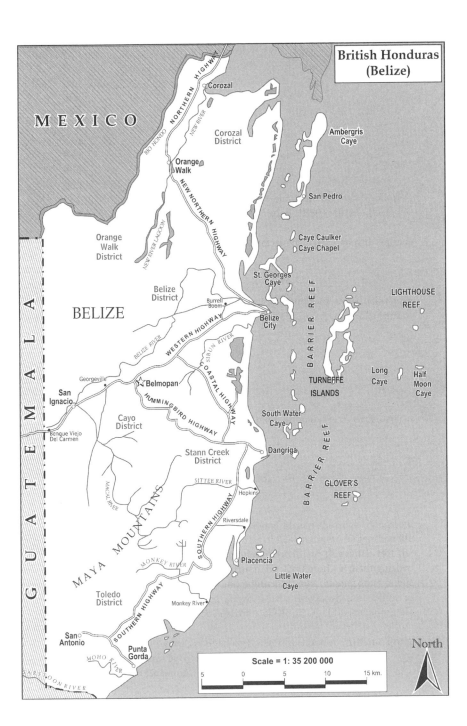

British Honduras (Belize)

MEXICO

GUATEMALA

BELIZE

Corozal
Corozal District
RIO HONDO
NEW RIVER
NORTHERN HIGHWAY
Orange Walk
NEW NORTHERN HIGHWAY
Orange Walk District
NEW RIVER LAGOON

Ambergris Caye

San Pedro

Caye Caulker
Caye Chapel

Belize District
Burrell Boom
St. Georges Caye
Belize City
BARRIER REEF
LIGHTHOUSE REEF

BELIZE RIVER
WESTERN HIGHWAY
SIBUN RIVER
COASTAL HIGHWAY

TURNEFFE ISLANDS
Long Caye
Half Moon Caye

Georgeville
Belmopan
San Ignacio
HUMMINGBIRD HIGHWAY
Cayo District
Benque Viejo Del Carmen
MACAL RIVER

South Water Caye

Dangriga

Stann Creek District
SITTEE RIVER
Hopkins
SOUTHERN HIGHWAY
Riversdale

GLOVER'S REEF
BARRIER REEF

MAYA MOUNTAINS

MONKEY RIVER
Placencia

Toledo District
Monkey River
Little Water Caye

San Antonio
Punta Gorda
MOHO RIVER
SARSTOON RIVER

Scale = 1: 35 200 000
5   0   5   10   15 km.

North

Prologue

WHAT DID YOU do in the colonial theatre, grandpa? This, I hasten to add, is a rhetorical question of general application and not one my own grandchildren have ever addressed to me. That they have not done so is understandable. Whereas the world into which I was born, in the third decade of the twentieth century, was coloured with many symbols and other impressions of imperial glory that induced in me a strong feeling of pride at being a member of the greatest empire the world had ever known (not least of these created by my accumulated stamp collection with its heavy emphasis on colourful stamps of the many and widespread countries of the empire; and 'wireless' programmes or gramophone records heard in my youth featuring the then popular South Australian bass baritone, Peter Dawson, singing in his deep rich voice, patriotic ballads including those of a Kiplingesque nature such as 'Mandalay' or, say, 'Boots') my grandchildren were born at a time when the age of British imperialism had all but disappeared and the word 'colonialism' was likely to arouse angry passions or be shrouded in shame, guilt or apology. Such a question, therefore, was unlikely to occur to them without some form of prompting.

Had they put such a question, how would I have answered? As a strolling player, sometimes performing only bit parts, I would probably have said, 'Not much of any significance' – although I did make a modest contribution, initially in the Colonial Office and British Honduras (now Belize), to which I allude further below. But to put that in perspective and help their understanding of our colonial past and its implications, it is necessary to sketch out an outline of the relationship between Britain and her colonies in the immediate post-1939–45 period, and those who served there, adding a glimpse of early British activity in the Bay of Honduras in the first phase of empire spiced with a few personal philosophical musings on colonialism. The hub of that relationship was the Colonial Office, formally constituted as a separate and independent department of state in 1854, having developed from the Committee for Trade and Foreign Plantations that had, itself, evolved from the Committee of the Privy Council for the Plantations created in 1660 to handle the administration of colonial affairs. And so I begin.

In 1947, having previously occupied the building on the southeast corner of Downing Street, the Colonial Office moved nearby to what was intended to be temporary accommodation in Great Smith Street prior to the construction of a proposed new office building. The secretary of state and his junior ministers, together with the geographical and many other key departments, were located in Church House (leased from the Church commissioners) with the remaining supporting departments housed opposite in Sanctuary Buildings. There was also a small outpost at 15 Victoria Street incorporating the office of the Colonial (later Oversea) Nursing Association responsible for the recruitment of nurses and a section that catered for the welfare needs of colonial students in Britain.

The main office was identified by an inn or pub type of signboard that appeared above the front entrance to Church House. On a Cambridge blue background it displayed a golden crown and the words 'Colonial Office' and, like a pub signboard, it swung in the breeze and wind. The ministerial suites occupied the first floor. As the lift ascended towards the upper floors, the various geographical departments were identifiable by plaques bearing the arms of the colonies whose affairs were dealt with on that particular level. On the sixth floor, some of the offices were formerly the sleeping quarters previously available to visiting clergy, thus providing their current occupants with the added facility of their own private bathroom and lavatory. It was on that floor that the West Indian Department, in which I once served, was situated.

Spluttered around the office were various tangible links with the past of which I cite a few. Foremost, was the portrait gallery along the corridor to the conference room in Church House, irreverently known as the 'Rogues Gallery', with its pictures of secretary of states past and present ranging from the aristocratic first, the Earl of Hillsborough (subsequently Marquess of Downshire) to the last, Fred Lee, a former trade unionist and Labour Party member of

1. Fred Lee, the last secretary of state for the colonies, with his private office staff on the final day, author second from right.

parliament – an interesting contrast reflecting the social and political transformation that had taken place over that time. In the conference room itself was a small white plaster cast bust of Colonel T. E. Lawrence, Lawrence of Arabia, who joined the then newly formed Middle East Division[1] in the early 1920s before slipping off into the lower ranks of the Royal Air Force, ostensibly seeking anonymity by enlisting as 352087 Aircraftman Ross. In the secretary of state's private office was what appeared to be an antique tea trolley: closer examination would have revealed that it was once a depository for files or other documents, the upper and lower trays of which were divided into spaces for papers relating to specific colonies of the day.

One territory named, if memory is to be trusted, was the Swan River colony, funded privately in 1829, which collapsed as an economic venture and was subsequently incorporated into the state of Western Australia. The walls of several offices were adorned with framed prints depicting colonial scenes, and many desks and window sills often displayed native wooden carvings or other mementos brought back by travellers or left by colonial visitors over the years. For those seeking specific detailed history, the well stocked shelves of the Colonial Office Library in Sanctuary Buildings and advice of the knowledgeable librarians who staffed it were always available to them.

When I joined the Colonial Office in 1950, its Secretary of State was responsible to Parliament for the affairs of over fifty colonies, protectorates, protected states and trust territories (ranging alphabetically from Aden to Zanzibar) covering an area of about two million square miles and embracing all continents: their populations estimated to total something in the region of seventy-seven millions.

From this it seemed not unreasonable to assume that the Colonial Office had a shelf-life extending well into the next millennium. The architects' model in the foyer of Church House of the proposed new office building to be erected on the site of the old Westminster Hospital, opposite the Abbey, gave added credence to this. Yet within sixteen years or so the Colonial Office was no more. The once proud colonial empire, on which the sun never set, had all but disappeared save for a few isolated specks of red on the world map representing a handful of small islands of doubtful economic viability or territories whose sovereignty was the subject of international dispute. In a fast changing world the pressure for self-determination by colonial peoples had given rise to a faster pace of decolonization than most pundits had envisaged.

The office in those days was an exciting place in which to work. A constant stream of overseas visitors, many in their country's colourful traditional dress, crossed its threshold to confer with ministers or departmental staff on serious local issues or take part in constitutional or economic conferences. Delegations would often include colonial governors whom, as I recall, were invariably tall with builds like those of modern international rugby forwards. Debates on colonial issues in Parliament were lively, sometimes passionate, and, in general, well informed. Telegraphic correspondence between a department and a colony was sometimes confined to terse, apt biblical quotations or, perhaps, classical allusions.

Thus, a proposal from a governor at odds with Colonial Office policy might draw the simple holding response, 'St Luke 16:26' ('between you and us there is a great gulf fixed'), while a considered reply was being prepared. Or a query about whether a rumour affecting a colony allegedly circulating in London was true might perhaps be answered equally tersely but gracefully by, say, 'Rumour is a lying jade'. One governor seeking advice from the office when he would have been better served by using his initiative about the disposal of certain sensitive documents was simply advised to 'light the blue touch paper and retire immediately'. He probably had an uneasy night's sleep as he dwelt on the last two words of the reply. And so on. To add to a vibrant atmosphere, a parliamentary division bell installed at Church House would suddenly burst into noisy life at unexpected moments for staff, to be followed by the Secretary of State and any supporting ministers in the building rushing headlong downstairs to a waiting car, or cars, that would then screech off to the House of Commons where their occupants would arrive breathless at the division lobbies just in time to vote at their party's call.

There were occasional moments of deep shock, such as for example when news was received of the ambush and assassination by terrorists in October 1951 of the British high commissioner to Malaya, Sir Henry Gurney. Also, there were touches of humour, misplaced or otherwise. One instance of this was when our printing and stationery department, which produced the colony name cards displayed before delegates at conferences (these were narrow folded white cardboard strips on which the name of the colony was stencilled in black), inadvertently transposed two letters in the name of the colony of Montserrat on the card placed before its representative at one of the West Indian conferences. To his chagrin and embarrassment and the amusement of other regional delegates he sat behind a name card proclaiming 'Monsterrat' until the error was rectified. Nowadays such an incident would be leaked to the media, which would blow it up out of all proportion; questions would be raised in Parliament with the Opposition calling for the resignation of the relevant minister and all and sundry would be demanding a public enquiry. But in those days humour was a greater force than political correctness and the media were more restrained and responsible.

Then there was the rare entertaining diversion. For example, in the early 1950s when a very young David Attenborough, then early on in his to be sparkling BBC career, arrived at the office and thereby generated much interest and excitement. He was organizing a visit to one of the colonies to put together a wild-life programme for television and had called on the relevant geographical department for background briefing. Although British television in those days was still in its infancy, the young Attenborough with his infectious enthusiasm for the natural environment was already attracting a cult following. That he was to develop into a national institution in later life was to come as no surprise to those early audiences. But to revert to his visit, work slowed down as many members of the staff, especially the ladies, sought to catch a glimpse of so handsome a celebrity. However, as already intimated, this type of diversion was the unexpected exception rather than the general rule.

The demise of the Colonial Office took place piecemeal. By the early 1960s some of the staff had already been siphoned off to form the new Department of Technical Cooperation, which subsequently blossomed out into the Ministry of Overseas Development (now Department for International Development). But with policy makers closely scrutinizing Britain's changing role in the world, deeper fundamental structural changes affecting staff were now afoot. In 1964, following acceptance by the government of the recommendations of the Plowden Commission's Report on future overseas representation, it was announced that the Colonial and Commonwealth Relations Offices would merge as soon as practicable in the second half of 1965; and that, meanwhile, a new diplomatic service would be created comprising the Foreign and Commonwealth Offices and the Trade Commission Services. In the light of this, a circular was issued to Colonial Office staff outlining two options: apply to be considered for transfer to the new diplomatic service (applications to be considered jointly by the personnel departments of the Foreign and Commonwealth Offices) or seek transfer to other branches of the Home Civil Service. The majority opted for the latter and, until their transfers could be effected, formed, together with their colleagues who had applied for the new diplomatic service, a residual rump of colonial expertise within the expanded Commonwealth Office.

Inevitably, as is the case with most mergers, not everyone was happy. The Commonwealth Office had been openly reluctant to take Colonial Office applicants for the diplomatic service under its wing on the grounds that such staff members were 'tainted' with colonialism and likely to be regarded with suspicion by newly emerged Commonwealth nations that had just shed its yoke. A few eyebrows were raised at this for, ironically, these were the very persons who had been instrumental in facilitating the decolonization processes and had a unique practical, as opposed to academic, understanding of the problems still facing the newly emergent countries. So what price experience? Was there another reason? Cynics at the time concluded that the Commonwealth Office's concern was to keep out such experienced staff in order to maintain its current staff's promotion prospects. But that's now an incidental almost forgotten passing blip on the screen of history.

Over the next year or so most of those in the 'rump' had transferred to posts in other home departments; and when on 17 October 1968 the Commonwealth Office was formally amalgamated with the Foreign Office under one secretary of state, only a handful of the old Colonial Office staff, of whom I was one, was absorbed into the new diplomatic service. Thus, henceforth, the affairs of the remaining colonies would inevitably be dealt with within Whitehall by staff largely inexperienced in such matters. However, this was not too serious a problem for the reality was that the decolonization process had by now been virtually completed. It was rightly anticipated that even after the main remaining colony, Hong Kong, reverted to China in 1997, the long established overall policy (namely that if any of the remaining territories declared their intention to become independent HMG would not stand in their way, but if they wished to maintain the status quo their wish would be respected) would continue to prevail, at least for the foreseeable future, while recognizing that territories whose sovereignty was under dispute internationally (British Honduras, the Falkland Islands and Gibraltar) posed special problems.

So the British Empire that had entered the twentieth century with all the appearance of the proverbial lion went out before the *fin de siècle* like the proverbial lamb. Some felt that Britain had acceded too readily to the postwar clamour for independence. But this took no account of changing world attitudes towards colonialism, or of a country whose resources had been significantly drained by the impact of the Second World War and now had neither the capacity nor the will to maintain and defend those territories in a changing world order. In all this, the prospect of a closer relationship with continental Europe was now overshadowing events. For the traditionalists one remaining loose end remained to be tied up before the end of the century: due recognition of the men and women of the colonial service (since 1954 renamed Her Majesty's Overseas Civil Service) who had devoted their lives to the economic, social and political development of the people living in the countries in which they served.

On Tuesday 25 May 1999, a service of commemoration and thanksgiving was held in Westminster Abbey, in the presence of Her Majesty the Queen and His Royal Highness the Prince Philip, Duke of Edinburgh, to mark the end of Her Majesty's Overseas Civil Service, the Centenary of the Corona Club and the Golden Jubilee of Corona Worldwide.

In his opening prayer, 'The Bidding', the scene was set by the Very Reverend Dr Wesley Carr, Dean of Westminster, with these words:

> For one hundred and sixty years, from before the beginning of the reign of Queen Victoria, through the height of Empire, to the era of today's Commonwealth, Her Majesty's Overseas Civil Service worked for the Crown and the colonies. Its duties concluded when Hong Kong was handed back to China.
>
> Today we gather at the heart of the nation, in Westminster Abbey where the permanent memorial to their service stands to recognize thousands of devoted people: those who managed this, the oldest of Britain's overseas civil services; those who worked in times of extraordinary change to sustain its tradition of loyalty to the crown and integrity in dealing with local governments; and the two clubs which were associated with members of the service – the Corona Club and Corona Worldwide.

We mark two endings: Her Majesty's Overseas Civil Service and the Corona Club.

Their commitments discharged, their memory remains in many hearts; we thank God for work well done; for duties borne bravely; and for friendships made and kept through the years.

When you have carried out all of your orders, you should say, We are servants and deserve no credit; we have only done our duty.

It was perhaps fitting that one of the hymns sung that day was Rudyard Kipling's enigmatic religious poem, 'Recessional', which the author, some years later in a letter to a cousin, attributed to his Wesleyan heritage. As he put it, 'Three generations of Wesleyan ministers … lie behind me … the pulpit streak will come out.'[2] Angus Wilson is sceptical of this claim in his biography of Kipling when he sets it against the latter's lifelong agnosticism and little apparent interest in his ancestry; but, in recognizing that his 'preaching streak' was undoubtedly present in both his mind and writing, accepts there was a superficial inheritance from his Wesleyan grandparents in terms of the work ethic, a hatred of frivolity, earnestness in life's purpose and a readiness to use the language of the Bible.[3] All this, however, was secondary to the interpretation of the poem, for its words were to have a significant impact in the country, either reflecting or influencing the attitude of some of the nation's 'movers and shakers'. For, beneath the cladding of biblical language, Kipling was undoubtedly warning the public against a tendency towards arrogance in respect of the empire and reminding it of the unpalatable fact that empires decline and fall as well as rise.

This poem, perhaps the most famous of his poetical works, was written in 1897 in the heyday of the empire to coincide with the celebrations to mark Queen Victoria's Diamond Jubilee on 22 June of that year. It was seen by some as a clear and sharp corrective to the imperial euphoria that had gripped the nation at the time. Wilson argues that part of it reflected a late Victorian climate that stressed the need for humility, awe, simplicity and decorum in those charged with governing the empire.[4] It also seemed to prophesy, or at least

envisage, its end. These sentiments colour the five oft quoted verses.
Remember how they go?

> God of our fathers, known of old,
> Lord of our far-flung battle-line,
> Beneath whose awful Hand we hold
> Dominion over palm and pine –
> Lord God of Hosts, be with us yet,
> Lest we forget – lest we forget!
>
> The tumult and the shouting dies –
> The captains and the kings depart –
> Still stands Thine ancient Sacrifice,
> An humble and a contrite heart.
> Lord God of Hosts, be with us yet,
> Lest we forget – lest we forget!
>
> Far called our navies melt away –
> On dune and headland sinks the fire –
> Lo, all our pomp of yesterday
> Is one with Nineveh, and Tyre!
> Judge of the Nations, spare us yet,
> Lest we forget – lest we forget!
>
> If, drunk with the sight of power, we loose
> Wild tongues that have not Thee in awe –
> Such boastings as the Gentiles use,
> Or lesser breeds without the Law.
> Lord God of Hosts, be with us yet,
> Lest we forget – lest we forget!
>
> For heathen heart that puts her trust
> In reeking tube and iron shard,
> All valiant dust that builds on dust,
> And guarding, calls not Thee to guard,
> For frantic boast and foolish word –
> Thy mercy on Thy people, Lord!

These words and thoughts were echoed and interpreted elsewhere. Kipling was persuaded to send a copy of the poem to *The Times*, which, on 17 July 1897, printed it with the comment that 'the most dangerous and demoralizing temper' into which the nation could fall was that of boastful pride in the empire.[5] *The Graphic* followed in similar vein, maintaining that the lesson the public should draw from the celebrations was that behind the rhetoric of empire was not only a sense of greatness but also of responsibility.[6] This reflected a significant movement that had been developing steadily throughout the Victorian period (initially inspired by a missionary zeal to propagate Christianity among perceived 'heathens' and subject them to Anglicized civilization, perhaps flowing from the anti-slavery campaign begun in the late eighteenth century): that of acceptance of a growing moral responsibility towards colonial peoples. However, in practice, it has to be admitted that morality unfortunately was to take a back seat to greed and power as British involvement in the European 'scramble for Africa', taking place around that time, began to have effect.

Despite this seeming ambivalence, the intellectual mood towards empire was undoubtedly changing. The jingoism that had greeted the start of the Boer War was to give way to moral revulsion at some of the methods used to bring about victory – for example, the setting up of concentration camps in which, as a result of poor conditions and mismanagement, more than 20,000 inmates (mostly children) died of disease or malnutrition. The country was anxious to restore its liberal image and old fashioned imperialism was in decline. 'Moral responsibility' was now on the agenda although implementation was inevitably slow.

This responsibility was to colour Colonial Office policy as the twentieth century advanced, resulting in the active stimulation of economic and social development in the colonies through, for example, various colonial development acts starting in 1929 with the creation of the Colonial Development Fund. Admittedly, it was not only enacted at a time of serious unemployment in Britain, but it was also tied to British trade and was no doubt conceived of as a means of helping to alleviate unemployment at home rather than general colonial development as such. None the less, it was to establish the

principle of grants for development, which then led to the introduction and operation of the Colonial Development and Welfare Acts
from 1940 onwards. Coupled with this was the guiding of colonial
territories towards responsible and representative self-government to
ensure that people had a better standard of living and freedom from
oppression. These enlightened policies also influenced the attitude of
those serving on the ground in the final phase of British colonialism:
there emerged a newer class of conscientious, talented and humani-
tarian administrators whose task it was to implement them. This
they carried out faithfully and effectively as history recognizes.

John Smith (chairman of the Corona Club) developed this theme
obliquely by reading an extract from Sir Gawain Bell's book, *An
Imperial Twilight*, which mused on the history of empire and how
policy adapted to modern needs:

> The history of the British Empire can be likened to a great
> tapestry. Its panels show an accumulation of hues and
> colours, of shapes and designs, of individuals and incidents,
> some sombre in tone, some vivid, there is struggle and
> success, achievement and disappointment, and sometimes
> failure. And throughout the broad extent of the canvas there
> remains a single and unbroken thread. It is a thread that has
> marked the latter stages of empire as it runs towards its final
> patterns. It is the thread that represents social and economic
> improvement, it is the thread of education and enlightenment
> and it leads to national consciousness and to the conclusion
> of the work. Here in the last panel of all there is portrayed the
> ceremonial lowering of the Union flag and its replacement by
> bright newly designed standards symbolic of unity, of
> freedom, of prosperity.[7]

Could there be a more fitting tribute to those responsible in the
postwar years for bringing about this comparatively speedy
transition from colony to full self determination, imperfect though it
may have been or seemed at times?

At the end of the service while those present were waiting to
depart for various receptions, a distinguished senior civil servant

sitting with his wife behind Florence and me, John Stackpoole, who was a contemporary in the Colonial Office, asked if I had noticed a significant omission in all the various tributes paid. 'You mean the lack of any mention of the Colonial Office?' I responded. 'Exactly,' he said. We agreed it was a pity that there was not even a nod in its direction. For, although those administering the territories on the ground were in the vanguard of the economic and social improvement of the indigenous populations, and in later years working themselves out of a job by introducing and implementing localization policies (that is to say, replacing expatriate officers with local equivalents in preparation for independence) the decolonization policies and timetables they were following were laid down by the Colonial Office whose equally dedicated staff (who, too, were working themselves out of a job although, unlike most of their colonial service counterparts, were invariably found alternative posts within the home civil service framework) had the delicate task of devising formulae that would allow government and opposition parties in the various colonies to accept the constitutional changes that were a necessary prerequisite to political independence. And it was, of course, the Colonial Office that introduced in October 1954 the transition from 'Colonial Service', a title that had been in use since at least the reign of William IV, to 'Her Majesty's Overseas Civil Service' and for the attendant provisions that would provide a measure of security for its members as their services increasingly came outside the old responsibilities of the Colonial Office.

Although too much should not be made of this omission, it does provide a convenient peg on which to hang a brief explanation of the structural hierarchy under which the colonies were administered. The Colonial Office and colonial service were two disparate strands of the whole colonial fabric. Sir Charles Jeffries (deputy under secretary when I joined the Colonial Office) described the former as 'nothing more or less than the Secretariat of the Secretary of State – the tool with which he does his work'. The colonial service, on the other hand, was the instrument responsible for administering the colonies on the ground. Colonial Office staff were members of the home civil service while those of the colonial service were in the employ of one or other of the various colonial governments.

Methods of recruitment and terms and conditions of employment were, therefore, different with the result that many colonial service officers in later years, as career prospects dwindled, felt that although swearing allegiance to the same sovereign, heirs and successors they were treated less favourably than their home service counterparts.

But could the creation of a fully integrated joint home and overseas service have worked? It would have required officers serving in the field in all the various disciplines to be subject to central control. Apart from other considerations, given a natural empathy towards those within their local jurisdiction, their probable inclination would have been to follow a different agenda to that decreed by Whitehall. Such a situation would inevitably have given rise to a conflict of interests, particularly if financial considerations involving United Kingdom subventions to the local economy and development were involved. From HMG's point of view it was important to retain control in such matters for, in the process of discharging its responsibility to Parliament, it follows that any payments to the local piper would require HM Treasury to call the tune.

This is not to say, however, that no thought was ever given to the prospect of creating a merged service. In the early 1950s, when career prospects in the colonial service were dwindling, coupled with drooping morale as the general movement towards decolonization gathered pace, together with the drying up of new candidates for recruitment, consideration was given in Whitehall to the possibility of amalgamating the administrative staffs of the Colonial Office and colonial service into one fused service. In the event, practical and financial obstacles proved insuperable; and the scheme that had been drawn up for what was provisionally described as a 'British Overseas Service', was finally dropped. None the less, the career insecurity and recruitment problems of the colonial service continued to be addressed, resulting in 1954 in the creation of Her Majesty's Oversea Civil Service, referred to above, which went some way towards their alleviation.[8]

Given that the occasion in Westminster Abbey was primarily to mark the end of Her Majesty's Overseas Civil Service (colonial service) the omission of any reference to the Colonial Office was, therefore, understandable, except in one important connection. The service was also to mark the centenary and ending of the Corona Club, the official link between the two services. Founded by the arch imperialist, Joseph Chamberlain – one of the leading advocates of that late Victorian dream (or delusion) in some quarters, an imperial federation and longest ever serving secretary of state for the colonies – it was open to anyone connected with colonial administration. A meeting ground for the staff of the Colonial Office, colonial service and Crown Agents for the Colonies and marked until later years by an annual dinner (a function described in the original constitution as a 'smoking conversazione') with the Secretary of State for the Colonies presiding. On these grounds alone a nod in the direction of the Colonial Office would not have come amiss. However, in highlighting the omission we were simply making an observation, not voicing a criticism.

Through my parent office I gained the opportunity to work as part of the overseas team during the period 1961–64, thus acquiring practical experience on the ground in the colonial theatre that was to become invaluable to me in my later career. In the 1950s it was recognized that certain grant-aided territories, namely colonies that could not meet their minimum needs from their own resources and had the deficit between revenue and expenditure met by HMG, should, wherever practicable, be given additional administrative assistance at outside expense through the secondment of Colonial Office personnel. British Honduras, Britain's only colony in Central America, which HM Treasury had been supporting financially since a devastating hurricane in 1931, was a case in point, for in addition to his normal responsibilities, its governor was required to deal with problems and other complications arising out of a territorial dispute with Guatemala in which the latter claimed sovereignty. So, in the later years of that decade, Ken Osborne was seconded to the colony to assist him. When his tour ended, I succeeded him. This, I may add, was not a one-sided interchange for the experience gained could often be utilized by the office when we returned.

Reference to British Honduras, a country about twice the size of Jamaica and roughly the equivalent of Wales, as being part of Central America invites a more precise definition of its geographical location. Bounded on the east by the Bay of Honduras in the Caribbean Sea, on the south by Guatemala, on the west mainly by Guatemala and partly by Mexico, and on the north by Mexico, it is in effect an English-speaking enclave in the midst of surrounding Spanish-speaking republics.

✿ ✿ ✿

It is against this general background that I have amused myself in retirement by recounting, in the anecdotes and reminiscences that follow, a few of my experiences in that territory in the hope that they may at some stage be of interest to my grandchildren should they ever pose the question with which this Prologue opened. In so doing, I have had recourse to some notes I retained, particularly in connection with some dispatches I initially drafted, but have relied mainly on memory – not perhaps the most reliable of sources drawn upon by some one now of an age where, for example, the purpose of entering a particular room is sometimes forgotten. In defence, however, these stories relate to incidents or events that are stamped on my mind, even though I recognize that in reciting them some of the detail may understandably have become distorted through selective memory, exaggerated or perhaps faded over the years. Interwoven with the situations and anecdotes are the occasional glimpses of earlier history to remind them, my grandchildren, and possibly others who may be interested in what I have recorded, of a now almost forgotten British presence in lesser known parts of the Spanish Main (defined here as the Caribbean Sea) and Central America.

At this point I should perhaps say a few words about terminology relating to semantics and political correctness. By the early 1950s the word 'colony' was beginning to carry a somewhat odious connotation for some people and it was common practice to substitute it with the words 'overseas territory'. Be that as it may, the latter is a vague expression with no specific meaning whereas the former makes it clear that the country concerned is a dependency of a parent state. I have, therefore, in subsequent chapters, stuck to the word 'colony' simply to emphasize this point and not to provoke the reader.

Furthermore, in my time in British Honduras, some people in the colony referred to it as 'Belize', one of the names given to the early settlement and, as it so happened, the country's post-independence name – though the change in nomenclature actually took place earlier, in 1973. That said, its recognized name during my second-ment there (since 1840, in fact) was British Honduras and Belize was the name of its capital city, so that is how I have generally referred to them during the colonial period. Also, the stories I tell and any historical references relate to events prior to the territory's attain-ment of political independence in September 1981. One other point needs to be made. As would be expected, some of the names in the following anecdotes have been changed to avoid possible personal embarrassment to any person or persons concerned.

In choosing a title for this collection of tales I was tempted, as a fan of Gilbert and Sullivan operas, to draw on Nanky Poo's popular rendering in *The Mikado*, of 'A Wandering Minstrel I', by adopting the words of the next line, 'A Thing of Shreds and Patches', for it would suggest a pot-pourri of personal tales relating mainly to my own experiences and observations. However, it was a temptation to be resisted because that was only part of what I had in mind. Underlying my autobiographical cum roving reporter attempt to cast a fleeting personal glimpse on administrative and social life in a narrow section of the colonial service in the early 1960s (supple-mented by three later visits) in a small and unfashionable colony moving steadily towards political independence, lies a broader theme – the unusual and fascinating history of British Honduras. This is a little known tale and not without significance in the context of British involvement in Central America over the past few centuries. I have attempted to draw these two themes together and, to some extent, they are complementary – a subjective snapshot in time, if you like, as viewed through expatriate eyes and put in a wider historical context. Consequently, it seemed to me that a more relevant title was appropriate, one relating to the story of the country in its many forms from inception to independence within the imperial framework. In short, I needed a title that focused largely on the song, as it were, rather than the singer. But what should it be?

In thinking about this I remembered three messages on roadside properties, variations on a theme, I once spotted in a single day on a journey between Belize and Corozal on the northern road leading to southern Mexico. The first, scrawled with black paint on rough boarding behind a wire fence at about mile sixteen, proclaimed that, 'TRESPASSERS WILL BE PERSECUTED'. Inside a larger property about ten miles further on was an even more belligerent message painted in white letters on what appeared to be an old school blackboard, namely, 'TRESPASSERS WILL BE SHOT'. Finally, just as I was entering Corozal, I saw outside a small church a poster declaring that, 'TRESPASSERS WILL BE FORGIVEN'. Its New Testament message came as a ray of sunshine after the harsh impressions of the other two. And, in musing upon it, I drew a parallel with British involvement in the colony in particular and the region, or even the world, in general. If, as the *Concise Oxford Dictionary* claims, 'trespass' is 'the unlawful or unwarrantable intrusion of another's lands, possessions or other rights', then the words 'colonialism' and 'trespass' are to some extent synonymous.

By this definition, Britain had trespassed in many countries in and near the Spanish Main and worldwide for centuries, so let us not beat about the bush. The driving force was not missionary zeal but an expansionist quest for commercial or strategic advantage. Britain was not alone in this. Other European maritime powers also actively carved up the world in their acquisition of empire; new factors stimulated the expansion of their commercial and political influence outside Europe with attendant consequences for themselves and the people of the areas in which they operated.

It could be said that this emergent geopolitical order, to which the terms 'colonialism' and 'imperialism' are often applied, was initially attributable to accident rather than design. But, once the maritime enterprises of the medieval period had opened up the world it was an accident waiting to happen. The great voyages of discovery accessed new minerals, raw materials and agricultural products. They also increased opportunities to trade and market the products of the industrial revolution, and provided new lands on which to settle surplus populations. In the light of these perceived advantages, global self-interest in a setting in which the principal European maritime nations vied with each other for supremacy soon governed colonialism and empire building. As this situation developed, the British (initially the English), who began to 'bleed' the Spanish empire by robbing its treasure ships rather than creating their own, gradually emerged as the supreme colonial power and, in so doing, introduced their own special stamp on the world with a resounding impact that still lingers today in various forms, some of which are touched on below.

In short, this was an age of expansionism and, consequently, various degrees of exploitation. Thus, many people in the previously 'undiscovered' world undoubtedly suffered from displacement, imported alien diseases, forced labour or other forms of coercion or exploitation – to say nothing of cultural shock. Yet, it should be recognized that oppression takes many forms and that human abuse was not confined to the colonial theatre. For most people in the world at that time life was, as Hobbes put it, 'nasty, brutish and short'. Even in the 'enlightened' twentieth century, including the post-colonial age, barbarism, wars, terrorism, racism, human exploitation and suffering in all forms and guises were, and still are, very much in evidence. This is neither to condone colonialism and its various unwelcome legacies, such as the lingering impact of slavery on its descendants, the creation of ethnic tension, and the conflicts resulting from the arbitrary delineation of artificial territorial boundaries, nor to make excuses. It is simply to underline the point that, when reviewing events with the advantage of hindsight, it is important to recognize the need to weigh emotion against an understanding of what has gone on in the world at a particular stage in its history.

However, such understanding is not always forthcoming. Although there was no shortage of critics in the twentieth century lining up to condemn British colonialism and to impugn its motives, however justified some of these criticisms undoubtedly were, there were, alas, too few champions coming forward to present the other side of that picture. There is another more positive story to tell about moral responsibility. As far as one can generalize in colonial matters, the British authorities (thanks largely to the world policing activities of the Royal Navy) brought order and stability to many areas like the Spanish Main that had previously been the haunt of buccaneers – many of whom were admittedly British – and, with it, economic and social development. And, as the empire became established, this pattern of progress was replicated in other colonial regions. British funds paid for schools, hospitals, roads and harbours and, especially in later years, attempts were made to develop local natural resources to improve living standards or combat poverty. Local involvement in government was gradually introduced.

As a result, many British traditions pertaining to law and order, social justice, political tolerance and parliamentary democracy continue to be practised in several former colonies. Indeed, the introduction and maintenance of a dispassionate legal system added a particular moral dimension to British rule, especially where the indigenous population recognized that the system protected them from local despots who would otherwise prey upon them. Also, with English now the universal language, they have been given a head start in the sphere of communications. So the ledger is not all in debit. Taking the cue from the extract from Sir Gawain Bell's book recorded above it seems fair to say that there are solid entries on the credit side too. For this reason, I venture to suggest that although the British undoubtedly trespassed in pursuit of empire, their presence was not entirely devoid of positive aspects from which some inheritors of their colonial legacy have benefited. And, in their own and others' interests, they did have the grace and wisdom to leave without fuss when local self-determination demanded it. Moreover, while accepting the inevitability and desirability of independence, British colonial rule has not always been replaced by a more enlightened system of administration – witness, for example, events in Zimbabwe in recent years under the administration of President Mugabe.

This prompts a radical thought. Since it is becoming fashionable for nations to apologize publicly for their ancient wrongs and thereby indirectly seek forgiveness, it occurs to me that it would be a pleasing contrast if some of those who had been trespassed against in the colonial context could express their forgiveness, thus putting the focus on the future instead of a past that can never be recovered. The world has before it the example of that noble South African statesman, Nelson Mandela, who not only forgave those who had trespassed against him and his people but also did something practical about it when he assumed presidential power through the establishment of the Truth and Reconciliation Commission. This sort of response has the virtue of drawing a line under what is now a phase of history from which lessons have been learnt and for which the current generation, which has long since made a psychological break with the imperial past, cannot be held responsible. Of course, given the prevalence of an understandably negative attitude towards colonialism, there is virtually no chance of this happening, so it is undoubtedly a pipe dream. But before dismissing the notion out of hand as quaintly chimerical, it is worth considering, in isolation, how British Honduras fits into such a seeming fantasy.

As hinted at already, generalizations about colonialism need to be treated with caution for, in the acquisition of the British Empire, the history of each particular territory tended to vary widely to take account of different times and circumstances. The origins and development of British Honduras underline this fact and, in a colonial context, it might be described as *sui generis* or, as we are more likely to say nowadays, a 'one off'.

Basically, in the seventeenth century a small group of British pirates turned log cutters settled around what is now known as the Belize River in the Bay of Honduras to pursue their newly adopted lucrative calling in what apparently was an unoccupied region claimed but not possessed by Spain. Until the early years of the nineteenth century they were subject to military and other attacks from the Spanish who tried hard to dislodge them from the settlement. Over the years their numbers grew and the acquisition of African slaves, with whom many of them intermingled to create an early socially accepted hybrid class of citizens (Creoles), saw the size of the settlement increase to several hundreds. These numbers were further supplemented in subsequent years by the arrival of compatriots and their slaves evacuated from the Mosquito Shore of Nicaragua in 1786; a number of Caribs from St Vincent in the Windward Islands; the absorption of Maya Indians as local frontiers were pushed back further and an influx of Mexican Spaniards fleeing from Yucatán Indians in the so-called Caste War around the mid-nineteenth century. Thus, a multiracial society grew and developed.

The dominant input and culture, however, remained British, which is how the early settlers and their descendants saw themselves, although the accent was on the English connection with its pride in political liberties despite an infusion of nationalities from its Celtic neighbours. The late Dr Roy Porter has observed in this context that even 'non-English Britons had little compunction about calling themselves English when it suited'.[9] Accordingly, like most of their colonizing compatriots at the time who invariably set up new England's wherever they settled, the Belize settlement saw itself as an extension of the home country. So, long before Rupert Brooke immortalized the thought and words, here again was yet another 'corner of a foreign field that is forever England'.

Yet, despite numerous petitions to London in the face of Spanish attempts to drive them from the area, Britain was not disposed at that time to accede to requests for colonial status. It was, however, finally and reluctantly ceded in 1862 and upgraded to crown colony status nine years later. Thereafter, a multiracial population generally regarded itself as British. But this was to wane over the years once political parties committed to self-determination were created; their policies then had to take account of growing Hispanic and Amerindian influences in pursuit of that objective. This resulted in its political leaders maintaining in the second half of the twentieth century that the time had come to dispense completely with outside hands, however loosely applied, on the reins of local government. Such a contention was consistent with the mood of the times although international complications slowed down the actual decolonization processes. Once the longstanding territorial dispute with Guatemala had been resolved, full political independence was finally achieved in 1981.

Another aspect of this outline of history, as seen primarily from the 'white' settlers' angle, was expounded in the approaching twilight years of empire by the late Professor A. F. Newton in his intro- duction to the first volume of the *Archives of British Honduras*:

> The story of British Honduras is certainly to be classed among
> the lesser chapters in the development of the Empire, for the
> numbers of those engaged were always small and their adven-

tures were little known even to their contemporaries. But it
has many points of interest and in some ways it is of significance. Among British colonies with the exception of Newfoundland, Belize has seen a collection of Englishmen[10]
managing to survive in spite of the attacks of their enemies
and the neglect of the authorities at home until they could
receive recognition, receive settled government and be
provided with proper organization as a firmly established
British colony. The struggle for existence lasted for nearly one
hundred and fifty years and it was not until the last quarter of
the eighteenth century that the colony was launched upon an
unthreatened life whereas its inhabitants could put forward
their energies without the fear that that they might be
sacrificed to imperial interests elsewhere.[11]

The stoism, courage, resilience and determination of the early settlers, embodied in 'the spirit of the bulldog breed' as perceived in
British folklore, was never in question. It was to find echoes in subsequent British history, especially in the epic Antarctic expeditions
of Scott and Shackleton; the trenches on the Western Front during
the First World War; and Dunkirk and the towns and cities in Britain during the Second World War to cite just a few examples
plucked at random. But, in his criticism of the home government,
Professor Newton seems to have taken insufficient account of the
diplomatic nuances involved in dealing with the problem of sovereignty in the area and other international complications arising from
it. Also, it is reasonable to assume that British foreign policy at the
time related to a commitment to trade rather than colonization *per se*
unless the two coincided. Furthermore, it should not be overlooked
that practical help and protection was invariably given in times of need
in those early years even before colonial status was achieved.

In reality, any theoretical trespass into Spanish land rights by the
early British settlers became academic once Spanish sovereignty in
the region was relinquished in the early years of the nineteenth
century. In fact, there is no evidence to suggest that indigenous
Amerindian interests were ever deliberately violated. But what do we
know about the administering colonial power, Britain, once colonial

status had been granted? Was there, to draw on the above definition of trespass, any 'unwarrantable' intrusion into local affairs?

Obviously, with responsibility for defence, external affairs, internal security and overall good government under the colonial system there would have to be some involvement that might be construed locally as intrusion, especially given the independent nature of the settlers/colonists and their determination to govern themselves. In that respect it could be said that Britain, as the administrating power, was trespassing in local affairs. Whether such intrusion could be called 'unwarrantable' depends on a point of view that is likely to be subjective. Even as far back as 1786, when the unfortunate Colonel Despard arrived as the first formal superintendent in response to the settlers' plea for a British government representative to assist and speak on their behalf, they turned against him and reacted strongly when he followed HMG's policies, which they maintained ran counter to their interests (see Chapter 9). Many entries in Burdon's *Archives* suggest that this pattern continued in the run-up to colonial status and thereafter. This applied especially to the period from 1892 to 1932 when, having created a remarkable political situation that was to give non-officials a majority in the Legislative Council and thus control of the key areas of finance and legislation, they were to all intents and purposes virtually self-governing (see also Chapter 9). From my reading of the history of the country, both as a settlement and a colony, its inhabitants were only too keen to accept the security and other advantages of colonial recognition but less enthusiastic about accepting its obligations and restrictions.

If a charge of trespass were to be levelled against Britain's colonial stewardship, what would be the case for forgiveness? Here it is important to recognize that the drive for colonial status in British Honduras came from within and was not imposed by a colonial power seeking to expand its empire. As already mentioned, this was indeed a status that was ceded most reluctantly. Although it was not granted until 1862, one none the less has to admit that the value of the logwood and subsequent mahogany trade ensured assistance from Britain when the early settlers were resisting Spanish attempts to dislodge them from their holdings. One also needs to say that without Britain's diplomatic, naval and military role over the years in protecting their claim to the lands they had acquired, their descendants and those of the many others who followed would by now have been absorbed as citizens into the republics of either Guatemala or Mexico instead of emerging as people of an independent multiracial nation within the Commonwealth.

Above all, let it be remembered that Britain's generous and I believe unprecedented gesture in retaining a temporary garrison of troops in the country after independence to safeguard its newly acquired sovereignty meant that such status could finally be achieved in 1981. If we add to this the economic aid given after the 1931 hurricane and budgetary and development aid in the postwar years (not least the rehabilitation funds made available after the 1956 and 1961 hurricanes), coupled with a timely recognition over the same period that political and constitutional reforms reflected prevailing attitudes towards self-determination, then the case for forgiveness is formidable. The various expressions of gratitude for the helpful role the mother country had played in the transition from colony to politically independent state I heard articulated at the 1981 independence celebrations (see Chapter 29), leads me to conclude that, at least in the emergent country of Belize, this has been tacitly recognized – hence the significance of the title chosen for these tales, 'Trespassers Forgiven'.

In conclusion, I am bound to add that, for my insignificant part, I feel privileged to have served in the Colonial Office during the post 1939–45 period, and also to have been associated with many colonial service officers in the field in several colonies whose idealism and devotion to duty in the interests of their 'flock' shone like a beacon in a world becoming more and more selfishly preoccupied with material possessions and rights rather than responsibilities. Also, in particular, with my local colleagues in the British Honduras civil service who, as localization policies gathered pace in pursuit of the goal of independence, not only grasped the baton of service passed on by earlier and current local and expatriate colleagues but carried it onwards smoothly and efficiently as they advanced towards the finishing line that would finally mark the end of colonial status.

This, then, is the background from which I emerge to recount for my grandchildren a few personal anecdotes of British involvement in British Honduras mainly in the early 1960s, but not exclusively so; and, in so doing , to superimpose them upon an outline of some of its coetaneous and earlier history. Significantly, it is part of a wider history now, alas, fast slipping almost furtively into the mists of time. But then it has to be recognized that our imperial past no longer inspires newer generations born into a multiracial and cultural Britain, many of whom are the children or grandchildren of former colonial subjects who have their own perception of what that past means to them. None the less, it is a history that deserves telling if only to remind such generations that the acquisition of empire took many forms and was more complex than many may have realized. And, in so doing, to introduce them, however indirectly, to aspects of the fascinating story of one of Britain's earliest, albeit less fashionable, colonial possessions, British Honduras, or Belize as it was once sometimes and now again called, set in the context of a wider British imperial presence in the area.

Chapter 1
En Route

STORED IN THE memory bank of my mind are a number of dates relating to personal experiences or family events that, when recalled, evoke vivid memories. One such date is Tuesday 11 April 1961, the day on which Florence and I and our younger daughter Susan (Janet was to join us a few months later after the end of the summer school term) set off for British Honduras, in those days a small, unfashionable and remote colony in Central America. Although parochial and limited in facilities, it was rich in human and practical situations that were to dispel any thoughts of boredom. Thus began three years of experience that were to colour our lives thereafter.

The day of our departure dawned grey and overcast with a hint of rain in the air. We had passages on board the SS *Camito* sailing from Southampton in the late afternoon; and, with the weather as it was, the prospect of a sea voyage to the then British West Indian island colonies of Barbados, Trinidad and Jamaica *en route* to our destination – never an unattractive one in my book – beckoned more strongly than ever.

Here I should explain that by the late 1950s the hitherto usual practice of colonial service officers travelling by sea on first appointment and to and from leave had generally become a thing of the past. The reasons for this reflected both a technical evolution in the way of travel and a fast changing global scene. As the world put the 1939–45 war behind it, the pace of life quickened and this, coupled with great advances in aviation techniques and marketing, meant that leisurely sea travel was fast giving way to the aeroplane. Furthermore, as constitutional advance on the road to independence gathered momentum in the remaining colonial territories, the services of expatriate specialist staff tended to become more and more urgently needed. Often they were required locally within days rather than weeks. Only air travel could meet this need. None the less, sea travel was still possible on a few routes in certain circumstances while some vestige of empire remained.

As current generations generally are unfamiliar with sea travel, except in the context of ferry crossings or cruise ship holidays, it might help understanding if I were to touch briefly on the significance of such travel in the colonial period – a significance that carries resonance of the empire in Victorian and Edwardian times and during the subsequent reign of King George V.

In those halcyon days the voyage 'out and home' was part of colonial folklore. This applied particularly to the Orient route and more specifically to India. For the new colonial appointee, soldier, missionary or businessman it was an opportunity to get acclimatized gradually; and, indirectly, to become exposed in a practical way to the extent of Britain's presence and influence in the world as the vessel (probably belonging to the P&O line) called at or passed by such outposts as, say, Gibraltar, Malta, Port Said and Aden on the eastern route thus enabling them to absorb the sights, sounds and smells of a mighty empire and maybe reflect on its power. For the older hand it offered a chance to relax in style after a long stint of duty or prepare mentally, after home leave, for yet another tour. The best and most comfortable berths for the hundred or so miles of the Suez Canal where the sun beat down mercilessly on liners travelling at the snails' pace regulation speed imposed by the canal authorities before facing the equally sweltering temperatures of the Red Sea, were the outer cabins on the port side and the reverse on the return leg. These were also the most expensive and occupied by senior colonial and military officers or rich civilians. Not surprisingly, therefore, 'port out, starboard home' became abbreviated to 'posh' and in that acronym form incorporated into the English language.

But that form of sea travel whether on the Far East, the East and West African, or the Caribbean routes has long since passed into the annals of colonial history. We now live in a different age in which countries and indeed continents can be reached within hours let alone days or weeks. And the empire as such has now gone and is almost forgotten. For anyone interested in drawing a comparison between transport in the two ages I leave the last words on this to those of a family friend, a contemporary in British Honduras, who, on reading this chapter in draft form, annotated perceptively against this particular passage:

> How many thousands travelled 'port out, starboard home' on similar boats to start a new life? The comparison now is odious. Nowadays it's a quick trip to Gatwick, two hours wait for the 'plane and expect to arrive the same day, hopefully without a thrombosis. Where has style gone I ask myself?[1]

Where, indeed! But back to the voyage on the SS *Camito*.

In the Caribbean at that time the Elder Fyffe Line had two vessels operating, the SS *Camito* and SS *Golfito*. They would leave Southampton in turn, at fortnightly intervals, to ship bananas from Jamaica. On the outward leg the particular vessel would take on the role of passenger ship as well as cargo carrier and provide a first-class service for fifty or so passengers. As it was no more expensive than air travel, and as I was not required to reach British Honduras before the end of April to take over from my predecessor, there was no official objection to my family and me proceeding by sea, which had the advantage of giving us, to some extent, an opportunity to get acclimatized.

Leaving northwest London, where we had stayed overnight with relatives, we took the underground to Waterloo station to catch the boat train to Southampton docks. During the journey we gazed importantly and perhaps self-consciously at our many cases and bags festooned as they were with various labels provided by the shipping line such as, 'Kingston' and 'Not wanted on Voyage', hoping that any inquisitive fellow travellers would associate 'Kingston' with Jamaica and not Surrey or Yorkshire – but you know how insular the English were in those days.

My father met us at Waterloo station and soon it was time to move onto the platform to board the train. This was the moment I was dreading. It was the first time since the war that we were splitting up as a family and, although Janet was to join us in September when she had finished college, it was not without heartache for everyone. My father, who was then in his seventy-third year, and I had been particularly close since the advent of the Second World War and he was clearly upset and puzzled about why I should want to go into voluntary exile, as he saw it. Although he did not mention or even give a hint of it at the time, I sensed that it had crossed his mind, as it had indeed mine, that in view of the length of my tour and considering his advanced age this might be our last meeting together. But, in the event, neither of us needed to have worried on that score. We were to say goodbye on numerous subsequent occasions over the next twenty years or so as I went off on other overseas assignments. Indeed, he was still very much around after my retirement and lived to the age of almost 98. But of course this was not foreseen at the time and the farewells were painful.

We parted in typical British fashion. All subjects except our departure were discussed until the last minute. Then, prior to boarding the train, there was a flurry of embraces and the shedding or suppressing of tears and before we knew it we were speeding on our way to Southampton docks.

My recollection of that train journey is now blurred. From what I recall, the London suburbs gave way to the green hills and fields of Surrey and as we crossed into Hampshire a huge hoarding alongside the track marked the advent by proclaiming that 'YOU ARE NOW ENTERING THE STRONG COUNTRY'. Strong, I was to learn later, was a renowned local brewer. Further along the line this was amended to read 'YOU ARE NOW IN THE STRONG COUNTRY'. And, before assimilating the message or passing another hoarding to tell us that 'YOU ARE NOW LEAVING THE STRONG COUNTRY', if indeed there was one, the train pulled in at Southampton docks station where an official from the shipping line met us, along with our fellow passengers.

✿ ✿ ✿

After clearing the usual immigration formalities the representative guided us towards the ship that was to be our home for the next twelve or so days. We threaded our way along the quayside dodging ropes, crates and other hazards until we reached the Elder Fyffe's berthing spot. Our preconceived notion was that the SS *Camito*, a banana boat and not primarily a passenger vessel, was going to look pretty tatty and puny in comparison with normal seagoing liners. In other words, our perception of a banana boat was of a dull cargo vessel. However, when we arrived at the gangplank we were pleasantly surprised. The SS *Camito* looked like a mini luxury liner. Painted white overall (except for the single funnel and masts that were yellow in colour with black trimmings) it looked spruce and inviting to the passengers it was to accommodate. For the voyage Captain R. W. Lundy, OBE, RD, RNR would be in command.

We presented ourselves to the purser who arranged for us to be taken to the cabins to which we had been allocated. Florence and I occupied a double berth outer cabin, and Susan, a single cabin on the deck below. A pleasant surprise greeted us on arrival in our cabin in the form of a bouquet of flowers from my youngest sister, Phyllis, and her husband, Stanley, with an accompanying card wishing us *bon voyage*. We then went along to the dining room for afternoon tea and a first introduction to some of our fellow passengers.

Back in our cabin the ship's engines, which had been throbbing softly since we came on board, seemed to alter pitch. Looking through the porthole I could see the docks buildings slowly moving backwards and realized that we were 'off'. It was surely a romantic and exciting moment. It evoked memories of old black and white films I had seen in my youth in which packed passenger liners or immigrant ships left the quayside to the accompaniment of a band playing 'Auld Lang Syne', with streamers being thrown and, invariably, families and sweethearts (now there is an old-fashioned word!) dabbing their tear-stained eyes. Or perhaps it evoked images of a troop ship leaving, say, at the time of the Boer War from a quayside crowded with soldiers, officers, top brass and families and, in the background, the regimental band playing 'Goodbye Dolly Grey'. This vision, however, soon faded when I recalled the crowded troop ships in which I had sailed during my own military service; they were accompanied by no such colourful sendoff, only Dickensian squalor below deck. But the occasion was not allowed to pass without some recognition. As we scrambled on deck to watch the departure there came over the ship's loudspeakers the rousing strains of 'A Life on the Ocean Wave' played by the band of the Royal

Marines. This, of course, turned out to be a recording and not a live rendering by the band itself, but it added colourful atmosphere to the occasion.

On deck we surveyed the scene. The usual port activity was evident. Staff involved in our departure watched patiently as we moved towards mid-stream and there was some last minute banter between them and crew members. Others clutching clip boards moved importantly to and from dockside sheds. An elderly couple looking frail and forlorn waved towards the ship, and a younger couple with their two small children who were at the deck rail close to us waved back. The man waving back, presumably their son, was openly weeping. Having endured similar feelings earlier in the day in saying goodbye to Janet and my own father, I silently sympathized.

Elsewhere the port was full of vessels of all sizes. Among them was the *Queen Elizabeth*, huge and majestic, towering above us. Warehouses, customs sheds and other buildings lined the quayside. Huge cranes and derricks, like the skeletons of giant long-necked prehistoric monsters, probed the sky. Seagulls screeched and wheeled overhead. We were indeed 'off'. It was too late now to turn back even had we wanted to do so.

As we moved into the Solent I tried to analyse my feelings and emotions. Relief, first, at having shed the burden of making arrangements, which in preparation for the appointment and transit were time consuming and exhausting. We were now in the capable hands of others. Anyone who has emigrated or taken up an overseas post of any duration will know exactly what I mean: clearing one's desk at work, disposing of home, storing furniture, getting kitted out with the appropriate clothes, having inoculations, bidding farewell to relatives and friends and so on. Also I felt apprehensive about leaving behind all that was familiar in exchange for the unknown. Intermingled with this was the stimulus and excitement of the challenge ahead, of the prospect of adapting to a new way of life and a new environment. These musings, however, soon gave way to a realization that a biting wind had now developed and it was time to return below deck and to contemplate instead the prospect of enjoying the cruise ahead. And so, in largely optimistic mood, with Southampton fading into the distance behind us and evening drawing in, we returned to our cabins to prepare for dinner, which in those days was a formal affair – black tie the rule rather than the exception.

The ship's dining room was set out like the first-class restaurant it was; tables pleasantly arranged with spotless linen, silver cutlery and gleaming crystal glasses. A pianist provided background music. The menu was à la carte and the cuisine and service excellent. The head steward, a small ebullient bespectacled Scot, fancied himself as a dab hand at making crêpe Suzettes. Wandering between tables at the 'dessert' stage with his trolley laden with utensils, mixture and alcoholic spirits he produced his offerings to much applause through a miasma of erupting blue flame with all the flourish and panache of a conjuror to the delight of his captive audience. The performance would have graced any stage show. As yet we had not the confidence to invite him over. When we subsequently left for bed we felt that we were now embarked on what is commonly known as 'the life of Riley'.

By morning we were to put a less rosy gloss on events. During the night the vessel had moved into the Bay of Biscay and the cruel sea had begun to demonstrate some of its strength. As we went down to the dining room for breakfast we were conscious of the ship being thrown up and down and from side to side by not insignificant angry looking waves. To keep one's balance in the circumstances was no mean feat. Having been weaned on films of the Wild West during my school days I likened the experience to that of a cowboy at a rodeo riding the wildest and most wicked mustang in the old corral without a saddle. At times I felt that if my heart was not in my mouth, my stomach certainly was. Undeterred, we managed to reach the dining room where the many vacant tables should have served as a warning.

If eating breakfast were not itself a disaster its aftermath certainly was. Only those who have experienced seasickness will know exactly how bad I felt. Green faced, I was reminded of an old radio sketch by the prewar Scottish comedian, Will Fyffe, who, portraying an old sea dog offering advice to a father thinking of sending his son to sea in the merchant navy, says 'if the boy has anything in him, the sea will bring it out.' Those words, with their veracity now personally confirmed, were recalled without amusement and a high degree of squeamishness. The next 36 hours or so were spent lying on my bunk with a restricted diet of sandwiches delivered by sympathetic stewards. Susan was in a similar condition while Florence, who, unlike ourselves and the nautical national hero, Nelson, was happily immune to all this rocking and rolling with its tendency to induce various states of nausea without fear or favour to the unfortunates.

Gradually, the weather improved. Blue skies appeared as if by magic and the sun began to radiate warmth. In a sparkling deep blue sea, porpoises gyrated and wheeled alongside the prow as if deciding to provide us with an aquatic escort. Flying fish, breaking the surface in shoals in spectacular fashion, glinting silver in the sunlight, entertained us with their quick bursts of flight, skimming the surface of the sea over long distances. So prodigious were their leaps that some unfortunately ended up on the deck of our vessel, in a manner reminiscent of Second World War Japanese kamikaze pilots, where they expired. A change of mood now came over the ship and its passengers. The swimming pool on deck was opened and games, of which deck quoits seemed to be the favourite, began to be played. Elsewhere, deck and lounge chairs were brought out and the less active read, dozed or sunbathed. In the evenings after dinner, bingo might be played or perhaps there would be some form of musical entertainment or a film. All this culminated in a fancy-dress ball before any of the passengers had reached their various destinations. And, of course, at dinner sessions we took turns, by invitation, to join the captain's table.

The passengers were a motley collection. Some, like us, were going out to the West Indies on first appointment and others in the public service were returning from leave or study. One retired married couple was on a round trip from Southampton to Jamaica and then back to Southampton. We found them all friendly and agreeable. Some were characters that could have stepped out from the pages of a classic Agatha Christie murder mystery. A rugged Roman Catholic priest of pugilistic appearance whose forearms were festooned with tattoos seemed an unlikely man of the cloth. By contrast in the religious fraternity was a quiet married couple, both Salvation Army officers on a missionary assignment. Then again, the wife of the couple on the round trip would walk up and down the deck with her cat, a Burmese, on a lead, which to my cynical mind seemed more pretentious than eccentric. And, of course, there was the inevitable ladies' man. This one, with sleek black hair, small moustache and obsequious manner, seemed to spend all his time flirting with female passengers, not with any success as far as one could see. In any event, he seemed more enamoured of himself than of those he was trying to impress. In short, he was a pale imitation of one's idea of a shipboard Lothario. We nicknamed him 'Neville the Devil'. Had any passenger been stabbed, shot, thrown overboard or poisoned in his or her sleep then I am sure that these characters would have been among the first to come under suspicion.

We struck up friendships with four people in particular – John Spence, Joyce Campbell and Desmond and Rita Brown. John Spence, whom I was to meet on and off in various countries in the Caribbean over the next twenty or so years was at that time an agronomist with the agricultural faculty of the University of the West Indies at the Mona campus, Jamaica (and subsequently professor at the Imperial College of Tropical Agriculture at the St Augustine campus in Trinidad) and returning from study leave in the United Kingdom. A tall, slim, cultured Trinidadian he had a relaxed manner and a nice quiet sense of humour. His father was a distinguished West Indian public servant, Louis Spence, who was currency commissioner for the Eastern Caribbean. John, himself, after retiring from academic life was to become a senator in the Trinidad legislature, but that was for the future. Joyce Campbell was returning to her native Jamaica having also been studying in the United Kingdom to complete her midwifery training. This she achieved successfully and was returning with the SCM qualification. A warm hearted bubbly young woman with an infectious laugh she was great fun. Desmond and Rita Brown, destined for Trinidad, were to provide a link with British Honduras as explained below and in Chapter 24.

Time on board passed in what seemed to be indecent haste and soon we were approaching our first port of call. Now, storm clouds of a different sort had appeared. Over the ship's radio we learnt that Cuban refugees based in Miami had launched an attack on the Cuban mainland. This was, as we were to discover later, the disastrous Bay of Pigs fiasco and it set alarm bells ringing in the heads of those of us going on to Jamaica and British Honduras, both of which are in close proximity to Cuba. In this context the attitudes adopted by the then super powers were crucial. Would the Soviet Union intervene and, if so, how would the United States react? In short, were we heading towards a potential war zone? But, as I said, the operation was a fiasco and, in the event, the super powers were confined to posturing. Although this development was a cause of anxiety, our thoughts were now distracted elsewhere: for we had arrived at what appears on the map as a small ham or tear shaped island, Barbados – among other things, the cradle of some of the most exciting and talented cricketers the world has ever seen.

✿ ✿ ✿

As one of its then oldest colonies, much British history is vested in Barbados. Unlike its sister islands in the area, it had since its colonization always been British. Occupied in 1627, it soon became an important sugar producing island and a key contributor to England's then valuable trade with the West Indies. Indeed, by 1700, though not much larger than the Isle of Wight, the island was exporting products more in value than all the English colonies on the American mainland put together.[2]

Over the years it came to be recognized as the most English of the West Indian islands. Victorian authors seemed particularly keen to highlight this fact. For instance, the historian James Froude, in his book *The English in the West Indies*, written after his visit to the colony in 1887, refers to 'that little England in the tropical seas'. Its nickname 'Bim' is expanded locally to 'Bimshire' to suggest a mythical county. This is in keeping with a flat island relieved in places by gently undulating hills and superficially giving the impression of some English counties. The Quaker abolitionist, Joseph Sturge, who visited the West Indies in 1837, the year of Queen Victoria's accession to the throne, to observe the delayed effects of the complete emancipation of the slaves following the Abolition of Slavery Act of 1833, wrote in the report of his self-appointed commission:

> Barbados is called little England, by way of pre-eminence, a name which it deserves, from the prevalence of English comforts and refinements; though among other features of resemblance to the mother country, we regret to notice, a great body of white paupers, and numerous licensed houses for the sale of spirits.[3]

The 'white paupers' were, conceivably descendants of the 800 or so followers of the Duke of Monmouth who were taken prisoner at the collapse of the Monmouth Rebellion in 1685 and transported to the colony as slaves, later supplemented by working-class Britons recruited as indentured labourers for work in the sugar fields. Over time both groups were considered less effective than black slaves and, consequently, made redundant and deserted by their employers.

Anthony Trollope, in his chapter on the colony in his book *West Indies and the Spanish Main* first published in 1859 (who incidentally found the ruling white class 'Bims' arrogant, conceited and boastful and little to his liking) wrote of 'little England as it delights to call itself'.[4] In *Westward Ho*, a novel not primarily about the West Indies but of adventure against the background of British political and commercial attitudes in the reign of Queen Elizabeth I, Froude's brother-in-law, Charles Kingsley, in a short chapter on Barbados that tells the reader virtually nothing about the island, none the less described it as 'that lovely isle, the richest gem of all tropical seas'.[5] However, it comes as a letdown, although perhaps no great surprise from the lack of detail in what he had written, to learn that he had not visited the island, or indeed the region, at the time of writing and that his vague but colourful description was based on his recollection of accounts told to him at his mother's knee, she having lived there as a child. This has shades of Richard Hughes's classic tale for children, *A High Wind in Jamaica*,[6] which is a more recent case of an author writing about a West Indian island before having visited it. However, it does not do to be too pedantic, for without literary and poetic licence imagination would be stunted. And away from the literary world there is a well rehearsed story, apocryphal or not, that on the outbreak of the Second World War, a message of support was sent to His Majesty's Government in London from the island's counterpart to the effect that 'Barbados is behind you'. How our enemies must have trembled! But all that relates to the past. What of the present?

We reached the island before dawn and anchored just outside Bridgetown. Being a small port, it was not possible in those days for larger vessels like the SS *Camito* to berth alongside the quay. Travel between ship and shore was by ferry. After breakfast we joined other passengers on deck where a colourful sight greeted us. From a ring of rowing boats grouped around the stern small boys, their brown skins glistening with water, were diving for coins that passengers threw into the sea. Not unreasonably, they would dive only for silver coins and their lung and retrieving capacities in this connection seemed to me nothing short of amazing. Then came the customs' launch with its crew dressed like British Jack Tars of the Victorian age; they wore traditional white naval rig and round straw boaters with the words 'HM Customs' on the surrounding headband. The scene could have been from a D'Oyly Carte production of *HMS Pinafore*, except that there was no accompanying music or lyrics.

By chance or by pushing, I cannot recall which, we managed to secure places on the first ferry to leave. It was a large dilapidated old motorboat that failed to inspire confidence. Laden to the gunwales and low in the water we crept slowly towards the quayside. That it never capsized seemed to me a miracle to which I hope my prayers made a contribution, but we made it without mishap. On shore a large crowd waited to greet visitors, new employees, returning friends or prodigal sons or daughters. Among them was Sir Grantley Adams, the island's first premier, whom I easily recognized from his many visits to the Colonial Office in connection with the proposed establishment of the West Indies Federation, of which he became the first and only prime minister (about which more will be mentioned below in connection with Trinidad).

Leaving the bustling dock area of Bridgetown, in company with John Spence, we headed for Broad Street, the city's main thoroughfare where Barclays Bank International was sited. There I changed some travellers' cheques in an air-conditioned building. It was the first time I had experienced this particular luxury and it offered great relief after the unaccustomed heat outside. From the bank we moved north along

Broad Street towards Trafalgar Square (like its London counterpart it has a statue of Nelson, though not on a column) and the South Bridge, taking in St Michael's Cathedral and the post office *en route*. Outside the latter I photographed a buxom local lady who was at that moment walking past with a bowl on her head from which a large fish protruded. After this preliminary sightseeing, and with Joyce Campbell now joining us, we arranged to see something of the island outside the capital. Our taxi took us through sugar cane fields and pleasant countryside to the Atlantic coast. Keeping to the coastline, following inlets, cliffs and sandy beaches shaded by tall coconut trees, and occasionally catching glimpses of fishermen's boats drawn up on the shore or out at sea, we reached Sam Lord's Castle, originally a small eighteenth-century plantation house belonging to the Lord family but now a tourist attraction. It was converted into an elaborate French style mansion early in the nineteenth century.

Sam Lord was a rich Regency buck about whom legend and fact are inextricably entwined. Guide and travel books tell us that he was an adventurer who lived well beyond his means and died in London in 1845 leaving behind huge debts. A legend, carefully nurtured to this day (no doubt to add colour to a tourist attraction) is that he and his cohorts lured vessels onto nearby rocks so that they could plunder them and thereby enrich his fortune. But there is no evidence that he was responsible for causing any of the 16 wrecks that occurred near his house between 1820 and 1841. Perhaps the main reason why his name endures today is because his 'castle' is unique among the remaining great houses in Barbados – indeed, possibly, in the whole of the West Indies. So, we have seen that, done that! Now it was on to Crane Beach with its beautiful white coral sands and wild Atlantic rollers crashing in. A stiff breeze tempered the heat somewhat, but it was still too hot for us unacclimatized visitors. We stopped at the post office there to post a few cards and then it was back along the coast road to Bridgetown and the SS *Camito*. We had 'done' Barbados in less than eight hours and the next port of call was to the south, Trinidad.

✧ ✧ ✧

Looking over the deck rail as we neared the island of Trinidad early in the morning, John Spence pointed out the Serpent's Boca, the neck of sea between Trinidad and the coast of Venezuela. Shortly afterwards we reached Port of Spain and tied up alongside King's Wharf. Colonized by Spain in 1577, the island had been under continuous British rule since 1797. What impressions would we form of it, I wondered?

We took a taxi to John Spence's mother's house where his car had been parked during his absence. Whenever I read that venerated novelist V. S. Naipaul's descriptions of his native Trinidad, I think of that wooden house set among numerous flowering shrubs in a dusty street, with its accompanying sights and sounds and, of course, the good humour and old-world courtesy of the local people.

My first impression of Port of Spain, later to be confirmed, was that the capital city lacked the old-fashioned pace and charm of Bridgetown. The extraction of oil and bauxite had given the economy a boost and this was reflected in the hustle and bustle of activity all around the business section of the city. In particular, traffic clogged the streets and driving was clearly not for the faint-hearted. John Spence was not among that number. With his casual typically relaxed West Indian style he drove us around with his right arm out of the window and resting on the roof of the car for much of the time in order to keep cool while, at the same time, giving us a running commentary of places of interest in his low musical voice. Outside Port of Spain we passed Chagaramas, one of the West Indian bases Britain leased to the United States during the Second World War in exchange for the loan of 50 ageing American destroyers. We saw pitch lakes, bauxite workings and Texaco oil fields. As a cricket lover a pilgrimage to the Queen's Park Oval was a must. It is in a beautiful setting, with Trinidad's northern range of mountains providing an impressive background. To my mind it is the most distinguished of the West Indian cricket grounds.

The highlight was a visit to the federal parliament building. At that time the idea that all the British West Indian islands should come together to form one unified political entity was still extant. Indeed, despite suspicions in certain quarters over the shouldering of costs, a customs union and freedom of movement between the

islands, all of which raised serious problems, the West Indies Federation formally came into existence on 3 January 1958. But dreams
tend to fade or, as an old popular song has it, 'never did come true'.
Suspicions persisted. Within two years of its inception Jamaica and
Trinidad were severely criticizing the federal government for
imperilling their national economic development. In September 1961
Jamaica held a referendum on whether or not to continue in the
federation and its electorate gave it the thumbs down. As a result,
Jamaica and then Trinidad pulled out. With Barbados or any of the
other smaller islands in a group either unwilling or in no position to
take over, it finally went out of existence on 31 May 1962, thus
consigning the federal dream to the pages of history.

So a radical experiment in regional unity came to a sad end. It has
to be recognized, however, that there was not at the time any real
sense of West Indian nationhood and love of cricket was about the
only unifying factor. The fact is that the Caribbean Sea tends to
divide and not unify the people of the many disparate islands.
Subsequently, Jamaica, Trinidad and then Barbados opted for
independence. The remaining islands in the Leeward and Windward
groups, with the exceptions of Montserrat and Anguilla, had their
status elevated to that of associated state. This gave them greater
local autonomy and edged them closer to independence, which,
following the example set by Barbados, they all achieved a few years
later. But these events had yet to unfold.

As it was, we toured the parliament building and, for the record, I
photographed Susan on top of the building holding onto a flagpole
on which the West Indian Federal flag, shortly to become defunct,
was flying. All too quickly our brief visit to Trinidad came to an end
and, having said goodbye to John in the knowledge that he would be
visiting us in British Honduras shortly, and Desmond and Rita
Brown (the latter had given us a message to pass on to her parents
who were in British Honduras) we were back on board the SS *Camito*
again. The next and final leg of our journey was to take us
northwards past the line of the Windward and Leeward Islands to
the east and then on to Jamaica.

✿✿✿

We entered Kingston harbour early in the morning of 24 April. The sun was burning hot even at such an early hour and the general impression of the immediate scene was that of colour and noise. After berthing and saying our goodbyes to the crew we were welcomed by Gei Eaton, the United Kingdom information officer, a very tall, slim man smoking a cigarette through a holder with some elegance. He kindly took us to his home for morning coffee and to introduce us to his wife (a local sculptress of some repute) and children; and then on to 'Green Gables' at Half Way Tree in the parish of St Andrews, the hotel where we were to stay for two nights until taking off on our flight to British Honduras.

'Green Gables' was a modest establishment providing little in the way of luxury. It was a small but clean hotel with a few bedrooms and offering simple meals, but the garden was exquisite. Exotic tropical plants and shrubs such as poinsettia and bougainvillea (the former named after Joel Roberts Poinsett, the first United States ambassador to Mexico, and the latter after the first French navigator to circumnavigate the globe in the eighteenth century) abounded. Everywhere, there were lizards, butterflies and, to our great delight, humming birds – the first we had ever seen, and we were enchanted. But there was a downside to this. As evening merged into night we found ourselves attacked by hordes of mosquitoes and this necessitated the use of mosquito 'coils', which, when lit, glowed and gave off fumes that acted as a repellent. And the unaccustomed (to us) chirping of the cicadas at nightfall delayed our dropping quickly into sleep when we turned in to bed.

At that time the hotel, guesthouse perhaps would have been a more appropriate description, was popular with British travellers of modest means. One of our fellow guests, staying there indefinitely, was an elderly former British army officer who had served in British Honduras and some of the West Indian island colonies prior to retirement. On quizzing him I found that his knowledge of British Honduras was limited mainly to polo and social activities, with his understanding of the current political and wider social scene very out of date. It was, therefore, of little value to me in terms of my assignment. He cut a sad and sorry figure. The impression I formed was of one of those tragic misfits who found it hard to adjust to the wind of change that had struck the British Empire in the post-1945 period: he was neither 'local' enough to understand or accept with equanimity the acceleration of the pace of self-determination now affecting Jamaica and the rest of the British Caribbean, nor sufficiently attuned to the economic, social and other changes in postwar Britain to retire comfortably there. Consequently, while worldwide inflation eroded the purchasing power of his modest pension, he remained on in the sunshine dreaming of the good old days when people knew their places. Had I the ability to write a play (perhaps in the style of the late Sir Terence Rattigan) set in a seedy hotel featuring the attitudes and values of some of the lower middle classes of the day whose financial resources failed to match their affectations or pretensions, then I am sure he would have found an automatic place as one of the characters in the plot.

That evening Joyce Campbell took us to her family home in an affluent part of Kingston where her family and friends received us with great warmth and we sat in the garden, talking, eating and drinking until the inevitable squadrons of mosquitoes drove us indoors.

The following day we had a look around Kingston. In those days it was possible for visitors like us to use public transport or wander around, even in the dock area, without being subject to abuse or worse. Unfortunately, a few years later the hostility of a small minority of locals was to make such ordinary events both unpleasant and even dangerous. That said, we found the city a lively, bustling place vibrating with noise, humour and energy. With the impressive Blue Mountains, the home of excellent but expensive coffee beans, providing the background, it whetted the appetite for an exploration of the whole island, but time did not permit that. As I was to discover in a later incarnation, Jamaica is perhaps the most beautiful of the former British islands in the West Indies. Rich in British history, it is also the final resting place of many British servicemen and colonial officials who died there from cholera, yellow fever and dysentery in the eighteenth and nineteenth centuries as tablets on the walls of the church at Port Royal, military cemeteries and the many references in *Lady Nugent's Journal*[7] bear testimony.

✧✧✧

That evening we packed our cases in preparation for our transit to British Honduras early the following morning on the weekly British Airways flight. We were up well before dawn. With so early a start we slept only fitfully, wondering if the taxi would arrive on time as ordered. It did and the driver called at 4.00 a.m. We reached Palisadoes Airport in good time and, still half asleep, boarded our flight, which took off at 6.00 a.m. After about an hour and a half we passed over the long line of white surf stretching over the Barrier Reef and then began to catch sight below of the blue and green waters surrounding numerous cayes (small coral islands) lying within. Shortly afterwards we landed at Stanley Field Airport where my predecessor, Ken Osborne met and welcomed us.

After introducing us to a few officials and other locals who were in the airport building at the time, he drove us into Belize along the narrow road that runs between the Belize River and the mango swamp adjoining the Caribbean Sea. He then took us to his home to meet his wife and daughters and, over refreshments, he provided us with an up-to-date briefing on local events and personalities. Thereafter, he drove us to Government House where we were to enjoy the hospitality of the governor and his wife, Sir Colin and Lady Thornley, who had kindly offered to accommodate us for the first few days after our arrival. Thus, in the formal atmosphere of that old white painted wooden building whose walls could no doubt tell a tale or two, we began an experience and adventure over the next three years, which, though I did not realize it at the time, was to prove invaluable in another colonial setting some years later.

So much for the prologue and setting of the scene – the stage awaits. Now, up with the curtain, enter our hero centre stage. Cue Chapter 2. *But soft, he speaks …*

Chapter 2
The Bung

I N MY OFFICIAL capacity in British Honduras I was cast in the image of 'Pooh Bah', that ubiquitous character in *The Mikado* who holds many offices at once. That is to say I wore three government hats (metaphorically, of course) at the same time and was secretary to many committees. Another, albeit incidental, resemblance to the world of Gilbert and Sullivan was that some of the situations in which I found myself during these roles would, I am sure, have tickled the Gilbertian sense of the ridiculous.

As principal secretary for external affairs I assisted the governor in the discharge of his responsibilities for foreign affairs. At that time there was a flurry of activity arising out of the long outstanding Guatemalan territorial claim to the colony that was to culminate in the breaking off of diplomatic relations with the United Kingdom early in 1961. But assisting the governor in that connection was not quite as simple and straightforward as it sounds.

The colonial hierarchy, like all other hierarchies, had its own distinctive chain of command. In that structure the chief secretary had a pivotal role – in effect, chief of staff to the governor and, as the second most senior officer in the administration, his locum-tenens during absences. It follows therefore that much of my work on external affairs was of necessity channelled through him.

Not surprisingly, therefore, I was also designated principal secretary (chief secretary's office) and, in that capacity, assisted him in all matters within his portfolio, including police administration, internal security, public service and the many general subjects not covered by specific government ministries. Accordingly, I was given an office in the secretariat in addition to the one allocated to me at Government House. My roles continued to expand. When the clerk to the Executive Council, a hitherto presumed apolitical local civil servant, was seen on an anti-government march in the ranks of the opposition party, another less sensitive post was found for her. A subsequent discussion between the governor (then Sir Peter Stallard) and the first minister, Mr George Price, saw me installed as her successor – in Executive Council of course and not on opposition marches. This role, which continued throughout the remainder of my secondment, throws an interesting light on the degree of trust and cooperation at that time, based on shared objectives in the political, economic and social fields, between the governing political party and the governor and his staff.

Now the purpose of this somewhat and seemingly egotistical introduction is not to emphasize my importance to the local administration, either real or imaginary, or to enlist sympathy on the grounds of overwork. Indeed, on the latter point. I welcomed the opportunity to be at the heart of many of the significant events affecting the colony. No, it is simply to explain how I came to be involved in the various and diverse incidents recorded in this and subsequent chapters.

It was not long after taking up post that I was plunged into the world of practical administration. This introduced me to a hitherto unknown aspect of public life, namely the attempted or perceived bribe, sweetener or bung – call it what you will – as a reward for a favourable decision. The sum of money was trivial. There was no wad of notes stuffed in a brown paper envelope. Indeed, it was more like a tip to a porter or waiter. But principle and integrity were involved. What were the circumstances and what was my reaction?

It was normal practice in the secretariat for the chief secretary, Michael Porcher, provided he was not delayed by visitors or meetings, to leave for lunch at noon. I would follow shortly afterwards. On the day in question this practice was being followed and I was just about to leave when the burly figure of Corporal Welby of the British Honduras police force came into the secretariat with a squat Maya Indian in tow.

Welby, a powerfully built local officer of good Creole pedigree and cheerful disposition, was at the time the designated immigration officer. He asked if the chief secretary were available to see him on an immigration matter. I said he had already left for lunch, adding, somewhat pointedly, that I was about to follow his example.

Undaunted, Welby brushed such personal considerations aside and said that it was a matter with which I had the authority to deal and, before I could say anything further, he launched into his story.

He explained that the accompanying Maya Indian (whose name I have long since forgotten, but for the purpose of this narrative I shall call Placido) was a Guatemalan national normally domiciled in that country. He had recently married a British Honduran woman from the Maya village of Soccotz and now wished to make his home at Benque Viejo on our side of the border. This, added Welby, was not unusual. There were many precedents. For, in practice, the Maya, who are tribal rather than nationalistic, tend to move freely over the border in their everyday pursuits in that part of the region. To them, the border between Guatemala and British Honduras is an artificial barrier designed by governments. But artificial barrier or not, an official permit of residence was needed before Placido could be allowed to settle permanently on our side. Such a document required the authority of the chief secretary or, in his absence, another designated officer, in this case, me.

Continuing, Welby added that he had checked all the relevant details, was satisfied that Placido was of good character and that this was a bona fide case that he could fully recommend for approval.

After studying the relevant immigration laws and regulations, which were available in the secretariat, and satisfied that the proper procedures had been followed, I somewhat pompously instructed Welby to inform Placido that, subject to any conditions laid down by the British Honduras immigration authorities, he would be allowed to live on this side of the border indefinitely and that I would sign the appropriate document to facilitate this.

In telling Welby to relay this decision, I had assumed that Placido did not understand English and that the lingua franca would be Mayan, Spanish, Creole or possibly some other form of pidgin English. To my surprise I was wrong on both counts. As my words were being loudly echoed in English by Welby, Placido clearly had already understood what was going on. Fishing around in one of his trouser pockets he pulled out a crumpled American ten dollar note and placed it on the desk in front of me. This he achieved without a flicker of emotion.

For a moment, the significance of this failed to register. Then I realized the implications. 'My God', I thought, 'a bribe: is this the way official business in the colony is conducted?' On reflection, however, I doubted whether it really constituted a bribe, as such, as it was proffered after my decision and, therefore, not an attempt to influence it. On the other hand, it was clearly intended as a *douceur* or sweetener for a favourable service rendered. Looking beyond semantics and sophistry, there was no doubt in my mind that an element of sleaze had now entered the proceedings. Placido must be made to understand that we British could not be bought.

There was, of course, no official code of practice on what to do in such circumstances. This was not necessary. Like many of my generation I was familiar with the stereotyped colonial official portrayed in novels read or films seen in my youth. From these I learnt with pride that 'our chaps' were incorruptible and concerned only with the well-being of the natives for whom they were responsible.

The effect and impact of the cinema in this connection cannot be overstated. In my formative years, especially in the 1930s, the imagery of empire was impressed upon me by a number of films carrying imperial connotations. These included *The Drum*, *Lives of a Bengal Lancer*, *Sanders of the River*, *Gunga Din* and *The Four Feathers*, to name just a few that spring to mind. Of these, *Sanders of the River*, a black and white film (in more than one sense) starring Leslie Banks and Paul Robeson, particularly impressed and influenced me and Sanders was to become my role model in my new duties. The part was played by Banks who portrayed a district officer or commissioner showing character and spirit while dispensing British justice to West African natives in the face of skulduggery initiated by the wicked tribal despot, King Mofalaba. In that role he appeared in sweat stained tropical kit, sometimes complete with pith helmet, pipe clenched between his teeth and looking suitably worried or serious at the messages of dastardly plots or native risings relayed monotonously by the war drums. All the perceived virtues of the imperial system were paraded on the cinema screen and received enthusiastically by audiences who lapped up like cream this display by 'our chaps' in the colonies on how they behaved in the face of threats to the rule of law. Sanders's integrity and devotion to 'his flock' was lauded musically by his faithful ally Chief Bosambo (played by Robeson) in a catchy repetitive number delivered in his rich base voice, which, if memory serves me aright, began something like this:

> Sandy the strong,
> Sandy the wise,
> Righter of wrongs,
> Hater of lies.

It goes without saying, after this, that Sanders ultimately triumphed over an evil despot and in so doing, as would be expected, displayed all the virtues and qualities that guided our colonial administrators as they built, governed and sustained the empire.

With the inspiration of Sanders guiding me and possibly the imaginary strains of 'Land of Hope and Glory' providing background music in my ears, I turned again to Welby and, with all the dignity I could muster, said, 'Please tell this man that we British consider cases on merit and are not influenced by inducements of any sort. He must, therefore, take back his money.' After Welby had complied, Placido continued to stare at me impassively for a moment or two. Then he again fished around in his pocket and drew out another ten dollar bill which he placed alongside the other one. 'Good Lord! Was he upping the ante' I wondered, on the premise that everyone 'has a price' or had he still misunderstood the nature of British officialdom?

Again I told him, via Welby, that he must desist from such attempted financial inducements and that if he persisted I would not approve his application for domicile. Either he finally got the message or had run out of money, for the fishing in his pocket for further dollar bills ceased. He reluctantly took back the 20 dollars, proffered in two instalments, and departed with Welby, application officially approved, but no doubt puzzled and somewhat concerned with the manner of the proceedings.

I learnt afterwards that the general practice in Guatemala, if there was no advance bribe, was for the recipient of any favourable official decision to clinch the deal by rewarding the government official con-cerned in some tangible way. The object was to show gratitude to the official, who would expect such an 'acknowledgment' and perhaps ensure that there would be no backtracking on the decision. That I had not followed what Placido had clearly regarded as common practice, tradition if you like, had seemingly made him uneasy. Possibly, he was concerned lest it might, perhaps, affect the future validity of his permission to stay in the colony.

However, my guess is that he need not have worried on that score. If official acceptance of the proffered dollars was to ease his concern and provide peace of mind then I am sure that Welby, a kind and helpful man, would have been only too happy and willing to help him out. When the first dollar note came across my desk his eyes widened. When the second followed they were shining. It may be, of course, that he was admiring what he thought was my technique in getting Placedo to up the ante. But he can, I think, be forgiven if he was also imagining what he could do with such a sum if offered to him. Modest as it now seems, 20 American dollars at that time would have been a significant boost to his pay packet.

In other words, it is possible to envisage a scenario in which Welby was able to persuade Placido that, as immigration officer, he was the most appropriate official to receive any financial show of gratitude and that, if it would help, he would be willing to cooperate. But I hasten to add that this is pure fantasy. I have no idea if there was such a sequel and I must be careful not to traduce an old and respected colleague – heaven forbid! After all, I was already aware that the local civil service matched its British counterpart in matters of correct behaviour in the carrying out of all its duties. But, as I subsequently discovered on travels to neighbouring republics, the 'greasing of palms' is an integral part of Central American culture and experience had already taught me that, in matters of this sort, it was best not to enquire too deeply.

Thus began my initial foray into the field of practical colonial administration and, with it, came the dawning realization that it differed widely from situations that would normally come across my desk in Whitehall.

Chapter 3
Baron Bliss

AT THE TIP OF the promontory running northwards from the mouth of the estuary of the Belize River,[1] which divides the capital city into two parts, known respectively as Northside and Southside, on the foreshore between the customs sheds and Fort George Park, is to be found, sited next to the lighthouse, a monument – the tomb of the late Baron Bliss, symbolically facing the Caribbean Sea. Enquire of local historians and you will be told that he was an adventurous, eccentric, wealthy English aristocrat who adopted British Honduras as his home in his last few days alive, which were spent offshore on board his luxurious steam yacht, *Sea King*. But who was he and what was his connection with the colony? Thereby hangs a tale: a fisherman's tale.

My first awareness of the lingering impact the late Baron still had locally came shortly after my arrival in the colony. With it came my first introduction into the mores of colonial protocol.

One morning, Michael Porcher sauntered into my office in the secretariat and, in an affable mood, asked if I knew that one of the features of the forthcoming public holiday would be the regatta in Belize harbour stipulated in the will of Baron Bliss. Having told him that I was vaguely aware of the significance of the day and the event he then disclosed that the governor had been pleased to invite Florence and me to watch the regatta from on board his launch, *Patricia*. Michael added for good measure that the other guests, in addition to His Excellency and us, were the attorney-general, permanent secretary of finance, chief justice and, with the exception of the latter who was a bachelor, their wives. As neither Florence nor I was much interested in sailing events and thinking that the day could be better spent on other things, I said something to the effect that I was most grateful for the invitation but regretfully would have to decline. This, as I was soon to find out, was clearly a *faux pas*.

Fixing me with a cold stare, as befitting a chief secretary having to deal with an ungrateful junior officer, Michael informed me sternly that invitations from His Excellency the Governor were tantamount to 'royal commands' and that, accordingly, the question of choice did not arise. Having been thus admonished and put straight, as it were, I thought it prudent to apologize with suitable obsequiousness for my naivety and hastily reversed my decision. But, in formally accepting the invitation, I must confess that I was not looking forward to the occasion with any great relish or enthusiasm.

In the event, my reticence in accepting was, to my mind, vindicated. Rain was falling heavily when we boarded the *Patricia* and for the next seemingly interminable hours the vessel bobbed up and down in Belize harbour. During that time I tried, without obvious success, to show interest in the activities of a number of yachts looking for the entire world like lost and bedraggled large deformed butterflies performing complicated and incomprehensible manoeuvres within the harbour. As if the rocking of the *Patricia* were not enough, the smell of diesel from the vessel's engines coupled with an unwise intake of gin and tonics was to induce in me a feeling of squeamishness that was to linger and spoil the rest of the day. Mercifully, the races were finally completed and by some miracle winners were identified, declared and suitably rewarded with silver cups for the owners and rum, beer or some other tipple for the crews. The rest of the day was our own.

Incidentally, this experience brought me up against another aspect of colonial life, namely the passion that lies within most British expatriate breasts for social recognition and adherence to the pecking order. Let me explain. Shortly after that event Florence and I detected a certain coolness in the attitude of some of our newly acquired friends and colleagues. From a few snide remarks I concluded that they resented the fact that we, as newcomers, had been invited to a function with the governor and the colony's senior officers while they, some of them long serving heads of department and their wives, had not. The irony of this did not escape me. We who had attended would willingly have spent the day elsewhere and those who had spent the day elsewhere would rather have endured the regatta to impress their friends who had not – in fact, shades of

Lord Macaulay's poem 'Horatius' in which 'those behind cried "Forward!" And those before cried "Back!"' The perversity of human nature certainly knows no bounds.

That said, and putting aside the complexities and nuances of expatriate colonial society, I resolved to find out what I could about the late Baron Bliss. If he was important enough to be recognized by, among other things, a public holiday, regattas, a special tomb and a cultural institute there must be a good reason for it. My enquiries revealed a well-documented and quite extraordinary story.

Henry Edward Ernest Victor Bliss, JP and fourth baron of the Kingdom of Portugal, was born in Marlow, Buckinghamshire, on 16 February 1869. He was educated at Cheltenham, succeeded his father to the barony in 1890 and married Ethel Wolton the following year. He had one great passion in life (and having just mentioned Ethel it would be courteous and perhaps true to add, apart from his wife), namely fishing. He was an ardent deep sea fisherman.

Always on the lookout for the challenge of new seas and larger fish to catch, he was seduced in the summer of 1925 by stories of the abundance of huge outsize monsters of the deep to be hooked around the cayes and the barrier reef of British Honduras, the second longest such reef in the world. These, among others, included king fish, sail fish, whale shark, barracuda, jew fish, amber jack, crevaille, Spanish mackerel, blue marlin, tarpon, grouper and black snapper. Additional bait dangled before him was the prospect of battling with fighting bone fish in the Belize River – in short, it was an angler's paradise and, not surprisingly, he became interested. In fishing parlance, having swallowed the bait, so to speak, he was hooked.

The following year he sailed to Jamaica in the *Sea King* and thence to British Honduras. Tragically, he was taken seriously ill within sight of the shore and, without ever landing in the colony, died in his cabin on 9 March 1926. And it was at this point that the story is given an astonishing twist.

According to all accounts, Baron Bliss in his last moments alive managed to get a local lawyer on board and made out a hurried will. And here is the curious and extraordinary thing to which I have alluded. Although, so far as is known, he had not been specifically aware of British Honduras until the year before his death, had certainly never set foot on its soil, had no previous connection with it or any of its people, and knew no more about it than its reputation as a deep sea fisherman's paradise, he nevertheless decided (after providing modest life annuities for his wife and some other legatees) to leave the bulk of his considerable wealth to the colony.

At that time, British Honduras was a particularly poor colony sorely in need of modern infrastructure. Part of the problem, as I shall amplify in a later chapter, was that the unofficial majority on the Legislative Council, drawn predominantly from the landowning and merchant classes, opposed any significant raising of taxes if it affected their commercial interests. Thus, with only limited funds available for investment in the public sector, even modest essential capital projects tended to be delayed or perhaps shelved indefinitely. Not surprisingly, therefore, the local authorities enthusiastically welcomed the news of this unexpected windfall arising out of the baron's death. Counting his chickens before they were hatched, if I may be forgiven for inflicting a poultry metaphor on a fishing story, the then governor, Sir John Burdon, announced to the Legislative Council that the baron's munificence would have a significant impact on the colony's future development. In this he reckoned without the all-pervading influence of HM Treasury in London, which claimed and received a substantial sum in income tax, surtax, and death and estate duties. None the less, a considerable sum remained that was to provide an annual income in the region of BH$ 40,000 (£10,000), which was a small fortune in those days. A trust fund was set up to administer the will: the trustees were the governor, colonial secretary (later redesignated chief secretary) and attorney-general, all expatriates with authority passing to their successors *ad infinitum.*

Under the terms of his will the baron specified that two official regattas should be financed each year, one in Belize harbour and the other in the Belize River, and that all other revenues should be used primarily to finance purely capital projects in the colony. In other words, building public amenities such as badly needed schools, health facilities, public buildings, libraries and so on were in general to be eschewed on the grounds that considerable sums would be required annually to finance the necessary recurrent expenditure needed for, say, the provision of staff and attendant accessories, which would quickly drain the trust of its income at the expense of numerous other much needed capital items. So, any exceptions would require recurrent costs to fall upon the local treasury and not the trust fund.

Typical of the projects the trust financed over the years up to the early 1960s were the cultural centre, the Baron Bliss Institute, which incorporates a theatre, the Burdon Canal, an industrial school for boys, roads, improvements to the water supply, public market structures, shore lights, electrical generating plants and so on. All these projects are, in themselves, practical monuments to Baron Bliss. But, of course, the two most tangible are his tomb and the public holiday on 9 March bearing his name.

Why did Baron Bliss leave the bulk of his wealth to British Honduras? This we shall never know, but we can speculate. The most likely, and simplest, explanation is that of a fervent deep-sea fisherman who finds himself dying in a fisherman's paradise and who then decides to leave the bulk of his fortune to the territorial custodians of that maritime Elysium. Another logical and equally plausible explanation, a variation of the first, is that the baron was a romantic and an eccentric and, just as other eccentrics tend from time to time to bequeath their fortunes to cats or dogs' homes, or to other animal institutions, so he left his to a place that he perceived to be a shrine of deep-sea fishing.

Yet, I still puzzle over the terms of his will and the riddle it poses. Is it likely, I wonder, that a dying man who had never set foot in the colony would manage, of his own volition, to stipulate so precisely how his legacy should be spent? Did the thought come to him by divine inspiration? Or did some local Iago with the colony's best interests at heart, of course, whisper seductively in his ear in a brain-washing session? Whatever the case, the terms could not have been more favourable for addressing much needed social and economic infrastructural needs, or, for that matter, the local love of boat races.

Pursuing this train of thought and allowing the imagination to run riot, a dramatic and even sinister scenario could be envisaged. A situation could be invented in which prominent local citizens with the inherited genes and blood of their pirate ancestors prompting their actions, aided by a devious lawyer, contrived to get the baron's signature on a prepared will made out in the colony's favour without him being aware of what he was actually signing. Now, there's a thought! But attractive as this may seem to those fascinated by the frisson of a 'black' story or conspiracy theory, it is not a scenario that stands up in practice. Apart from anything else, Baroness Bliss and the other legatees also allowed the revenues from their annuities to buoy up the trust fund after their own deaths. This, to my mind, suggests that the magic of the British Honduras fishing grounds had cast its spell over the whole Bliss family and circle. So this leaves one of the other two explanations advanced above. Was he a besotted fisherman or an eccentric? Perhaps he was an amalgamation of the two. 'You pays your penny and makes your choice!'

However, speculating on his motives at this distance in time is not only idle but also purely academic. The legacy was made and is now history. Game set and match, or, perhaps, hook, line and sinker would be a more appropriate expression.

That, in essence, is the strange story of Baron Bliss and its relevance to the colony's history. Inherent in the thread that runs through it are the unpredictability and idiosyncrasies of mankind, a theme much exploited by novel, film and TV writers. Sir Arthur Conan Doyle elegantly defined and, almost poetically, elaborated upon this theme in the opening sentences of his story, *A Case of Identity*:

'My dear fellow' said Sherlock Holmes (in conversation with Watson as they sat on either side of the fire in his lodgings in Baker Street) 'life is infinitely stranger than anything that the mind of man could invent. We would not dare to conceive the things which are really more commonplace of existence. If we could fly out of that window hand in hand, hover over this great city, gently remove the roofs and peer at the strange things going on, the strange coincidences, the plannings, the cross purposes, the wonderful chain of events working through generations and leading to the most *outré* results, it would make all fiction with its conventionalities and forseen conclusions most stale and unprofitable.'

Nowadays, a more impatient age, the same sentiments would be put more succinctly and prosaically simply by opining that 'fact is stranger than fiction'. This brings to an end the curious story of Baron Bliss in relation to British Honduras. Students of the empire might see it as a mere footnote to an insignificant page of imperial history. Put in that wider context it would be an understandable reaction. But, to others, imbued perhaps with a romantic streak, it might serve as a timely reminder of the generosity and humanity as well as the unpredictability of mankind. A few might even interpret it as a unique early example of voluntary economic aid to a developing country.

As time goes by the memory of Baron Bliss and his legacy will inevitably slip quietly into history, even in Belize as British Honduras was once and is now again called. Outside the territory it is likely to remain virtually unknown except to a handful of expatriates who have served there or perhaps a few tourists who picked up the story during their travels. But to my mind it is a singular and fascinating item of British colonial history, so extraordinary that it is surely worth telling and preserving.

Chapter 4
It's Clean

OUR COMMISSIONER of police, Bruce Taylor, was the very model of a modern senior colonial police officer (*circa* 1960s). He was well experienced in law enforcement generally and in all aspects of police control, organization and administration. Moreover, he had previously served in India, Malaya and East Africa where internal security situations (a common feature of several territories at the pre-independence stage) had added a further valuable dimension to his already wide experience. Possessing an equable temperament, he was an ideal man for any administration to have around, especially in times of crisis.

In his early forties, of average height and with piercing blue eyes, Bruce fitted well into the local social scene when invited to functions, but he was not really part of it. Because of his wife's indifferent health, he seldom entertained at home. At cocktail parties he enjoyed the occasional drink but eschewed small talk and gossip. However, his forthright manner and penchant for blunt comment sometimes upset particularly sensitive people. Once a fine athlete he would give glimpses of his former prowess on the tennis courts and cricket field.

He was popular with all ranks of the British Honduras police force where he was recognized as being firm but fair. He was also well regarded by all the governors and chief secretaries under whom he served. Although he sometimes had difficulty subscribing to policy decisions he might regard as 'a bit too liberal', he none the less could always be relied on to follow such policies with the utmost loyalty once they were laid down. In that respect he typified the old traditional British civil and colonial service attitudes at their best. In short, British Honduras was extremely fortunate to obtain the services of such a dedicated and experienced officer in charge of its police force.

When the vacancy arose, Bruce was about to leave East Africa with seemingly no other job in sight. With a wife and four young sons to support the possibility of landing the post attracted his interest. However, the salary offered was less than he was already receiving as a senior police officer; and British Honduras was not the most salubrious of places for his wife whose health was somewhat worn down by the climates and pressures of life in the troubled places in which they had served. After much consideration and heart-searching, he applied for and was offered the post, which he accepted. The ultimate inducement was the status of number one in the police department and, with it, the chance to run his own show for the first time.

As already intimated, Bruce Taylor's character was beyond reproach. His integrity and loyalty were never in question. Neither friendship nor financial inducement would ever persuade him to go against his conscience when it came to upholding the law, both in spirit and the letter. When, for instance, Norman Stalker, our chief auditor, had the jacket of his expensive brand new suit stolen, and the culprit arrested a day or so later, no amount of special pleading by Norman could get it back. 'It will have to remain with the police', said Bruce, 'as evidence for the magistrates court'. Unfortunately for Norman, the accused escaped and went on the run. The jacket remained at police headquarters as evidence pending his rearrest, which never happened. By the time he finally got his jacket released, the trousers to the suit (and indeed the spare pair also) had become worn out. But, despite Norman's displeasure, shrouded to some extent by his good humoured recital of these events, Bruce's conscience undoubtedly remained clear.

Yet, if he had an Achilles heel, it was in respect of his private motorcar. As commissioner of police he had at his disposal an official saloon car and a Land Rover for which he was allocated an official driver, all provided by the force. But, on his arrival in the colony, he succumbed to temptation and bought for his private use a large second-hand convertible Chevrolet, which was to become his pride and joy. The bodywork was metallic bronze in colour and this, coupled with gleaming chromium headlamps, bumpers and other parts, gave it a most impressive and luxurious appearance. Each morning his driver would be conveyed by Land Rover to his residence (opposite mine) where he would back the long and sleek Chevrolet out of the garage ready to take his master to police headquarters in Queen Street. With the hood of the vehicle down, Bruce would on most occasions sit alongside the driver looking both important and resplendent in full uniform. He much preferred this arrangement to the use of official vehicles when travelling to and from his home and office. But, alas, a cloud was about to descend on such simple satisfaction and with it a suspicion that our paragon of law enforcement might have feet of clay.

One day on a visit to police headquarters, I noticed on entering his office that not only did he look despondent but his body language confirmed it. 'Anything wrong, Bruce?' I ventured. 'I should bloody well think there is,' he said, 'read this.' With that he handed me a telegram from the Miami police department asking him to be on the lookout for a number of vehicles stolen in that state and now believed to be either in Mexico or British Honduras. Details of make, colour, engine number and so on were listed. Being less than quick on the uptake in trying to absorb this information, I enquired about its significance. 'The significance,' he snorted, 'is that one of the cars listed as stolen is my Chevrolet.' He added that he should have realized when he bought it comparatively cheaply from a smooth, fast-talking American that something was not quite right when the latter kept insisting that 'it was clean'. 'I thought he was referring to the condition of the bodywork and upholstery,' said Bruce.

> I now recognize he knew it was 'hot' and was trying to convince me that all was above board. He convinced me all right – and having the nerve to flog it to the commissioner of police, to boot! Bastard! Now I am in the invidious position of being the receiver of stolen goods and the butt of local humour.

Recognizing his dilemma and having no solution of my own con- sistent with the law, I commiserated and asked what he was going to do about it. 'I don't know', he said. 'If I give up the car, I will get no recompense and, on my salary and with my commitments, I cannot afford another. I will have to think about it.'

As the car remained in his possession until he left the colony on the completion of his contract some two years later, he must have given the matter considerable thought.

In the expatriate world of Belize in those days, Bruce's dilemma soon became known and invariably grist to its gossip mill. Moralists among its number professed to be outraged at a hitherto squeaky clean law enforcement officer who was now seemingly failing to return stolen goods. A few, including myself, argued that we did not know all the facts and it was not inconceivable that Bruce had declared the presence of the stolen vehicle to the Miami authorities who then considered, on reflection, that the cost of recovery outweighed its value. Most, however, thought it a huge joke.

Like most jokes, its humour and impact dulled with repetition and before long the matter became stale and ceased to be a talking point. New subjects for gossip superseded it. New butts for malicious humour were found.

As already mentioned, Bruce retained possession of the car during the remainder of his service. Shortly before his final departure, he sold it. A few who claimed to be in the know, said that he took great pains to assure the buyer that the vehicle was 'clean' – meaning the state of the gleaming bronze metal-coloured bodywork and freshly-vacuumed upholstery, of course. But given the malicious humour of the informants, I suspect that this was apocryphal. But who am I to spoil a good story?

Chapter 5
The Mosquito Shore and Other Imperial Links

ST JOHN'S CATHEDRAL, standing like a sentinel watching out over Government House and its front lawns, is to my mind distinctive without being a particularly attractive or inspiring building, although the colourful flamboyant trees and tropical shrubs gracing its grounds undoubtedly tend to offset some of its exterior plainness. Built with public funds in the early nineteenth century from bricks that once provided the ballast for British ships trading with the settlement, and under construction for 14 years, it has little obvious aesthetic appeal. Native woods were given emphasis in its interior, the roof being constructed of sapodilla with mahogany beams and pillars providing supports for the west gallery. The original wooden spire that may once have enhanced its architectural style was removed in 1862 for structural reasons and the present brick upper section added in 1926.

To some, perhaps, it stands as a drab monument to the Anglican faith or as a general reminder of what religion and traditional ways of worship in 'God's House' meant to earlier generations. Other more inquisitive and imaginative people may sense within its rough brick outer walls a whiff of history worth pursuing, a history dating back to its very early years when, as the first Protestant Episcopal church in Spanish America, the Anglican diocese radiating from it extended as far south as Costa Rica. An important feature of this was that for a quarter of a century or so after its dedication in 1826, the kings of the Mosquito Indians from the eastern shores of Nicaragua (usually described as the Mosquito Shore), wishing to maintain their link with Britain and the church, were crowned at St John's and their children baptized there – although the first of these coronations actually took place as long ago as 1815. Probe this connection more

2. St John's Cathedral.

deeply and the vista of a much earlier and wider imperial past is
revealed.

Because of British involvement in the affairs of both the Belize
settlement and the Mosquito Shore, there was a period when their
destinies were to some extent intertwined. Although that association
was not bracketed as close as, say, Rogers and Astaire, Holmes and
Watson, Laurel and Hardy, ham and eggs, salt and pepper, or horse
and carriage (nowadays love and marriage hardly applies), they each
had lines out to the other as neighbours with similar aspirations and
facing similar threats to their continued precarious existence.
Indeed, it is virtually impossible to tell the story of one without
reference to the other. Those stories are set against the backdrop of
the area's developing history, particularly the intense competition
between Spain and England over trade originating in the Bay of

Honduras, most pertinently the trade in logwood and then mahogany beginning in the early colonial era. But, to put that in context, I start with the wider picture.

Under a papal bull of 1494, the pope arbitrarily divided the east and west of the then undiscovered New World between Spain and Portugal, assigning to them all lands including offshore islands and seas. Shortly afterwards, however, a Portuguese expedition breached the dividing line in the Americas defined under the Treaty of Tordesillas and established a colony in what is now known as Brazil. Spain had occupied very little of this extensive territory when, in 1587, Queen Elizabeth I issued a forceful declaration of policy in response to Spanish claims to a monopoly of trade and colonization in the west implicit in the pope's edict. Consistent with her Protestant faith she not unsurprisingly called into question the assumed papal right to carve up the world in this way and also the propriety of any ensuing action to prevent other nationals from settling or trading in areas not inhabited by the Spanish.[1]

The upshot was that as the Spanish attempted to build an empire in the region, British pirates and adventurers, among others, moved in to steal the fruits of that empire once harvested and dispatched in treasure ships *en route* to Spain. Hopes that this situation could be resolved peacefully after the suppression of piracy in 1667 under the Treaty of Madrid, proved optimistic. Further friction arose specifically over the lucrative logwood trade that Spain had originally monopolized. This was a timber to be found almost exclusively around the Bay of Honduras and was then a much coveted commodity in Europe used by dyers in the textile industry. When the trade attracted British cutters to the region, Spain attempted to dislodge them from the settlements from which they were operating.

I first became aware of the close connection between the Belize and Mosquito Shore settlements in the late 1950s when, while working in the West Indian Department of the Colonial Office, I dealt with a letter from a person in the Netherlands in which a photocopy of a document purporting to be a deed of land held on the Mosquito Shore was enclosed. The person wanted to know if the deed was still valid and, if so, was the land of any commercial value? This involved some research, which revealed a classic land swindle and accompanying human misery. But that research, admittedly gleaned from a variety of secondary sources and developed further in subsequent years, introduced me not only to the close cooperation between the two settlements but also to a much wider British involvement in and around the Bay of Honduras in the seventeenth, eighteenth and nineteenth centuries, which, for reasons of space and relevance, cannot adequately be developed within the compass of a single chapter. None the less, some account of that involvement is necessary if one is to develop the story of the relationship between the Belize and Mosquito Shore settlements, the land swindle and a wider imperial presence. I have, therefore, sketched out below for the general reader a potted version of that history touching upon the salient features.

With most of our school history textbooks on the New World focusing on British involvement in North America and, in particular, on the settlement of the 13 states on the eastern seaboard of what became known as the United States of America and the subsequent revolution, coupled with the struggle for Canada, it tends to be overlooked that there was a time in the seventeenth and eighteenth centuries when Britons also established a number of settlements on the swampy fringe of the bulge of the Central American mainland. These were strung out along the coastline of the Bay of Honduras from Yucatán to Costa Rica, extending in one particular instance, further south to Panama. Maps of the period show British settlements around Campeche and elsewhere in the Yucatán Province of Mexico, the Belize (Honduras or Bay) settlement as it was then sometimes referred to, the Mosquito Shore and some of the neighbouring offshore islands. The settlers were, for the most part, originally buccaneers who had settled down to the business of logwood cutting, but not exclusively so.

Towards the end of the seventeenth century, for example, the Scottish founder of the Bank of England, William Paterson, led an expedition to Darien on the isthmus of Panama where he hoped to establish a Scottish settlement financed mainly by a group of his country's merchants seeking new trading outlets in what was thought to be a key strategic location for investment and commercial opportunities. Much of Scotland's national wealth was poured into the scheme, with contributions from small savers as well as large investors. Initially, there were English subscribers, but these were withdrawn because of parliamentary disapproval in London where the proposed settlement was seen as a threat to English trade and a possible cause of war with Spain.[2] Indeed, the latter made it clear that it would regard such a settlement as aggression.[3]

More unfortunately, the site was ill chosen, for situated as it was on a malarial swamp few of the would-be colonists survived the malignant tropical diseases or climate. In the event, the adventure turned out to be a complete disaster. Paterson's wife and daughter died there, along with many others, and he too barely escaped with his life.[4] The financial losses incurred by the catastrophic failure of this enterprise had an adverse affect on the overall Scottish economy and worsened the existing poverty of many of its people: thus, it undoubtedly contributed to the circumstances leading up to the Act of Union between England and Scotland in 1707 when political independence was traded for economic advantages. And, as I shall explain in more detail later, attempts had been made earlier in the century to set up on religious grounds a British settlement on the island of Providence off the Mosquito Shore. But such endeavours were undoubtedly exceptions to the general pattern centred on the logwood trade.

At first, Spain had a complete monopoly in logwood (or Campeche wood as it was also called). It originally attracted a high price, as much as £100 a ton at one time – a very high price indeed for those days. Once British pirates became aware of its cash value, it was not long before they began to prey on Spanish logwood ships. Thereafter, following the suppression of piracy, it was only a short step before they engaged in logwood cutting for themselves at various points along the coast of the Yucatán Peninsula, particularly in Campeche, despite Spain prohibiting foreigners from undertaking such activities.

The first British settlement of logwood cutters of which there is clear evidence was near Cape Catoche on the northern coast of Yucatán.[5] Others subsequently established included San Paulo, Suma Santa (adjacent to the Laguna de Terminos), Triste in the Bay of Campeche, and Cozumel,[6] an area extending southwards from the

River Hondo to the mouth of the Belize River and Mosquito Shore. But it has to be accepted that old habits tend to die hard and, given human nature, the probability is that until late in the seventeenth century the two callings of logwood cutting and piracy remained interchangeable.

Throughout the eighteenth century the status of logwood cutters caused conflicts in the area and repeated friction between Spain and Britain. By that time the monopoly in logwood had passed from Spain to the British cutters and the importance of this cannot be over estimated. In the early part of that century, Britain generally regarded imports of sugar and other products from its West Indian possessions, together with logwood from the Yucatán Peninsula, as more valuable than all the other products exported from the mainland American colonies, or even trade with India, which was where the future development lay.[7]

Despite a growing demand for mahogany for the burgeoning furniture industry in Europe gradually overtaking the logwood trade, the latter was to remain important until late into the nineteenth century when the production of synthetic dyes started to render it obsolete, though some exports continued until the early twentieth century. The value of its trade to the British economy did not escape the attention of the cutters. For example, in a submission to London in February 1783, designed to press their claim for colonial status and fully aware of the contribution to British wealth and power flowing from the logwood trade at that time, petitioners from the Belize settlement claimed that they were producing sufficient to satisfy not only the home market but re-exports to much of continental Europe, particularly Italy, Portugal, France and the Netherlands, but also Russia. Moreover, they added, supply was beginning to outstrip demand to the extent that the price per ton had fallen to about £10 on which His Majesty's Customs imposed a duty of £1 per ton. Not only did this help the exchequer, but the prevailing low price assisted the competitiveness of British clothing manufacturers, especially in the export market. The trade also provided employment for 7700 British seamen.[8]

However, during that century almost continuous European conflicts with ripples spreading across the Atlantic to the Caribbean and the Americas threatened the settlers' very existence and survival became their overriding consideration. This involved all manner of hardships and hazards. In all of this, as already suggested in the Prologue, they displayed enough courage, fortitude and stoicism to warrant a special place in British imperial history.

Because of their isolation they were vulnerable to political pressures or military attacks from Spain, and their ships were liable to seizure. Among the first to succumb were the Campeche and northern Yucatán settlements shortly before or during the so-called War of Jenkins's Ear (1739–49), although these were, in any event, becoming less economically viable due to over exploitation or untenable because of Spanish harassment. As we learn from general history books, this war broke out over Spain's insistence on the right to intercept and search other nations' shipping for plundered goods or what they regarded as 'contraband' (that is to say goods not authorized for foreign trading under the terms of the Treaty of Utrecht) thus creating tension in the area and alarm among certain commercial interests in London that saw their lucrative livelihoods, based on such 'illicit' trade, threatened.

Against this background a certain Captain Jenkins from the West Indies station appeared before the bar of the House of Commons with a shrivelled ear in his hand. Lifting the flap of his wig he told horrified members that it was his ear that the 'barbarous' Spanish had cut off after pillaging his ship, torturing him and insulting Britain and its king. What he omitted to add, lest it might affect the drama and intent, was that it had been sliced off by a cutlass blow in a scuffle with a Spanish customs officer who had boarded his ship off the coast of Cuba and that the affray had taken place seven years earlier.[9] The ear had been preserved in brandy ever since. Current wags were no doubt subsequently tempted to observe that 'this was to bring matters to a head'. And so it did.

Although both nations made an effort to solve peacefully the dispute this incident had raised, they were up against the powerful determination of the British merchants who were in no mood to be denied unrestricted access to the trade of the New World. Under pressure from their parliamentary representatives and public outrage (induced but not generally whipped up by the affected commercial interests) Walpole, the government leader designated First Lord of the Treasury (and to all intents and purposes Britain's first prime minister) reluctantly declared war on Spain and its ally, France, Britain's other maritime and commercial rival. In this he acted against his better judgement. Appalled by the shrill display of jingoism[10] that had manoeuvred him into this position, he was said to have observed at the time that, 'They now ring the bells, but they will soon wring their hands.'

Inevitably, it was a war entered into with little conviction and concluded with neither honour nor glory. Essentially a maritime operation, the British strategy was to seize ports on both coasts of Spanish America. But, apart from Admiral Vernon's temporary success in capturing Porto Bello on the Panama isthmus, which could not be held, the venture generally failed and is regarded without pride in the annals of British military and naval history. It came to an end with the Treaty of Aix-la-Chapelle in 1749.

By that time the centre of the logwood industry had shifted southwards to the Belize settlement. Many of the dispersed and displaced settlers from the now deserted settlements of Campeche and Yucatán found their way there or to the Mosquito Shore, which was also an important source of logwood. Thereafter, both settlements maintained close contact and were able to offer each other a convenient refuge in times of threat or need. Thus, in 1754, for instance, when the Spanish drove the settlers out of Belize, they fled to the Mosquito Shore before returning home the following year. And when the latter was evacuated in 1786 under the Convention of London the evacuees were settled in the former. And there are numerous other examples of common help and cooperation. But, back to the treaty of Aix-la-Chapelle, which was to provide a short prelude to another threat to the continued existence of both settlements, this time from a totally unexpected quarter although neither was made aware of it.

When the War of Jenkins's Ear ended in 1749 it was to provide an uneasy breathing space among the European powers before the onset of the Seven Years' War in 1756. The latter was to see Britain use the activities of the logwood settlers as a potential expendable pawn in European diplomatic circles.

In 1761, the fifth year of that war when it looked as though France was about to negotiate a separate peace settlement with Britain, there were indications that, fearing that such a settlement would be at its expense, Spain was preparing to ally itself with France to prevent this happening. In a pre-emptive move the Cabinet authorized the British ambassador to Madrid to offer the withdrawal of all British log-cutting settlements in the Bay of Honduras if Spain remained neutral.[11] This failed to do the trick and Spain entered the war two years later, only to find itself on the losing side. In the subsequent peace of 1764, which finally recognized the settlers' right to cut and export logwood, Britain did not require it to cede anything else. Thus, agreement to Spain's continuing insistence that no military fortifications should be erected was a sop to its theoretical sovereignty in exchange for recognizing the settlers' rights to continue their log-cutting activities.

A map of British possessions in the Bay of Honduras drawn by Thomas Jeffrey, the royal cartographer, and dated February 1775, throws an interesting light on the names by which the two main settlements were known at the time.[12] The area that came to be called British Honduras is simply depicted as being occupied by 'The Logwood Cutters' with the northern boundary shown as the River Hondo and, surprisingly, long before it was ever recognized internationally, the southern boundary as the Sarstoon River. Also represented in traditional red shading among the numerous offshore cayes, is Turneffe Island. The area generally referred to as the Mosquito Shore carries the double name 'Moskitos Sambos'. At that time the Mosquito (Moskito, Mesquito or Misquito) Indians, an Amerindian people, and the Sambos inhabited the northeastern shore of Nicaragua. The Sambos were a group of hybrid Afro-Amerindians descended from runaway Negro slaves, many of whom had fled to the Mosquito Shore from their Spanish masters in the Caribbean, and intermingled with the local Indians. Some people believe that 'Sambos' is the collective name British buccaneers gave to them and may have derived from one of their respected leaders at the time, Colonel Samboler.[13] It is a word I suspect is now politically incorrect, though it was still in vogue during my childhood. Both our daughters read Helen Bannerman's *Little Black Sambo* first published in the late Victorian era, which was then still a popular children's book. The Mosquito kings came from that group of Afro-Amerindians. The map also shows the Bay Islands of Rataan (Ruatan) and Bonnaca, off the coast of Honduras, as British possessions.

Yet, in one respect the Mosquito Shore, unlike the other settlements in the area, might be described as the joker in the pack. This is because, although the initial British presence was almost certainly directly related to piracy, there was also a religious dimension. That involvement, which included the protection of the Mosquito Indians, began in 1630 when the 2nd Earl of Warwick, an English adventurer, colonial administrator and advocate of religious tolerance in the newly formed American colonies, assumed responsibility for managing the Providence Island Company, which administered the island of Old Providence off the Mosquito Shore.

Warwick had devised an emigration scheme, financed by private venture capital, for the settlement of British colonists in those parts of the West Indies and of South and Central America not occupied by the Spanish or other foreign powers. Its aim was to attract people wanting to establish a free Protestant empire overseas along the lines of the Pilgrim Fathers who sailed for North America in the *Mayflower*. In the event, the settlement on the Mosquito Shore lasted for 12 years before the Spanish sacked and destroyed it.[14] Although out of favour at the English court because of his Puritan sympathies, Warwick's association with the local Indians did not affect British protection, which, through the captain general in Jamaica, continued throughout successive reigns until, as mentioned earlier, British settlement ended in 1786 under the Convention of London. At that stage, many of the settlers and their slaves moved northwards to Belize where they were granted land under the administration of Colonel Despard – a story I will come to in a later chapter. Even then, notwithstanding that move, British protection of the Indians was to continue until the middle of the nineteenth century, and even beyond.

When Nicaraguan troops entered Mosquito territory (Mesquitia) in 1894 and the Indians appealed to Britain for help, the British, with US support, intervened by landing forces at Bluefields. Later that

year a convention was signed incorporating Mesquitia with Nicaragua and, at that stage, the British and American forces withdrew.[15]
The Mosquito Indians, for their part, were intensely loyal to Britain
and seemed to regard their territory as part of the British Empire.
Consistent with this was their practice from early on until the
change of venue to Belize, to have their kings crowned in Jamaica,
from which British influence in the area radiated. Relations between
Jamaica and the Mosquito Shore, however, went even deeper than
that, for Jamaica Assembly archives record a military agreement in
1720 with Jeremy, then king of the Mosquito Indians, for assistance
in subduing a rebellion of Maroons – runaway Spanish-speaking
slaves who occupied the Cockpit region of Jamaica.

There are several references to this close connection in *Lady
Nugent's Journal*. She was the wife of Lord Nugent, governor of
Jamaica from 1801 to 1805. For example, in an appendix, she
records how news was received of the assassination of George II by
the Mosquito people. The text of the relevant letter was addressed to
the governor and government of Jamaica and dated February 1802:[16]

Sir,

We beg leave to Acquaint you that we have had here a
General Meeting with the greater part of our officers to advise
your Honour of our present Situation and are very sorry that
our King George the 2nd was assassinated in his house on the
10th of August last by the people from Sandy Bay they robbed
the house of all Arms and Ammunition none of us to Leeward
of this knew anything of it, we have since elected his Br
Stephen King for life we are in great need of a Supplie of
Muskets Machets Powder Ball and Flints, falling axes & small
hatchets as we are afraid of an attack by the Spaniards as soon
as the dry Season setts in which is soon and we never liked
the Spaniard and King George when alive allways looked up
to the English for assistance in Arms and Ammunition and we
still look upon them as our Allies and would be very happy
they return to Black River we will clear the land for them
ourselves. …

King Stephen is in great need of some Cloth and would be

greatly obliged to his Honour to send some such as Osnaburgs
Checks and Platillas [?] a dozen pair of Pistols and Swords.
Notwithstanding we elected King Stephen we leave it intirely
to the determination of the British Government to be directed
for the Appointment One.

   We beg leave to remain with the greatest Esteem,

Sir.

   Signed by the following with their respective marks:
General Marshall Wayatt, General Robinson, General
Perkins, Major Jasper Hall, Colonel Quaco and Captains
Thomas Pitts, Smith, Abraham and Ross.

The reference to the previously abandoned British settlement at
Black River is of particular significance because it was the setting of
the subsequent swindle mentioned above to which I shall return
shortly. But first a little more history is needed to set the scene.

   With the invasion of Spain by Napoleon's army in 1808, political
movements were set up in Mexico and the other Spanish possessions
in Central America to espouse the cause of independence. The
achievement of independence by the early 1820s led to the creation
of a new political entity, the Central American Federation, in 1823.
It also gave the Mosquito king an opportunity to reassert the
independence of his territory from Spanish sovereignty, theoretical
though that sovereignty was. This upheaval was to have economic as
well as political repercussions beyond the Caribbean. Businessmen
and speculators in the City of London, for instance, were undoubtedly watching the situation with interest, sensing new entrepreneurial opportunities. The Mosquito Shore in particular, which
Britain never fully gave up despite the Convention of London
mentioned above and which was now virtually a British protectorate
inhabited by friendly natives, seemed to offer promising opportunities for commercial exploitation. This included possible involvement in the construction of a shipping canal through the narrow
isthmus of Central America to link the Atlantic and Pacific Oceans, a
project that had been bruited about for some time and was now
beginning to be taken seriously. Inevitably, however, there were also

minor speculators whose activities were distinctly dodgy; prominent among these was a certain Scottish adventurer, Sir Gregor McGregor, a tartan 'Arthur Daley' of the day.

In 1819 McGregor somehow secured from the Mosquito king a concession of land in Poyasia near the mouth of the Black River where, as intimated above, reminders of a once thriving British settlement survived in the form of run-down wooden buildings with rotting timbers, rusty and deteriorating machinery and a variety of discarded tools and other implements. Until sacked but not occupied by a Spanish force in 1780, it was the largest British settlement in the Bay of Honduras with considerable agricultural and timber potential that was being profitably exploited. Two years later the Spanish returned to take over its fortifications, but shortly afterwards were forced to surrender in a counter-military action led by Colonel Despard, to whom reference has been made above.

Having parcelled this land into lots, Mc Gregor issued a seductive brochure announcing the formation of a new Gold Mine Company and painting a lyrical picture of a veritable El Dorado offering rich pickings only waiting to be exploited by immigrants assisted by available and willing native labour. The brochure imaginatively depicted the area as a beautiful and productive sub-tropical paradise blessed with the amenities of civilization – in other words, the so-called 'State of Poyais' had a well-ordered government and established capital at San Joseph. The promoter of the company was designated 'His Serene Highness, Gregor, Prince of the Poyasia, Cazique of the Poyasia nation, Defender of the Rights of the Indian tribes etc' and, as befitting his regal title and standing, he would sign commissions and other documents relating to the company as 'Gregor P'.[17] His business agent, a Mr George Alexander Low, was accorded the rank of colonel and the illustrious title (with res-plendent insignia to match) of Adjutant General of the Poyasian Army.

Well, if you are going in for a swindle, why not do it in style by invoking the presence of the aristocracy and all the attendant trappings among the usual exaggerated honeyed blandishments? Surely W. S. Gilbert had this sort of situation in mind in *The Gondoliers* when the Duke of Plaza Toro (who having turned his own dukedom into a limited company) trills:

In short if you kindle
the spark of a swindle,
lure simpletons into your clutches,
or hoodwink a debtor,
you cannot do better,
than trot out a Duke or a Duchess.[18]

Of similar view, 'His Serene Highness Gregor' went even better and trotted out not only a prince but a cazique. This had the desired effect of luring droves of simpletons into his clutches. And so a classic scam produced a classic outcome.

Wily McGregor clearly had the public weighed up when he designed his prospectus calculated to bring in 'a nice little earner'. Dangle the prospect of easy profits or a short cut to wealth before their eyes and gullible people will inevitably be attracted in a manner reminiscent of moths around a flame. A century earlier, a classic example of the dangers of speculation in an age that had not yet grown familiar with its tricks is to be found in the history of the South Sea Company. This had been founded in 1710 to trade, mainly in slaves (the *asiento*), with the Spanish American colonies, but Spanish restrictions on the trade under the Treaty of Utrecht of 1713, upset the financial calculations. However, by the time King George I became governor of the company in 1718 confidence had become unbounded and, though it had no assets whatsoever behind it, the enterprise was soon paying 100 per cent interest. This became known as the South Sea Bubble, which, when it burst, brought financial ruin to most of its shareholders. Into a frenzied financial fever over trade with Spanish America the unscrupulous, venal and corrupt preyed on people's naivety. Thus, in 1720 there was a vast outpouring of a wide variety of company promotions with much speculation in their shares. As this grew it attracted numerous fraudulent companies that were floated to batten onto the sudden orgy of speculation. Some of the schemes beggared belief. For example, one company invited shareholders to invest in a scheme 'for an undertaking of great advantage but nobody to know what it is'.[19] Many others were equally incredible, including one for importing jackasses from Spain, to which considerable funds were pledged.[20]

I shall now fast forward a century to after the collapse of the Spanish American empire when, with the memory of the South Sea Bubble now faded, fresh generations were persuaded to part with their money in another investment boom based likewise, though not exclusively, on investment prospects in Spanish America. Indeed, among the companies vying for investment funds at the time was one that proposed 'to drain the Red Sea with a view to recovering the treasure abandoned to the Egyptians after the crossing of the Jews'.[21] Well, I ask you! But full marks for nerve and imagination. As that flamboyant American showman Phineas T. Barnum once observed, 'there's a sucker born every minute.' However, despite that evident truth, we should not stray from events on the Mosquito Shore.

In short, hundreds of Britons gambled their life's savings, and many even their lives, on McGregor's highly publicized and speculative miniature South Sea Bubble mark two. Although clearly a swindle, it was marginally within the law in the sense that the land and buildings outlined in the prospectus did exist and a small amount of gold had been panned out of the river silt. Unsurprisingly, however, it was far from being the 'promised land' that McGregor had portrayed, in fact quite the reverse. On disembarking after a long and uncomfortable voyage across the Atlantic – it should be remembered that this was still the age of sail – these people found, as one of their number put it, 'nothing but a few wretched huts, with no one to receive them, no shops, [and] no provisions or good water'.

They were soon in a desperate plight, for most of them were unused to manual work or 'roughing it' in any way. Starvation loomed large and many of them died of privation or disease. Eventually, news of their situation reached their compatriots in Belize. Superintendent Codd reacted immediately and early in 1823 dispatched two prominent local citizens, Messrs Bennett and Wallby, to investigate their plight. They confirmed 'an accumulation of Misery beyond conception' and brought back 60 of the worst cases to Belize for early relief.[22]

Now that the facts were known, the settlers acted with speed, vigour and compassion. A Colonel Hall was dispatched at once to the area where, among other things, he noted the newly turned graves of over seventy dead Britons. Picking up such possessions as they still had, he shipped the destitute survivors to Belize. About fifty were settled on smallholdings in Stann Creek (now renamed Dangriga) with tools and labour to give them a start – though many of these were to find agricultural labour too strenuous for them. The sick were looked after in hospital and 49 were shipped back to Britain at the settlement's expense. Overall, expenditure on the refugees, exclusive of private subscriptions and gifts, was given as £4290, which was indicative of the settlers' early growing social consciousness and responsibility.[23] Among the expenses listed in the first ever recorded annual financial estimates, in the archives for 1808 and published that year, is an entry described as 'Incidental expenses for humane and charitable purposes', thus confirming the settlers' social awareness.[24]

Naturally, a report on the situation was relayed to the authorities in London by Superintendent Codd. In acknowledging it, the secretary of state informed him that the king had approved the action he had taken and that His Majesty was also pleased to notice 'the arduous personal exertions of Messrs Bennett and Wallby'.[25] But the story does not end there.

At the beginning of September 1823, the so-styled adjutant general of the even more fictitious Poyaisian army, Colonel Low, arrived in Belize with his family to protest to the magistrates against the unlawful disposal of his property and that of his friends, including Sir Gregor McGregor. He refused to produce any form of authority or identity.[26] In reporting this further development to London, the superintendent admitted that Colonel Hall, who had brought back the last batch of survivors from the Mosquito Shore, had seized a number of possible items of value and had subsequently sold them to defray his expenses. But he went on to add that, far from anyone in the settlement profiting from all the human misery and suffering experienced by those whom McGregor had duped, they had rescued them, paid the passages of 49 to England and had looked after the remainder at public expense. In refuting the charges he was fuelled by indignation that not only had compassion and altruism governed the settlers' intervention on behalf of the refugees, but also that one of the perpetuators of the whole crooked scheme was now challenging him, especially given that many, including himself, had experienced the misfortune and indignity of having been infected with fever caught through contact with sick refugees.[27]

The story continued to run. In London, the McGregor faction submitted a memorandum to the secretary of state that repeated his allegations about the seizure and sale of property, specifically citing the action of one of the original rescuers, Mr Marshall Bennett (an enterprising local merchant heavily engaged at that time in entrepôt trade with the newly emerged Central American states) whom they claimed, with the support of the superintendent and magistrates, forcibly carried off their labourers and servants.[28] This was followed by the publication and circulation of a pamphlet entitled *The Belize Merchants Unmasked* in which it was alleged that three of the magistrates were responsible for the downfall of the Poyaisian settlement.[29] The latter sued Low for libel, but the jury acquitted him on the grounds that there was insufficient evidence to prove that he was the author of the pamphlet.

This brought to an end the McGregor saga as far as the Belize settlement was concerned – well, er, not quite. A faint echo of his continued interest in the area was subsequently heard. On 8 July 1825 the secretary of state notified Superintendent Codd of Sir Gregor McGregor's intention to occupy either the 'island of Rattan' (Ruatan) in the Bay of Honduras 'or some of the adjacent islands without the authority or sanction of His Majesty's Government'.[30] I have found no evidence that he did so, but he was obviously not short of ambition, perseverance and a thick skin in his incessant pursuit of gullible people and easy pickings.

When the story came out in Britain, many of those who had followed it were probably astounded to learn for the first time that the empire had a footing on the Central American mainland. And no doubt there would have been a fluttering in the dovecotes of Whitehall and in the chanceries of the newly formed Central American republics, as they pondered over the international implications. For example, was this Poyasian settlement an infringement of the 1786 convention forbidding British occupation on the Mosquito Shore? Or had that convention lapsed on the recent break-up of the Spanish Empire in Central America? In that event, what was the present status of the Mosquito Shore in international law? More specifically, had the Mosquito king been in his rights to grant a land concession to McGregor? And so on.

But this was the age of the Pax Britannica. Without asserting any territorial rights either in Belize or the Mosquito Shore, Britain proceeded to act as though such rights had long existed. Thus, in practice, Belize was regarded as a colony while the Mosquito Shore was pro tem a protectorate.

With the colonial status of Belize now seemingly assured, further recognition was accorded when in 1826 the Mosquito Indians formally switched the venue for the coronation of their kings from Jamaica to St John's Cathedral. But by now a new factor had entered the political equation, namely the role to be played in the area by the newly established United States.

In a fast changing international climate, the fledgling United States was busily reassessing its attitudes and policies towards the area at its backdoor. It was determined not to allow any other European power to occupy the vacuum that the collapse of the Spanish Empire in the region had created. Therefore, in 1823, President Monroe declared in a published edict (known subsequently as the Monroe Doctrine) that, in effect, the United States would not tolerate such moves. In other words, the whole of the American continent was to fall within its sphere of influence and, if there was going to be any exploitation it would be the power to do it. At that stage it was in no position militarily to implement such a policy and there is evidence to suggest that it counted on Britain's commercial, military and naval clout to prevent other European powers intervening in the affairs of the newly-independent republics. Indeed, the catalyst for the renowned Monroe statement was a suggestion in 1823 by the British foreign secretary, George Canning, that Britain and the United States should issue a joint statement warning the continental Europeans against intervention in Latin America.[31] The American authorities considered this unnecessary on the grounds that their statement did not call for public British support; such support was in any event forthcoming because Britain's desire to carry on trade with the new Latin American republics was the real reason for its opposition to the re-establishment of other European rule.

So, for many years after the Monroe Doctrine was pronounced, Britain acted as though its principles did not apply to it. British involvement in the area continued to expand, particularly under Lord Palmerston's stewardship as foreign secretary. In 1839 the superintendent of the Belize settlement, Colonel Macdonald, retook possession of Ruatan in the Bay Islands and, despite protests from the state of Honduras, the home government sustained his action.[32] Thereafter, *de facto* possession was maintained and, to provide local stability, magistrates from Belize were appointed to serve there.[33]

In 1841, two years after taking possession of Ruatan, the enterprising Macdonald, accompanied by the king of the Mosquitos, proceeded to the port of San Juan south of the Mosquito Shore and, in the latter's name, attempted to dispossess the Nicaraguan commandant there. Macdonald had apparently acted on his own initiative and the Nicaraguan authorities remained in San Juan.[34] Nevertheless, the policy of supporting the Mosquito Indians was encouraged and, in 1844, it was decided to appoint a British Resident on the shore. The post was given to Patrick Walker,[35] Macdonald's secretary, who took up residence at Bluefields. The territory was locally renamed Mesquitia and the Indians were presented with a flag that bore a striking resemblance to the Union Jack.[36] Three years later the British government announced that the Mosquito king's territory extended from Cape Honduras to the San Juan River and, since it was under British crown protection, the British could not view with indifference any encroachment on his lands. Shortly afterwards, in January 1848, Walker, emulating Macdonald, proceeded to San Juan with the king of the Mosquitos where he hauled down the Nicaraguan flag and hoisted that of Mesquitia. Nicaraguan resistance was crushed by the arrival of two British gunboats and San Juan was renamed Greytown in honour of the then governor of Jamaica.[37] Subsequently, in 1852, Ruatan, Bonnaca and four neighbouring islands were incorporated by royal proclamation into the short-lived colony of the Bay Islands.

By now this overt British activity was beginning to set alarm bells ringing in the United States, especially as the long held dream of the need for a trans-isthmus canal between the Atlantic and the Pacific had now gained wide acceptance. The idea of piercing Central America at some point had occurred to the Spanish as far back as 1534,[38] when they became aware of the relative position of the two oceans, but the technology to turn this dream into a reality was not then available. In the event, a railway through the narrow Isthmus of Panama was the first technical advance to be exploited, but the transit of ships was the ultimate aim.

Among other schemes, in 1846 a Frenchman (whose countrymen were already contemplating linking up the Mediterranean Sea with the Indian Ocean at Suez) published a plan to join the two oceans via Nicaragua. It was based on ideas that had been in existence since the time of the early Spaniards. The key to this was the linking of the great inland waterways of Lakes Nicaragua and Managua. It was believed that access to these waterways from the Atlantic side was feasible in or near the River Juan and, from there to the Pacific, various passages of egress were possible. The proposed scheme, the brainchild of a French entrepreneur called M. Belly, was based on a feasibility study an engineers officer from the United States army, Colonel Child, had conducted some years earlier.[39] The latter's findings had never been costed and, at most, even after considerable dredging, would have led to the construction of a canal only 17 feet deep, which would have excluded the transit of large seagoing vessels. Furthermore, there were problems. For a start, such a canal would impinge on several national sovereignties and there was no guarantee that it would be a truly internationally operated waterway. Above all, there was a strong suspicion that M. Belly was little more than an adventurer of no substance whose main aim was to float a company of doubtful propriety for his own financial advantage. In the event, his scheme failed to get very far beyond trying to negotiate for concessions with the presidents of Costa Rica and Nicaragua and publishing a prospectus so grandiose that it would undoubtedly have earned the admiration and respect of Sir Gregor McGregor.

The canal project then gained impetus for a seemingly unconnected reason. Texas was annexed in 1844 and, four years later, following the war with Mexico, the United States acquired New Mexico, Arizona and California. While the US authorities were naturally anxious to see US citizens populate these territories as quickly as possible, and encouraged them to do so, an even greater stimulus for mass migration westward was the discovery of gold in California on 24 January 1848.[40] This was to attract mining pioneers who arrived in large numbers the following year. Among these so-called 'forty-niners', as older generations may recall, was the fictional father of 'Clementine' in Percy Montrose's once popular ballad of that name originating in the Victorian age. At that time, around the mid-nineteenth century, most of the uncharted territory west of the Mississippi, which settlers had not yet occupied, lay across difficult terrain, including mountain ranges and deep or fast flowing rivers. Starvation and disease were ever present hazards and sometimes the route was through hostile Indian controlled country, though probably to a lesser extent than Hollywood films were to depict in the following century. With great distances to overcome, primitive transport and little physical protection, it was virtually impassable except for the most determined or optimistic westbound pioneers. The practical response to this situation was to seek a route from the Atlantic to the Pacific through the narrow waist of Central America.

Accordingly, many prospectors and other migrants poured into the isthmus in their thousands. Most, to avoid various hazards, had chosen the Panamanian route to California in preference to an alter-native service Cornelius Vanderbilt's steamship company provided via the San Juan River and Lake Nicaragua. Although the American-financed 48-mile stretch of the Panama Railway was opened in the 1850s to help facilitate this (and indeed earned millions of dollars before being sold in 1877 to the incoming French canal company for the formidable sum of US$ 25 million),[41] interest in the construction of a canal heightened. As the United States government began to focus on a wider Central American trajectory, it found that, despite the Monroe Doctrine, which was now integral to its foreign policy, the British remained strongly entrenched on most of the Atlantic seaboard. Apart from Belize, the latter had revised their interest in the Mosquito Shore, where mahogany operations were taking place, and in Ruatan in the Bay Islands, to which several hundred Britons had emigrated from the Cayman Islands. Above all, the Americans had now become acutely aware of the importance of the Mosquito Shore connection because, if the Nicaraguan canal project were to materialize, a right of way would be required across the territory over which Britain claimed sovereign rights.

It was against this background that the United States began to question Britain's rights in the area. With the importance of trans-isthmian communications now enhanced, cooperation between the two countries was clearly essential and, in the ambiguously worded Clayton–Bulwer Treaty of 1850, they jointly agreed to promote the construction of a canal that was to be 'free and open to all nations' and to secure its neutrality by 'refraining outside powers from occupying, fortifying or colonizing any part of Central America, including the Mosquito Shore'.[42]

The problem with treaties, however, is that self-interest tends to open them to different interpretations. The United States thought that Britain should abandon all territories in the region, including the controversially acquired area south of the Sibun River in Belize, which transgressed the London Convention of 1786 and which the Americans had long contended belonged to Guatemala.[43] Presumably to underline their proclaimed predominance in the hemisphere, the US view was based on a general enforcement of the Monroe Doctrine. More specifically, it might also be seen as the reflection of a fear that such an extended British presence in close proximity to the Atlantic entrance to a proposed trans-isthmus canal could pose a threat should relations between the old and new powers become strained.[44] In the event, a compromise was reached under which, against their inhabitants' wishes, Britain handed Ruatan over to the Republic of Honduras and the Mosquito Shore to Nicaragua. For its part, the United States agreed to the southern boundary of Belize at the Sarstoon River. No doubt this was an early example of the challenge to the Pax Britannica by a fledgling Pax Americana, a challenge that was to increase as the United States began to flex its international muscles and that ultimately, as the twentieth century advanced, resulted in the latter superseding the former as the dominant world power. But now the borders of British Honduras had finally been defined.

The rest of the tale is now well-recorded modern history. Britain and Guatemala signed a treaty on Belize in 1859. However, a dispute over interpretation kept a Guatemalan claim to inheritance of the territory from Spain smouldering and sometimes flaring up until the settlement, now a colony, achieved independence in 1981.

The construction of the projected trans-isthmus canal, in which there was still a residual British interest arising from the Clayton–Bulwer Treaty, was to take place later rather than sooner. In the event, the favoured route turned out to be through Panama, not Nicaragua; and Colombia (of which Panama was then a department) awarded the contract to a French company, though the United States was monitoring developments closely in the light of its own interests. As its power grew, commercial and strategic considerations (including a determination to create a united Atlantic and Pacific battle fleet) demanded easy access to each ocean through the isthmus instead of the existing time-consuming long haul around the Magellan Straits. For the present, however, the initiative for realizing this dream lay with the French.

The internationally renowned French diplomat/engineer who had supervised the building of the Suez Canal, Ferdinand de Lesseps, arrived in Panama in 1881 and, after a preliminary survey, decided on a route along the Chagres River and the Rio Grande.[45] After several false starts due, among other physical obstacles, to poor planning, yellow fever, malaria, torrential rivers and impassable mountain ranges, coupled with allegations of fraud, the operating company, the Compagnie Universelle du Canal Interoceanique, collapsed as an economic venture in 1889. It was reorganized as the Compagnie Nouvelle du Canal de Panama six years later. Eventually, Colombia authorized the company to sell all its rights and properties, including the canal-building rights, to the United States.

To facilitate this, in 1900 the United States entered into negotiations with Britain to secure the abrogation of the treaty of cooperation the two powers had signed half a century earlier and which, theoretically at least, remained a juridical obstacle. Consequently, both sets of negotiators devised a new draft agreement based on the Suez Canal model and imposing similar restrictions on United States control. When it was examined in Washington against a background of nationalistic fervour in which the spirit of the Monroe Doctrine was vociferously invoked, it raised a political storm. Congress and the Senate, as well as influential organs of the press, strongly criticized the restrictions Britain proposed on behalf of the wider international community on American rights of control (not involved in the financing and building of the project) as flagrant outside interference. Some were in favour of going ahead and ignoring the earlier obligations, but calmer heads prevailed. In a welcome return to diplomacy both parties finally agreed to a new accord providing, among other things, for the canal, when built, to be wholly under the control of the United States. This arrangement, known after its respective American and British negotiators as the Hay–Paunceforte Treaty, was regarded as superseding the Clayton–Bulwer Treaty of 1850 that called for joint construction.[46]

Britain's agreement to leave the construction solely to the United States clearly reflected the former's waning power, political interest and involvement in the region since the middle of the nineteenth century. It turned out to be a fortuitous decision, as subsequent events, beginning when the Colombian senate rescinded the decision to sell the canal rights, unfolded. This aroused the fury of the Panamanians who countered by declaring their independence of Colombia in November 1903. The upshot was a war between the two countries involving US intervention and leading to its subsequent recognition of the new republic against Colombia's wishes. Thereafter, the Compagnie Nouvelle du Canal de Panama sold its holdings to the United States in 1904 under what some would regard as dubious, though understandable, circumstances.[47]

Work on the canal began shortly afterwards in concert with a determined drive to eradicate the malignant tropical diseases that were decimating the work force. Other formidable physical and technical obstacles were finally overcome and, on 14 August 1914, the canal was opened to international traffic. Although its construction must rank as one of the wonders of the modern world its cost in human and financial resources was a heavy one to pay. However, none of this was envisaged when Britain and the United States concluded the Clayton–Bulwer Treaty way back in 1850 when the former was the dominant international power in the region. The reality now was that this mantle had been assumed by the latter, leaving British Honduras as the sole surviving symbol of a British role in Central America, which began in the seventeenth century and was to end before the close of the twentieth.

◇ ◇ ◇

Such is a glimpse of Britain's active and colourful involvement on the Spanish Main over the course of four centuries. Since this phase of its imperial history, Britain's global power has faded and its former glory has lost lustre in the eyes of current generations. This history is probably only of marginal, if of any, interest to most Britons today. But what does it mean to the British Honduran (now Belizean) public in general? How much of this history features in their sense of the past? What is more pertinent, perhaps, is what history is taught in schools to help shape a Belizean sense of national identity? This invites what is, in effect, a local footnote to the wider history outlined above.

Close to St John's Cathedral is a girls' secondary school, St Hilda's, with a primary mixed school nearby, and whenever I attended my office at Government House early in the morning I would enjoy the sometimes plangent but ever haunting sounds of the hymns the children sang as they began or ended morning assembly. From its numerous renderings, it was clear that the famous old hymn 'From Greenland's Icy Mountains' was a well-established favourite. As I dwelt on Bishop Heber's words – 'From Greenland's Icy Mountains/ from India's coral strand/where Africa's sunny fountains/Roll down their golden sands' – I would reflect on what they meant to children living in Central America to whom such places were simply words. If history was their next lesson, the textbook would almost certainly have been the Paternoster Press publication of *History through Maps and Diagrams*, covering the political, economic and social development of Britain and the Commonwealth. The import of this struck me forcibly. While they were singing or learning about events thousands of miles away in countries or continents that most of them would never realistically envisage, let alone visit, their school curriculum failed to include the colourful and romantic events leading up to the establishment and initial development of their country. So far as I know, during my secondment little of their history entered the school curriculum. For an explanation, we need to look for clues in tradition, the influence of religion and a changing political scenario.

In the first place, a cultural and historic background ensured that the local education system operating in the secondary schools traditionally followed the British model with similar courses and examinations. Accordingly, detailed local history played no part in the curriculum. Within and outside the classroom, general interest in the past focused on the Battle of St George's Caye in 1798 when their Creole forebears repelled the final Spanish attack on the settlement. Its significance was that henceforth this particular external threat to their existence was at last removed. Not surprisingly, therefore, the anniversary of that victory, 10 September, was adopted as the national day. As children would learn and sing at school, the ballad of 'The Tenth Day of September':

> It was the tenth day of September,
> In ninety eight *Anno Domini*,
> When our forefathers won the glorious fight –
> The Battle of St George's Caye.
>
> Then cheer them, hail them!
> Let our grateful loyal hearts not fail them,
> As we march and shout and sing with merry glee:
> The Battle of St George's Caye!'

This omission was further complicated by the educational system being run along largely denominational lines with the Roman Catholic Church assuming a dominant role, thus reflecting its following in the territory. Missionary bodies, with substantial financial support from the government, ran the majority of the numerous primary schools. At the secondary stage there were, during my secondment, seven recognized schools (of which four were Roman Catholic, two Anglican and one Methodist) and two private secondary schools, both of which were Roman Catholic. This situation allowed the various churches to command and exert an influence on pupils that extended beyond the realms of religion and into the wider affairs of society – and they seized this opportunity.

At one level, they were able to ensure that church objectives often took precedence over academic considerations. At another, they were able to impose upon students whatever political and social interpretations they favoured. The Roman Catholic Church was particularly active in this direction with many of its priests, especially American Jesuits, using the influence of their office to disseminate an anti-colonial and anti-British bias. So, in addition to pursuing church objectives, they took upon themselves a secondary role – that of coming to bury British colonialism and influence and not to praise it! In local political terms, some of them were undoubtedly instrumental in providing tacit political backing to the decolonization and foreign policies of the People's United Party (PUP) under George Price. This religious dimension was to play a part as subsequent developments unfolded.

By the mid-twentieth century, new factors were beginning to influence events. The most significant of these was that the population had become more multiracial and multicultural in its composition and political outlook. Latin American and Amerindian ethnic groups were beginning to challenge the supremacy and British orientation of the majority Creoles. In fact, in those early days of decolonization, many young, emergent (mostly Catholic-educated) nationalist politicians were advocating that the country form a closer alliance with Central America as opposed to the prevailing Colonial Office proposal for a close federal association with the British West Indian islands and British Guiana. Foremost among these politicians was George Price, who was ultimately to emerge as the leader of the main political party, PUP. In a nationalist context, Price, the son of a Creole father and Mayan mother, articulated the ethnic sentiments of his parents and of the growing Latin American presence in the society.

On the political stage he played down the country's colonial past and British connection to further his contention that the country's history lay in the ancestry of the indigenous Maya of Central America who were the original inhabitants. His aim was to impress upon all local ethnic groups that their cultural affinity was with other Central American countries and not with the British West Indies. Initially, his tactic worked, for it broadly represented public opinion, especially in the towns. The PUP's main support came from ordinary Creoles in Belize who were apprehensive about labour migration from overcrowded West Indian islands flooding the labour market at their expense, but, despite its predominantly Creole leadership, the party's focus on Mayan identity also appealed to the Indians, Mestizos and Ladinos, who likewise opposed closer political association with the West Indies.

However, in pushing the Central American connection too strongly, Price began to alienate sections of the Creole elite, which subsequently broke away to form the opposition National Independence Party (NIP). One controversy was sparked off over the name of the country. Citing Spanish historical sources, Price claimed that its original name had been Belize, which derived from two Maya words '*be*' (meaning land) and '*likin*' (meaning to the east), in other words land east of the major Maya centre of Tikal in neighbouring Guatemala. A later source suggested that the word *beliz*, which means 'muddy water' in Yucatán Maya, might offer a more plausible derivation, for this could be said to chime with a description of the Belize River or the fact that the original settlement was built on swampland. However, both these and other interpretations contradict the time-honoured and widely accepted local view that the name Belize is a progressive Spanish corruption of the surname of a Scottish buccaneer Wallace (Walis–Valiz–Baliz), who was believed to have been active in the area in the seventeenth century.[48] Yet another, albeit less popular, view is that the name is derived from the French word *balise* meaning beacon. Thus, to some people it seemed as if history was being rewritten in a revisionist way to nudge the country towards the Central American orbit.

In short, changing circumstances were shaping British history in the region as they were that of its colonial offshoot in Central America. The shift in emphasis was now away from a focus on the traditional past towards more radical thoughts about the present and future. The challenge from other racial, cultural and religious groups in the society to the political influence of the dominant Creoles accentuated this change. In particular, as the move towards decolonization began to gather pace, the gap widened between those who favoured a possible association with Latin America and those who preferred to see the country's future in the Commonwealth with the rest of the British West Indies. In the event, as disillusionment, economic reality and other practical considerations set in, the Central American dream faded and the political pendulum swung back to the traditional past prior to the country's acquisition of independence within the Commonwealth in 1981 – although ironically by that stage its name, British Honduras, had been changed to Belize.

How this developing history is to be interpreted, written and presented locally to schoolchildren and others, so they see from where they have come as they chart the political and international direction in which they wish to go is, of course, something that local historians and educationists have in all probability already addressed. Yet, interesting as this may be, it has to be recognized that it is but a footnote to the main purpose of this chapter, namely to present an outline of a wider British presence in the region to which the logwood and mahogany cutters in the Bay of Honduras contributed.

As I have already intimated, that history has received little general attention in Britain. This is not altogether surprising: as that acute observer of his fellow countrymen and prolific imaginative writer of fiction, H. G. Wells, once opined, '19 Englishmen out of 20 knew as much about the British Empire as they did about the Italian Renaissance'. If he was referring to detail, then I suspect he was not far out. Although most of the great British public at the time were undoubtedly unaware of much of the detailed history of empire, they were certainly aware of its wider imagery, which was indelibly imprinted on the national psyche and reflected and articulated in A. C. Benson's words set to Elgar's music in the imperial anthem, 'Land of Hope and Glory' – hence Aldous Huxley's pointed observation about the British public *vis-à-vis* British Honduras in the extract recorded earlier. So, if the above account adds to a better understanding of one small part of that past empire it will have served some purpose, especially if it stimulates interest in a forgotten British role in and around Central America.

Above all, it serves as a reminder to current generations that in our imperial past we used, as is said nowadays in another and somewhat vulgar context, 'to put it about a bit'.

Chapter 6
806

I HAD NOT BEEN LONG in the colony before I realized that local interest and involvement in one's private life, often in the guise of being helpful, tended to create unwelcome complications and lead to unforeseen trouble. While this undoubtedly added spice to life it also played havoc with one's nervous system. Take, for example, some of the situations involving such a mundane object as my private motorcar.

It is now axiomatic that possession of a motorcar by most adults in the United Kingdom is the rule rather than the exception. That was not so in 1961, though signs of the present-day love affair with the car were already discernable through increasing sales figures and the burgeoning construction of new roads and motorways. On a personal level, although I had learnt to drive during my military service in the Second World War, I had no vehicle of my own when the 'swinging sixties' arrived. When my letter of appointment made it clear that I would need a car because there was no public transport in British Honduras, I realized that I needed to address the questions of make and model. In other words, given the poor state of roads in the colony and the limited facilities for servicing and maintaining a car, it was important to know what would be an appropriate model to purchase. On this I consulted my predecessor, Ken Osborne, who was still in post pending my arrival.

In his reply he told me that he was the owner of a Morris Traveller that had proved absolutely reliable. However, he suggested that as the newly arrived chief secretary had brought out a Hillman Minx, for which there was a local agent who could provide servicing and spare parts, I might wish to consider one of that make. Helpfully, he added that it would be tactful, status being what it is in the colonial hierarchy, to purchase a standard model as the chief secretary had the 'L' version. Armed with this information I ordered a 1.5 litre

Hillman Minx Special Saloon, light green in colour. This was shipped on the Elder Fyffe vessel taking us to Jamaica, the SS *Camito*, and from there a United Fruit Company vessel transhipped it to Belize where it was brought ashore by lighter and delivered to the Queen's Warehouse to await customs clearance.

Once the usual formalities had been completed, and registration and insurance effected, the car was on the road with its white number plates bearing the large figures 806 in black with the name of the colony in small letters above and the words 'Land of Opportunity' below. Although this suggests, quite rightly, that only a little more than 800 private cars were registered and on the road at that time, there were many other vehicles such as taxis, goods vehicles and motor coaches in everyday service. Another incidental point of marginal interest was that cars belonging to members of the Executive Council and to a few other high officials were provided with a form of personalized number plates. For example, the first minister, chief secretary, chief justice and, say, the minister for local government would drive around with special white number plates bearing the initials in blue, 'FM', 'CS', 'CJ' and 'MLG' respectively. And so it went on along the hierarchical line. From this one can deduce that there were many ways in colonial society of separating the establishment wheat from the common general public chaff. However, let us get back to the narrative.

Being a new car and of a colour not hitherto seen in the colony, 806 soon became a focus of attention. Among its early admirers was a group of prisoners from the local gaol whom I found one morning clustered around the vehicle. Here I should explain that in British Honduras prisoners were, and still are, required 'to sing for their supper', as it were. That is to say they were expected to provide some community service towards the cost of their upkeep. This usually took the form of grass cutting with machetes around government buildings and public grounds under the supervision of a warder. One of them, showing particular interest, told me that he would like to own such a vehicle one day. I smiled sympathetically but did not comment. This was perhaps just as well for I subsequently learnt that he was an inveterate thief and that this was the reason for his present incarceration. Although car theft was not hitherto part of his repertoire, he looked the sort of enterprising character who could adapt given the chance. To be on the safe side I nervously enquired about the length of his sentence and in that knowledge calculated that with good luck (that is to say mine as opposed to his) he would still be 'inside' when my tour in the colony ended. However, his tendency to give me a friendly wave whenever he spotted me driving around in the car while on his grass cutting outings did nothing to dispel my anxieties on that score.

As already mentioned, car servicing was to some extent available, but what about cleaning? On this I inherited from my predecessor the services of David, a Government House orderly whom I engaged to give 806 a weekly wash and brush up. What I was soon to discover was that despite his commendable energy and enthusiasm, reliability and tact were not included among his strong suits. At this point I seemingly digress, but with a purpose that I hope will soon become apparent.

One of David's official duties was to serve as a drinks waiter at Government House cocktail parties. As members of the governor's 'inner circle' what could be more natural, therefore, than for the chief secretary and me to engage his services at similar functions of our own? However, although he was a model of deference at Government House parties he seemed to regard himself more as a guest than a waiter at my 'dos'. To say that he drank more than he served would be an exaggeration, but that was the general impression I formed. Certainly, he tended to imbibe liberally and on many occasions the outcome was for him to berate the usual hard core (that is to say, those who invariably stayed on talking and drinking long after most of the other guests had left) by telling them forcibly that they ought to be ashamed of themselves for abusing their host's hospitality. Good old David was always protective in his own distinctive way. Fortunately, no one was embarrassed by these familiar outbursts. Indeed, they added to the evening's entertainment.

One morning at Government House I was told that His Excellency wanted to see me straightaway. To this message was added a rider to the effect that he was not in the best of moods. I was already aware of this from seeing him earlier in the day. The reason was that a handwritten note about social engagements the following day, which he had sent to his private office for copy typing, had been reproduced and returned to him with a glaring error of Freudian proportions. A new temporary local typist had apparently misread the reference to his wife 'Lady Betty' and had typed it up as 'randy Betty'.

Whether he was upset because this was a story that would undoubtedly go the rounds of local society or whether he thought that the new typist knew something about his wife's private life that he did not, were questions I thought prudent not to raise. What was not in dispute was that he was very annoyed.

When I made my second visit that morning I could sense that his mood had not improved. Glowering at me over the top of his spectacles as he sat behind his desk he addressed me more in anger than sorrow. He came straight to the point. 'In future', he began, 'if you want to call on the services of any of my personal staff at any time, perhaps you would have the courtesy to seek my permission first.' This took me aback and I assumed that he was referring to the use of David at social functions at my home. But glancing out of his study window in that split second when I was searching desperately for some plausible excuse or appropriate apology I could see immediately what he was on about and it was not waiter service.

In a secluded part of the western side of the front lawns of Government House, opposite St John's Cathedral, was a metal ramp on to which Government House cars were driven for cleaning or inspection from underneath. As my eyes focused on this I could see 806 on the ramp with David, having hosed it down, giving it a loving polish. It looked immaculate and gleaming in the morning sunlight. By contrast, the governor's large black Austin Princess by the side of the ramp, on which he should have been working, looked travel stained and badly in need of a clean before its next outing.

Now the governor was very sensitive about the Austin Princess, which had been purchased for reasons of prestige. With its gleaming (when cleaned and polished) black bodywork, luxurious upholstery, an interior as large as a London taxi, silver crowns front and rear instead of number plates and the Union Jack flying from the bonnet whenever he was its passenger, he undoubtedly saw it – as possibly did the locals too – as a palpable symbol of British sovereignty over the territory and a boost to his status. Unfortunately, that aura of prestige was overshadowed when the Guatemalan consul in Belize obtained an identical model. That too, was to be seen on the streets. Thus, by implication, the consul was asserting parity with the governor on the basis of his country's territorial claim to British Honduras or *Belice* as they called it. At first it carried no number plates, but the police quickly reasserted British authority by pointing out that this was illegal and accordingly insisted that the appropriate plates be displayed. Although some locals dismissed the incident as a huge joke, the governor was not included in their number. Not surprisingly, he saw it as an attempt to undermine his position. It was against this somewhat sensitive background that he probably saw the cleaning of 806 being given priority over the Austin Princess by a member of his personal staff (and at Government House at that) as tantamount to rubbing salt into an already open wound.

Having by now grasped the reason for his pique I said that I assumed he was referring to David cleaning my car, which I could now see going on through the window; I said that I would speak sternly to him to avoid any repetition. This was to drop another clanger. His Excellency reminded me in somewhat chilly tones that David was one of his personal staff and that if any 'speaking' was to be done he would be the person doing it. Thus admonished I retreated from the room conscious that my popularity rating, if any, had nose-dived, to put it mildly.

Once David had received the expected dressing down from the governor, we arranged for the weekly clean of 806 to take place at the secretariat or at my home whenever he had time off from his duties at Government House. But this was to give rise to problems of another sort. Shortly afterwards reports came to my notice that on such days David would be seen driving my car around the city and surrounding areas with a girlfriend in the passenger seat. Worse was to follow when I learnt from the police that he held no driving licence and, indeed, had never taken, let alone passed, a driving test. So 806 and David parted company. But the former's adventures continued.

With Belize under several feet of sea water during the visitation of

Hurricane Hattie a month or so later (see Chapter 13), any motor vehicles submerged under it were written off for insurance purposes. This was because, apart from rendering the engine and electrical parts virtually useless, the potential corrosive effect of sea water on the bodywork was ruinous. The chief secretary's Hillman, which had been parked at police headquarters during the hurricane and totally immersed in sea water, fell into that category. His subsequent insurance claim was speedily met leaving the vehicle to be sold for whatever price it could attract as scrap or for spare parts. My car, by contrast, had been safely housed at Airport Camp where a colleague's wife had driven it with my family on the afternoon before the hurricane struck. Thus, it was undamaged. Unfortunately, however, as soon as the road to Belize was clear for traffic, it was used to drive Florence into the city to see what damage had been done to our house. As ill luck would have it, the journey through several inches of sea water and piles of salt-impregnated mud and debris was to set in train a process of corrosion that was to eat away the bodywork of 806 and shorten its life span significantly. Had I recognized this at the time, I too might have put in a successful insurance claim. As it was I was left later to reflect ruefully on the vicissitudes of life. For the moment, however, the scene was set for yet another development.

At police headquarters, all vehicles belonging to the force were under the care of Sergeant Meads, a first-class local motor mechanic. He was quick to acquire the chief secretary's Hillman for a nominal sum. Having then stripped and cleaned all the moving parts and effected the necessary rewiring, it was not long before he had it up and running on the road. Shortly afterwards he approached me to say that, since he was now familiar with the workings of a Hillman, he would be only too happy to maintain my vehicle as well. This was a tempting offer, for not only was he a skilled mechanic but he also operated from a well-equipped workshop. So 806 found itself in the police compound for regular attention, but so much for expectation. Its performance seemed to deteriorate rather than improve. After a few weeks the reason became apparent.

One day when I had reason to lift the bonnet of 806 I noticed that the radiator and, on closer inspection, the battery and alternator were not the originals. A horrible suspicion prompted me to take a close look at Sergeant Meads's newly-acquired vehicle and my suspicion was confirmed. From that inspection it was clear that he was replacing dodgy parts in his own vehicle with those in better condition taken from mine. When challenged he naturally protested his innocence and professed to be hurt by my 'wild and unjustified allegations'. But both I and 806 knew the truth. Thereafter, I sought the assistance of mechanics from the army garrison whenever repairs or maintenance were needed.

In the event, 806 survived the trials and tribulations of colonial life in general (and the attentions of Messrs David and Meads in particular) and it was shipped back to Britain at the end of my tour. There it remained a faithful servant for a short time until the effect of sea water corrosion on the chassis rendered it unsafe for the road. So, with only 28,000 miles on the clock, it was consigned to a breakers yard where it probably suffered the further indignity of cannibalization before ending up as scrap metal.

Though not overtly sentimental I retained the vehicle's British Honduras number plates intending to mount them on the walls of the garage of my newly acquired house. It was the least I could do for an old and trusty (er, rusty) friend. But the 806 gremlins were to strike once again. The plates disappeared when a person or persons unknown walked off with them together with a few garage and garden tools. Thus was severed my last tangible link with the car; but, as the foregoing surely demonstrates, images of those locals who were involved with it one way or another during its service in the colony still lurk in my memory. To say nothing of reminding me of the strain they had put on my nervous system. It is all part of life's rich pattern, I suppose.

Chapter 7
1931 Hurricane

ALTHOUGH WE ARE given to understand from Eliza Doolittle's elocution lessons in the musical version of Shaw's *Pygmalion* (*My Fair Lady*) that 'urricanes 'ardly 'appen, it should be recognized that their relevance in this context is to the English counties of 'ertford, 'ereford and 'ampshire and not British 'onduras, er Honduras. Hurricanes, known as either cyclones or typhoons in other tropical regions of the world, are an annual climatic feature of parts of the Caribbean and America. Not only are they part of life but, invariably, the harbingers of death and destruction. When my family and I arrived in British Honduras we soon discovered that the impact of a devastating hurricane in 1931 was etched upon the national psyche. But what is a hurricane and what happened on 10 September 1931?

Hurricanes spawn in the Atlantic Ocean east of Barbados. They begin as high winds that develop into tropical storms. Once wind velocity increases to 75 miles an hour and over they are classified as hurricanes. At that stage they were in the 1960s given female names from an alphabetical list prepared annually by the Miami weather bureau, which monitors them closely. They normally strike in the months of August, September and October.

When a hurricane passes over the surface of the sea, the wind raises a ridge of water. Should the centre (eye) of the storm strike a coast its effect is to generate an unnaturally high tide, which, depending on the location, can bring terror and devastation to those affected. Most at risk from this menace of high winds and tides are the northern islands in the Caribbean, the eastern seaboard of Central America and the southern states of the United States of America. The death toll can be considerable and the damage to standing crops (especially tree crops like bananas, coconuts, citrus and cacao) and housing can be catastrophic.

Although the pattern has fluctuated, British Honduras has suffered from occasional visitations over the years. Few instances in early times are recorded in any detail, possibly through the loss or destruction of public records, but it is known that there were hurricanes in 1785, 1805, 1813 and 1864. The country appears to have escaped severe damage during the nineteenth century; the absence of any significant storm between 1864 and the early part of the twentieth century possibly gave rise locally to the erroneous belief that the colony was outside the hurricane belt. A severe hurricane causing great damage and loss of life in 1931 rudely shattered that belief. Thereafter, they were to become relatively common. The south was hit in 1941 and 1945 and the north in 1942 and 1955. These were all seemingly eclipsed in 1961 with the visitation of Hurricane Hattie about which more will be mentioned separately elsewhere.

Any reference to hurricanes in British Honduras during early 1961 would invite recollections of the 1931 storm. People's memories focused on the devastation and loss of life involving immediate family, other relations and friends. The hurricane took place on 10 September (a national holiday commemorating the Battle of St George's Caye in 1798 when the settlers repelled a potential Spanish invasion) and the eye of the storm passed over Belize at about half-past three in the afternoon.

A graphic account of the events is recorded in A. H. Anderson's, *A Brief Sketch of British Honduras*, published in 1954, extracts from which are as follows:[1]

On September the 10th, 1931, after a lifetime of immunity, Belize was struck by a hurricane of short duration but considerable intensity in which wind velocity exceeded 132 miles an hour. Roofs were torn off and houses swept off their supports. The sea was driven into the town in a swirling flood some five feet deep carrying with it scores of large and small seacraft which added considerably to the terrible destruction wrought by the wind and the water. Fortunately, the wind abated in the early evening and although still dazed hundreds of willing workers were soon engaged in rescue work. The following morning Belize presented a weird sight: almost every building damaged, scores were roofless, many had collapsed and others were torn to pieces and scattered over a wide area. The streets were jammed with masses of wreckage interwoven with telephone and electric power supply wires and coated inches thick with a particular evil smelling mud.

The greatest loss of life occurred in the Mesopotamia area which was reduced to a few heaps of tangled wood. The East Indian community at Queen Charlotte Town, was almost entirely wiped out along with its village. The Women's Poor House at the Barracks had disappeared into the sea along with its inmates and duty staff and the nearby Government Wireless Station had been put out of commission. The Public Hospital had sustained damage and the Fort area had been dotted with boats and barges of all descriptions and the wrecks of the houses they had mowed down.

Hundreds of willing workers tackled the appalling task of collecting and burying the dead in long trenches hastily dug by prison and other labour. In the Mesopotamia area in particular the piles of wreckage were packed with dead bodies which were difficult to extract. The sun beat down with terrific intensity and it was soon realized that the work of recovering bodies in this area would not keep pace with climatic effects. The worst piles therefore were drenched with gasolene and turned into huge pyres.

It was unfortunate that when the hurricane struck, the Capital was packed not only with unemployed labourers but with scores of country visitors attracted by the annual 10th September celebrations of the Battle of St George's Caye and the death toll could not be accurately computed but was probably around 1000.

The reference to 'unemployed labourers' refers to the impact of the great economic depression then affecting the whole world, which had hit British Honduras particularly hard. Demand for the country's timber and agricultural products had declined significantly and this had a knock-on affect on those employed in connected service industries. As usual, in the main it was the unskilled labourers who lost their jobs, predominantly in Belize.[2]

Once in discussion about the hurricane with Mr George Price (at that time designated first minister, who was a pupil at school in the year it struck) he told me that the high death toll was attributable to the illusion of calm induced as the eye of the hurricane passed over the city in the early afternoon. In the lull, most of the population came out of their homes or shelters to try to rescue the large numbers of people trapped under fallen buildings or to witness the phenomenon of the sea receding a great distance towards the cayes. As they gazed out to sea, the wind suddenly changed direction and, within minutes, a huge tidal wave swept in over the city with great force, drowning many citizens as it did so, particularly those still pinned under buildings and their would-be rescuers. By the time the waters had abated night had fallen and it was too dark even to assess the situation properly. That had to wait until the following morning when the full extent of the disaster, in terms both of the death toll and of damage to homes and property, was realized and relayed to the outside world.

Powerful though the force of the hurricane undoubtedly was, another powerful force was soon asserted – the resilience of the human spirit. Once the population of Belize had come to terms with the shock of the impact of the hurricane and grief at the heavy loss of life, they (and here I draw on the words of a popular song of the 1930s that could perhaps be applied in this context) 'picked themselves up, dusted themselves off and started all over again'. In short, they began to rebuild their lives rather than to bathe in self-pity.

Visiting the colony about a year later during his travels to the Caribbean and Central America the distinguished author Aldous Huxley emphasized this when he recorded his first impressions of Belize in his book, *Beyond the Mexique Bay*:

> Walking through the streets, one saw but little traces of the great calamity of 1930 [*sic*] when the hurricane blew the sea in a huge wall of water right across the town. A heap of bricks, it is true, was all that was left of the principal house of

God; but Mammon, Caesar and the Penates had risen fresh
and shiny from the ruins. Almost all of the private residences
and all the Government offices, all the shops and warehouses,
had been rebuilt or repaired. The town as a whole looked
remarkably neat and tidy. Even a tidal wave may have something to be said for it. It does at least clear away the slums.
Our government and municipalities are less brutal; alas, a
good deal less effective.[3]

While the physical signs were soon covered up, the mental scars
remained, with memories of the events of that September afternoon
etched on the minds of all those who were present. Indeed, the
subject was still a strong talking point at dinner or drinks parties
when my family and I first arrived in the colony 30 years later. In
fact, one soon learnt to avoid guests who would make one's eyes
glaze over with their repetitive accounts of what happened in the
1931 hurricane. A parallel might be drawn with some servicemen of
my generation who, following their demobilization after the Second
World War would preface their conversations with remarks such as
'When I was in Sidi Barrani', or perhaps 'When we landed on D-Day
plus two', to quote just a couple of examples. Little did I know then
that within a few months the 1931 hurricane bores would be
superseded and put in the shade by the 1961 hurricane bores, among
whom I would feature prominently.

The fact is that not having experienced a hurricane before, neither
I nor most of my expatriate colleagues were able to grasp the full
significance of these local stories. We needed no convincing that a
hurricane could present a terrible and terrifying ordeal, but despite
the relayed experiences of the 1931 survivors we had only the
haziest notion of what to expect before, during and after the event.
This was to change in October 1961 when we were about to be put
to the test with the visitation of Hurricane Hattie. How we coped is,
as already mentioned, the subject of later chapters.

Chapter 8
Loaves and Fishes

ALTHOUGH A NON-SMOKER, I keep on the desk in my study a small ashtray that serves as a receptacle for paper clips and other incidental stationery items. It is about four inches long by two and a half inches wide, made of opaque glass and coloured Cambridge blue. With its slightly raised sides and ends it resembles a shallow rectangular dish. At its centre is a circular badge, surmounted by the imperial crown depicting what seems to be a chess style castle with a serpent encircling the lower battlements. Around the badge are the words '224 Squadron Royal Air Force' with its motto '*Fedele All Amico*' underneath. It marks the occasion of a goodwill visit to British Honduras in early 1961 by three Shackleton aircraft from Coastal Command based in Gibraltar.

I subsequently learnt from the Ministry of Defence that the badge actually portrays a rock on which there is a tower enshrined by a serpent drinking from a lamp therein. The design is based on the arms of the town of Otranto in Italy where the squadron was formed during the First World War. The motto (which translates as 'Faithful to a Friend') is a reference to that campaign.

Although RAF planes landed at Stanley Field Airport from time to time, so-called 'goodwill' or 'showing the flag' visits such as this one were infrequent, in fact few and far between. As a result, fewer airmen would be seen in the colony than members of the other British armed forces. The army had been stationed in British Honduras since the nineteenth century and soldiers of all ranks were an integral part of the social landscape. Jolly Jack Tar was also a familiar and welcome visitor. Destroyers and frigates paid regular goodwill visits, surveys of local waters were often undertaken and the Royal Navy could always be relied on to provide all sorts of practical assistance in the event of hurricanes or other natural disasters. But, though eclipsed in familiarity compared with the other two services, the key role of the RAF in the defence of the colony was fully recognized and appreciated. Therefore, much was to be made of the impending visit of the three Shackletons and their crews.

Once the dates of the visit had been settled, the civil and military authorities met under the chairmanship of Sir Colin Thornley, the governor cum commander-in-chief, to arrange a programme. This included flights over specified areas, courtesy calls and cocktail parties. The army would accommodate the crews at Airport Camp. There was one free day in the programme, Sunday, and I was asked to ascertain from the local British expatriate community whether they wished to entertain the RAF visitors that day. On this I con-sulted my good friend and neighbour, John Hall, our hospital administrator.

Away from his official duties, John was also the dynamic secretary of the Belize Club, an institution we were trying to steer away from its reactionary 'whites only' image and reputation. Not only that, with his drive and experience of sporting clubs in Britain, he was also moving it in the direction of a family rather than a predominantly male oriented establishment. It was in his Belize Club capacity that I consulted him.

Having served in the RAF as a pilot officer in the Second World War he was very willing to help organize something for members of his old service. He took soundings from club members and the upshot was a proposal that we should hire the government launch *Lolette* and spend the day at Rendezvous Caye, a small idyllic coral island on the edge of the barrier reef. It was assumed that our visitors would be both charmed and delighted with such a relaxed setting and outing.

I should perhaps mention that an alternative venue was con-sidered, Goffs Caye. This was another of our picnic spots. Pleasant, though lacking the charm of Rendezvous Caye, it offered an interesting if tenuous historical dimension. In recent years skeletons had been found on the nearby English Caye when tidal waves uncovered some of the island's coral sand. Reference to the colony archives indicated that these were probably the bones of some of the crew of HMS *Blossom* who, like so many of their colleagues in the

Caribbean in those days, had contracted and died from yellow fever. In August 1860 the vessel was lying off English Caye, having been placed in quarantine there because of fever on board. It was essentially a reserve venue, however, and one to be considered only if we learnt that other groups were planning to visit Rendezvous Caye on the same day as we were.

The army authorities were content with this proposal and said that they would like to include some of their own personnel. In that event they would contribute their own launch, the *Lord Nuffield*, so a joint enterprise was agreed. In view of the military involvement and the fact that the local expatriate group was prepared to meet the cost of drink for the whole party, we were allowed to obtain supplies from the NAFFI store at forces prices provided the order went through the officers' or sergeants' mess. This offered a useful financial saving.

The Sunday morning dawned with sunshine and blue skies as usual. At about 10 a.m. we all assembled at Customs House Wharf. The *Lolette* and the *Lord Nuffield* were already at their moorings with their engines running. Army trucks, having discharged their passengers, now began to offload the hard and soft drink that had been ordered. This was shared between the two vessels. With picnic baskets already on board the party set off in high spirits.

Like a charabanc outing to the coast on a bank holiday, the party mood was evident from the word go. Within minutes cold Heinekens were being quaffed and the empty squat green bottles consigned to the sea bed where, in a few hundred years or so, marine archeologists will no doubt be examining them and trying to piece together their history. So, the pattern of the day had been set. At the way things were going would the drink, especially the beer, hold out? John Hall and I had our doubts.

For me, travelling to the cayes, several miles offshore, was always a delightful experience and that day's visit to Rendezvous Caye was no exception. Within a few hundred yards of the wharf the sea began to change colour and, it seemed, texture. The murky impenetrable green/grey of the waters near the shore began to turn translucent and then merge into clear crystal. Gazing into this one could see not only the sea bed but also marine vegetation and a variety of fish. From the

Lolette's rail it was like looking at the sea bed through a plate of clear glass. Nearing the caye, a sandy sea bed was to give the kaleidoscope of colour yet another attractive twist by presenting the surrounding sea in a warm green and golden hue.

About fifty yards from the caye some of the more enterprising spirits, including several of the airmen, dived overboard into about twenty feet of clear water to swim to the shore and possibly to clear their heads of alcohol fumes. Within minutes they were shouting 'look at these big fish'. From the deck of the *Lolette* we gazed in horror at the sight of a shoal of very large fish, four to five feet long I would guess, shooting under the swimmers looking for all the world like missiles that had been fired from an artillery rocket launcher and hurtling towards some distant target. From their sinister, lean, hungry and vicious appearance it required only a split second to identify them as barracuda whose voracious and predatory reputation tends to strike terror in the minds of swimmers in Caribbean waters. Fortunately, they passed through in a flash before any in the group had realized the potential danger, so there was no panic. The fact is that nature being what it is the barracuda showed no interest in the humans, or were possibly scared of them, while the humans (unaware of the type of fish or their reputation) showed no interest in the fish other than some excitement about numbers and size. But for those of us who would have been held to account had the incident resulted in tragedy it was a traumatic and sobering experience. After that brief buzz of excitement the rest of us disembarked and sought out shady spots under palm trees.

Rendezvous Caye is little more than a small coral island about the size of a football pitch with the width running from east to west. The breakers, which could be seen on the barrier reef several hundred yards away to the east, somehow protected the sea around us, making it still, calm and inviting to swimmers. There were surprisingly many palm trees on the island and some scrub. Soldier crabs were in abundance but the real treat was to watch the large birds, brown pelicans, osprey and man-o'-war (frigate bird). Of particular delight was the sight of these large pelicans plunging into the sea, beaks outstretched after the fish on which they live, with all the poise and grace of top competitors in an Olympic

3. Rendezvous Caye.

diving final. Though uninhabited except for occasional visits from local fishermen and weekenders like us, there was a house on the western side. It was originally an old village police station that had been taken down and rebuilt on the caye to provide a retreat for senior officials. But in recent years it had been neglected and was now in dilapidated condition. None the less, it added charm to the setting.

In idyllic surroundings and in pleasant and agreeable company we spent a glorious day swimming, eating, drinking and talking, not necessarily in that order, until the time came to leave. There were a few diversions. Dennis Malone trod on a sea urchin and felt the full impact of its long sharp spines – a painful experience that attracted a few unorthodox suggestions for their removal, which will be known to those who are familiar with the Caribbean and sea urchins. Then Major Barry Matthews, the officer commanding the Royal Hampshires, never one to forget the role of the military in the colony, decided to use the occasion to try to make radio contact with his headquarters at Airport Camp by way of an experiment. Such contact between the cayes and the mainland was invariably unpredictable because of atmospheric conditions. So we were treated to a monologue that went something like this: 'Sunray calling, Sunray calling. Can you hear me, can you hear me? Over.' Either the operator at the other end could not hear him or refused to play, for the conversation was one-sided after several abortive attempts. But it added to the entertainment.

It was late afternoon when we reboarded the *Lolette* and *Lord Nuffield* for the mainland. Exposed to sun and fresh air, the effect of exercise and drink contributed to heavy eyelids and a soporific mood that was in sharp contrast to the party atmosphere prevalent on the outward leg. Even so, the 'hard core' were still at it, imbibing the 'dreaded Heineken' (the export version of the brew was particularly strong, hence the locally applied adjective). Their stamina was phenomenal. As we disembarked, and before going our separate ways I remarked to John Hall that I was pleasantly surprised that the drink had held despite the sustained attack upon it. 'A miracle', he responded. 'There had probably been nothing like it since the feeding of the multitude in the miracle of the loaves and fishes.' That, I thought, was a singularly apt biblical simile.

The Shackletons and their crews departed next day around noon. After takeoff they swooped low at little above roof height over the expatriate government quarters at Newtown Barracks by way of a salute. Then they were off to Jamaica. A rumour was started that the aircraft noise of this manoeuvre so frightened some of the elderly inhabitants of Belize that it induced a few heart attacks. But, like most rumours going the rounds of the expatriate community, it was unfounded.

It used to be said in the days of horse transport that 'after the Lord Mayor's show comes the dust cart.' In other words, after the parade, pomp and pageantry the clearing up begins. In the context of the RAF visit this meant sending out letters of the dunning variety to the expatriate participants for their contribution towards the cost of hiring the *Lolette* and the drink consumed. Once the bills arrived from the local treasury and the army officers' mess I did the calculations and appropriate letters were sent out. The cheques came in, often with a note of appreciation and sometimes a reference to how low the cost had been for what was provided. But a cloud was soon to descend on this mellow atmosphere.

When John Hall received my letter about payment due, he called on me to say that there must be some mistake because he was still awaiting the drinks bill from the army. I then learnt he had assumed that, as secretary of the Belize Club, he was responsible for ordering the drink through his contacts in the sergeants' mess. He was unaware that I had already acted by ordering separately via the officers' mess. In short, between us we had double ordered. The seemingly endless spring of cold Heinekens that invited the simile of the miracle of the loaves and fishes was no longer relevant or fitting. For 'miracle' read 'cockup!'

I was left in the embarrassing position of having to send out supplementary bills when the second drinks account arrived. The reaction, to put it mildly, was lukewarm and many of the comments less than complimentary. In the space of a few days my reputation as an organizer had, as the wartime RAF would have put it, 'Gone for a Burton'. Fortunately, I suffer from no illusion that life is fair, but I vowed never to organize anything similar in future if I could avoid it. The miracle of the loaves and fishes, indeed!

Chapter 9
Eighteenth- and Nineteenth-century Characters

I T IS A MOOT POINT whether a Central American backwater like British Honduras, first as a settlement and later as an early colony, created or attracted the many diverse characters who flitted across its stage. By 'characters' in this context, and here I draw on the *Oxford English Dictionary* definition, I mean those whose particular style, idiosyncrasies or personal individuality mark them out as distinct from their neighbours. To put it another way, those whose distinctive presence and behaviour bring colour and incident to the lives of the rest of us.

Topping the charts would, in my view, be two of the early administrators: the first formally appointed superintendent, Colonel Edward Marcus Despard, and the first fully fledged governor, Roger Tuckfield Goldsworthy, CMG (later Sir Roger). These were figures from the eighteenth and nineteenth centuries respectively. Their stories, depicted below, add detail to the wide British involvement in that part of the world in those days and the international ramifications connected with that presence mentioned in earlier pages. The opportunity is also taken in the succeeding chapter to continue the narrative into the twentieth century by introducing a few of the many less illustrious, but none the less interesting, local characters whom I met during my own service in the colony.

The origin of the post of superintendent has its roots in the history of the region. As I have already mentioned, Spain claimed sovereignty over the territory without actually occupying it. Then, under a treaty between Spain and Britain in 1763, following the end of the Seven Years' War, the former, having failed to dislodge the settlers, finally recognized their right to cut, load and carry logwood within a loosely defined area between the Belize River and the River

Hondo subject to restrictions relating to agriculture, fishing and fortifications. They were also excluded from the cayes. The settlers tended to ignore these restrictions while the local Spanish authorities tried to impose them. Petitions for colonial status were submitted from time to time, but London consistently turned them down. For example, on 6 June 1774 the then secretary of state, Lord Dartmouth, informed the governor of Jamaica, Sir Basil Keith (who had taken up the settlers' cause), that 'where there is no territorial right no jurisdiction can be exercised.'[1]

Despite consequential friction, the settlement continued to exist until war broke out again in 1779 when Spain joined France, the Netherlands and America against Britain in the American War of Independence. Before news of its outbreak reached the settlers, Spanish forces landed at St George's Caye (also known at that time as Cayo Casina, which was then in effect the settlements' administrative centre) and carried the population off to Mérida in Mexico. From there they were shipped to Havana, Cuba, where they were incarcerated under appallingly harsh conditions. Thereafter, the settlement virtually ceased to exist until peace was declared in 1783. The terms of the resultant Treaty of Versailles, signed that September, were a disappointment to the returning settlers. All that Britain had demanded on their behalf was that the right to cut logwood be reconfirmed and that the boundaries for this 'concession' be more clearly defined by representatives of Spain and Britain.

The settlers, some of whom were apparently still in exile, protested at what they saw as a raw deal and betrayal by the home government; they, along with representatives of their commercial interests in London, then pressed hard for the appointment of a superintendent who, with the support of an appropriate executive authority, would speak on their behalf. For such a post they suggested Lieutenant Colonel Despard who was well known to them from his military and administrative service in the region (to which reference is made below) as indeed he was to Governor Campbell of Jamaica, under whose authority he had served and who supported the suggestion in reference to Whitehall.[2]

Despard, an Anglo-Irish Protestant from County Lei, alternatively

known as Laoighis and formerly as Queen's County, was a British
army officer and colonial administrator. He entered the army in 1776
and rapidly rose to the rank of colonel. After serving in Jamaica he
was sent to the Central American region in 1781. There he was made
governor and commander-in-chief of the new British possession of
Rattan (Ruatan) Island, off the Honduras coast, and soon afterwards
of the British Mosquito Shore. During earlier military service in the
area as a lieutenant attached as an engineer to the 79th regiment
(Liverpool Blues), he served with the then Captain Horatio Nelson
(at that time commanding HMS *Hinchinbroke*) on the Nicaraguan
coast in a brief campaign in 1778–79 against the Spanish, who were
increasing their naval and military activity locally. The objective of
that campaign was to annex that territory, thereby cutting Spain's
South American possessions off from its Central American ones and
so gain access to the Pacific. Also, a proposed attack on San Juan
might, incidentally, be seen as a gesture towards avenging the
'outrage' at St George's Caye mentioned above.

On that occasion, a British naval/military force under Colonel
Polson captured the port during an operation in which both Despard
and Nelson played prominent heroic roles and held it against
counterattacks until a disastrous outbreak of yellow fever among the
troops led to an untimely evacuation. Suffice it to say in this connection that in those days Caribbean and Central American postings
were dreaded for health reasons, that during the campaign three-
quarters of the 1800-strong force (including most of HMS
Hinchinbroke's complement of 200 men) died from fevers and that
very few of the survivors, including Nelson, escaped infection from
malaria. The expedition was deemed a military failure, with only
Despard and Nelson coming out of it with their reputations
enhanced.

Despard's military reputation was further enhanced in August
1782 when, by now promoted to the rank of lieutenant-colonel, he
commanded a successful expedition to reclaim the Black River
settlement on the Mosquito Shore from the Spanish forces that had
captured and occupied it some five months earlier. Thereafter, he
returned to Jamaica but was back again in the region in May 1784
when, having been promoted further to the rank of full colonel, he

was appointed as one of the British commissioners appointed to delimit the boundaries of the Belize settlement under the Treaty of Versailles alluded to above.

On 1 December that year, at the age of 33, Despard was appointed superintendent of the Belize settlement. In confirming the appointment the Secretary of State, Lord Sydney, wrote to him in the following terms:

> His Majesty has been graciously pleased to appoint you to regulate and superintend under the Governor of Jamaica His Majesty's affairs within the district which the late Treaty of Peace has been allotted to the Logwood cutters upon the coast of Yucatán, and prevent any quarrels and Disagreements between his subjects who may be employed there and those of His Catholic Majesty inhabiting that neighbourhood.[3]

The avoidance of direct control between the superintendent and London and vice versa was, of course, a sop towards acknowledging Spanish sensitivity over sovereignty.

At the same time, Lord Sydney wrote to the then Governor of Jamaica, Clarke, reporting that Despard had been so appointed and giving details of the terms and the salary to be paid (that is £500 a year). But fearful of an impending Spanish attack against the Mosquito Shore, he went on to direct that Despard 'with his knowledge of the Settlers and the Native Indians' should continue to serve there until that threat had subsided. Unfortunately, it was not until nearly two years later, June 1786, after two local requests for his presence, that he arrived in the settlement to assume that office. By that time a new and significant development was about to unfold that was to put him on a collision course with both the settlers and London.

Subsequent to the Treaty of Versailles, diplomatic negotiations between Spain and Britain resulted in the Convention of London, which was signed on 14 July 1786. Article 1 provided for the evacuation of the Mosquito Shore and the islands adjacent to it. In return, Spain agreed, among other things, to an extension of the Belize settlement southwards to the Sibun River, and to the rights to cut mahogany as well as logwood and to engage in market gardening for local consumption. The reoccupation of St George's Caye was also conceded, though forts, garrisons, plantation agriculture and the formation of any formal system of government were still prohibited. A Spanish commissary, accompanied by a British equivalent, would monitor adherence to these stipulations on half-yearly visits. To that extent, Spanish claimed sovereignty remained carefully preserved. This, however, was to spotlight a growing problem. In the absence of any formal system of government for the settlers there was no legal basis for law making or enforcement.

In place at the time was a primitive democratic system operated by seven local magistrates, elected annually at a public meeting (see below), whose task was to enforce a kind of customary law and generally administer the settlement's affairs on the basis of consensus derived from public meetings. The magistrates' role was something akin to that of an executive council, judiciary and magistracy combined; and the forum of the public meeting, which was open to the small number of property owning settlers, could reasonably be regarded as the equivalent of a legislative assembly. The system was given some sort of official cachet and recognition when these customs were recorded in a document known as 'Burnaby's Code' during a visit from Jamaica in 1765 by Admiral Burnaby. The importance of this code lay not so much in the general laws based on long accepted custom that it contained, but in the initial quasi-constitutional practice relating to the magistracy and public meeting that it recognized and that reflected the settlers' perception of freedom to run their affairs in their own way.

However, although a framework of simple basic laws or practices existed, there was little corresponding sign of order. Indeed, a state of near anarchy existed. It seems clear from reports by captains of naval vessels visiting the settlement that some of the early inhabitants were undoubtedly inclined towards every form of crime, including murder, coupled with a bent for creating all forms of public disorder and confusion.[4] A parallel of sorts might perhaps be drawn with situations prevailing in the frontier towns of the United States of America when the pioneers moved westwards and became the subject of many subsequent Hollywood films. With no effective system of law enforcement to combat this lawlessness, the result was that crimes went unpunished, apart from the strong extracting personal revenge from the weak. Yet, as the settlement developed, the majority of the population began to recognize and generally accept the need for a legally established and vigorously enforced code of law. This was to give rise in numerous petitions to the declared aim that 'the laws of England' should be extended to them. This aim was finally achieved in November 1840 when the superintendent of the day was authorized to issue a proclamation on the authority of Her Majesty Queen Victoria directing that 'the Law of England to be the law of the Settlement or Colony of British Honduras'.[5] That, incidentally, was the first reference to the territory as 'British Honduras' and nominally a 'colony'. But this development runs ahead of the narrative. The fact is that in 1786 law enforcement was seemingly an intractable problem.

When Despard arrived in the settlement that year, the role originally envisaged for him two years earlier had changed. The main responsibility now committed to him was to enforce observance of the terms of the London Convention. As he was to be accused later of observing them too rigidly, it seems only fair to reproduce his revised terms of reference as conveyed to him in a letter by Lord Sydney:

> His Majesty expects that you will on your part, most rigidly fulfil the several stipulations contained in the said Convention, and you do let it be publicly known and understood by all HM Subjects under your superintendence, that if any of them are found to be acting in contradiction to the spirit and intention of the present Convention, that such proceedings will be disavowed by HM and they will, on account of such misconduct forfeit every claim to His Royal Protection and Support.[6]

This was, indeed, Strong stuff!

Two further missives from Lord Sydney followed. On 31 July 1786 Despard was informed that the bulk of the settlers evacuated from the Mosquito Shore would be removed to the Belize settlement and that he should do his utmost to assist and support them.[7] A few weeks later, on 17 September, he was told that the convention had been ratified and that the way was now clear for the agreed six-monthly visits from a Spanish commissary.[8] On each occasion he was reminded yet again of the need to enforce rigidly the stipulations of the convention.

The original settlers (Baymen), who dominated the commercial timber activities, immediately understood its implications and how it would affect their way of life. On learning of its ratification they dispatched a petition to London protesting at its one-sided nature. In particular, they pointed out that even with the southward extension to the Sibun River, there was insufficient land available to provide an economically viable future for themselves, let alone the evacuees. Furthermore, they resented Spain's refusal to allow plantations for export crops and expressed unease at the prospect of six-monthly visits by a Spanish commissary.[9] Understandably, however, they failed to foresee at that stage the factor that was to have the greatest impact: the future suppression of their primitive existing form of government.

Their worst fears were soon realized. In the event, the influx of evacuees (Shoremen) totalled 537 white and free persons and 1677 slaves.[10] These thus outnumbered the Baymen by a ratio of about four or five to one.[11] Following royal instructions to give the Shoremen preference over 'all other persons whatsoever in the distribution of the new district',[12] Despard settled them on the new lands south of the Belize River. This had the affect of incurring the wrath of the original settlers who argued that these displaced people were being given preferential treatment at their expense. Consequently, a number of acrimonious disputes arose in which some Baymen saw the superintendent's intervention as favouring the newcomers. But, in practice, all this was to become academic. With an increased population in an area now too small to provide all of them with a living, it was not long before there was an inevitable encroachment beyond the extended boundaries, probably into unoccupied areas extending to the west, north and as far south as the Sarstoon River, despite the disapproval of the superintendent and all other authorities concerned with implementing the terms of the convention. When Despard reported on the situation to London, which apparently on occasions involved the use or threat of Spanish troops in attempts to enforce these terms, he was in principle supported in his actions by Lord Sydney who, in his criticism of the settlers, added that 'His Majesty was much displeased at their conduct.' But there was a sting in the tail of that dispatch when the secretary of state implied in respect of the land disputes that had arisen, that Despard was his own worst enemy in his handling of the matter and that had he adopted a more diplomatic stance he might have prevented such disputes from arising.[13] Whitehall conveniently swept under the carpet the fact that he was following his terms of reference as consistently instructed, and had no local legal powers or support. But by then the authorities there were being subjected to pressure from commercial interests in London, which were beginning to see the superintendent's actions as a possible threat to their suppliers' livelihoods.

If Despard had got away to a bad start over the allocation of lands to the displaced Mosquito Shore migrants and the resulting boundaries issue, more trouble was to follow shortly afterwards. In 1787 the visiting Spanish commissary ordered and arranged for the destruction of vegetable gardens on the grounds that all cultivation was prohibited under the terms of the convention. This was clearly an incorrect interpretation as the actual prohibition concerned plantation crops grown for export and not those grown for local consumption. Although Spain subsequently issued orders allowing such cultivation to take place, the settlers spoke bitterly of their condition as tantamount 'to subjection to Spanish rule'.[14] This feeling spilled over in their attitude towards Despard who was accused of outdoing the Spaniards in his adherence to the Convention while, at the same time, neglecting their own interests. Other complaints against him were that he was full of self-importance and domineering. Thus was generated a head of steam that was to result in suggestions to Whitehall that he should be recalled or, if he were to stay 'that the settlers should not be censured for complaining against him'.[15]

Matters came to a head on 30 May 1789 when, in compliance with a demand from Gual, the Spanish commissary who claimed that the existing form of administration contravened the convention, Despard abolished the system of magistrates. At a public meeting on 5 June, the courts and magistrates were formally dissolved. At first sight it looked as though he had fallen for a carefully laid Spanish trap. Obviously, the settlement could not be sustained or continue to exist without some form of government and judiciary, even one as primitive as that established under the magisterial system; under the circumstances, the settlers' position was now seemingly untenable. In other words, it seemed that the abolition of the settlers' crude form of civic government could only be construed as a shrewd Spanish move to achieve this end and either bring them under their control or force them to abandon the settlement. But perhaps there may have been a deeper reason. In 1704, during the War of the Spanish Succession, Britain captured Gibraltar and, under the Treaty of Utrecht of 1713, its newly acquired sovereignty was acknowledged. This rankled with Spain, which thereafter until 1782, when General Elliot's forces successfully withstood the last attempt to blockade the territory, not unnaturally sought its return through direct military action and siege. Therefore, by turning to diplomatic as opposed to military methods, Spain may have reasoned that persuading Britain to give up the Mosquito Shore settlement in exchange for concessions in the Belize settlement, their control of the latter might be used as a bargaining lever for the return of Gibraltar. If so, they were to be disappointed. Events proved otherwise.

Now, having grasped the danger facing them, the settlers approached Despard with a request to introduce a new system of administration 'in order to avert the ruin of the Settlement which would result from a total cessation of Justice'.[16] Ignoring the convention and possible Spanish reaction, he promulgated a new system for their acceptance based on the elective principle, but autocratic in the sense that he gave himself the power to veto the proceedings of the elected representatives and to dismiss them at will. None the less, by a vote of 130 to 24, it was accepted, presumably as a makeshift arrangement. Numerous petitions submitted subsequently to London, probably organized by the dissidents (presumably the Baymen) and supported by their allies (the British merchants trading with the settlement) protested strongly against the so-called despotic form of administration. In particular, they contended that it was not right for a small body comprising the superintendent and 15 elected representatives to have the power to abrogate laws and regulations; all appropriations of funds, they argued, should be controlled by 'the people' and not the superintendent. More generally, they maintained that:

> Englishmen can never brook the despotic government of an individual. We have tasted the sweets of liberty and hitherto have never forfeited our right and title to that valuable blessing. ... Is it just that His Majesty's Superintendent possessing no judicial authority whatever shall abrogate these laws and substitute his own will and fist in their stead? We humbly concede that the people to be governed are of all others the best judges of the local regulations necessary for the good and peace of the Settlement.[17]

Here, indeed, was an echo of the political principles their compatriots had articulated with such resonance in the North American colonies a few years earlier being extended to colonists in other British possessions in the region like, for example, Jamaica and Barbados. It was probably also a wider reflection of the independent nature of eighteenth-century Englishmen generally, whether at home or abroad, many of whom were attuned to or influenced by the political philosopher John Locke's doctrines on the rights of citizens *vis-à-vis* the powers of rulers.

After a few months Despard found that the system was unworkable and he abolished it. Shortly after that he called upon the public meeting to elect a committee of 15 to devise a plan for a temporary government, and then two months after that 12 'Conservators of the Peace' were appointed to try offences with the assistance of a jury.

By that time, Whitehall was showing signs of alarm at what was going on. On 2 October 1789, Lord Grenville notified Despard that, in the light of allegations to the effect that his conduct was causing general dissatisfaction among the settlers, he proposed to send a Colonel Peter Hunter to 'Honduras', under the direction of the governor of Jamaica, to report on the situation there, to look into the

causes of disputes and to propose measures for reform.[18] Despite
maintaining that he would 'not deliver any decided opinion on his
[Despard's] conduct until he receives justification of it from the
Superintendent' (in this case Hunter), Grenville wrote again a
fortnight later informing him of his suspension from office in favour
of Hunter immediately the latter arrived in the settlement; he also
said that he should either return to Britain or remain until the latter's
report had been received and considered in London.[19]

Hunter arrived on 10 April 1790 and immediately re-established
the previous form of civic government. However, the subsequent
election for magistrates in which Despard had surprisingly submitted
his name as a candidate, produced an astonishing result. Despite
having petitioned for his removal on the grounds that he was
dominating and full of his own importance, he was now returned at
the head of the poll. Of course he had no intention of assuming such
a subordinate position. His purpose in standing clearly had been to
demonstrate to the authorities in London on his return that he had
the backing of the majority of settlers and that the calls for his
removal had come from a powerful minority seeking to maintain its
power and preserve its commercial interests. Until he embarked for
England with his local (probably common-law) black wife and
young son on 3 June that year, and before Hunter's report was completed and submitted, he spent his time preparing his defence
against the allegations the settlers and British merchants trading with
them had directed at him. Shortly before his departure he forwarded
to the secretary of state, Lord Grenville, a petition relating to his
service in the Bay of Honduras from 1784 to 1790, which was a
staggering 312 manuscript pages long, plus a 494-page appendix.[20]
Eight days later he submitted his answers to the merchants' complaints. This was to take up 75 manuscript pages.[21] What impression
would all this make on Whitehall?

Inherent in this situation were three disparate strands that were to
come together to produce a tangled skein of potential and actual
confusion and conflict and to make Despard's suspension and recall
inevitable – these were personalities, self interest and imperial policy.

Without doubt and perhaps unavoidably given his personality and
military background, Despard was bound to clash with the inde-

pendent minded and undisciplined local population. As a senior army officer and 'gentleman', Despard probably had more in common with the Spanish authorities whom he met in the course of his duties than with the settlers whom he probably rated no higher than those whom Lord Erskine had described in another context as uncontrollably licentious 'brutal and insolent soldiery'. This may account for the accusations that he held the settlers in contempt. As a soldier, strict adherence to orders would have come naturally to him. Although he had spent much of his time in the region engaged in hostilities against the Spanish, this would not necessarily have deterred him from rigidly following instructions from Whitehall about the need to ensure that the settlers complied with the stipulations of the convention, irrespective of their wishes. It was in this context that Despard found the settlers frustratingly refractory, particularly when they showed no sign of observing the provisions of the treaty.

Lurking beneath the surface of these turbulent personalities was yet another divisive human trait, self interest. The introduction of comparatively large numbers of evacuees from the Mosquito Shore obviously altered the settlement's population balance. That, coupled with the competition it would likely introduce to the profitable timber industry, especially mahogany extraction, which had now overtaken logwood as the main export and which the now minority earlier Belize settlers monopolized, no doubt created alarm in the ranks of the latter. This would have been accentuated further when the superintendent abolished the old form of government that had for so long suited their purpose and replaced it with one that might see power drifting out of their hands into his and perhaps towards the newcomers whose interests he appeared to be favouring. Given that their power base, and with it their dominant commercial interests, now seemed under threat from Despard's actions, the obvious tactic open to them was to engineer his removal and seek restoration of the status quo. They and their business associates in London achieved this through petitions and by successfully lobbying the home authorities. With the involvement of ministers, policy issues were now to come into play against a background of domestic political unrest and outside threats to national security.

It should be understood that Britain's main interest in the Belize settlement was the contribution its resources were making to the overall British economy – in short, trade. It was also necessary to keep an eye on the sovereignty issue Spain raised. The British government would have expected Despard to pursue both aspects of this policy with tact and discretion so as 'not to rock the boat', as it were and, in so doing, not to raise irrelevant side issues that would find their way onto ministers' desks in Whitehall. Yet, here was an ostensibly avoidable situation in which not only were business interests in Belize and London up in arms against him, but he had also taken independent action that ran counter to the London Convention and affected Anglo-Spanish relations. Consequently, ministers had now been drawn in at a time when they were confronting more pressing and important domestic and overseas issues.

Although the British government would have required Despard to use his initiative in guiding and implementing policy according to his judgement of local circumstances, it follows that it would not have expected him to disregard it. Why then did he abolish the existing system of elected magistrates at the Spanish commissary's request without referring the matter to Whitehall through the governor of Jamaica? This was a major policy decision that lay beyond the terms of his authority and area of competence. He could easily have avoided getting caught up in local controversy by placing the responsibility for the decision on the shoulders of those best able to deal with it. Even more puzzling, however, was why he then committed a complete *volte face* by assuming the reins of government for himself? This totally violated the convention and neither Spain nor Britain could have approved of it. One can only conclude that he saw an opportunity to take over the settlement and 'lick it into shape' by installing an old-style conventional colonial regime. What was Spain's reaction? Having persuaded Despard to abolish the magistracy, why did it fail to protest when he replaced that system with one that was constitutionally more advanced? This presented yet another puzzle!

To the British in Whitehall, seeing their representative in the settlement overturn the old magisterial system to create a new form of government with himself at its head must have looked suspiciously like a coup to introduce an unauthorized form of colonial rule. His tampering with the existing primitive form of administration to achieve such an end was clearly the last thing they wanted. In fact, Lord Grenville's instructions to Colonel Hunter before he took up his appointment were to declare Despard's innovations null and void and to restore the old system. He then added more significantly that he was 'to discourage any measures on the part of the settlers, which could lead to a Settlement of a more extensive nature, to the establishment of anything resembling a Colonial Government in the way of exercising territorial sovereignty'.[22] Hunter followed these instructions faithfully and the status quo was restored.

It is now clear that the home government regarded Despard as a dangerous maverick who should not be allowed to return to the settlement and was too unbalanced and unreliable to be considered for any other comparable post. Indeed, though the charges the settlers and their business associates made were by and large ultimately dismissed, the British government refused to employ him further. On 4 October 1791 the then secretary of state, Lord Dundas, notified him of that decision in the following terms:

> You were informed by Lord Grenville at the time of your suspension of the impression His Majesty's Servants had received of your conduct from the Papers then before them. That impression not being done away either by the points which have been objected to, or the other documents to which you have referred in the Narratives which have been transmitted from Honduras, I have now only to inform you that His Majesty does not conceive it will be for the advantage of His Service to reinstate you in your appointment of Honduras.[23]

As if to underline its finality, the government decided not to fill the post of superintendent, which had become vacant a few months earlier following Colonel Hunter's departure.

This situation, we may assume, only served to fuel the burning sense of injustice Despard felt at the turn of events, especially with his career now in tatters and his future uncertain. Accordingly, he continued personally to protest at the loss of his appointment and demanded reinstatement and compensation so violently that he was twice imprisoned in subsequent years on no specific charge. It is conceivable, however, that the government's spin doctors of the day may have hinted that he was suspected of involvement with dissident groups planning subversive activities against the state stemming from the then growing clamour for political reform at home and the turbulent political situation in his native Ireland leading to the Act of Union of 1800 incorporating that country into the United Kingdom. And, as subsequent events suggest, there may have been more than a germ of truth in this.

As a soured and embittered man he began to associate with dissidents who had grievances against the crown and ruling establishment. It was in this context that he later became associated with an alleged plot to assassinate the king, capture the Tower of London, seize parliament and take control of national institutions such as the Bank of England and post office. In 1803, he, along with a group of 32 English, Irish and Scottish dissidents, including some soldiers, was arrested at the Oakley Arms public house in Lambeth in southeast London, where they had met to conspire, and subsequently charged with leading the plot. He was also accused of inciting the military to mutiny. The accusations were so improbable that, if proven, even in those 'unenlightened' days, his mental state must surely have been questioned and some allowance made for it. But this was the nineteenth and not the twenty-first century and people's psychological problems counted for little at a time when the security of the United Kingdom was perceived to be at risk.

Here it will be recalled that he returned to London in the aftermath of the American and French revolutions, at a time when the British ruling classes feared a real threat to their interests from similar radical ideas being imported into Britain. The subsequent ongoing conflict with the French under Napoleon Bonaparte, and the grim prospect of an invasion of England by his troops using other parts of the kingdom as a back door for their operations, further heightened the climate of fear. The authorities were particularly concerned about the situation in Ireland. Then, the revolutionary spirit of the age, which helped fan the ever smouldering embers of Irish grievances against England and the imperial government in London, burst into flames in 1798 with the Irish Rebellion and, with it, a state of anarchy. French exploitation of this situation, especially the activities of that country's agents, added further fuel to the conflagration. The situation was exacerbated in June of that year when a small body of French soldiers (about a thousand) under Humbert landed in Ireland and reached Killala Bay in County Cork. There, after some initial success, the local militia forced them to surrender within a month. That October an even larger force sailed into Lough Swinney only to be defeated and dispersed.[24] Although this barely touches on the Irish problem shortly before and after the Act of Union in 1800, and with it a fear of France gaining a foothold in that country from which to launch an invasion of England, it does provide the background against which Despard's alleged actions would inevitably have been judged.

When he and his fellow conspirators were brought to trial, Lord Nelson, with whom, as I mentioned above, he had served in the combined land and sea expedition at San Juan in 1779, testified on his behalf. He strongly praised him for his loyalty and gallantry, especially during the ill-fated Nicaraguan operation when so many other officers had been struck down with disease. 'We served together on the Spanish Main,' he said; 'we served together in the enemy's trenches ... slept on the same ground,' adding that 'Colonel Despard was then a loyal man and a brave officer.'[25] Yet, despite this high-profile intervention by so renowned a heroic and popular public figure, and a paucity of openly corroborated evidence produced at the trial, he was none the less convicted of high treason and sentenced to be publicly hanged, drawn, quartered and beheaded: he was the last person so convicted to receive such a barbaric sentence that was not subsequently commuted. He, together with six fellow conspirators, was executed on Monday 21 February 1803, protesting to the last his innocence of the charges against him but failing to disclose details of the intrigues in which he had undoubtedly been involved.

In the event, fearing that a groundswell of public sympathy for a once publicly acclaimed military hero could conceivably develop into rioting at the scene of the execution if the sentence were fully observed, the authorities decided to invoke their statutory discretion to waive 'quartering' and to limit 'drawing' to a token enacted within the prison yard.[26]

After the execution, Nelson demonstrated his friendship yet again through a further intervention, this time on behalf of Despard's Afro-Caribbean wife, Catherine, by urging the government to provide her with a pension or some other form of financial provision.[27] He was again unsuccessful, but by highlighting her plight a private bene-factor was encouraged to come to her assistance.[28]

By any reckoning, this was a tragic end for a man who had hitherto given brave, conscientious and loyal service to the crown. The epithet 'unfortunate', which was frequently attached to his name in later years, was not without justification. In fact, it is tempting to believe that had he not been appointed superintendent of the Belize settlement he would not have suffered such a fate. The old cliché that he was the wrong man in the wrong place at the wrong time would appear apposite in this case, for time and time again the fates conspired against him. When he was nominally appointed in 1784, the settlers assumed that his main duty would be to represent them and look after their interests in an executive capacity. However, it seems that his primary task, according to the terms of his appointment, was to keep the peace between them and the neighbouring Spanish authorities. When he actually assumed office almost two years later he was then charged with the more specific task of ensuring that the settlers rigidly observed the terms of the London Convention. The upshot was that in trying to follow his orders from Whitehall some settlers came to regard him as a domineering and self-important tyrant, even a traitor to his fellow countrymen. He was having to confront the classic dilemma that many senior colonial administrators faced in later years: how to square the circle between the wishes and aspirations of the dominant local population with the policy directives and attendant instructions of the home government.

But his dilemma was even more acute than that, for he was never in a position to wield any executive power and, in the absence of local support, he had no means of enforcing either his will or his instructions from Whitehall. In this regard, his situation was much like that of a captain of a seagoing vessel trying to follow a course yet having to rely on the goodwill of a crew intent on going in a different direction; then, when he finally takes over the helm, his masters, fearing he is heading into dangerous waters, quickly relieve him of his command. The events that followed his return to England clearly had much to do with his passionate sense of injustice turning into an overriding obsession.

However, the last word, and his epitaph, should perhaps be left to the settlers. Some 23 years after his execution he was accorded high praise in the 1826 local *Almanac* (the first officially authorized account of events in the settlement and its history that was to serve as a model for what was to become known in future years as the Annual Report) for his action over 'the difficulty' Gual's demand to abolish the old administrative system created. 'He saved, by a bold and steady hand, the inhabitants from a destructive trap set by the Spanish Crown … his efforts were defeated by those who selfishly cringed to Spanish despotism.'[29] From this I deduce that, in retrospect, it was felt that his decision to establish an alternative system not only foiled a Spanish attempt to assert sovereignty in a way calculated to make the settlers' situation untenable, but also served notice that something more sophisticated than the old constitution had become appropriate. Had there been no local protest at this, or had Britain taken a stronger line with Spain, something akin to colonial status might have been achieved sooner. However, given the British government's reluctance to change the status quo at that time, that is mere conjecture. None the less, that this eulogy was recorded within the lifetime of people who remembered his service in the settlement is significant and surely goes some way towards restoring his hitherto loyal reputation.

✿ ✿ ✿

Having replaced Despard, Colonel Hunter restored the status quo and left the settlement in March 1791. From then until Colonel Thomas Barrow was appointed as superintendent in January 1797, the settlement reverted to administration by magistrates. By that time Britain was again at war with Spain and it was Barrow who organized the defence of the settlement that was to end in the defeat of the Spanish forces at the Battle of St George's Caye on 10 September 1798. Thereafter, the appointment of a superintendent was put on a permanent basis. When Spain relinquished its control in the region in the early nineteenth century, both Guatemala and Mexico claimed sovereignty over the area, with varying degrees of emphasis. However, when a legislative assembly replaced the public meeting in 1854, the settlement came closer to acquiring colonial status. Then, in 1862 Britain formally assumed sovereignty when by royal warrant the territory was declared the colony of British Honduras with the title of the then superintendent, Sir Frederick Seymour, changed to that of lieutenant governor but still operating under the aegis of the governor of Jamaica. The new colonial constitution lasted for 17 years.

Friction between the landed and commercial interests over sharing the taxation burden led to petitions from the public claiming that members of the assembly were misusing their powers for personal use and requesting a change in status. In response, in 1879 the territory was accorded the status of a crown colony (that is to say government by the governor in council). That year, on the authority of Queen Victoria, a legislative council was introduced in which provision was made for five official (including the president) and four nominated (unofficial) members with the lieutenant governor as its president. Although it was not realized locally at the time, in practice this arrangement provided for an official majority since the governor, in his capacity as president of the council, was allowed a casting vote. This was to sow the seeds of conflict that would sprout when the next constitutional change took place. Such was the country's political background that, as Despard's experience suggests, the locally perceived role for crown-appointed superintendents and their gubernatorial successors was to oversee the colony's affairs generally and not to take the initiative in government – that being the assumed prerogative of local representatives who, in particular, had no intention of sacrificing their traditional right to exert financial control.

The next change came within the next decade with a challenge to the connection with Jamaica. This issue had rankled for some time because local people resented the colony being made to appear subordinate to a territory with a governor who had little knowledge of, or even interest in, its affairs. At last, the Colonial Office acknowledged the problem and took action. On 7 October 1884, it severed all ties with Jamaica and from then on, by letters patent, the title conferred on the crown's representative was His Excellency, Governor and Commander-in-Chief. With that the first fully-fledged governor with direct access to London was installed. He was Roger Tuckfield Goldsworthy, a former soldier and experienced colonial administrator.

Goldsworthy had served with distinction as a soldier during the Indian Mutiny and thereafter, from 1868 to 1874, as inspector of police in West Africa, more specifically Sierra Leone, Nigeria and the Gold Coast. He served as colonial secretary in Western Australia from 1877 to 1881 and in St Lucia from 1881 to 1884;[30] now he had his own command, but in retrospect it was probably too much of a promotion for him. After six controversial years embracing two tours, his actions were to set in train a series of events that were to plunge the colony into a constitutional crisis leading to an alteration in the balance of political power locally, which, indirectly, was to retard political and economic development for the next forty or so years.

In my time in the colony, the only mention of Goldsworthy I ever heard was in connection with his expedition to the Cockscomb Mountains in 1888 (see Chapter 23). I therefore assumed that his term of office had been comparatively trouble free. However, during research into another matter in the library of the old Commonwealth Society in Northumberland Avenue, London, in the mid-1980s, I came across sources that associated him with sleaze, corruption and maladministration, accusations that subsequent readings confirmed. Furthermore, it was also evident that such was his unpopularity that, just as the early settlers were quick to engineer the dismissal of the first superintendent, it did not take their descendants long to demand the removal of their first full governor. The well-documented story[31] begins shortly after his arrival in the colony when he quickly ruffled feathers.

A primary reason for his unpopularity was over the implementation of the Siccama Committee's report on improving the sanitary
conditions of Belize by filling in swamp areas in the city, as well as
dredging the harbour and the two principal canals into which domestic sewage (euphemistically called night soil) was, and still is,
deposited. Here I should explain that the city, like Topsy, 'just
growed'. Having developed from the site of an old shipping point for
logwood and mahogany and originally built partly on sand dunes
and partly on infilled swampland, the houses needed (and some still
need) to be raised 'on stilts'. And, because the city is only a few inches,
if at all, above sea level, storm-water drainage, sewage disposal and
drinking water supplies have always presented perennial problems.

Baron Siccama, a Dutch engineer from British Guiana whom the
Colonial Office had sent out in 1880 to advise on how to improve the
capital's sanitation, which was notoriously poor and considered to be
a health hazard, devised the proposed improvement scheme. Because
the canals (which were little more than open sewers) had become
clogged with 22 years of accumulated sewage, and because in the
past there had always been a rise in the incidence of yellow fever in
the territory if raw sewage was dredged out of the canals and left
exposed, there was a recommendation to dispose of the dredgings
out at sea. True to his autocratic style, Goldsworthy rode roughshod
over the committee's recommendations with respect to this public
works project. It began when, without taking competitive bids, he
awarded the contract to one of his cronies, a Mr C. T. Hunter, a
Scottish-born engineer whose ability to complete the work satisfactorily was questionable. The local view was that he was unreliable
and that there were others who were better qualified for the job. He
was also a member of a so-called 'Scots clique' made up of highly
influential merchants and landowners who exerted considerable
influence over the colony's administration and, among other things,
controlled most if not all of the unofficial seats on the Legislative
Council.

The dredging of the Northside Canal was completed satisfactorily
in 1885 without incident. But then, at Goldsworthy's instigation, the
government allowed Hunter to deviate from his contract by dredging
the Southside Canal in the hot season and failing to dispose of the

sediment at sea. In the event, raw sewage was dredged and deposited along the canal banks. There was an immediate local outcry, which was further inflamed when Goldsworthy appointed Hunter's brother, Dr Alexander Hunter, as colonial surgeon at an inflated salary over the heads of better qualified and more popular local candidates. Although a member of the committee that had earlier advised on health precautions in respect of the operation, he now changed his mind and advocated indiscriminate dredging and dumping, opining that no health hazard would result from his brother's proposed operations despite having previously maintained that indiscriminate dumping would 'be unsavoury and nothing less than madness'.[32] Soon afterwards both yellow fever and a disease known as canal fever became endemic. The upshot was that the regular labour force refused to go near the canal and the contractor was allowed to use low-cost prison labour.

Resentment and anger against Dr Hunter lingered on and was further fuelled when he retired from his post of colonial surgeon in 1888 after serving for only a very short time and was awarded an unprecedented pension to which local opinion, unsurprisingly, maintained he was not entitled. But this, yet again in this chapter, is to run ahead of the narrative.

In October 1886, after two years of the Goldsworthy administration, the local treasury had gone from a healthy surplus to a deficit. This appears to have been due to wholesale squandering instigated by the governor, often to the financial advantage of his local associates. Therefore, there was a great relief and satisfaction shortly afterwards, except in the ranks of his cronies, when he was recalled to London.

Goldsworthy departed on 2 November 1886. According to contemporary reports, a large crowd saw him off by shouting abuse and carrying large banners proclaiming equally rude slogans. After receiving a full military salute from a guard of honour formed by the West Indian Regiment stationed there he embarked from the wharf behind Government House. As the barge drew alongside the breakwater he was loudly hissed and booed. When, as a witness described it, he replied 'with an obscene gesture', missiles were thrown at him.[33] Here the mind boggles over the words 'obscene gesture'. If he

had cocked a snook, then surely that would have been contemp-
tuous rather than obscene. So was it, one wonders, a generally
recognized lewd hand gesture? Maybe it was the well-practised
inverted two fingers vertical personified by that forthright horseman
and show jumper, Harvey Smith. Or was it perhaps the upward
thrust of the middle finger, which I am reliably informed carries the
vulgar connotation of 'up yours', or words to that effect? But, leaving
aside such fascinating and intriguing speculation, the fact is that no
love was lost between Goldsworthy and the local population. No
plaintive rendering of 'Auld Lang Syne' was to send him on his way,
only abuse. And so a despised governor departed for good – or so it
was thought.

Following Goldsworthy's departure, Colonial Secretary Henry
Fowler took over the reins of the colony's administration and,
bowing to general public feeling, cancelled Hunter's contract and
confiscated his dredging equipment. This move, though generally
popular, was legally questionable and Hunter sued for breach of
contract and damages.

Meanwhile, while he was on leave Goldsworthy's reputation in the
colony sank to a new low when it was reported from London that he
had been arrested and fined for striking a police officer. He was
under the influence of drink at the time and had apparently been
trying to engage the services of a prostitute.[34] The Colonial Office
took a jaundiced view of the incident, but, despite this further blow
to his already damaged reputation, reassigned him to British
Honduras for a second tour. Although formal objections were made
to his proposed return, accompanied by memoranda listing the
administration's alleged sins during his two years of office, his
reappointment none the less stood. This did nothing to improve his
relationship with the bulk of the colonists and further allegations of
corruption ensued. Finally, a controversial award of damages to
C. T. Hunter in 1890, arising belatedly from the canal cleaning affair,
stoked up vociferous public anger in influential quarters. This, as
intimated earlier, had far-reaching affects on the constitution, the
infrastructure and social development.

Hunter's action in suing the government created a local legal
problem in that the then chief justice declined to take the case on

the valid grounds that he had been involved in the preparation of the original contract, had given legal opinions on points therein and was, therefore, an interested party. Under the circumstances, both parties agreed to accept arbitration on the basis of equity. The case went to three arbitration sittings. The first two in Belize in 1888 ended in deadlock when Hunter, in the first instance, contested the proposed award as being too small and, next time, refused to accept one of the two arbitrators. After dragging on for two further years, arbitration moved to London where he was awarded $29,000 in damages and compensation.

This award, regarded locally as excessive, provoked a public outcry among representatives of the mercantile and landowning elite. Apart from Hunter being generally unpopular and a crony of Goldsworthy's who had clearly misused a government contract to further his personal profit, it now came to light that because of a loan made to the claimant's brother, the colonial surgeon Dr Alexander Hunter, six years earlier that was still outstanding, the arbitrator the government appointed was not a disinterested party to the affair. On this point, although the acting attorney general gave his opinion to the governor that this was 'a circumstance calculated to bias the mind of an arbitrator and sufficient grounds for inter-ference in a Court of Enquiry',[35] Goldsworthy was unmoved.

The matter was ventilated at a public meeting on 6 March at which, in the light of the changed circumstances, objection was voiced to the arbitration proceedings being held in secret in London rather than in the local Supreme Court. Accordingly, a petition, which every influential merchant and resident landowner in the colony signed, was sent to the secretary of state asking for the award to be set aside and the newly appointed chief justice to be instructed to try the case in open court. Before the Colonial Office had time to consider it, however, Goldsworthy pre-empted the issue by intro-ducing a motion in the Legislative Council on 16 April to make funds available to pay Hunter the award. In the same session he proposed a bill to increase land tax. The ex-officio members (the governor's men, as it were) supported both proposals but this was neutralized when the corresponding number of unofficial members unanimously opposed them. Goldsworthy then used his casting vote as president to force them through. At that juncture the unofficial members stormed out of the meeting and subsequently sent a letter to the secretary of state protesting at Goldsworthy's high-handed action.[36] Whether in exercising his casting vote he was governed by established procedure that required him to vote for the motion in the event of deadlock, which became common in later years, is a matter that is now academic. The fact is that his action fuelled local resentment against him still further.

At yet another public meeting a week later the action taken by the unofficial members was endorsed and, led by representatives of the mercantile and landowning elite (now known as the Peoples' Committee) widened the issue further by demanding constitutional changes leading to greater representation in government and against what they maintained was the open despotism of crown colony rule as administered by Goldsworthy. The demand for constitutional change was clarified at a subsequent public meeting when it was resolved that 'the unofficial members of the Legislative Council should not resume their seats until the composition of the Council has been changed to give the unofficial element a majority.' It was also resolved in this connection that the elective principle based on franchise qualifications should be reintroduced.[37] But, as Goldsworthy pointed out to the Colonial Office, these demands, if conceded, were tantamount to handing over executive power to selfish local interests, especially as the proposed franchise was not universal but limited to a virtual handful of wealthy citizens, to wit, the merchants and landowners.

As the gravity of the situation slowly dawned on the Colonial Office, there could have been no doubt in the minds of its officers that Goldsworthy's autocratic and insensitive actions were what had stirred up the agitation for so significant a change in the constitution. Although they would have recognized that a common feature of crown colonies was the tension that invariably existed between official and unofficial members of the various councils, they would have regarded the governor's typically cavalier approach on this occasion as a serious misjudgement that could and should have been avoided.

Against this background he was finally recalled in October 1890 in the hope that a locally-accepted diplomatic successor would find a way out of the impasse. This time the break was final and there was no question of the proverbial 'bad penny' turning up again. Indeed, he was transferred to the governorship of the faraway windswept Falkland Islands, which, given its remoteness and lack of facilities even by British Honduran standards, many people at the time might have regarded more as a punishment than as a 'sideways transfer'.

Neither Colonial Secretary Melville, who stepped in as acting governor on Goldsworthy's departure, nor the latter's successor Major Alfred Moloney (who got away to a terrible start when, after only two weeks in the colony, his wife died of yellow fever to be followed three weeks later by the death of his private secretary from malaria)[38] could extract concessions from the elite who by now had the bit between their collective teeth and were determined to press on with their demands. This emphasis on the 'elite' rather than on 'public opinion' is deliberate. For, despite all the rhetoric bandied around at the time, particularly in the local press, it was predominantly the representatives and employees of the commercial and landowning classes, and not the public at large, who attended the relevant public meetings and drafted and sent off the petitions to the secretary of state. And so, with neither side willing or able to budge, the impasse continued throughout most of 1891.

A particular problem arising out of this was over the legitimacy or otherwise of legislation the Legislative Council passed in the absence of the unofficial members. This came to a head when the courts challenged a bill to increase certain customs tariffs on the grounds that, at the time of the amendment, the council was illegally constituted. The chief justice ruled in favour of the appellant. The question of an appeal to the Privy Council's judicial council then arose with neither side confident of the outcome and, therefore, reluctant to pursue the matter or to see it pursued.[39] This left the initiative with the Peoples' Committee and the Colonial Office desperately casting around for a compromise.

Finally, in December, on learning that the elite was willing to compromise by giving up demands for the elective principle in exchange for the unofficial majority, the secretary of state, Lord Knutsford, responded with a weak and botched up formula, which, in effect, saw executive power transferred from the governor to an unofficial majority that could now veto any legislation and financial matters that clashed with their own interests. His response was to reduce the number of ex-officio members on the Legislative Council to three and increase the number of nominated unofficial members to no fewer than five, thus conceding to the unofficial members the majority for which they had been pressing. This was done on the understanding that he was not consenting 'to any alteration of the Law which would preclude the Queen from appointing additional ex-officio members and to restoring the official majority at any future time should circumstances make it expedient'.[40] This constitutional change took effect in 1892.

In trying to extricate itself from the constitutional mess Goldsworthy had landed it in, the Colonial Office was manoeuvred into a position where British Honduras remained a crown colony nominally but not in practice. The elite had got its way. It could afford to give up the elective principle because in the appointment of the unofficial members the only nominees from which the governor could choose sprang from the ranks of a tiny literate and administratively competent group within the population – in other words, the same commercial and landowning class that would have been the beneficiary had the elective principle been observed. Thus, executive power would henceforth be wielded according to their interests and not by the governor and his officials. Theoretically, of course, the secretary of state could always restore the official majority, but unless the circumstances were right that would inevitably spark off yet another constitutional crisis.

Not surprisingly, this change gave the representatives of the merchants and landowners control over the future of the colony for the next 40 years. During that time they consolidated their position in government to the detriment of the authority of subsequent would-be 'progressive' governors who were now placed in the anomalous position of being answerable to the crown but unable to insist on local adherence to imperial policy. It was also to have a significant impact on the public at large, for the elite ensured by all means in their power that there were no significant taxes on their profits or properties; consequently, there were only limited public funds available for sorely needed infrastructure and other public works or social services. This policy of putting profit before all else was to lead to years of neglect and that situation, too, was indirectly attributable to Goldsworthy.

But the wheels of change are always turning, however slowly. In 1932, the year after the devastating hurricane and during the Great Depression, which sent most of the world economies reeling, the colony became dependent on British budgetary aid and needed its help to raise a reconstruction loan. HMG would only guarantee the loan if reserve powers for the governor were incorporated into the constitution, thus enabling him to effect measures he considered essential whether the council assented to them or not. This was reluctantly conceded. Thereafter, the formation of political parties, stimulated by occasional labour unrest and moves towards universal adult suffrage were to see in 1954 a majority of elected members, over nominated and official members combined. So, with the break-up of the elite, the road towards a more representational political system was now opening up and subsequently realized.

I suspect there was more to Goldsworthy than the negative description above suggests. For a start, he led the first expedition to explore the Cockscomb Mountains in the Stann Creek District. Also, in trying to break the impasse over a territorial dispute with Guatemala (see Chapter 16) and to enhance British interests in the region, he floated the idea of building a railway between the Peten region of Guatemala and the colony that would link up with the lines then being projected between that country and Mexico. In so doing, he suggested the Colonial Office discuss this option with Guatemala on the basis of common interest, which, if acceptable to it, might then lead to the latter dropping its territorial claim. What he also had in mind in the adoption of such a scheme was that by opening up communications with Guatemala and other surrounding states, the colony could once again become the centre for entrepôt trade with the whole of Central America.[41] Both the colonial and foreign offices liked his proposal, but it foundered on treasury objections based on 'the present condition of the finances of the country'.[42]

Although the proposed railway idea revealed original thinking and a hitherto unsuspected seam of diplomacy, the suggestion about entrepôt trade resurrected the memory of a former trading practice that had existed decades earlier at a time when the colony was the conduit for British trade with some of the countries of the newly formed Central American republic. As Spain withdrew from the region, the demand for British manufactured articles and other goods then flooding the world's markets increased considerably. In 1824 it was estimated that the settlement was exporting British goods shipped via Jamaica to the value of £1,600,000 a year and buying in return goods worth £1,700,000 over the same period.[43] This highly profitable source of trade enriched a new class of wholesalers and retailers, many of whom were Scottish, who owned firms in Belize and who, as already intimated, were destined to exercise a particularly powerful political influence over the local elite. A triangular entrepôt trade between Jamaica, Belize and Central America continued for several decades before competition from other exporters and importers, mainly from the United States, using an increasing number of new shipping services and trading directly with the individual Central American republics, weakened and then eclipsed it. Therefore, as far as British Honduras was concerned, there was little prospect of a revival of such a lucrative trade in the late nineteenth century.

On that note, with Goldsworthy having departed, it is time to end our glimpse at his turbulent, colourful and, some might add, fascinating contribution to the colony's history.

✦ ✦ ✦

This brings to a close the saga of two unpopular administrators. In their different times in the settlement and colony respectively, they shared many similarities. Despard was the first formally appointed superintendent and Goldsworthy the first fully-fledged governor with direct access to London. Both came from upper-class families steeped in military tradition[44] and both had been soldiers who displayed heroism in the field. As colonial administrators, both had caused constitutional confusion requiring intervention from White-hall. Both were regarded in the same quarter as proverbial bulls in china shops. Both were strong willed, single minded and seemingly lacking in political sensitivity. Both were recalled because of intense local feeling against them engineered largely by powerful minority commercial interests. In their defence, however, it should be recognized that the settlers and colonists in their different times were collectively and individually wild and fiercely independent; whoever was appointed to administer their affairs would undoubtedly have faced local hostility at one time or another.

But their fates were quite different – for Despard it was the gallows and dishonour, for Goldsworthy a knighthood, a further appointment as governor of the Falkland Islands and, presumably, a state pension. Lady Luck is undoubtedly fickle in disposing her favours.

What is not in dispute, surely, is that Despard and Goldsworthy were characters of such stature that some people today may be inclined to imagine them as more fictional than real. They certainly added colour to the history of British Honduras as it unravelled over the years. They also showed that in those days being offered official appointments to administer the settlement and subsequent colony was not unlike being invited to sup from a poisoned chalice. Whether their careers or destinies would have been significantly different had they been appointed to another territory is anyone's guess. But reverting to the thought posed in the opening sentence of this chapter, I cannot help but think that, though their genes may have moulded their characters, the unusual nature of the local environment and situations in which they were called upon to serve undoubtedly influenced their actions. I would suggest that it was six of one and half a dozen of the other.

Chapter 10
Twentieth-century Characters

AS CHARACTERS, Messrs Despard and Goldsworthy are hard acts to follow. They reflect earlier ages, other times and other personalities, but it is not necessary to be either famous or infamous to be categorized as a character. In British Honduras in the 1960s I met many people in all walks of life whose presence struck me and whom I regarded as characters. They demonstrated, if demonstration be needed, Shakespeare's oft quoted shrewd and vivid observation that 'All the world's a stage/And all the men and women merely players/They have their exits and their entrances.' From these players I select a few characters at random. Take, for example, Paddy.

It will come as no surprise to learn that Paddy was an Irishman, a vagrant whose presence in the colony was never satisfactorily explained. Of medium height with closely cropped hair and a stubbly chin, not always in daily contact with a razor, he was to be seen on most days wandering in or around Belize. Wearing sandals, a collarless shirt and faded blue jeans cut off below the knees (long before it became fashionable for young people to adopt such a style) he looked much like a middle-aged Huckleberry Finn or latter day Robinson Crusoe and was easily recognizable. How he made a living or where he was accommodated was not obvious and, I must confess, failed to attract my interest at the time. His only visible means of support was the belt holding up his trousers. Yet, though he would call daily at the homes of British expatriates asking for hot water with which to make tea in the little blue billycan he carried around with him, he was not a beggar and would refuse all offers of food and drink. A familiar figure, he caused no trouble, gave no offence and was generally regarded with tolerance and amused affection. Little did we suspect in the summer of 1961 that, within a few months, the outside world would become familiar with his photographic image.

In the chaos and devastation following the impact of Hurricane Hattie that November, a visiting press reporter spotted Paddy wandering along the southern foreshore in his usual attire. As he looked the part of a hurricane victim his presence offered a photographic opportunity too good to miss. A click of the camera shutter and his image was captured to appear as a full-length photograph on the front page of a British tabloid, and possibly elsewhere, with a caption underneath identifying him as one of the many British Hondurans who had lost everything in the hurricane. And, to be fair, he looked the part. When I saw the newspaper I could easily imagine how much sympathy the photograph would have evoked. Meanwhile, the real victims who were trying to rebuild their lives and probably their houses somehow seemed less photogenic. In the event, the publicity proved too much for Paddy and shortly thereafter he was seen walking along the northern road towards Mexico and away from the colony. Who could blame him? There was so much devastation in Belize and elsewhere in the country that few people had time for anyone not involved in relief work or rehabilitation. No doubt, he had been painfully reminded that, unless one lived or worked there, life in the hurricane belt was not worth the candle.

Was there another explanation for his disappearance? Expatriate gossip was quick to suggest that Paddy's photograph in the outside press would indicate his current whereabouts and thus expose him to the attention of, say, a deserted wife, a cuckolded husband, the police or perhaps a string of creditors. This all seemed very unlikely given Paddy's general conduct, but you know how tongues wag in a parochial atmosphere! The fact, however, is that whatever his reason, his departure deprived us in the post-hurricane era of a familiar figure who, until then, had been part of the rich pageant of everyday life in Belize. In short, we missed him.

✿ ✿ ✿

Regularly moored at the customs wharf was the small motor vessel MV *Heron*, which in the 1960s left Belize every Tuesday and Saturday for points south. Crowded with passengers and heavily laden with freight its main destination was Puerto Cortes in the Republic of Honduras where, among other things, it discharged and received the colony's mail. Its skipper was Captain Georgie Goff, a tough and grizzled old sea dog who, according to the local grapevine, was an active smuggler of hooch into the United States during the days of prohibition there. With such a reputation, the local authorities subsequently eyed him suspiciously. Indeed, they were so suspicious that during the early days of the Second World War he was, I was told, interned locally for a short time because of allegations that he was seen signalling by torchlight to German submarines supposedly operating in the Bay of Honduras. The intent or purpose of his involvement was never satisfactorily explained to me, but it seemed so unlikely as to be laughable. However, it would appear that once the hysteria and gossip had died down, common sense prevailed. It was recognized that if Goff were up to anything untoward it was more likely to be connected with something far less dramatic and more to his personal financial advantage. So, with his reputation somewhat restored, but still partially in the shade, he came back into circulation and steadily built up a flourishing business that included importing and agency work as well as involvement in the profitable activities of the MV *Heron*.

He was not part of the establishment and therefore was never seen on the regular cocktail party circuit. However, he was approachable and I always found him a gruff but lively companion and thoroughly enjoyed talking to him. He never gave anything away, whether that was personal information or a concession that could result in financial loss or disadvantage to him. In this he was true to himself. His forebears were among the principal earlier settlers (Goffs Caye appears on early maps) and in my imagination I earmarked him as a typical descendant of the early buccaneers who held sway in that area until the late seventeenth century. Underneath his gruff exterior, an unsuspected softer side occasionally came to light – but not often.

✿ ✿ ✿

Another swashbuckling captain, this time a military one, was Captain Francis Reginald Gilpin Milton, MC. Having survived the First World War, in which he served in the Royal Artillery, he was unable to settle down to civilian life in England after demobilization, so, deciding to leave, he boarded the first available vessel sailing westward and landed in British Honduras where he settled. In his early years there he was associated with such diverse enterprises as sponge farming and various forms of agriculture. As a police inspector during the 1931 hurricane he successfully controlled a large panic-stricken crowd at police head-quarters in Queen Street. He served as private secretary to the governor, Sir John Burdon for a while and, as assistant editor to the committee responsible for producing the *Burdon Archives*, he compiled the index for its first volume. In his later years he performed various jobs for citrus growers and other farmers in the Stann Creek Valley.

Every so often he would come to Belize for a weekend and, on those occasions, he would invariably gravitate towards the Belize Club to meet old friends and enjoy a bout of hard drinking. At the bar he would be full of bonhomie as well as liberal quantities of whisky. According to how well he knew you, one might be addressed as 'old darling' or 'old cock'. He was full of life and eman-ated great warmth and good humour. His presence invariably led to a happier atmosphere at the club, albeit a noisier one.

Sadly, he met his end in a tragic way. Towards the end of the 1960s his body was found in the bush along Hummingbird Highway with signs of having been mauled by a large animal, possibly a jaguar. Whether he died of natural causes and an inquisitive or hungry animal subsequently pawed his body, or whether an animal actually attacked him, are questions I am unable to answer, for I was then working in London and the news of his death reached me second or third hand without much detail.

I cannot, however, help but feel that the manner of his death was predestined. He was one of those people who found the lure of adventure irresistible and, as such, was probably unlikely to die peacefully in his sleep in a comfortable bed. So, here was one old soldier whom fate decided, despite the popular old song, should not be allowed to 'simply fade away'.

✧✧✧

On another tack, it was difficult to reconcile the lithe and handsome fire-eater performing at the Saturday night cabaret at the Bamboo

Bay night club with the trader of East Indian ancestry to be seen daily in the streets of Belize driving his pony and trap at a brisk pace from one place to another. But it was the same man. I never knew his name but he was generally referred to locally as 'Coolie', though not in a disparaging or racially motivated way – in fact, the nickname was completely devoid of malice.

On stage for his performance he was transformed. Clad in a loin cloth, his brown body glistening with oil and his long dark shoulder length hair tied up in a pony tail, he cut an impressive figure. His act, if you regard playing with fire as entertainment, was spectacular if not a downright hazard to the audience, the building and perhaps even the performer. In complete contrast, his act was immediately followed by that of the club's cook, a local Creole woman of ample proportions who, once her culinary duties had ended for the day, performed her secondary role as a belly dancer.

There was always an air of expectancy and perhaps a whiff of apprehension when the fire-eater appeared on stage for the reasons already inferred. And this was justified. One night, arriving late, he rushed from the street into the kitchen where he hastily changed for his performance. Throwing his trousers and shirt across the wooden screen that shielded the open kitchen door from the rest of the club, he dived back into the kitchen to pick up his prop, the flaming brand, ready for his performance. Making his entrance a bit more hastily than usual, flaming brand aloft, he inadvertently caught his clothes alight together with the wooden screen as he passed by. By the time he was belching forth his own spiral of flame on stage an even larger fire was underway outside the kitchen. Fortunately, the cook, wearing Eastern style dress for her stage performance, and other members of the club's staff were able to douse the flames with buckets of water. Although the fire-eater's act was sensibly brought to a close, after some delay the cabaret was resumed, with the belly dancer performing in a smoke filled atmosphere still buzzing with excitement and suppressed panic. Here I must emphasize that these performers were simply two very ordinary local citizens. But it was the presence and activities of such characters that more than compensated at the time for the absence of modern cinema, theatre and television.

✿ ✿ ✿

A collective group of characters was Lord Bayfield's band, which was often engaged to play at dances at the Belize Club. They were good musicians but naturally more at home with Caribbean music than traditional waltzes and quicksteps played in the style and tempo of, say, Victor Sylvester, whose band inspired British trippers of the light fantastic in the postwar years. In general, they coped not only with the traditional dances but also with the new Western dances then coming into vogue such as 'the twist', described at the time as akin to someone leaving a shower who then vigorously dried the lower part of the back with a bath towel while at the same time stubbing out a cigarette with a big toe.

Its leader, Lord Bayfield, was, predictably, not part of the British aristocracy. He was simply one of a long list of band leaders and calypsonians in the Caribbean with a penchant for acquiring a title such as Lord, Earl or Duke. Neither he nor any other members of his group ever adopted airs and graces or were condescending towards the *hoi polloi*. They were staunch democrats in the sense that they regarded any function at which they performed as something for them to enjoy as much as for those dancing or listening to their music, and they undoubtedly did. This was the advent of the 'swinging sixties' and the narcotically inclined had slipped the conventional leash in all manner of means without inviting general social censure. Consequently, between numbers they tended to sample the waters, so to speak, or perhaps smoke a roll of the dodgy stuff. This could, and often did, produce interesting results.

The usual effect was that as the evening wore on the tempo tended to become erratic; then a bum note might be struck or even greater disharmonies ensue. If the musicians had really enjoyed themselves the odds on them being in a fit condition to play the last waltz in any recognizable form or time would lengthen dramatically. In such situations it could be said that MacNamara's band had nothing on that lot!

✿ ✿ ✿

A singular character was Herr Dinger, the German proprietor of the Belle Vue Hotel, a seedy establishment on the southern side of the Belize River near Court House Wharf. Like the dual character Jekyll and Hyde he displayed two distinct sides to his nature. On the one hand he was eccentric, aggressive and irascible. On the other he was cultured and talented and could, if the mood took him, be pleasant and charming. Some evenings at the hotel, when he was not arguing with his guests or attending to their needs, he could be found (in dress shirt, bow tie and monocled) seated at the organ he had installed in the foyer thundering out snatches of Wagner, Bach or Beethoven, leaving his chain smoking wife to serve the Wiener schnitzel and cabbage while trying, often unsuccessfully, not to drop cigarette ash on the food.

When he could find time off from his hotel duties, Dinger enjoyed deep sea fishing. To this end he had bought himself a small motor vessel and, adopting the British love of the pun, called it the *Humdinger*. This play on his name appealed to his sense of humour and he was forever explaining the joke to anyone who would listen and perhaps to some who would not.

Alas, humour sometimes has a nasty habit of rebounding adversely on the originator. One night a person or persons unknown approached the vessel and, with a deft flick of a paint brush, transformed the name from, the *Humdinger* to the *Hun Dinger*. The Teutonic rage that ensued was so intense that the culprit or culprits were careful to conceal their identity for fear of physical assault. On that occasion, however, Herr Dinger might have been forgiven for displaying his darker side, but his quick temper made him vulnerable to people who found it amusing to 'get him going'. A much misunderstood man, always flying off the handle, he was an early version of another hotel proprietor – albeit a fictitious one of television fame – Basil Fawlty. So, for one reason or another, life was never dull or quiet whenever he was around.

✿ ✿ ✿

There was a bright young set in Belize around whom many cultural and social activities centred. When, for instance, the British Council sponsored the University of the West Indies' extra-mural department to produce *The Taming of the Shrew* at the Bliss Institute in July 1961, it was no surprise to find that the key roles had been allocated to many of those who made up that set – in particular, Douglas Fairweather as Lucentio and Terry Gegg (one of a charming bevy of Gegg sisters) playing the part of Katherine. Outside the cast, another of its leading lights, Mario Valdez, was able to display his artistic talents as one of the two scenery painters. This, however, was a leisure activity, for at that time the British Honduras Broadcasting Service employed him as an announcer. His task was to introduce the 7.00 a.m. news from the BBC's external service (or from the Voice of America if atmospheric conditions made that impossible) and follow that up by playing gramophone records interspersed with public announcements and time checks.

Mario was a charming young man with an agreeable personality. Nothing ruffled him and he never allowed his work to interfere with his social life. Consequently, his nocturnal activities often caused him to arrive rather late at the radio station. Whenever this happened the studio technicians would cover for him by relaying the news and playing records without comment until he arrived. Then, when he did turn up, say at 7.25 a.m., he would announce at the earliest opportunity that the time was 7.15 a.m., thus attempting to give the impression that he had got to work on time. After the next record the time would shoot up to 7.30 as he adjusted to the time shown on the studio clock. For those listening to his programme and relying on knowing the exact time, this subterfuge could be disconcerting. When the governor (in this case Sir Peter Stallard) realized what was happening he became obsessed with the time checks. After listening to the news each morning, he would be on edge as he waited to hear the time announced and then to check it against his watch to see if there was any discrepancy, as there often was. On several occasions he suggested to the minister for broadcasting and information that he should replace Mario with a more reliable early riser. The minister would promise to look into the matter, but Mario remained in his post. In British Honduras in those days family, friendship and political ties carried more weight than gubernatorial power. Then there was …

Chapter 11
Cricket: Lovely Cricket

CRICKET IS A POPULAR sport in British Honduras although it lacks the intense competition and near religious fervour that it generates in the British West Indian islands and Guyana. In 1961 there were nine clubs competing in the Belize area, fourteen in the villages and eleven in the out districts. There was also a secondary school competition. Outside Belize, games were usually played on communal grazing lands where pitches were far from true and outfields not conducive to confident ground fielding. Within the capital, the main ground was the MCC sports stadium at Newtown Barracks, although most games were played virtually opposite on a nearby stretch of waste ground between the road and sea.

Although British Honduras had never reached test match status it received some international recognition with the visit of the MCC West Indian touring side in 1960, the first ever visit from an England test eleven. It was this occasion that led to the creation of a specially enclosed ground designed for cricket and major sporting events and designated the MCC Sports Stadium. A one-day game was played and the visitors won in a close contest. More importantly, it led to a great revival in the game locally. So seriously was the visit taken in the colony that when the British Honduras constitutional talks took place in London early in 1960, one of the prominent delegates, Albert Cattouse (also president of the Belize Cricket Association) asked me to obtain for him a copy of the *MCC Cricket Coaching Book*, then in vogue. This was achieved by a visit to Foyles Bookshop in Charing Cross Road. Thereafter, he could be seen studying it intently during quiet periods in the discussions. No doubt, like Baldrick in the TV programme *Blackadder*, he was devising a cunning plan. Obviously, he had got his priorities right.

The Belize Club, the team for which I played, consisted of a motley collection of expatriates and included several excellent players. The star, whenever he could find the time to play, was the chief justice, a Barbadian who in his younger days had played for his country in the interisland competitions and had represented the West Indies at international level. Then in his fifties, with a corpulent figure and always wearing, when playing, a harlequin type cricket cap, he could be taken for an elderly Billy Bunter, but once at the crease he was more like that grand old man of cricket, W. G. Grace, both in appearance (though unbearded) and ability. His repertoire of shots and the grace and style with which he played them were a delight to watch. He also bowled slow leg breaks with all the cunning of W. G. His practice was to go on at the end where the batsman was facing the sun and then toss the ball up high so that the latter trying to follow it often lost the flight in the sun's glare. He was a charming man and only once did I see him ruffled at a cricket match, though in discussions on cricket at various association meetings he voiced strong views at what he believed to be an unsporting practice then creeping into the game – namely persistent short-length fast bowling, which he not unreasonably maintained was putting batsmen at risk of serious injury as well as reducing the scope for playing hitherto classic strokes such as all the various drives. But let us now revert to the occasion when he was 'put out', in more than one sense of these words.

The Belize Club was playing Rovers (a team consisting mainly of local professional and business men and civil servants) at the recreation area at Newtown Barracks opposite the MCC stadium. It was here that the famous but tragic American aviator, Charles Lindburgh, is said to have landed in his celebrated monoplane 'Spirit of St Louis' when he visited the colony in 1929. Although this in itself has nothing to do with cricket it gives some idea of the length of the strip, several hundred yards. In width, however, there were on average no more than 100 yards between the road and the sea. Wickets were pitched horizontally between the two. Such were the circumstances when the chief justice (always referred to as 'CJ') was at the crease on that particular day.

Going in to bat as usual at the fall of the second wicket, he had his customary cautionary words with the other striker, 'no quick singles', which was reasonable given his age, girth and movement, which was an amble rather than a sprint. Runs were coming at a steady pace and the 'CJ' was performing as effectively and stylishly as ever when he played a defensive shot that trickled towards mid-on who bent and slowly picked it up. Assuming prematurely that it was now a 'dead ball', he moved majestically out of his crease to pat down some offending spot on the pitch in the way knowledgeable players do, confident that local convention decreed it was safe to do so. As he performed this little ritual he was shocked to find his stumps shattered by mid-on's throw, which was accompanied by a terrific shout of, 'How's that?' Gerald de Freitas, the umpire at the bowler's end and our chief information and broadcasting officer, was looking out to sea at the time. The shout so startled him that, though the decision was not his to give, he instinctively raised his finger in the gesture of dismissal before he quite realized what had happened. The square leg umpire also raised his finger, so the 'CJ' was given out – run out – twice over. He began his walk back with a dark frown on his face.

In all this, the only elated person was the fielder whose accurate throw had hit the wicket. He was a Jamaican by the name of Brown who was a keen and competitive player but, as a newcomer to the colony, not yet familiar with local custom. Most of the other members of the fielding side were looking aghast. The tension in the air was possibly analogous to that in the Victorian workhouse when Oliver Twist had the temerity to ask for more while the others waited for the inevitable reaction. The fact was that no local person would normally appeal against the 'CJ' on a cricket pitch. If he thought he was out, say, to a catch behind to the wicket keeper, he would, as a sportsman and gentleman, 'walk'. But to appeal willy-nilly for the dismissal of so eminent a personage as the 'CJ', bearing in mind that you might be arraigned before him on some future day, was something no prudent local would contemplate in the village atmosphere of the colony. The general view was that Brown had now better watch out and woe betides him if he ever has the misfortune to appear before the courts on even a minor charge. To his credit, the 'CJ' would not be drawn on the merits or otherwise of his dismissal; but he none the less left the distinct impression that he was not amused.

Despite this clash with convention, Brown settled down smoothly into local society and became quite prominent in the local cricketing world. In fact, he became so prominent that when it was decided to broadcast the final of the Hunter Cup between the village of Crooked Tree and the police over the British Honduras Broadcasting Service, he was regarded as the obvious choice of commentator. As a Jamaican he had all his countrymen's ability to talk at length on any subject, which he usually did. So, for him, the role of commentator presented no problems. More like Brian Johnson than John Arlott, he babbled on in high humour and not without perception. A great source of amusement for him on that occasion was that, of the eleven Crooked Tree players, seven were named Tillet and so were the umpire and the scorer they had brought along. To add to the confusion, three of the police side who came from the village also bore the name of Tillet. On switching on the radio to get the score from the match I heard a delighted Brown chuckling away as he exclaimed, 'He's out. Caught behind. So it's Tillet, caught Tillet, bowled Tillet, given out by umpire Tillet and recorded in the score book by scorer Tillet. And the next batsman to the crease is Tillet.'

While few fixtures ever aroused serious emotion, differences did occasionally arise over the nuances of the game. A particular instance of this took place in a game played at the MCC sports ground between a team from the British army garrison and Rovers. It was a tight game. The army, chasing a modest total, had lost a lot of wickets and, to win, needed to take runs at every opportunity. At a critical point in the game the Rovers' bowler ran up to the wicket to deliver the ball, but on spotting that the batman at the non-striker's end was out of his ground backing up, stopped in his stride and whipped off the bails. There was an appeal and the batsman was given out.

Back in their dressing room, the members of the army team were furious. They maintained that convention demanded that the non-striker should have been warned that he was transgressing the rules and only if he persisted in blatantly backing up, would it have been reasonable to run him out. But if tempers were high then they were to reach boiling point minutes later when the next batsman in did exactly the same as his predecessor and so did the bowler. Two batsmen out to unsporting behaviour was the claim of a furious army side, which fortunately had no access to weapons at the time or a massacre might have ensued. The Rovers' team was unmoved and went on to win the game. To it, the army non-strikers were trying to gain unfair advantage and were given out under the rules of the game. Most of the spectators present agreed with that reasoning, but some were persuaded by the army point of view. The upshot was that an animated buzz reverberated around the ground from which one could hear such remarks as, 'It's de convention,' and 'What's dis convention? Show me in de rules.' I often think of this when I hear pundits observe that sport helps to promote harmony between nations.

British Honduras cricket also had an international dimension at that time, albeit a narrow one. For a few years an annual game, sponsored by Walter Soundy, a rich coffee grower who had contributed a Spitfire to Britain in the dark early days of the Second World War, was played on a home and away basis between the Belize Club and a team from San Salvador in Central America. A club tie, common to both sides, was struck to mark these meetings: against a maroon background it had the repeated motif of a volcano spewing out a cricket ball. I was a member of the team that visited San Salvador in 1963.

Travelling via San Pedro Sula in Honduras and Guatemala in an ancient Dakota aircraft of Second World War vintage, which had seen better days, we arrived in San Salvador on a Friday afternoon to be allocated to families that would accommodate us during our stay. My host was Max Parroti, the number two at the British embassy. That evening we were guests at a local sports centre where, after a buffet supper, we were introduced to various local drinks, including the potentially lethal Screwdriver cocktail, which was to set us off on an alcoholic weekend. The following morning we arrived at the ground in Walter Soundy's *finca* (coffee estate). With its manicured outfield, smart pavilion, big scoreboard, sight screens and a perfect wicket, the setting was delightful. It was a gem of a place and, of course, there was a blue sky and sunshine. Winning the toss we batted. All went well until we discovered a large barrel of draught beer behind the pavilion, which we learnt was intended for the players. This we broached and while the effect was to do wonders for our morale it did nothing to improve our cricketing ability – quite the reverse, in fact. We were all out shortly after tea for a total in the region of 150. The home side, which included a couple of players schooled in the English minor counties league and a quartet from the oil company, Dutch Shell, which had played for a leading Dutch side in the Netherlands, Flamingoes, showed no mercy. By the close of play they were not far short of our total with all wickets still intact.

That evening the British ambassador hosted a cocktail party in our honour in the gardens of his residence to meet local guests. Because he had a subsequent dinner engagement, he charged me ('as Whitehall's representative', as he put it) to ensure that every one left promptly at 8.00 p.m. Well, I tried, but as fast as I got the team members away from the bar and outside the house, they were back in again via the back entrance to the garden. A refusal to serve them with more drink stopped this caper but not before the clock had ticked around to about 8.30 p.m. The ambassador seemed to hold me responsible. Fortunately, I was not called upon to serve on his staff in my future incarnation as a member of Her Majesty's diplomatic service.

The next morning, Remembrance Sunday, saw us in the Anglican church to mark Armistice Day. With splitting headaches we gazed dispiritedly at the hymn board, which listed the three hymns for the service:

388
2
154

Was this an omen of what to expect on the scoreboard after our opponents' resumed their innings an hour or so later? Alas, it was something like that. They batted nearly all day before declaring and then bowling us out again. And this time we could not blame a barrel of beer. But with the prospect of another social night ahead of us our spirits brightened. Yet socially, as the Duke of Wellington observed in another context, it was 'hard pounding, gentlemen.'

We returned to British Honduras the following day. Despite a disappointing result we managed to console ourselves with the thought that, like missionaries, we had carried the flag of cricket into heathen (cricket-wise) country. Some club members suggested, when this thought was voiced, that if we were missionaries it was on behalf of brewers and distillers rather than cricket. But such cynicism is only to be expected. In life, as in cricket, 'you can't win 'em all!'

Chapter 12
Hurricane Hattie (1)

W AS THE PATH Hurricane Hattie took to British Honduras in 1961 determined entirely by chance, a caprice of nature as it were, or was it predestined and written in the stars? The question arises because a Jamaican Cassandra's prophesy earlier in the year had been realized. However, to make sense of this remark, it needs to be put into context.

Hurricane Hattie, the most intense hurricane of its kind to move into Central America since the devastating Hurricane Janet crossed the Yucatán Peninsula in September 1955, struck British Honduras in the small hours of Monday 31 October 1961. In its wake a significant number of people died and thousands were left homeless, hungry and depressed. I shall expand on this brief outline later, but first a little background might be helpful.

On taking up my duties in the secretariat, Michael Porcher told me a curious story – a story, as it turned out, with a purpose. He said that while passing through Jamaica on his way to take up his current appointment as chief secretary about two months earlier, he met an old lady who, on learning of his destination, told him that a terrible hurricane would strike the colony later in the year. Although he confessed to me that he was not unduly superstitious, he added that his instinct was to take the oracle's warning seriously on the grounds that *obeah*[1] (witchcraft) was prevalent among large sections of the Jamaican population and that the old lady who had approached him was possibly someone who practised that black art. To heed her warning, therefore, was to adopt a practical form of insurance cover.

In the light of this I was told to take down and dust off the existing hurricane precautions plan and to bring it up to date after drawing on the experience and expertise of a newly constituted central disaster committee, of which I was apparently the secretary. The necessary action was set in train straightaway and numerous meetings were held to this end. The committee, which reported to the governor, sat under the chairmanship of the chief secretary. It comprised members of Executive Council, principal secretaries, heads of departments, senior police officers and representatives from the British army stationed in the territory and the local volunteer force. The army's contribution was immensely valuable both in terms of planning and practical help. At that time it was provided by the splendid Z Company of the Royal Hampshire Regiment under its commanding officer, Major Barry Matthews, and subsequently carried on equally diligently and effectively in following years by the British garrison at Airport Camp, initially under its commander, Colonel G. T. Anderson.

At the same meeting the chief secretary also passed on to me advice given to him in his previous post in British Guiana (now Guyana) by the governor, Sir Ralph Grey (later Lord Grey of Naughton), to the effect that in any crisis or emergency it was prudent to keep a close record of events. The rationale for this is that such events tend to become the subject of subsequent inquiries, usually in pursuit of scapegoats and, therefore, the inquisitors are likely to consider information recorded at the time more reliable and acceptable than recourse to memory. This advice I was to remember and act upon as the events of Hurricane Hattie unfolded.

By August the hurricane precautions plan had been fully revised, with procedures laid down and potential shelters included, strengthened or discarded on safety grounds. It was not long before the plan was put to the test because the first hurricane of the season, Anna, would shortly be moving towards British Honduras. Fortunately, as it crossed the coast south of Belize it was downgraded to a tropical storm and there was no loss of life or serious damage to property, although many trees and crops were flattened. In optimistic mood we concluded, prematurely as it happened, that the oracle had been right about the territory but hopelessly wrong about the impact.

Indeed, as the weeks passed the prophesy was beginning to ring more and more hollow, for the end of October was fast approaching and with it the end of a normal hurricane season. Then, on 27 October, the Miami Weather Bureau began to issue reports that suggested that a powerful storm was brewing up in the southwest

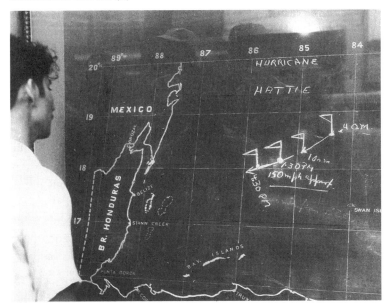

4. Anxiety and tension mount. Path of Hurricane Hattie is plotted as it moves closer to British Honduras.

Caribbean that threatened Jamaica, Grand Cayman and Cuba. Two days later it changed course and swung towards British Honduras. As it approached the coast, the highest winds near the centre were estimated to be moving at 150 miles an hour with gusts of up to 200 miles an hour. It now seemed inevitable that the hurricane would hit the colony and hit it hard – and it did.

At this point it might be of interest to compare how the warnings announced locally in 1931 differed from those announced in 1961. For the earlier date the first public intimation of an impending hurricane came during the 10 September celebrations when Governor Burdon told an audience he was addressing that Pan American Airways had sent him warning of an approaching hurricane. But 30 years later, with a regular flow of reports from the Miami Weather Bureau, it had become possible to plot Hurricane Hattie's progress locally and to relay the information, along with attendant advice, to the general public by radio. For those living in the hurricane belt, the service the Miami Weather Bureau provides is not only highly invaluable but also greatly appreciated.

Setting aside for the moment a detailed account of Hurricane
Hattie's visitation (which is the subject of the next chapter) I should,
perhaps, explain how it came to be written. That an official report
would be needed was a *sine qua non* for such occurrences. It was also
equally apparent that it would have to be produced in the secretariat,
which effectively meant by the chief secretary, by me, or by the two
of us together – I was therefore left with no illusions about not
having to play my part. Accordingly, I made sure that, while the
storm was raging, the logbook (diary) in the operations room was
kept up to date with barometer readings, messages in and out and all
other relevant information. Afterwards, bearing in mind Michael's
advice to keep a close record of events during a crisis, I made notes
based on personal experiences and observations and from
information gleaned or extracted from all those who were actively
involved.

Towards the end of January 1962, when the various government
departments were starting to deal with everyday matters again
(although the machinery of government was still creaking under the
weight of residual hurricane and reconstruction problems), Michael
raised with me the need to produce fairly soon a report on the
hurricane to send to the Colonial Office in London for the record. I
sketched out an outline of the material I had assembled for his
information and from that we agreed to the content, direction and
format of the proposed report. The emphasis was to be on facts
recording the affect of the hurricane and its aftermath on the whole
territory, giving as much detail as was available with the addition of
only a minimum of covering comment. He then told me to draft it,
although he recognized that, with normal official duties taking up
the average day, the task would undoubtedly have to be accomplished out of hours.

There was also another obstacle to overcome, namely the need to
find a suitable place in which to write. It needed to be away from too
many interruptions and all the distractions that were a feature of life
in the secretariat, especially at that time. In this connection I should
mention that Florence and our daughters had recently returned from
Jamaica, to which they and others had been evacuated at the beginning of November, but that in the continuing absence of electricity,

dearth of potable water and need for structural repairs, our house at Newtown Barracks remained uninhabitable. Fortunately, friends came to our rescue by finding us temporary accommodation close to the Caves Branch of the Sibun River on the Hummingbird Highway, fifty or so miles west of Belize. Although without electricity and our water having to be drawn from a well, it provided a welcome oasis of calm compared with the hustle and bustle of the clearing-up operations in the capital. I was able to spend time there at the weekends and during a couple of those visits, working under the incandescent light of a hissing Tilley oil lamp, I would write up the report in longhand after the family had retired to bed for the night.

Once completed and typed up by my efficient and indefatigable secretary Mrs Lillian Dakers, it was approved by the chief secretary and subsequently, with the governor's agreement, submitted to Executive Council, which endorsed the recommendation that it be transmitted to the Colonial Office. For anyone interested in undergoing the vicarious experience of what it is like during a hurricane and its immediate aftermath, and the problems involved, that report is reproduced as Hurricane Hattie (2) in the next chapter.

Given that the object of my description of Hurricane Hattie's impact on the country was 'to tell the story as it happened', it might at times seem repetitive or tedious. However, to reiterate, the intention was to produce as full a record as possible covering all aspects of the disaster. Inherent in that account is a reminder that it is essential for the responsible authorities to have a plan available covering pre- and post-hurricane situations, while recognizing that Murphy's Law (more commonly known as sod's law), which decrees that if anything can go wrong it will, requires flexibility and adaptability in actual practice. Equally important in their considerations is the recognition that law and order often break down in such situations, and unless quickly brought under control, chaos and confusion are likely to follow. Not least, it also needs to be recognized that a considerable amount of logistical expertise and organization are required to collect and distribute incoming relief supplies. In British Honduras in 1961 we were fortunate to be able to draw heavily on the expertise of the British armed forces (and the United States military in the early days) working in close cooperation with the local authorities, whose own contribution was equally significant.

An essential part of that contribution was the pragmatic and community spirited response of many British Hondurans from all walks of life (notably political representatives, civil servants, other public servants including teachers, doctors and nurses, people working in voluntary organizations and other volunteers) whose whole hearted efforts, once the extent of the damage became apparent, went towards either implementing policy or ensuring that its directives were fulfilled. If one had been looking for a catch phrase to describe that period, 'all shoulders to the wheel' could have been applied.

As for the prophesy with which this chapter began, who can tell if the sudden and surprising shift in the direction of Hurricane Hattie on 30 October was attributable to chance or destiny, whichever you call the mystery that governs our planet and our lives? The fact is that each year hurricanes occur in a roughly defined corridor with varying outcomes. And even if it is maintained that a particular event such as a hurricane is predestined, is there any reason to suppose that the information is registered in some sort of retrieval bank ready to be tapped into by someone practised in the art of witchcraft, or with the ability to read the stars, a crystal ball or tea leaves? With due respect to Nostradamus and the author of *Old Moore's Almanac*, I must declare myself a sceptic.

But that attitude reflects the mind. In my heart I am reluctant to accept that the Jamaican Cassandra's prophesy was little more than an inspired guess. For it was her pronouncement that enabled us in British Honduras to focus on hurricane precautions in 1961 and, by so doing, leaving us better able to prepare and then cope with the impact of Hurricane Hattie – conceivably leading to the saving of lives. It was, therefore, perhaps unfair to attribute the credit for this in the following official account to the actions of the Central Disaster Committee and not to her. But some might attribute that to destiny.

Chapter 13
Hurricane Hattie (2)

1. A report on Hurricane Hattie, which struck British Honduras on 31 October 1961. This report is divided into six sections:

2. It is not the object of this report to assess the damage to crops and property caused by the hurricane, or to discuss the problems of rehabilitation. They are matters of vast importance but of such magnitude that they must be and are being addressed separately. That said, the purpose of this report is to place on record the events that occurred shortly before, during and immediately after the visitation of Hurricane Hattie to this country and to set out the position to date. The account is not exhaustive, for it deals only with some aspects of the disaster. It is lengthy, but that is not surprising given that the hurricane devastated the capital and the next largest town and affected in one way or another the lives of about 40,000 people out of a total population of 90,000. Thus, there is much to report.

5. Hattie leaves its visiting card with devastating effect.
Belize, 1 November 1961.

General Picture in Outline

3. The general picture is that Hurricane Hattie approached the
   eastern seaboard of British Honduras towards the end of
   October from the northeast and moved, in a gentle curve, into
   the Maya Mountains and from there into Guatemala. The eye of
   the hurricane probably passed between St George's Caye and
   Turneffe Island, striking the coast near Mullins River. Estimates
   of wind velocity experienced locally vary considerably. Those
   who remember the 1931 hurricane here think that the Hattie
   winds were in the region of 150 m.p.h. in the centre. Others put
   the wind force much higher. But, the fact is that our
   meteorological instruments (that is anometers and other wind
   gauges) were either destroyed in the hurricane or were unable
   to record winds of the force experienced so that no speeds can
   be confirmed. Winds of 125 m.p.h. (that is to say the maximum
   speed the instrument could record) were, however, recorded at
   Stanley Field Airport. Furthermore, the assistant director of the
   Caribbean Meteorological Organization (Jamaica branch) who

visited this country shortly after the hurricane struck, expressed the opinion that winds gusting up to speeds of between 150 and 230 m.p.h. were probably experienced. This echoes the estimates provided by the Miami Weather Bureau, which was monitoring events.

4. There was virtually no hurricane damage in the northern part of the territory (namely the Corozal and Orange Walk districts) and very little damage in the Toledo District in the south and southwest. The most affected districts were Belize, including the cayes, Stann Creek and Cayo.

5. The official death roll is 262. This figure includes persons missing but presumed dead. A breakdown of the figure by districts is as follows:

Belize City	94	
Belize Rural	53	(of which 49 were on cayes)
Stann Creek Town	60	
Stann Creek Rural	54	(of which 46 were in Mullins River)
Cayo	1	

General Picture in Detail

6. Now for the picture in detail. Hattie was first reported as a tropical storm on 27 October in the vicinity of San Andros Island off the coast of Nicaragua, about 420 miles southeast of Belize City. The report originated from the Miami Weather Bureau. Subsequent advisories reported that Hattie had intensified and had become a hurricane. The forecasts were that it would travel in a northerly direction towards Jamaica, the Cayman Islands and Cuba. Indeed, it appeared that Grand Cayman Island was directly threatened, and HMS *Troubridge*, which was on its way to Belize City, was diverted to Kingston. There was nothing in the advisories to suggest that British Honduras was going to be severely affected.

7. On 30 October, however, the picture changed abruptly. Miami Weather Bureau Advisory No. 11 issued early that morning (time of receipt in British Honduras approximately 0700 hours local time) reported that the hurricane had turned sharply in a

westerly direction in the night and was now heading for the Chetumal area of Mexico. The reason for this surprising and sudden shift of direction may possibly be attributed to a cold front coming down from the United States of America across the Gulf of Mexico and the northwestern Caribbean, which deflected Hattie from its northerly course. The report added that the hurricane was still growing in intensity and it was estimated that there were winds of over 140 m.p.h. at the centre with gales extending out 200 miles to the north and 140 miles to the south. Tides of 15 feet were forecast where the centre would hit the coast. The position of the hurricane at that stage was latitude 18.6 west. It was travelling in a westerly direction at a speed of between 12 and 15 m.p.h.

8. It was evident from this information that, short of a miracle, some parts of British Honduras, particularly the Corozal District, were likely to be affected. Accordingly, at 0800 hours local time, the chief secretary declared the final warning stage, Red II, in the Corozal District, and the precautionary warning stage, Red I, throughout the remainder of the country. These warnings were conveyed to each of the districts over the 'Peter Fox' police wireless network and announced at regular intervals over BHBS (British Honduras Broadcasting Service). An advance precautionary and rescue team comprising PWD (Public Works Department) and nursing personnel was immediately dispatched to Corozal. Its orders were to take whatever precautionary measures it considered necessary and then stand by at Orange Walk. In view of the threat to the northern district and probably the Belize District also, British Honduras Airways sent its two aircraft south to Melinda and to Punta Gorda. But, as it happened, the hurricane struck south and the one at Melinda was destroyed on the ground.

9. At 0830 hours, the Central Disaster Committee, under the chairmanship of the chief secretary, met in the police operations room to consider the situation. Their unanimous view was that the situation was extremely dangerous but that Red II should not be declared throughout the whole territory until the next advisory from the Miami Weather Bureau (expected at 1030

hours local time) had been considered by them. They did, however, instruct:

(a) that immediate steps should be taken to shutter up all public buildings, including shelters, in Belize City;
(b) that immediate steps should be taken, wherever practicable, to evacuate people living on nearby cayes; and
(c) that BHBS should remain continuously on the air until further notice.

10. In the event Red II was declared throughout the whole territory at 1100 hours local time. This decision was taken after consideration of the awaited advisory, which reported that the hurricane was still growing in intensity and that it might now strike the Mexico–British Honduras coastline further south than originally forecast. It was now recognized that the threat from Hattie was far greater than previously thought. In fact, so great was it thought to be that the possibility of a general evacuation of the whole coastal belt was considered and only ruled out reluctantly on the grounds that it would be unfeasible. The hurricane arrangements decided upon earlier in the year were then set in train in Belize City.

11. An operations control headquarters was set up at police HQ comprising three controllers (principal secretary (CSO), military intelligence liaison officer and superintendent of police) and four duty officers, namely two police inspectors, one officer from the Royal Hampshire Regiment and one officer from the British Honduras Volunteer Guard, under the direction of the chief secretary. This control was maintained throughout the period of the hurricane. Public shelters were opened and manned by wardens, police, Red Cross workers and boy scouts. Special teams of police and PWD workers took up prearranged positions in the city ready for rescue and search operations. Rescue columns of the Royal Hampshire Regiment and the British Honduras Volunteer Guard stood by at their respective headquarters; the former at Airport Camp and the latter in Belize City. A number of PWD vehicles and most of the heavy

plant were taken to Mile 22 on the Western Highway in an attempt to disperse transport. A forestry road clearing unit, under the charge of the conservator of forests, was sited at Roaring Creek. In the districts the district commissioners took whatever measures they deemed appropriate.

12. Hurricane advisory No. 13 reported that the centre of the hurricane was, at 1600 hours local time, located near latitude 18.1 north, longitude 85.8 west and moving westward at a rate of 8 m.p.h. Winds had increased to 150 m.p.h. at the centre and gusts of 200 m.p.h. were reported. It was now estimated that it would strike the coast around the Chetumal–Belize City area (probably near the capital) that night or before the forenoon on Tuesday 31 October. That advisory, like all others, was announced over BHBS and there seems little doubt that the information encouraged those who could leave the city to seek shelter in other districts (especially the Western District) to do so. Similarly, it led many others who might otherwise not have done so to seek refuge in the public shelters in Belize City.

13. An inspection of all the public shelters in Belize City by a member of the Central Disaster Committee between 1900 and 2100 hours on 30 October showed that they were filling fast and that it would not be long before the majority would be filled to maximum capacity. By about 2300 hours the majority were full. As a shelter became full, the BHBS would relay the news to the public who were then advised to go to specified shelters where room was still available. In the event, four of the city's fourteen public shelters (St Catherine Academy, Pallotti High School, St John's College and the Princess Margaret Youth Hostel) still had space spare, thus suggesting that those who sought the safety of a public shelter were in fact accommodated.

14. At 2100 hours the barometer reading in the operations room was 29.62. Shortly afterwards the first minister arrived and remained there until the following morning. At 2200 hours the barometer reading was 29.61 and thereafter it began to drop steadily. At 2300 hours the reading was 29.58. Advisory No. 14 from Miami received shortly afterwards gave the centre of the hurricane as being about 100 miles east-northeast of Belize City

at 2200 hours local time. It was estimated that the centre would reach the coast, not far from the capital, about noon (whether this was EST or local time was unclear) the following day. Tides some 15 feet above normal were reported. At 23.15 hours the United States consul in Belize City telephoned to ask whether a US hurricane reconnaissance plane could be given permission to fly over British Honduras the following day. This the chief secretary readily gave.

15. At midnight the barometer reading was 29.53. Outside the operations room the wind began to increase to gale force and it began to rain. By 0100 hours on 31 October the wind was reaching hurricane force. The barometer reading at this point was 29.44. By 0200 hours the wind had increased to a force probably over 100 m.p.h. and the barometer had fallen to 29.21. At 0300 hours the barometer fell to 28.93 and at 0400 hours to 28.68. By this time the wind had increased steadily in intensity and gusts possibly between 150 and 200 m.p.h. were experienced. In the immediate neighbourhood of the police operations room it was observed that corrugated iron sheeting was being blown off roofs and that some wooden buildings had begun to collapse or disintegrate. The force of the storm increased further and by 0500 hours the barometer reading had dropped to 28.35, the lowest point recorded in the operations room during the hurricane. At that stage part of the ceiling in the operations room collapsed necessitating the control team to move to another room.

16. High winds and heavy rain continued, but during the following half hour the barometer, though vibrating violently, ceased to fall and finally commenced to rise, thus indicating that the centre of the storm was passing at the time. (It was *guesstimated* to be passing about 35 miles to the southwest). At 0600 hours the barometer reading had risen to 28.90, an encouraging sign. But the danger, now of a different sort, was far from over. A foot of water was observed in the police station yard. This rose steadily and by 0800 hours it had reached an estimated depth of 10–12 feet. The barometer continued to rise steadily and, shortly afterwards, the flood water began to subside. By 10.30

hours the wind force was light to moderate. The barometer reading was 29.50 and the depth of water in the police station yard was down to about three feet.

17. It was evident, from dawn onwards, that Belize City had been severely damaged. But it was also recognized that the eye of the storm had not passed over the city and that some area to the south, possibly Stann Creek, had been struck even harder. The first action, therefore, was to try to establish immediate contact with all the districts and with the outside world. Between 1200 and 1230 hours, through the radio system the police contacted their stations in Corozal, Orange Walk, Progresso, Benque Viejo, El Cayo, Barranco and Punta Gorda. The reports received from these stations were in the main reassuring, although hurricane force winds were still being experienced at that time in the Cayo District. They were, however, unable to establish contact with Crique Sarco, the airport and Stann Creek. Fears for the latter increased accordingly. Meanwhile, an army signals unit working side by side with the police signals section made several attempts to establish contact with Airport Camp and its HQ in Jamaica. Atmospheric conditions at the time were poor. They were, however, able to pick up a message that the former was transmitting to the latter to the effect that the army had cleared the runway of debris at Stanley Field and, although very few of the normal facilities were available, aircraft could land there. Unfortunately, BHBS was unable to help in establishing contact with the outside world. Although both broadcasting and telecommunications transmitters had been able to switch to an emergency power supply when the city's mains power had failed at 0100 hours they finally went off the air at 0300 hours when their aerials were blown away. They were to be out of action for several days.

18. At 1500 hours one of the police operators managed to establish contact with a radio ham operating from Mérida in Mexico. Through the latter, messages calling for immediate assistance were passed to London, the governor of Jamaica, the governor-general of the West Indies, and the United States and Canadian authorities.

HURRICANE HATTIE (2)   169

Outside Relief Measures

19. It was not long before outside assistance was forthcoming.
Relief food supplies and other outside aid arrived on a massive
scale from the United States, Mexico, the Central American
republics, Jamaica and, of course, the United Kingdom.

20. On Wednesday 1 November, an advance contingent of 16 USAF
personnel arrived at Stanley Field Airport in a C-130 transport
aircraft carrying initial stocks of medical supplies, trucks and
three large field kitchens. The US destroyer *Corry* arrived and
established a medical aid centre at the Holden Memorial
Hospital while another, *Bristol*, was deployed off Stann Creek.
On 3 November the US aircraft carrier from Florida, *Antietam*,
carrying supplies of medical equipment and food, started operating offshore with 23 helicopters. In these aircraft, 48
American doctors visited all parts of the country and a naval
medical team undertook mass anti-tetanus inoculations in the
Stann Creek area. The helicopters were also used to drop food
supplies into isolated villages in the distressed areas. The United
States task force operated in conjunction with the British
authorities and cooperation at every level was of the highest
order.

21. The Mexican response was swift and generous. Within a few
hours of the extent of the disaster being known to them, their
authorities arranged to dispatch food supplies from Chetumal.
Medical and other supplies, including blankets, arrived by air.
The Guatemalans were also quick to respond. Supplies were
brought in by air and sea and several sick patients were
evacuated to hospitals in Guatemala at the invitation of
President Ydigoras. They also contributed medical teams and
firemen. That the Guatemalan government subsequently
attempted to make political capital out of the aid its country had
given does not detract from its generous assistance at a time of
need. Other Central American republics, notably Honduras and
San Salvador, also gave speedy and welcome assistance.

22. In Jamaica considerable amounts of food, transport and building
supplies were assembled and shipped to this country. On 6
November, 11 doctors on the staffs of the UCWI and Kingston

public hospitals arrived to strengthen the medical department. On the same day 100 members of the Jamaican constabulary arrived to assist in the emergency arrangements (see paragraph 34 below). Five members of the Jamaican forestry unit were also flown in to assist the local forestry department generally. Other personnel, including a housing and planning adviser, Red Cross workers and water engineers also arrived.

23. Supplies from the United Kingdom first arrived by air. RAF Shackletons operated a shuttle service between Jamaica and Stanley Field Airport. Apart from bringing in essential supplies and personnel, this service proved invaluable in the evacuation of certain families who had lost their accommodation. HMS *Troubridge* arrived off Belize on 2 November bringing troops and supplies from Jamaica. A medical team from the ship set up headquarters at the Bliss Institute where they performed a herculean task of giving inoculations against tetanus, typhoid and paratyphoid, in addition to dealing with minor casualties. They were ably supported by members of the Royal Army Medical Corps. An RAF team also arrived and set up a medical unit. Commander Peynton-Jones, naval adviser to the West Indies federal government took over as queen's harbourmaster and worked miracles in getting the docks back into operation. On 7 November HMS *Londonderry* arrived with relief stores. It was followed a few days later by HMS *Vital*, which once again marked the deep sea channel into Belize harbour.

24. It should also be mentioned here, otherwise it might be overlooked, that the first aircraft bringing relief supplies came from the Bahamas. The plane landed after dark on the night of 31 October – a somewhat hazardous operation. A three-man medical team from that country, under a senior medical officer, arrived later.

25. Assistance was also forthcoming from within the less affected parts of the territory. Surplus food supplies were brought in to Belize City from Orange Walk, Corozal and Punta Gorda on the day following the hurricane; and a limited amount of transport was also made available. In regard to transport, it should be recognized that practically all vehicles that had remained in

Belize City had been immersed in sea water and it would take several days, at least, to have some of them back on the road, if at all.

Internal Relief Measures

26. Before outside relief arrived three important tasks had to be achieved. The first was for the army at Airport Camp to establish contact with control headquarters in Belize City and vice versa. To this end, the chief secretary sent a two-man team on the afternoon of 31 October with instructions from the Governor to OC Troops. With the airport road impassible, they travelled by river in a motorboat they had hired; but progress was slow because in places timber jams and barges blocked the Belize River. Just before Haulover Bridge, and shortly before dusk, they met a patrol led by OC Troops, which was *en route* to Belize City in the army leisure boat, the *Lord Nuffield*. It was learnt that another patrol had been dispatched by road. Both patrols reached the city that evening.

27. The second task was to clear the roads and thus establish communication between Belize City, Stann Creek and Cayo. Two army relief columns were dispatched, one to Stann Creek and the other to Cayo. Meanwhile, the forestry road unit was clearing the roads between Roaring Creek and El Cayo (the main town in the district) on the Western Highway, as well as along the Hummingbird Highway between Roaring Creek and Stann Creek, which fallen trees had blocked in many places. Progress on the latter was set back several hours because the approach to the bridge over the Caves Branch of the Sibun River had subsided considerably as a result of heavy flooding. This had to be filled before road traffic could cross and other blockages dealt with. Due mainly to the efforts of a Hummingbird Development Corporation employee operating a Caterpillar tractor, and the assistance of the army relief column, the necessary work of filling and repairs was carried out on the afternoon of 1 November. In the meantime, a party of six soldiers under the command of a sergeant marched to Stann Creek and arrived there at 0800 hours the following morning to be followed

shortly afterwards by the main column. The other army column dispatched to El Cayo reached the town, but was subsequently cut off for a time by heavy flooding on the Western Road near Roaring Creek.

28. The third task was to establish a central food storage and distribution centre in Belize City from which the whole country could be served. It was essential that the people in the distressed areas should receive food supplies quickly. With this in mind, the chief secretary, late on the evening of 31 October, instructed his principal secretary to set up at the Marketing Board, in concert with the marketing officer, an organization to achieve this end. It should perhaps be explained that normally the Marketing Board is the country's storage centre for locally grown rice and beans. It consists of two warehouses (one large and one small) and one rice milling shed. Much of the rice stored there prior to the hurricane had been immersed in sea water and would shortly be unfit for human consumption. On the morning of 1 November about one foot of water covered the floors of all the buildings and thick mud was everywhere. This had to be cleared before proper storage could be effected. The first step afterwards was to salvage any rice that had escaped the flooding and then to send any available transport to the airport to collect the relief supplies already beginning to arrive. The army unloaded these supplies and they were initially stored in the hangar there. It was also necessary to take over the cargoes of ships in the harbour consigned to local merchants who were now in no position to take delivery of them. These were to be stored together with the food the government had ordered that was arriving by sea. Existing stocks of certain foods held by local merchants were requisitioned in order to introduce a balanced food distribution. Furthermore, in addition to establishing a relief food storage centre sufficient to keep the entire population of the country fed for several weeks, the Marketing Board was now responsible for getting food out to certain feeding centres and ensuring that there were sufficient supplies to implement the food distribution system that was subsequently introduced. Food was also supplied on a commercial

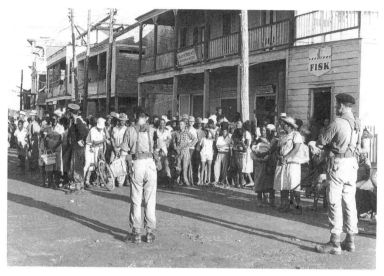

6. Waiting for emergency supplies of food and clothing. Soldiers from the
Royal Hampshire regiment and police organize orderly queues.

basis to the Orange Walk, Corozal, Cayo and Toledo districts.
On 4 November the principal auditor and other senior civil servants joined the Marketing Board organization as the need to
account for supplies coming in and going out was becoming
obvious.

29. The effects of the hurricane in Belize City and the districts were
as follows.

Events and Effects of the Hurricane in Various Places

Belize City

30. It is virtually impossible to convey in words the scene witnessed
around noon on Tuesday 31 October. The initial picture was
one of chaos and devastation. Nearly all the buildings in the city
had suffered damage of some sort and many were completely
destroyed. Very little property escaped damage entirely. Some
public buildings, notably Government House, the customs
buildings, mental hospital, TB ward, prison and the Belize
Hospital – to name but a few – were severely affected. Debris
and seaweed were everywhere and the streets were still about

two to three feet under water and mud. Walking was virtually impossible and some people travelled through the streets in dories. Motorcars or collapsed buildings blocked some streets. Electricity and telegraph poles had fallen and their tangled wires added to the other obstacles. The swing bridge that connects both sides of the city was out of alignment, though it was still possible to cross it on foot. There was no electricity, very few cooking facilities and only a little potable water. As already indicated, timber jams and barges blocked in places the already swollen Haulover Creek; flood water had lifted boats that had not been tied to the mangroves some distances inland where they stayed high and dry in various positions. Indeed, some boats, including one of more than forty feet in length, were washed several hundred yards inland and were to be seen in several parts of the city. Timber blown from nearby timber yards littered the mangrove swamp along the side of the river, as did petrol and diesel drums that had floated away from the 'Shell' depot. Some 78 prisoners from the Belize prison, who were released on parole when the hurricane badly damaged the prison's inner columns and gates, wandered aimlessly through the city. Inmates from the mental hospital also took to the waterlogged streets when the building's main gate and peripheral walls collapsed. This early picture was so grim and depressing that it may partially account for many citizens' subsequent behaviour.

31. Early in the day reports of looting began to trickle in. During the morning it was reported that men in dories were breaking into shops and business premises on a looting spree. A liquor store opposite the Paslow Building was one of the first places broken into. The following day widespread looting occurred and it was necessary for the police to use tear gas on occasions to disperse the offenders. In general, however, the police were unable to cope at this stage, which was not entirely their fault. Very few had been trained to deal with a situation of this sort. Furthermore, even after the water had subsided many streets were littered with debris and movement was difficult. Thus, it was not easy for them to reach the points where looting had

been reported. Above all, it should be remembered that many of them had been on duty continuously since before the hurricane struck and that they too were naturally worried about their families and homes. The main incident, however, took place at the Marketing Board when a large crowd broke into the huge warehouse and began looting bags of rice. The civil authorities, backed by soldiers from the Royal Hampshire Regiment under the command of Major Glynne Lewis and Major Albert Johnson of the British Honduras Volunteer Guard, very quickly brought the situation under control. Tear gas was released to disperse a section of the crowd, but otherwise no force had been necessary. Much of the rice taken was wet and would have been useless had it remained at the Marketing Board for any length of time. Also, it is probable that the rice, along with food taken from shops the previous day, served as a cushion against hunger for many people.

32. That day, 1 November, the governor, Sir Colin Thornley, invoked his special powers under the British Honduras constitutional ordinance to declare a state of emergency. A curfew between 1900 and 0600 hours was imposed throughout the stricken areas. The same day he requested HQ Caribbean in Jamaica to provide troops for immediate relief work. In response, the commander of the Caribbean area, together with the commanding officer of the first battalion, the Royal Hampshire Regiment, flew over immediately to discuss the situation with him.

33. The following day emergency regulations were put into force prohibiting free movement between the districts without the authority of the commissioner of police or anyone authorized by him. These regulations were designed to prevent the needless influx of people into the distressed areas, which would only aggravate an already difficult shelter and food problem.

34. Responsibility for maintaining law and order was given to the military commander under Hurricane State of Emergency (No. 3) Regulation, 1961. This was done because it became obvious that the police could not cope with the situation at that stage. Unfortunately, the use of armed troops at the initial stage gave

rise to subsequent rumours and reports that martial law had been declared. The arrival of troop and police reinforcements from Jamaica gave such a boost to the morale of the local police force that the civil authorities were able to resume control shortly afterwards. The troops were then used for guard duty, patrols and rehabilitation work. But that was still in the future.

35. In the event, 40 soldiers of the Royal Hampshire Regiment arrived in Belize City early in the afternoon of Thursday 4 November and, assisted by sailors from HMS *Troubridge*, tackled a growing security threat in the capital. Further reinforcements arrived over the next three days. The public was urged to cooperate fully with the authorities and the following is the text of a bulletin that Information Department staff distributed in the city and relayed over police hailers:

> The Government, the Army and the Navy are working closely together and in full agreement to overcome the disastrous results of the hurricane.
>
> They are all agreed on what is required to be done and in the immediate future, as these measures become possible.
>
> These measures of which you will be informed by all means available to us, will require the cooperation of all the people, which we earnestly beg you to give – otherwise measures of compulsion will be taken.
>
> Food supplies will be guarded and anyone seen looting or pilfering public or private property will be shot dead.
>
> We all appeal to you, in the interests of yourselves and your fellow countrymen in other areas which have been badly damaged, to give us your full cooperation.
>
> Arrangements have been made to provide food for all which will work, provided there is full cooperation all round.

36. Only once was it necessary to use force to guard food supplies. On 4 November a group of men was caught looting in the Brodies warehouse. They were challenged and twice called upon

7. Major Glynne Lewis foreground and author, police hailer in right hand,
behind, waiting to re-enter Marketing Board warehouse
having cleared it of looters.

to halt. Shots were fired at two of the men attempting to escape.
One unfortunately was killed and the other wounded in the leg.

37. The powers to shoot on sight were conferred upon the military
commander under section 4 of the Hurricane State of
Emergency (No. 3) Regulation, 1961.

38. The internal security situation was brought under control
shortly afterwards. The only other incident worth recording
occurred on 7 December when a crowd of about 100 people,
including women and children, broke into the premises of the
Belize Supply Company and stole hardware to the approxi-
mate value of $1000. The incident took place while the
manager and his assistant were at lunch. The reason prompting it was far from clear. The police arrived and the looters
dispersed. Two arrests were made and convictions were
obtained.

39. Starting from 4 November, troops from the Royal Hampshire
Regiment's first battalion were used to provide guards in the
dock area, the prison, the Guatemalan consulate (at the request

of the Guatemalan consul-general in Belize City), the Marketing Board and many other vulnerable points such as food distribution centres and government property. They took over from the US Army the feeding points the latter had established, and at one time were responsible for feeding between 6000 and 7000 people. Guards were provided for those shelters still occupied. A burial squad working in conjunction with the civilian authorities helped to dispose of the dead. They impressed some civilian labour and provided guards to control queues at feeding points and at food and clothes distribution centres. They requisitioned any transport that was required. Last, but not least, they assisted generally and introduced 'goodwill' patrols to ensure that the need for inoculation was kept before the public and to see that the old and needy were cared for. They withdrew from Belize City on 23 November and were replaced by the Worcestershire Regiment, which had come in from Stann Creek.

40. Other branches of the army gave valuable assistance. The Royal Army Service Corps (RASC) was responsible for unloading and storing the relief supplies that came in by air. The Royal Army Medical Services (RAMS), working in conjunction with the director of medical services, kept a very close eye on the public health situation and was responsible for many thousands of people being inoculated. The Royal Engineers assisted in general repair work and in clearing streets and roads. They also helped in the planning and initial construction of the refugee camp at Hattieville (see paragraph 43 below). A section of the Royal Signals was responsible for producing an emergency telephone system.

41. The need to provide food for the people of the city in the aftermath of the hurricane was of paramount importance. Most people had lost whatever supplies they had and provision stores were either destroyed or closed. Shops were closed because sea water had rendered their supplies useless or because their owners feared that reopening them would be an invitation to looters. The immediate problem to resolve was how to feed the people. On 1 November, food kitchens were set up at the Red

Cross headquarters and Militia Hall and meals were provided from there. Obviously, two centres were inadequate for this purpose and a further eight feeding centres, four on each side of the city, were established shortly afterwards. This arrangement, although it served the immediate need was not entirely satisfactory. After a few days, plans were made to ration food and to allow people to cook for themselves. Ration cards were issued for this purpose and food distribution centres (staffed by civil servants, school teachers, church and other voluntary workers) were set up. The issue of free food on this basis continued until 25 December.

42. It was difficult to obtain labour immediately following the hurricane for street cleaning and other manual tasks. This was understandable given that many men were anxious to patch up and mend their own homes before giving any thought to helping others. Some were still suffering from shock. There were others, however, particularly the naturally indolent, who had no intention of helping and, for them, the provision of free food destroyed any plan they may have had to work. In the main, labour had to be coaxed; but, at times, it was necessary to impress men for essential tasks. Men employed on immediate post-hurricane work got $1 a day and a cooked meal at their place of work in addition to their rations. After the initial stage the rate was increased to $2 a day and the daily cooked meal was dropped. In the third and final stage, they were paid the normal basic minimum wage and their ration cards were withdrawn.

43. The position at the time of drafting this report (end of February) is that Belize City is slowly getting back to pre-hurricane conditions. Streets have been cleared and great strides have been made in recent weeks towards clearing refuse and debris from housing lots, which had become the breeding ground of rats and flies. Until they are completely cleared there is still the risk of a serious epidemic breaking out. Much remains to be done. But thanks to the efforts to clear the city and a recent spell of cold weather the danger may be said to have receded. The majority of shops are open and reasonably

well stocked. There was a tendency after shops had reopened for some shopkeepers to increase their prices. As result, by 20 November it had become necessary to impose price controls on certain basic commodities. However, although the prices of some goods are higher than they were before the hurricane, there are indications that they are settling. The harbour is fully operational and the merchants are carrying out their normal business. Many houses have been repaired on a patch and mend basis. More, perhaps, could be done on rebuilding houses; but until a decision is taken on the proposal to build a new capital city inland, patch and mend is the order of the day. Most government buildings and some government quarters have been repaired up to a basic minimum standard. Six- and eight-inch pipes are bringing in the city's water supplies and there is no shortage of kerosene and gas for cooking purposes. Electricity has been restored to practically all households. The curfew, which in the New Year was still imposed between 2300 and 0500 hours was lifted on 31 January. The city's three cinemas are open, as are a number of clubs. The daily newspapers, the *Belize Times* and the *Belize Billboard*, are being published, though there is no sign as yet of the evening paper, the *Daily Clarion*. Schools have reopened, but they are short of textbooks and it will be some time before they are back to normal. BHBS is functioning, though still not at full power. The overseas telegraph unit is fully operational. Despite the heavy strain imposed upon it by the weight of the many aircraft that landed there carrying relief supplies, Stanley Field Airport is still open to air traffic. This was only possible because the PWD undertook a considerable amount of repair work. There were 1132 movements of aircraft in November, in other words four times the normal volume. A considerable number of people have gone to Hattieville, the refugee camp established on the outskirts of the capital. It is a self-contained camp with its own shops, schools, church and police station. A field hospital is being built there and a town board is being formed.

44. The total number of dead in Belize City is officially stated to be 94.

Belize District

45. Heavy floods and high winds caused widespread damage in the mainland section of Belize District. Villages near rivers were particularly hard hit, but fortunately casualties were light. Many of the thatched houses in villages were either destroyed or badly damaged and crops suffered considerably. At Gales Point, where the village was virtually wiped out, one death, a child aged two, was reported. The only other deaths were at Manatee Beach (one death reported) and Salt Creek Lagoon where two deaths occurred. Villagers in the district have been given assistance with roofing material and food. It is still necessary to continue to provide some assistance on the basis of need.

46. The cayes were less fortunate. They were particularly exposed to Hurricane Hattie's wrath and were hard hit. Some 49 people on the cayes were officially reported to have lost their lives. The most deaths (14) occurred at Caye Caulker and the immediately succeeding paragraphs give an outline of what happened there.

47. Caye Caulker is about 25 miles northeast of Belize City. There were 105 houses and 402 people living there before the hurricane.

48. On 30 October, advisories announcing Hurricane Hattie's course were heard over BHBS and at 1500 hours that day the village council and police called a meeting to warn all villagers of the impending hurricane and to advise them to batten down their houses and secure their boats and dories. Accordingly, the villagers complied with this advice and took their boats to the two creeks, one of which is in the north and the other to the south of the village.

49. Five families consisting of 31 people took shelter in the Roman Catholic school, a large wooden building raised to about four feet off the ground.

50. The wind began to freshen at about 1600 hours and one hour later heavy seas began to pound the beach. The wind, which was increasing in intensity, was then coming from the northwest. At 2100 hours the wind switched direction to the southeast. It was later estimated that the gusts were probably in the vicinity of 175–200 m.p.h. Large swells began to roll over the caye at around

midnight. At 0300 hours on 31 October the schoolroom collapsed and 14 of the occupants, 13 of whom were under the age of eleven, were washed away to sea. Only four bodies were subsequently recovered. Of the 105 houses on the caye, only 20 remained. All those remaining were severely damaged.

51. According to the surviving inhabitants the main damage resulted from five distinct waves. From tide marks still to be seen on the caye the water rose to a height of 15 feet in places. The water receded at about 0900 hours.

52. Similar conditions were experienced on other cayes. In the Turneffe Islands, a group of small cayes, three people lost their lives at Berry Caye, seven on Soldier Caye, six on Caye Bokel, ten on Calabash Caye and one at Bull Bay. There were some spectacular and almost unbelievable occurrences. At St George's Caye wind and water drove channels across the island dividing it into three. Saddle Caye has disappeared entirely and is now about four feet beneath the sea. Others have been severely damaged and their structure altered to varying degrees.

53. The terror people experienced on some of the cayes can best be illustrated by an account of what happened to Mr Allan Neal, which the district officer for Belize has recorded.

54. 'Mr Neal is a plantation worker on Caye Bokel, which is the most southerly of the Turneffe Island group. At 1700 hours on Monday 30 October strong winds were experienced there and Neal, a man of 33 years of age, and his four children aged 5, 7, 8 and 12 respectively took refuge in their house. Rain fell heavily at 2100 hours. The wind grew in intensity from the northeast and the house collapsed causing the family to take shelter under part of it. About midnight the wind abated and there was a lull of about ten minutes. Mr Neal did not realize that this was the eye of the hurricane and, accompanied by his children, tried to reach his dory, which was about fifty yards from the house. Before he could do so, the wind turned round to the southeast and, with it, the sea. A large wave lifted him into the sea separating him from his children. He did not see them again.

55. Neal drifted with the tide and wind for about six miles in a northerly direction. His hand then found a tree, which he hung

onto. At 0500 hours on 31 October, when the winds had dropped and the tide had gone down, he saw that he was in the Turneffe Lagoon. He swam and walked until he reached the Turneffe mainland where he stayed for the next 12 days, living on coconut water and jelly awaiting rescue. He was picked up by boat and brought to Belize City.'

Stann Creek District

56. In terms of comparative damage, the Stann Creek District was perhaps the hardest hit. The eye of the storm struck the coast near Mullins River, causing immense damage to the town and to four villages in particular – Mullins River, Hopkins, Sittee River and Seine Bight; 113 people lost their lives. There were 60 deaths in Stann Creek Town, 46 in Mullins River, 3 at Sittee River, 2 at Hopkins and 2 at Blair Athol.

57. The situation in Stann Creek town followed closely the pattern of the one in Belize City described above. Hurricane precaution arrangements were set in train on Red 1 and then it was simply a matter of wait and see. Many people, however, were quite confident that even if Hattie struck British Honduras, the southern part of the country, including Stann Creek, would escape its impact. The false alarm caused earlier in the year by the unrealized threat of Hurricane Carla, which struck the United States, may have contributed to this complacency.

58. Shortly after midnight in the early minutes of 31 October heavy rains fell and winds began to increase. The winds reached somewhere in the region of gale force at 0200 hours and hurricane force about an hour later. At this stage they were coming from the west, but they gradually veered round to the south. This took about one hour. It continued blowing hurricane force (probably over 150 m.p.h. and gusting over 200 m.p.h.) from the south but changing slowly to the southeast.

59. At 0500 hours the tide swept in and began to rise. It continued to do so until about 0900 hours when it began to recede, the winds having again returned to the south. On the south side of the town, in the vicinity of Havana Bridge and in low-lying places, the water rose to a height of between ten and twelve feet.

On the front street and in the neighbourhood of the police station, it rose to between four and five feet.

60. Between 0900 and 1000 hours the winds began to abate. Gusts became weaker and sporadic. At the same time the water receded. At 1100 hours it was possible to get into the streets. The scene was one of utter devastation. The police and others took immediate action to rescue people trapped in or under houses and to succour the injured. A group of citizens under the direction of the town board undertook the collection and disposal of the dead.

61. As might be expected from the direction of the winds, the southern part of the town was the most severely damaged. Indeed, the section south of Havana Bridge was virtually flattened. The northern section, though heavily damaged, fared better. In particular, the police station, hospital, convent and church were left in reasonably good condition. Some 90 per cent of the buildings in the town were either completely destroyed or badly damaged.

62. Work began that afternoon to clear the streets of debris and other obstacles and it continued for the next few days. Work was also begun to repair buildings and the pier, to clear the airstrip and to build temporary shelter for the homeless. As stated in paragraph 27 above, a sergeant and six men of the Royal Hampshire Regiment arrived in the town at about 0800 hours on 2 November to be joined later by the remainder of the platoon. The district officer, elected representatives and the platoon commander discussed the situation and, on their orders, two food centres were established to feed the population with food initially requisitioned from local merchants, and then supplied by the US destroyer *Bristol*, the RASC depot at Stanley Field Airport and the Marketing Board. This arrangement continued until 7 November.

63. On 1 November a medical officer and two nurses arrived from Belize City to assist the resident medical officer in the Stann Creek Hospital, which at that time cared for about 100 patients.

64. The US destroyer *Bristol* arrived and anchored off Stann Creek on 2 November. The ship's crew unloaded food supplies

(mostly canned foods) and 350 blankets, many of which actually belonging to the ship's personnel. They helped to establish the feeding centres and also set up a soup kitchen that they themselves operated. It is understood that 21,000 lbs of food was unloaded from this ship.

65. Two days later United States naval helicopters arrived in the town bringing in further food supplies and medical teams (see paragraph 20 above). Apart from assisting in the town they also covered most villages in the district with their operations.

66. On 7 November, a company of the Worcestershire Regiment arrived and took over from the detachment of the Royal Hampshire Regiment. The splendid cooperation between the civil and military authorities was maintained and continued until the Worcestershire Regiment pulled out on 22 November.

67. The combined civil and military authorities organized the town from top to bottom. All food was commandeered and held in a central store. From this, four commissariats were set up, each serving a section of the town. All able-bodied men were required to work for food and, as in Belize City, a unique system of payment was introduced. A chit system was evolved whereby a single man was given a chit for $1 in payment for a day's work and a family man $2. These were then taken to the commissariats where they were exchanged for a specified amount of food. In short, unless there were good reasons why a person could not work, this was a case of no work no food. If a person decided not to exchange his chit for food he would be credited with the equivalent amount in cash.

68. As it turned out the chit system was probably the best that could have been adopted in the initial shock phase when it was essential for every able-bodied man to help in the clearing up operations.

69. On 8 November HMS *Londonderry* arrived off Stann Creek and visited villages along the coast delivering food supplies and providing medical services. HMS *Vital* followed a few days later.

70. Mullins River was the hardest hit of all the villages. It caught the eye of the hurricane and was virtually wiped out. Only three of the 300 buildings – the police station, the Roman Catholic schoolroom and the teacher's quarters – were standing after the

storm had passed. Even those buildings were badly damaged and 46 people (of whom 33 were minors) lost their lives. It was estimated that here the tide rose as high as 20 feet in places. Losses of livestock, crops and trees were extremely heavy. The navigation light by the police station and the jetty were both completely destroyed.

71. At Hopkins all but two of the houses in the village were destroyed or seriously damaged (about 95 per cent). There was heavy flooding. Water up to a depth of two feet remained in the village for several days after the hurricane had passed. Two people lost their lives.

72. Seine Bight is a comparatively large village with a population of about nine hundred. Although 60 per cent of housing was destroyed or severely damaged, no lives were lost.

73. The settlement at Sittee River, which is very scattered, was badly affected. Three lives were lost.

74. Most of the citrus trees in the Stann Creek valley were, surprisingly, left standing. The forest throughout the area, however, was totally devastated. Trees had been stripped of their bark and looked as though they had been worked over by a high pressure sand blaster. In many instances they were without leaves and in some cases unidentifiable.

75. Much rehabilitation work has been undertaken in the Stann Creek District. In the town, business is almost back to normal. The market is functioning and the cinema has reopened. Regular classes have been resumed at the Roman Catholic and Methodist primary schools. Some homeless families have already been moved to the Silk Grass housing project.

76. The Silk Grass housing site is situated along the road to Mango Creek about twelve miles from Stann Creek Town; 137 small houses are being erected there to house homeless families from the district.

77. Food is still being issued to the town and villages on the basis of need. In an attempt to persuade farmers to return to their lands and to encourage others to take up agriculture, government are giving farmers in the Carib and Silk Grass reserves subsistence allowances while they work on their farms.

Cayo District

78. Most of the damage that occurred in the Cayo District was attributable to flooding although many thatched houses were destroyed or damaged by hurricane force winds. The district was hit some hours after Belize City and Stann Creek Town were struck.

79. Winds a little above hurricane force struck the Cayo District about noon on 31 October and continued for three to four hours. Shortly afterwards the Mopan and Macal rivers rose to incredible heights, certainly over forty feet in many places, as a result of flash flooding. In El Cayo the river rose to about two to three feet from the floor of the Hawksworth Bridge, which stands at 52 feet above the normal flow of the river. At Barton Creek the water covered the road to a depth of eight feet while, at Roaring Creek, the depth of water covering the road was estimated at 12 feet. Many villages were virtually submerged. The flooding lasted for almost a day. A second flood occurred in some villages along the rivers a day or so later.

80. Because of the heavy flooding in the river section of El Cayo, supplies of food in some shops, including the two principal ones, were destroyed. This caused an immediate food shortage in the town and a local disaster committee was quickly formed to deal with the situation. Relief supplies were obtained from several sources. For example, the local Roman Catholic priest donated 87 bags of flour, each containing 50 pounds, and one local merchant gave 189 bags of flour that were wet from the flooding but nevertheless fit for consumption – and no doubt included in his subsequent insurance claim. Oranges and grapefruit were available from nearby farms. These supplies were subsequently supplemented by eight loads of food dropped in the town by US helicopters. As soon as the road to Belize City was again open, supplies were also obtained from the Marketing Board. As the situation stabilized the latter began to supply the local shopkeepers on a commercial basis.

81. Helicopters dropped food in the villages to alleviate any immediate need.

82. The town of El Cayo escaped major damage. Only 24 thatched

houses were blown down and most of these have since been rebuilt. There is no shortage of food. In the villages many thatched houses were destroyed and severe damage to crops sustained. Calla Creek, Macaw Bank and Saturday Creek were particularly hard hit. At Saturday Creek the corn crop had not been harvested and was completely destroyed when the nearby river rose and the flood swept over the *milpas* (agricultural land cleared by burning). At the other two villages much of the crop had been harvested and stored, only to be destroyed when the flooding reached eight feet in many of the houses. In yet other villages the corn crop was left on the *milpas* because villagers could not get to them for a few days – apart from the flooding, the forests had been badly hit by wind, thus blocking the trails and paths – so the corn began to germinate and was ruined.

83. In the villages, despite the shortage of bay leaves for thatching due to the trees being damaged, many houses have since been repaired; also, beans and seeds have been planted for future crops. In general, however, there is a food shortage in the villages and many people there will have to be assisted for several months to come.

84. One person, a man of 70, lost his life. His death was probably caused by drowning. No lives were lost in any of the villages in the district.

Other Districts

85. The other districts in the country, namely, Orange Walk, Corozal and Toledo, were more fortunate. The district officer at Orange Walk had taken all possible hurricane precautions on 30 October. Buildings were shuttered up and people were moved to shelters. Patients were moved from the hospital to the upper floor of the police station, which was considered a safer building. Throughout the following morning, up to about 0830 hours, winds of 40–45 m.p.h. with occasional gusts of between 65–70 m.p.h. were experienced. The town and the surrounding villages were virtually untouched by the winds, although crops were affected. The situation in Corozal and the surrounding district was almost identical. In Toledo District strong winds

were experienced during the morning of 31 October. Between noon and 1430 hours that day the winds possibly reached hurricane force; thereafter, they abated. In the town of Punta Gorda eight houses were destroyed and twenty-three damaged. In the villages there was some damage to houses and crops. No lives were lost in any of these three districts.

Conclusion

86. It is worth recording that not a single life was lost in a public shelter in Belize City. This was more than mere luck. Earlier in the year the Central Disaster Committee had instructed the Public Works Department to examine all existing public shelters and to report back to them on their ability to withstand hurricanes. As a result of that report, the committee decided to remove the Eden Cinema and Cathedral Hall at the Holy Redeemer School from the list of public shelters on the grounds that they were unsafe. In the event, both buildings collapsed during Hurricane Hattie and it is probable that many lives would have been lost had they been retained as public shelters. Five additional shelters were added to the official list. As recorded elsewhere in this report, anyone who wished to weather the storm in a public shelter was able to do so.

87. Other prearranged plans, notably those for the disposal of the dead, were effective. Relief columns for devastated districts and road clearing also worked smoothly. In short, having regard to:

    (a) the intensity and size of Hurricane Hattie;
    (b) the fact that Hattie was a freak storm and there was less warning time than usual; and
    (c) given the limited finances available at the time for expenditure on hurricane precautions, the Central Disaster Committee can reasonably claim to have emerged from the storm with its colours flying. Nevertheless, a large number of lessons have been learnt and many improvements in the pre-hurricane arrangements are to be adopted this year.

88. Post-hurricane arrangements were less satisfactory. This was

largely because the committee's plans did not really cover the situation created by the unexpectedly wide impact of Hurricane Hattie. In this connection it should be mentioned that the committee had devised individual plans for different situations predicated on the assumption that the storm would hit a particular area. The advent of Hurricane Anna earlier in 1961, when these arrangements were introduced, suggested that they were satisfactory. Notwithstanding this, the committee did none the less consider and visualize a wider situation in which Belize City, together with a substantial part of the country, might be devastated, but came to the conclusion that if such a situation occurred normal services would be so dislocated that it would be impossible to formulate an effective plan in advance for dealing with it. However, in the light of experience, it would appear that a good deal of additional planning can be undertaken for coping with post-hurricane measures even in an emergency of the magnitude of Hurricane Hattie. This planning is already in train.

February 1962

Chapter 14
Hurricane Hattie (3)

B Y THEIR VERY nature, most official reports (especially those on military actions or natural disasters) are couched in impersonal terms and the preceding one is no exception. Therefore, in presenting an overall picture, individual personal experiences tend to be kept largely in the background. Yet, as the vivid account of Allan Neal's terrifying ordeal on Caye Bokel illustrates (in paragraphs 53–5 of Chapter 13) it is only through such glimpses of human drama that the true impact of recorded events, such as a hurricane, can be conveyed and understood.

Of course, it is impossible to record the personal experiences of all 40,000 or so people affected one way or another by Hurricane Hattie (or for that matter the experiences of those from outside involved in the ensuing relief operations) but, as I was close to the centre of events as they unfolded, it may be of interest if I record details of a few of my own personal experiences, together with supporting anecdotes, as a sort of postscript to the official report. In so doing, however, I am conscious that there are many others with more colourful and interesting stories to tell if only they would come forward.

Once it became clear on 30 October that Hattie was about to clobber us, arrangements were made for some of the families of those assigned for hurricane duties, including mine, to be accommodated temporarily with army families at Airport Camp where the height of the ground reduced the threat from the predicted tidal waves. With concern for their families to some extent relieved, those involved were now able to go about their emergency duties less encumbered with personal considerations. My duties were to be performed at the control centre at police headquarters in Queen Street where, as one of three controllers, I was to find plenty to do.

Early on that still and muggy evening, the sky suffused with a peculiar hazy and seemingly ominous yellow hue, I visited all the hurricane shelters to assess how they were being used. They were filling up fast. The occupants' mood was one of calm stoism as they patiently and philosophically accepted the inevitable. Thereafter, I returned to the control centre to await the impact of the impending hurricane, details of which have already been recorded in the preceding chapter.

At around 2.00 p.m. the following day, with still no contact with the army at Airport Camp, Captain Nigel Woodward of the Royal Hampshire Regiment (then attached to the governor's staff) and I were deputed to try and reach the camp by river with a message for the commanding officer from the governor, Sir Colin Thornley, who had now assumed overall command. When we reached the Belize River at a point on North Front Street between the swing bridge and British Honduras Distributors the situation looked hopeless. The still swollen river was so littered with timber and all sorts of other debris that it seemed inconceivable that any vessel moored in the vicinity could have escaped destruction or serious damage. Yet, by some miracle, we managed to find the owner of a small motorboat who was both able and willing, after we had negotiated a deal, to take us up-river. Because of the various obstacles in the river, navigation was difficult and progress was not only painfully slow but also hazardous.

Daylight was beginning to fade when, just before Haulover Bridge, the *Lord Nuffield*, the small army leisure boat carrying troops, came into view with Major Barry Matthews, commanding officer of the Royal Hampshires in the prow looking for all the world like the vessel's figurehead. For the occasion he was wearing a traditional Tank Corps black beret with his own regimental badge prominently displayed, and elegantly (or let's face it, ostentatiously) drawing on a cigarette through a holder – a nice touch of panache in a tight situation and one in keeping with the best British army traditions.

Following a brief mid-river powwow during which I ascertained news of my family, we accompanied the *Lord Nuffield* back to our starting point and then to the control centre where, in a series of meetings with Barry Matthews present, the Central Disaster Committee discussed the current situation and planned the next day's actions. At about 7.00 p.m. the chief secretary made me responsible for collecting and distributing relief food supplies (and with it hiring or requisitioning necessary transport) in concert with the admirable, hardworking and efficient local marketing officer, Fred Moody; we were to operate from the Marketing Board.

With no electric power in the city and the streets barely passable, it was obvious that nothing practical could be achieved that night, so I decided to walk home to see how my house had stood up to the wrath of Hurricane Hattie. I was aware that, being of concrete construction, it should have withstood the force of the winds, but as it was sited within 100 yards of the open sea I was concerned about the effect of tidal waves. The trudge home was more difficult than I had anticipated. Indeed, the journey through unlit streets was nightmarish.

Wading through several inches of sea water and mud while trying to avoid fallen telephone and electricity poles and a tangle of connected wires was time consuming and tiring; the mass of debris intermingled with the sludge, consisting mainly of timber and corrugated iron roofing from collapsed wooden buildings, presented a further hazard. While negotiating such debris in Eve Street I inadvertently trod on a submerged batten through which, as I was to discover painfully, a large rusty nail was protruding. The nail pierced the sole of my right shoe and entered my instep so deeply that I had difficulty releasing it from my foot. Fearing tetanus I retraced my steps to the Belize Hospital in which, in passing, I had spotted a glimmer of light. Nearing the main entrance I could see that the hurricane-force winds had badly damaged the structure of the building and, as I was to learn, the sea had swept in covering and ruining beds, stores and equipment. Fortunately, all patients had been evacuated before the hurricane struck. Also fortunately, for me that is, two nurses were still there having arrived earlier to treat a few hurricane casualties and subsequently to start cleaning up as a prerequisite for getting the hospital back into service. Under the light of a flickering oil lamp they applied a dressing to my foot and, to be on the safe side, gave me a tetanus booster. It was a comfort to know that both the spirit and practice of Florence Nightingale was still abroad in times of crisis. The dressing was to some extent academic. With still having to trudge through about half a mile of waterlogged streets to get home, it was obvious that it would become dirty and sodden before I got very far, but it gave me a welcome psychological boost. And so I carried on to my home at 24 Newtown Barracks.

Despite the darkness I could see that the house, with its windows boarded up against the winds, was intact structurally save for the disappearance of the wooden palings that had surrounded the lower floor where the water tank and laundry were housed. The tidal waves at that part of the coast had swept in to a height of about fourteen feet and had lapped the floor of our living quarters, leaving behind a coating of grey mud, a dank atmosphere and an unpleasant smell. With no electric light, torch or any other form of illumination, I groped my way into the main bedroom and lay down fully clothed on a wet mattress trying to collect my thoughts.

I was now beginning to feel the effects of the past 36 hours, for the adrenalin that had kept me going while I had something positive to contribute had evaporated. The cumulative effects of lack of sleep, little food and drink, painful foot and worry about how our elderly parents and other family members in Britain might react to the news of the hurricane induced in me a sense of depression and conceivably a touch of self-pity. But then, on reflection, I recognized how much better off I was compared with those who had suffered bereavement or were homeless. And with that more reassuring thought I fell into a deep sleep.

A few hours later I awoke feeling stiff, numb and unable to move my limbs easily and, with my foot throbbing painfully, I became convinced that I had contracted tetanus. However, this momentary feeling of panic soon passed when I realized that the probable cause of the stiffness and numbness was the affect of sleeping on a damp mattress. None the less, while anxiously awaiting the approach of dawn, I thought it prudent to remain awake to monitor any further aches and pains. With no further alarms, I greeted the dawn with relief.

Cleaning myself up as best I could in the circumstances, I limped off to the control centre through the still muddy, debris-littered streets before setting off for the Marketing Board, where I hoped to obtain a hot drink and perhaps some food. So much for hope or expectation! Instead I received the news that a large crowd had broken into the main Marketing Board warehouse where looting was now in full swing. The chief secretary ordered me to 'get down there immediately and get the situation under control'. So, accompanied by Major Glynne Lewis, the military liaison officer attached to the local police force, Major Albert Johnson of the British Honduras Volunteer Guard, three soldiers from the Royal Hampshire Regiment and three policemen, I limped off with a sore foot and empty stomach. I should add that I was armed with a police loud hailer through which to address the crowd we were about to confront.

Fred Moody, whose normal job was to buy and sell local agricultural produce through cooperative and other farming organizations, met us at the Marketing Board and, after a brief discussion of our proposed role *vis-à-vis* relief supplies, he explained that a large crowd had invaded the main warehouse where rice was stored and that individuals were busily walking off with huge sacks of it. Looking through the front door of that building the scene at first glance – and for that matter, on second and third glances – was chaos. Water covered the floor of the warehouse to a depth of about a foot and, among a swirling mass of humanity of all ages, bags of rice, each weighing a hundredweight, were being passed through side doors and windows where other staggering bodies carried them off to all parts of the city. It was a rupture defying process.

My military colleagues, the two majors, were keen to clear the building straightaway through the use of tear gas. But, as the perceptive Moody observed, the rice had been immersed in sea water and would only be edible if cooked and consumed reasonably quickly. To retain it in the warehouse, where it would only sprout and rot, would serve no useful purpose. As it was, it was now being distributed among the community and thus helping to relieve hunger. An additional factor, to my mind, was that the looters were in fact doing us a favour by unintentionally clearing the warehouse voluntarily, thus providing valuable floor space for the incoming relief supplies now beginning to arrive in the country.

In the face of murmurings from my military companions to whom law and order were the only considerations, I agreed with Fred Moody that we should defer action until more of the wet rice had been removed. So through the loud hailer I informed the crowd inside the warehouse that they had just 20 minutes to take what they could after which time they would be forcibly ejected. This gave urgency to their activities, which were redoubled. To emphasize the time factor I gave a countdown as each five minutes passed. At the end of 20 minutes, however, Fred and I felt that we still needed more floor space, so I issued a final ten minute warning adding, that after that time, tear gas would be released to disperse anyone still left in the building. The result was a further commendable flurry of activity. But, inevitably, not everyone was out of the warehouse when the ten minute extension was up.

The moment the final ultimatum expired the two majors could restrain their instinct for action no longer. Albert Johnson (who in his normal official capacity was our magistrate and the district officer for Belize) suddenly fired his revolver into the air inches from my left ear, presumably to signal that time was up. It may be that I was startled by the proximity and loudness of the shot, but it seemed to me that the bullet struck one of the iron roof girders only to ping and ricochet around the others in the manner of a steel ball bouncing off the pins on a bagatelle board or on a pin table to be found in an amusement arcade. In this case, however, I had no idea of where it would end up. To add to this feeling of personal danger my military colleagues had generated, my good friend Glynne Lewis, a gung ho Canadian serving with the British army, joined the action by lobbing in a tear gas canister. Unfortunately, such breeze as there was sent the gas drifting back in our direction and we, coughing and spluttering, were forced to retreat. The effect was to leave us with red-rimmed eyes and a building we were unable to enter for the next hour or so. On a positive front, the situation was restored and once the warehouse became habitable we could get down to the task to which we had been assigned – a farcical start, perhaps, but not the last to be experienced over the next few days.

It is to state the obvious to say that the task of receiving, collecting, storing and distributing relief food supplies is dependent on sufficient transport being available. In our case, there was an immediate shortage in the capital because immersion in sea water had rendered many trucks and lorries useless. However, such government vehicles that were available and others hired from less affected districts enabled us to make a start, but many more were needed. To this end, the power to requisition, for which provision had been included in the emergency regulations, was invoked. The police, army and civil servants were the agents used for this purpose. Unfortunately, this was to give rise to situations in which left and right hands did not know what the other was doing. Thus, an already requisitioned truck leaving the Marketing Board, say to collect a consignment from the airport, might be further requisi-tioned *en route* and, despite the driver's protests, brought back empty under guard to its starting point. A large 'R' painted on the wind-screen of such vehicles brought this frustrating time- and fuel-wasting antic to an end.

Then we had to face the unlikely problem we had with prisoners. When the hurricane damaged the outer structure of the Belize prison, leaving gaps in the walls, an unusual but sensible course was taken to release the prisoners temporarily on special parole until such time as the prison could be repaired and properly staffed. However, many of the prisoners soon realized that, despite the pleasures of freedom, wandering aimlessly around a devastated city was less attractive than prison life with regular meals. So they returned *en masse* to demand their rights, so to speak. With few warders on duty they were confined on a loose rein. Indeed, a truck was provided and, driven and controlled by prisoners, it would call at the Marketing Board to collect their daily rations. After a few days when proper checks began to be instituted, it became apparent that the truck was calling for rations several times a day, with its occu-pants claiming that they were helping in the distribution process, which they were, in a manner of speaking. While appreciating this show of public spiritedness, cynical officials could not help but suspect that they were supplying relatives, friends and possibly a growing black market with extra provisions. Obviously, this little caper had to be stopped quickly. Accordingly, other arrangements were made for the collection and supervision of their rations. In the short term, military guards were placed at the prison while priority was given to repairing and restoring its outer structure, including the walls.

As the volume of relief supplies increased, it was necessary to keep tighter control on the flow of provisions and other goods coming in and out. A group of civil servants was employed for this purpose under the supervision of the principal auditor. It was in this connection that the chief justice, Sir Clifford de Lisle Innis, came into the Marketing Board one morning and expressed the wish, as he put it, 'to make myself useful'. After discussion, he said that he was quite content to be one of the tallymen checking supplies in and out. So, equipped with clipboard, a supply of paper and a pencil he joined the team. It was, however, of short duration. After about an hour he came to me and said that, with great reluctance, he would have to find something else to do. By way of explanation he drew my attention to one of the workers unloading supplies and said, 'that man has just approached me to ask if I remembered him. When I said that I could not recall a previous meeting, he reminded me that he had once appeared before me in court and that I had given him a custodial sentence.' This added, Sir Clifford, was rather embarrassing, even though the man concerned was clearly not harbouring a grudge. The incident had also caused him to wonder whether there might be others in the building to whom he had dispensed justice over the years. I suspect, however, that he was more concerned about the possibility of meeting a former client of a violent nature who felt that he had been sentenced unfairly or too harshly and was still nursing a grievance. But speculation aside, he had made a valid point. In such a small and closely integrated community this sort of situation was a fact of life and I agreed entirely with what he had said and proposed. So exit from stage the 'CJ'.

As already indicated, for reasons of space and other practical considerations, the foregoing is a recital of just a few of my own personal experiences. But before concluding I would like to expand on this by adding extracts from an article contributed by John Hall (our hospital administrator in the early 1960s) about a decade later to a hospital magazine in Newfoundland, where he and his family had settled, in which he described his family's terrifying experience when the hurricane struck. Its special relevance is that it relates to the damaged Belize Hospital where I stopped for treatment on my journey home on the night of 31 October:

> My wife, myself and three relatively small children, the youngest a baby in arms, together with the Principal Nursing Officer and her dog, moved in with the Hospital Matron who occupied a first floor apartment in the hospital grounds less than eighty yards from the hospital. Nothing could be done but wait and see. ... At about 10 p.m. the first winds began to flow although not too severe at first. Before midnight a 30-foot eucalyptus tree which had been the pride of the hospital grounds fell, fortunately not in our direction although it completely wrecked my car parked in the hospital parking lot. Following this, things got really tough, the winds persisted and reached terrifying proportions. ... To add to our discomfort the glass French doors opening out onto the veranda shattered and the corrugated roof blew off into the night, no doubt adding to the wreckage elsewhere. This left us standing in an upstairs flat in water up to our knees with torrential rain pouring in on us with nothing left to do but wait and pray that the storm would pass completely and we would not suffer further agonies if the eye of the storm should pass over us only to return with redoubled venom, It turned out later that this was to be the unfortunate fate of Stann Creek. The hurricane raged for several hours of darkness. ... The lower segment of the hospital was completely gutted and all equipment lost. The private patients' wing was blown into the sea.

With that additional account, these few personal experiences and anecdotes can be drawn to a close. However, one piece of information that may come as a surprise to those present when the hurricane struck, and that only a handful of local people knew about at the time, is that while we were still reeling from the impact of Hurricane Hattie, its successor, Hurricane Irma, was reported to be heading in our direction. Although monitored closely, the threat was not made public lest such news caused further public demoralization or even panic. Fortunately, this 'wait and see' policy paid off when we were spared what would have been a devastating second blow. However, it would perhaps be unwise to conclude from this that hurricanes, like proverbial lightning, never strike in the same place twice.

Chapter 15
The Boy(s) Stood on the Burning Deck

I T WAS ONE THING on top of another, or, as my dear mother used to say when problems built up, 'It never rains but it pours.' No sooner had we begun to recover from the impact of the hurricane and its immediate aftermath, and were turning our attention to the formidable tasks of rehabilitation and reconstruction, than another danger threatened. This time it was a blazing cabin cruiser adrift in Belize harbour and heading towards a cluster of shipping in a manner that those directing the fire ships that helped to repel the Spanish Armada would have applauded. Disaster loomed large and the chief secretary and I witnessed the whole fascinating drama. But let me start at the beginning.

We were a few weeks into December 1961 and life in Belize was beginning to show signs of slowly returning to normal. Other people had taken up the street clearing programme that sailors from HMS *Troubridge* had started and many streets were now cleared or partially cleared of debris. Houses were slowly being patched up or rebuilt. Food, fuel and other essential supplies were coming in. Some shops were reopening. Although the swing bridge connecting the two sides of the city was still out of alignment and open only to pedestrians, a temporary pontoon bridge (heavy steel plates mounted on barges) straddled the Belize River from east to west close to the Pallotti Convent and was open to road traffic. Colder weather than usual helped to abate fears of a possible outbreak of an epidemic or fire hazards, but the task of rehabilitation and reconstruction had only just begun and it was necessary for the administration to keep on top of events. To this end the Central Disaster Committee still met each afternoon to iron out problems and plan action for the next day.

With the arrival by sea of relief food supplies, building materials, equipment, fuel, generators and other essential goods, Belize harbour was heavily congested with shipping. The damage the hurricane had caused to the docks and harbour accentuated the problem and tight controls were needed if chaos was to be avoided. However, as mentioned earlier, we had been fortunate to obtain the temporary services of Commander Peynton-Jones, naval adviser to the West Indies federal government in Trinidad, as Queen's harbour master. Not only did he, with the collector of customs, Leo Bradley, perform the herculean task of getting the docks back into service and was now organizing the smooth flow of shipping in their unloading operations, but he was also to become a principal character in the story that is about to unfold.

During one of the afternoon meetings of the Central Disaster Committee, reference was made to the density of shipping in Belize harbour and the chief secretary, Michael Porcher, decided to visit the docks to judge the situation for himself. As usual, my role was to play Pancho to his Don Quixote or, put in a more modern context, Robin to his Batman. So, at 8.00 a.m. the following morning, we set off on foot for the harbour, a distance of about half a mile.

Having left the secretariat and passed the Scots Kirk and market, we crossed the swing bridge to turn right into North Front Street. We immediately came across the fire station, a large corrugated-iron garage that housed two old Ford motorcars with solid tyres (*circa* the 1920s), which would not have looked out of place in one of the old silent black and white movies featuring the Keystone Cops. The local fire superintendent, Steve Huesner, was as usual organizing maintenance on the vehicles as we passed. We noted that the rum and liquor store next door to the Belize Estate & Trading Company, which had been looted on the morning of the hurricane, was still closed and boarded up. We also noted that the street, which only a few weeks earlier had been widely littered with debris, was now comparatively clean. On the opposite side of the road, all that remained of the Eden Cinema was a tangled skeleton of metal girders. We reached the now reopened hardware store opposite Angel Lane and passed the Marketing Board, which as usual was bustling with activity. We then proceeded on to Customs House Wharf from which we could see that there was an impressive array of ships already in the harbour and others queuing up to come in.

Leo Bradley and Commander Peynton-Jones (the latter incidentally a member of a distinguished British naval family) were both waiting to meet us and to explain the overall situation to us. Once these formalities were over we then wandered along the quayside to where a large cabin cruiser, which had just arrived, was moored. Our arrival there coincided with the owner and his wife, both Americans and known to the chief secretary, stepping ashore and we stopped to exchange courtesies. As we were chatting we were, as they say, rudely interrupted. Whoosh! There was a terrific explosion in the cabin cruiser and almost immediately it burst into flames. As we were only a few feet away at the time, the question of self-preservation became our immediate priority.

Michael, whose awareness of danger was obviously keener than mine, hurled himself to the ground, conjuring up a picture of a rugby player diving at the knees of an opponent who has just broken loose. Although one could only admire the speed, grace and vigour of the movement, its execution was not without personal pain and discomfort. The dive to the ground was to result in a badly damaged knee, which subsequently required a visit to the hospital, a tetanus inoculation and several stitches. My own reaction, as befitting a more junior officer, was slower. But, to be fair, I was taking account of another factor. With the explosion, which was later attributed to the ignition of a leaking gas-cylinder, a large object, a barrel or possibly the heavy iron cylinder itself, shot into the air like a launching space rocket. Conscious of the rule in physics that maintains that 'what goes up must come down', I had the uneasy feeling that it could descend on me. This seemed a greater danger than the threat of the vessel exploding completely, so, rather than trying to emulate the chief secretary's painful dive, I kept my eye on the rising object. While I was thus gawping, a customs officer, perceiving the threat of fire extending to nearby shipping, cut the cabin cruiser's mooring ropes with a machete. It then began to drift out into the harbour gently propelled by the current. Meanwhile, the fire brigade was hastily called.

As the blazing vessel drifted towards other shipping in the manner of the fire ship simile pictured above, Commander Peynton-Jones immediately recognized the potential danger. Leaping aboard a nearby tug, possibly with the command, 'follow that boat', he set off in pursuit. Coming alongside the burning vessel, he clambered on board and with great courage attached a towline from its stern to the tug. He remained on board as the tug began to steer slowly towards the quayside where the two fire engines were now stationed, their crews busily rolling out hoses. The fire superintendent, Steve Huesner, who had arrived with the engines and crews, was also a man of action. Unwilling to be a passive observer, he too felt that his place should be at the actual scene of the blaze. A motorboat took him there but when he arrived the gallant naval officer waved him away, presumably on the grounds that he would both be in the way and expose himself unnecessarily to danger. Undaunted, Huesner dived overboard from the motorboat, swam to the cabin cruiser and somehow hauled himself aboard. One can only imagine what words actually passed between the two men, but an exchange of words there clearly was. From the quayside we could hear only muffled voices. We could, however, see two wildly gesticulating figures looking for all the world from that distance like puppets on a string performing an angry Punch and Judy sequence.

Aside from this diversion the burning vessel, now emitting more smoke than flame, was slowly but surely approaching the quayside under the power and guidance of the tug. Anticipating their role, and more than keen to apply the *coup de grâce*, the crews of both fire engines were waiting and ready with hoses already sending powerful jets of water into the harbour. At last the tug brought the smouldering cabin cruiser into range.

The full force of water from the hoses struck the vessel, but the initial result was not quite as expected. Although it would be true to say that the hoses were on target, their powerful jets struck the midriffs of Huesner's and Peynton-Jones's bodies and drove them around the deck. How they were not blasted overboard was perhaps a miracle. There they were, slipping and sliding around while the firemen adjusted their aim. To someone of my generation it evoked memories of old-time fairgrounds where table tennis balls (more commonly known in those days as ping-pong balls) used to rise up and down at varying heights on jets of water as targets on rifle ranges. Having effectively drenched and disabled our two heroes, the next effect of the combined hose power was to fill the vessel with so much water that it was now in danger of sinking. With reluctance, the intrepid firefighters turned off their hoses, but it was clear from their expressions and comments that they felt they had scored a triumph, but whether they did more good than harm is a matter of opinion.

The still slightly smouldering vessel, which was now charred and much the worse for wear, was brought along the quayside and again secured to its mooring. The bedraggled figures of Peynton-Jones and Huesner, drenched to the skin and looking decidedly battered, then came ashore: the former was obviously aggrieved that his moment of glory had been dimmed by the latter's dramatic intervention, which he undoubtedly deemed irresponsible at least and foolhardy at best. But danger had been averted, so all's well that ends well – though it is unlikely that the vessel's owners, insurers or the chief secretary, whose wounded knee was now very painful, would agree. As the fire engines departed and Peynton-Jones and Huesner left the scene, it only remained for me to arrange transport to get Michael to the Belize Hospital and then to his home. Once that was done, I would report to the governor on the morning's developments.

Here I should mention that in the period between the visitation of Hurricane Hattie and the incident recorded above there had been a change of governors. The previous incumbent, Sir Colin Thornley, had been due to retire in November at the completion of his tour and the name of his successor had been announced, so Sir Colin and his wife left as originally planned. The farewell ceremony, which took place at the Fort George wharf, followed the usual pattern of a guard of honour, in this case provided by the Royal Hampshire Regiment, the British Honduras Volunteer Guard and the police force, which the governor inspected. Having then said his farewells to local politicians, dignitaries and senior civil servants, he and Lady Thornley boarded a naval launch to take them to the HMS *Troubridge*, bound for Kingston, Jamaica. From there they would fly home to Britain. As they boarded the naval launch the police band, true to tradition, struck up a version of 'Auld Lang Syne' with instruments that had, unfortunately, suffered badly from having been submerged in sea water during the hurricane. Although the rendering was somewhat dodgy, tinny and discordant, the tune was none the less recognizable and it introduced a note of poignancy into the proceedings. It was said afterwards that this moment brought tears to the eyes of Sir Colin and his wife. But whether the cause was sadness at leaving, the prospect of retirement on a modest pension or a pained reaction to the police band's delivery was not to my knowledge ever explored.

Sir Colin's successor, Sir Peter Stallard, flew in on an RAF Shackleton aircraft about a fortnight later. He was wearing full governor's white uniform complete with cocked hat and plumes, and the same team that was present at Sir Colin Thornley's departure greeted him. But any thoughts that Sir Peter was a man for pomp and ceremony were soon dispelled. Just as Sir Colin represented an older, more paternal and traditional colonial approach, so Sir Peter introduced a whiff of informality, coupled with a determination to prepare the people of the colony to take over the reins of their own destiny. In short, he was one of a new breed of colonial administrators who not only advocated early independence but who also helped prepare and sometimes nudge colonial people towards that end. But I digress: all I really wanted to say was that it was to Sir Peter Stallard that I now reported.

As I gave my verbal report, he was highly amused. 'What larks!' he commented. Being a practical man, however, he added that as the chief secretary was *hors de combat* he expected me to chair the afternoon's meeting of the Central Disaster Committee and combine with it the role of secretary. 'Good experience for you,' he further added before disappearing for his lunch. 'Thank you very much,' thought I by way of a silent rejoinder, owing more to sarcasm than servility. This brings the story as such to an end.

There is, however, a footnote. Both Commander Peynton-Jones and Steve Huesner received recognition in the 1962 honours list. Presumably, both awards were an acknowledgement of their post-hurricane activities. But I would like to think that part of that recognition extended to their initiative and bravery in dealing with the blazing vessel aimlessly adrift in Belize harbour and the potential danger surrounding it.

Years later, on the occasions when Michael and I met and the subject of Hurricane Hattie and its aftermath cropped up (as it invariably did), he would refer to that incident with the words, 'What a morning that was!' We would then chuckle over the events, but for me that morning was to add yet another drama to a series of dramas that followed the hurricane, as later chapters reveal. 'It never rains but it pours' thus seemed to me a more pertinent observation. I am sure that both Commander Peynton-Jones and Steve Huesner – the boys (well all right then, men) who stood on the burning deck of the cabin cruiser and were drenched to the skin for their pains would have endorsed that sentiment. What larks, indeed!

Chapter 16
Incursion

C AN YOU RECALL what you were doing early in 1962 when news of the Guatemalan incursion filtered through? I am glad you asked that question, for it enables me to resurrect and give an account of a now long forgotten incident that initially gave rise to alarm and subsequently developed comical overtones before descending into farce. Its significance can only be understood by reference to Guatemala's territorial claim and its military implications. So what was the incursion about and why was it taken seriously? Let me set the scene and then provide the account which, incidentally, answers the question posed above.

Without digging too deeply again into the history of the region, suffice it to say (as already mentioned in earlier chapters) that the Guatemalan claim had its genesis in the early nineteenth century following the collapse of the Spanish Empire throughout Central America and the subsequent emergence of new republics. Two of them, Guatemala and Mexico, then laid claim to the Belize settlement. This was predicated on their perceived assumption that, as the inheritors of Spanish sovereignty in the region, the settlement now came under their authority. Of the two, the Mexican claim possibly had greater legitimacy on the grounds that, hitherto, the Belize settlement had always fallen under the direction of the captain general of Yucatán in southern Mexico. However, although it may be argued that Mexico was the only 'successor' state with a legitimate interest in its southern neighbour, it became clear early on that it was prepared to accept the status quo for a number of reasons and, in the event, did not press its claim strongly. So it is only the Guatemalan claim on which we need dwell.

In the mid-nineteenth century, when the United States was showing active interest in the region following the Monroe Doctrine warning to the European powers that Central America was now a 'no go' area for them, Britain entered into treaties with the republics of Honduras, Nicaragua and Guatemala. With respect to the latter, early negotiations indicated that Guatemala was prepared to drop its claim to the Belize settlement in exchange for unspecified compensation, an opening that both British and Guatemalan envoys pursued. After further diplomatic activity a final draft treaty was produced that contained two key articles. In Article 1 the Guatemalan government recognized British sovereignty over the Belize settlement within its existing frontiers. The other article of importance was Article 7 in which both governments agreed:

> to use their best efforts by taking adequate means for establishing the easiest communications (either by means of a cart road, or employing the rivers, or both united, according to the opinion of the surveying engineers) between the fittest place on the Atlantic coast near the settlement of Belize and the capital of Guatemala.

Britain and Guatemala signed the resultant treaty on 30 April 1859. As far as Britain was concerned this met United States objections to a European presence in Central America based on the Monroe Doctrine and cleared up once and for all doubts over the sovereignty of British Honduras and the extent of its boundaries. The Guatemalans were also content. Abandonment of their claim, however tenuous, wounded national pride and the implementation of Article 7 was the inducement insofar as it represented a form of compensation.

The significance of their interest in such a road or river link is explained by reference to an atlas. All of Guatemala's west coast borders the Pacific Ocean. Its only access on the Atlantic side, however, is a narrow 14-mile stretch at Livingstone between Honduras to the south and British Honduras to the north at the Sarstoon River. Access to the sea around the capital, Belize, would open the way for the Guatemalans to exploit the forestry area of the Peten (just beyond the settlement's western border at Benque Viejo) as well as giving them a toehold in the settlement that might possibly be exploited later for political ends. But instead of settling the matter the treaty was to set off an unresolved series of further negotiations reflecting Byzantine characteristics. A simple guide to these is outlined as follows.

Given that it required action to be taken conjointly, it was not surprising that difficulties soon arose over the two countries' interpretations of their responsibilities under Article 7. The Guatemalans argued that it was compensation for Article 1 and that Britain should take the initiative in implementing it. Britain, however, took the view that there was no connection and that if any road was to be built it would have to be done conjointly, commensurate with any conceivable commercial benefits that might derive from it.

The initiative Britain actually took was to understand the words 'taking adequate means' (contained in Article 7) to mean making a survey, which was undertaken in 1860. The cost of the proposed road following this was around £150,000 and, in a convention in 1863, Britain agreed to contribute £50,000 of this to be paid in instalments of £10,000 depending on the progress of the road that Guatemala was to construct. The convention was due to be ratified within six months, but the time lapsed and Guatemala (then facing internal upheaval) asked for a delay, which Britain refused to grant. The latter thereafter held the view that because the financial details had not been agreed within the time specified, the whole undertaking to build the road had collapsed.

The issue then remained dormant until 1933 when Guatemala unsuccessfully raised the question of Article 7 once again. Four years later it requested United States arbitration. Britain refused but expressed willingness to allow the problem to be put before the International Court of Justice at The Hague. Guatemala was agreeable to this provided the case was based on equity and not on a legal interpretation. Britain, however, insisted on the latter. From then on, the matter was to surface from time to time with varying degrees of intensity until the colony achieved independence. Although there was no evidence that the Guatemalans would ever use armed force to achieve their territorial objective, it was a possibility that could never be entirely ruled out. Yet, even in Britain's darkest days during the Second World War, the Guatemalans made no attempt to exploit the situation militarily. But there was a late scare.

In his diary for 3 May 1945 the British Chief of the Imperial General Staff, Sir Alan Brooke (later Field Marshal Viscount Alanbrooke) recorded:

> In the middle of the crumbling of Germany suddenly wild rumours appear that Guatemala is going to attack our colony of Honduras! Much discussion at COS meeting and much time wasted: only force available is a Canadian battalion in Jamaica. Colonial Office must be approached and Foreign Office informed owing to repercussions in America etc. In the end it turns out to be a bad forest fire in Guatemala which had necessitated employing most of the Army to put it out. This had put Honduras nerves on edge. They saw ghosts everywhere and wasted our time unnecessarily.[1]

Early in 1948 rumours of a Guatemalan invasion were again so rife in British Honduras that the governor requested military help from Britain. As a result two warships were dispatched: the cruisers HMS *Devonshire* and HMS *Sheffield* arrived off Belize and marines were landed. Shortly afterwards a detachment of the Gloucestershire Regiment arrived and took up positions on the border. This led the Guatemalans to protest to the Americans, who expressed confidence that the two governments would find a way out of the situation. Thereafter, the British military presence was strengthened and any perceived Guatemalan threat taken more seriously.

A new factor now entered the political equation, namely the probability that before long the colony would seek independence from Britain. The prospect in such an event of sovereignty passing to a third party (the people of British Honduras) touched Guatemalan sensibilities and, at each stage of constitutional advance, relations with Britain became increasingly strained with resulting uneasiness in the colony. In 1960 a constitutional conference was held in London at which a decision was made to introduce greater local autonomy through the creation of a ministerial system and, early the following year, the Guatemalans broke off diplomatic relations with Britain. There was obviously a considerable amount of tension in the air during the ensuing months.

8. First step towards independence. British Honduras delegates with
Secretary of State Ian Macleod, at constitutional conference in London, 1960.

Given the Guatemalan claim to British Honduras, or *Belice* as they
called it, reflected in the slogan *Belice es Nuestros* (Belize is ours),
and the fact that its government occasionally pressed that claim with
the hint or perceived threat of force, the understandable British
response was to reinforce the local military garrison more strongly,
mainly as a deterrent but capable of defending it. It was against this
background that the reported incursion was taken seriously. Indeed,
it was to put the military and the colony's civil authorities onto a
state of high alert. So when did I first become aware of what was
happening? Here I attempt to answer the question posed in the
opening sentence of this chapter.

Late in the afternoon of Sunday 21 January 1962 I was sitting at
home reading a recent copy of *The Times* the governor had passed on
to me when the telephone rang. The call was from the chief secretary
who said he could not explain why over an open line but that I
should come to Government House right away. When I arrived I
found the governor, Sir Peter Stallard already occupying the room in
which executive council meetings were held. With him were the first
minister, Mr George Price; the chief secretary, Michael Porcher; the

garrison commander and senior army officers; the acting commissioner of police, Ronnie Watson; the military intelligence liaison officer, Major Glynne Lewis; Colonel Fairweather of the British Honduras Volunteer Guard and Leo Bradley, the controller of customs, who was responsible among other things for government launches. The chief secretary then briefed me on the situation.

He explained that a short time earlier, the acting commissioner of police had informed the governor of a wireless message received from the police detachment in Punta Gorda, headquarters of the remote Toledo District. It reported the arrival at 10 a.m. in Pueblo Viejo (a village five miles from the border) of an armed party of about twenty Guatemalan soldiers who had lowered and burnt the Union Jack flying on the village flagpole and hoisted a Guatemalan flag in its place. Some shots were alleged to have been fired but no casualties were reported; the party then proceeded on foot to the village of San Antonio, 12 miles away, and arrived at 4 p.m. On receipt of this information the two-man police detachment at San Antonio was instructed not to engage in armed resistance. No further information was available and there was no prospect of obtaining any before dawn the following day, Monday, because with the antiquated wireless equipment it was impossible to maintain radio communication during the hours of darkness. With no road link with the Toledo District the only physical contact was by sea.

It was against this background that the assembled group discussed the situation. It was decided that one platoon of the Royal Hampshire Regiment should proceed to Punta Gorda forthwith in the government launch *Patricia* to arrive there the following morning. In addition, at dawn, a light aircraft with Major Glynne Lewis aboard would fly to Punta Gorda on reconnaissance and land on the small airstrip there if the Union Jack was still flying from above the police station. The officer commanding the Caribbean area was then informed of the emergency and asked to make reinforcements ready. A special guard was placed on the Guatemalan consulate for its protection and other local military precautions were taken. And, of course, the various authorities in London were alerted. Nothing further could be done that night and we were to meet again the following morning.

Early on Monday morning, 22 January, we received a disquieting report from Punta Gorda to the effect that ten Guatemalans had taken a truck from San Antonio and driven to within three miles of Punta Gorda where they had entered the bush; the police detachment there proposed to offer no resistance even though it numbered fourteen and had nine serviceable rifles at its disposal. It was also reported that a further party of 200 Guatemalans had arrived at Pueblo Viejo during the night.

In the light of this report, the governor summoned his advisers for an 8 a.m. meeting at Government House. A message was immediately sent to Punta Gorda ordering the police to hold the town at all costs and to expect a platoon of British soldiers to arrive at about 11 a.m. Other military deployments were made locally. At that meeting, the elderly minister of culture and education, Mr J. W. Macmillan (Mac), who had accompanied the first minister, introduced an echo of 'Dad's Army' into the proceedings by recalling his service with the local volunteer guard in the Second World War and displaying a hitherto unrevealed streak of belligerence by wanting 'to get at 'em' himself, maintaining that he still knew how to handle a Bren gun. As he was clearly well over military age and normally of a mild and seemingly nervous disposition, his uncharacteristic outburst provided some light relief. Henceforth the governor, who had a tendency to give people nicknames, always referred to him in private conversation with the chief secretary and me as 'the Bren gunner'. But I digress.

By 10 a.m. the aerial reconnaissance had been completed. The aircraft had landed at Punta Gorda from where Major Glynne Lewis had reported that the Guatemalans in the area were not in uniform and that no large body of persons (the 200 previously reported) had been seen either at Pueblo Viejo or on the road to the east. Subsequently, the bulk of the Royal Hampshire Regiment platoon, which had disembarked at Punta Gorda at 11.25 a.m., left at once for Pueblo Viejo, but leaving behind a small section to help Major Glynne Lewis and a body of armed police search the bush around Punta Gorda.

Meanwhile, we tried to make sense of the events. From the facts then available it appeared that there might be three possible explanations for the incursion. First, the Guatemalan authorities had originally organized the foray but then had a change of heart that had resulted in a botched operation. Second, some maverick had acted on his own in an attempt to curry favour with the president by supporting the republic's territorial claim. Third, a political opponent had attempted to embarrass the president by mounting a 'heroic' gesture calculated to demonstrate that actions speak louder than words. At that stage, however, we were of course unaware of all the facts and consequently still groping in the dark for an explanation.

In view of the information obtained from the aerial reconnaissance in the Toledo District and the absence of any military activity on the western border in the El Cayo District, reinforcements from Jamaica were not called for although the officer commanding the Caribbean area was asked to continue to keep them on stand-by.

Given the parochial nature of local society, by this time such information as was available was already in the public domain, but most citizens in Belize reacted only with quiet interest. Of course, in this, they were comforted in the knowledge that about a hundred miles separated them from any perceived danger and that no road existed over part of that distance. There was no attempt to demonstrate outside the Guatemalan consulate, from which staff continued to enter and leave normally. As often happens on such occasions, some people allowed their imagination to run riot and, at 4.15 a.m. on Monday morning, two police officers on street patrol claimed to have seen a force of twenty or more aircraft flying over the city in a southerly direction. The acting commissioner of police doubtless warned them afterwards to keep off the rum in future while on duty.

The following morning the leader of the incursion's identity became known. He was Francisco Sagastume, a political opponent of the Guatemalan president and an unsuccessful candidate in the recently held election for a representative for the administrative district of the Peten. We also learnt that he was headstrong, rabidly anti-colonialist, but to his credit (and here I venture a *non sequitur*) a worthy captain instructor of the Guatemalan fire brigade. From this it seemed fair to assume that the third of the possible explanations mentioned above was the most likely: that is to say the incursion was the work of a political opponent trying to embarrass the president by engaging in a 'heroic' (if unfruitful) gesture by at least being seen to take positive action over the territorial issue.

Recognizing by now that a headstrong maverick minor political opportunist and not the Guatemalan authorities had instigated the incident, the governor issued a press release to that effect, primarily to allay any potential or lingering local fears of serious fighting involving their lives and property. This stirred up the local political cauldron. *The Belize Billboard*, the mouthpiece of the opposition National Independence Party (NIP), took him to task for being so naive as to absolve the Guatemalan government of complicity. At the same time, this organ of the local press also used the incident to print highly emotional and wildly tendentious allegations about the assumed intention of the ruling People's United Party (PUP) to deliver the country into the hands of the Guatemalans. This was based on its editor's interpretation of George Price's claim that the country's economic and political destiny lay with Central America. Of course, as befits the opposition party press in most democratic countries, all this was good, political, over the top, knockabout stuff without too much regard for the facts. But irrational or otherwise, constantly on the minds of many citizens, particularly the Creoles, was a fear of Guatemala as a predatory neighbour. This was illustrated when followers of the NIP marched under a large banner, on the 10 September parade that year, proclaiming paradoxically 'NATIONAL INDEPENDENCE PARTY – WE NO WANT INDEPENDENCE!' But looking beyond the paradox, the real message being imparted was that they would be happy to achieve independence in the context of the Commonwealth with its democratic traditions and parliamentary systems. They did not want an independence that would see the country sucked into the Central American orbit and ultimately, so they claimed, into the arms of Guatemala.

Meanwhile, back in the Toledo District that morning, the net was closing around the infiltrators. Revolver in hand, Major Glynne Lewis, in company with the stalwart squaddies from Hampshire and the local constabulary, were hot on their trail in the area around Punta

Gorda. One surrendered and not long afterwards Sagastume and three of his followers were captured. The others were caught two days later.

When Sagastume and another prisoner were brought to Belize that afternoon for questioning, the full extent of the limited incursion became apparent and with it the end of the emergency. Locally, the military were 'stood down' and the Commander, Caribbean Area, was informed that reinforcements would not be required.

From the examination of the prisoners it was, at last, possible to piece together all the events of the past few days. Dissatisfied with what he regarded as the president's weak attitude towards Britain *vis-à-vis* British Honduras, Sagastume decided to take matters into his own hands. Together with ten compatriots and a British Honduran friend he left Peten for San Luis on Thursday 18 January. There, seven more were to join the party. At this point, he told them that his aim was to search for mahogany as he proposed to go into the timber business. The following day, Friday, the party travelled on foot to Pulsilha where they slept. On the Saturday, Sagastume engaged two Indian guides to show the way to Pueblo Viejo. They spent that night in the bush. Throughout their march from San Luis he commented on the size of various mahogany trees and, at times, stopped to place sticks in the ground marking, he said, the sites of future roads for extracting logs. When about to cross the border he told his companions that the intention was to mark out a trail to Pueblo Viejo to facilitate the transport of logs, which would be finally exported via Punta Gorda. He also handed out some firearms, ostensibly for hunting food *en route*.

However, on arrival at Pueblo Viejo he and his immediate cronies not only lowered and burnt the Union Jack and ran up the flag of the Organization of Central American States (ODECA) but also tore down pictures of Her Majesty the Queen and His Royal Highness the Duke of Edinburgh and burnt them together with the lowered flag. He did not leave the ODECA flag there because, he said, he needed it later. With these gestures he then told his bewildered companions that they were now on a mission to liberate *Belice* and said to the villagers that he and his group were Guatemalan soldiers – hence the original report to reach Belize City. At this unexpected and unwelcome news, nine of the party and the two guides took fright and disappeared into the bush at great speed in the direction from which they had come. They no longer feature in the narrative.

Despite this setback, Sagastume managed to rally the remainder and they then trudged 12 miles though the rain to San Antonio where he addressed a hostile crowd of villagers in both English and Spanish on the purpose of his mission. The policeman on duty, who by then had received the instruction not to resist, asked them to leave and when they refused he took it upon himself to arrange for a truck to take the party on to their declared destination, Punta Gorda. Three miles short of the town they stopped the vehicle and took to the bush. I have already described what happened next other than to say that the police detachment at Punta Gorda, with adequate .303 rifles and ammunition at its disposal, could easily have disarmed the infiltrators (whose total armament consisted of two .22 rifles, one .38 calibre pistol, one shotgun and one .44 calibre pistol without ammunition) had they the determination to do so. As it was, they obviously felt in this case that discretion was more appealing than valour and they conveniently assumed that the 'no resistance' instruction to their colleagues at San Antonio also applied to them.

This then was the extent of a reported incursion that had caused the local civil administration and the supporting military apparatus to be placed on a state of high alert. In short, it was little more than a half-baked scheme devised by an undoubtedly unstable minor Guatemalan politician with a political axe to grind that would have caused the inmates of a mental asylum to shake their heads in disbelief. On becoming acquainted with the facts one did not know whether to weep with relief at what was virtually a non-event or laugh at the bizarre antics of the participants. But matters of this sort can never be taken lightly for it was not inconceivable that the incursion could have been the real thing. However, as we learnt at school (or was it Sunday school?) 'things are sent to try us' and, in being tested, the local civil and military reaction was not found wanting.

That said, this allusion prefaces a reference to a trial of a different sort, in the courts. Tracking down the infiltrators and capturing them was one thing: deciding what to do with them once they had been taken prisoner was another. At first they were held on charges of illegal entry. This made it easy for the followers to be dealt with and deported without much fuss. But, as the ring-leader, Sagastume presented a special case. Local opinion was vociferous in demanding that he be put on trial not only for his actions but also *pour décourager les autres* (or whatever the local translation into Creole, Spanish or Maya might be) should any of his compatriots be tempted to chance their arm in a more determined manner at some future date. In the event, he was arraigned before the chief justice in the Supreme Court on 26 February on three counts – attempting to procure an alternative government, sedition and illegal entry involving armed force. The trial took place before a jury in open court and he was naturally allowed legal representation. The upshot was that he was found guilty on all three counts and sentenced to ten, ten and two years respectively, all sentences to run concurrently.

With the law now having taken its course and justice seen to be done, another form of symbolism was required, namely to replace the Union Jack and royal portraits at the village of Pueblo Viejo. To this end the chief secretary Michael Porcher and Major Glynne Lewis travelled to San Antonio where arrangements had been made to take them onward to the village on horseback. There, they ceremoniously hoisted the flag and were photographed doing so. If my memory serves me correctly, it appeared in one of the British tabloids with an appropriate caption as well as in the local press. Although a good horseman, Michael had been away from the saddle for a long while and for some time afterwards he complained of saddle soreness. Not so the gallant major, who in previous incarnations had served in the Royal Canadian Mounted Police and subsequently with a regiment of Hussars in the Indian Army. On horseback and in full regimental dress uniform he was in his element.

The scene now returns to Belize where the governor was considering the full implications of Sagastume's incarceration. The uncomfortable fact was that, though a low profile character in his own country, while in our prison his political supporters were able to embarrass the Guatemalan president and government by pressing for his immediate release – a situation that could only strain relations between Britain and Guatemala and keep the sovereignty issue in the spotlight. On the other hand, if they pardoned Sagastume too quickly, the opposition political party in British Honduras would no doubt see it as evidence of the ruling party's determination to placate a predatory neighbour whom they were willing to embrace at the expense of the colony, aided and abetted by the representatives of Britain. The preliminary conclusion the governor and his advisers drew was that Sagastume should not serve his full sentence and that, if favourable circumstances presented themselves, he might be pardoned administratively at some appropriately early moment.

So Sagastume spent that summer in Belize prison, not the most salubrious of establishments but no doubt a more humane environment, I would guess, than its equivalent across the border. There was, however, yet another twist to this tale.

One morning, while at Government House a few months later, His Excellency told me that he had just heard that Sagastume had physically attacked the chief prison officer, Campbell, and that he had asked the latter to call and report details of the incident to him personally. He arrived shortly afterwards, hatless and with his khaki drill uniform sweat stained as usual. Around his forehead was a clean white bandage. The sight he presented was of a walking wounded of First World War vintage leaving a casualty clearing station in the field with a minor head injury. After commiserating with him the governor enquired: 'How did it happen, Campbell?' 'Sagastume, Sir,' he replied, adding by way of explanation, 'he hit me over the head with a piss pot.' Just like that, right out loud, bloody rude! Now, even in those enlightened late postwar days, governors tended to be treated as demigods and no ambitious expatriate with sights set on advancement in the service would dare to speak in front of 'His Excellency' in such a forthright manner. But Campbell, an honest outspoken local officer, had no such inhibitions. To him a spade was a spade and a piss pot was exactly that and not a chamber pot as the delicate might refer to it. All this tickled my sense of humour and I could only suppress a fit of the giggles by pinching the top of my thigh sufficiently hard to inflict pain. For his part, the governor took it in his stride and simply said 'poor Campbell' as he continued his quizzing. As for the reason for the attack, which was less damaging than the bandage suggested, if I ever knew it has long since been forgotten.

At the beginning of September, Sagastume submitted a petition to the governor expressing regret at his escapade and the trouble it had caused and appealing for clemency. It was no longer a live issue in local political circles and the governor assumed, quite rightly as it turned out, that he could exercise his powers of clemency, as the constitution provided, without creating local protest meetings. This he did on 17 September 1962. Sagastume returned to Guatemala the same day and, from then until now the incident has slumbered in the ever accommodating and embracing bed of history. Following its exposure, it can now be returned to its somnolent state with little prospect of being awakened again in a hurry. But, if nothing else, I can recall what I was doing around tea time on Sunday 21 January 1962, when this little storm in a teacup arose with seemingly hurricane implications, or worse.

And so ends a tale that began in a climate of high drama and petered out in an atmosphere of low farce. But it was an example, albeit an exceptional one, of the sort of situations that continually intruded on the lives of colonial administrators in small colonies, such as British Honduras, which served to keep them on their toes in a manner reminiscent of slip fielders to fast bowlers in Test matches fully expecting every snick off the bat to come to them at any time and at any height. But had the story been fictional and hatched in the fertile imagination of a latter-day William Shakespeare, then I am sure that he would have had no hesitation in recalling a familiar but apt title, *Much Ado About Nothing*.

Chapter 17
The Mark of Cain

W HEN PLANS WERE drawn up for a proposed visit by HRH the Duke of Edinburgh to certain South American and Caribbean countries in the spring of 1962, British Honduras was not included in the original itinerary. There was nothing unusual or significant about that. At that stage of colonial history, royal visits to dependent territories (except to attend independence celebrations) were generally infrequent and normally connected with some special event or occasion. As HRH the Princess Margaret had visited in May 1958 (incidentally, this was the first occasion in its history that a member of the royal family had ever visited the territory) it was obviously felt that another royal visit so soon after that would, to draw on a cliché of the day, 'be over-egging the pudding'. But Hurricane Hattie, which had tried to wipe parts of the country off the map, had the contrary effect of putting it on the map, so to speak, in the minds of senior officials in the Colonial Office. Accordingly, Buckingham Palace was approached to ascertain whether HRH was able and willing to extend his tour for a brief visit to British Honduras to give recognition to the reconstruction efforts then underway and (wait for it!) provide a bit of a fillip to local morale. On the understanding that it would be brief and completed within one day, 'the Palace' indicated that HRH would be pleased to cooperate.

The proposal was then put to the governor, Sir Peter Stallard, who was only too happy to accept. Not only would such a visit demonstrate to the local populace that their ordeal was recognized in the highest echelons of British society but it would also take the form of a thank you to those officials, civilians and soldiers who had been, and were still, working hard to get life back to normal following the hurricane. And, of course, there was always the possibility accompanying such a high profile visit of extracting from aid funds a small additional tranche for some much needed infrastructural improvement (the resurfacing of a road for example) on the royal route into Belize. In the less affluent colonial hierarchies, such practical considerations were never far from the mind.

Once the visit had been confirmed and the date (4 April) notified, the governor asked the chief secretary, the garrison commander and me to attend a meeting with him to discuss a local programme. Obviously, he said, there would have to be an opening and closing ceremony at the airport to mark HRH's arrival and departure and, of course, time allowed for travel from the airport and back for departure. Also, time must be found to visit the garrison's headquarters. In addition, the governor proposed to give a reception for a limited number of guests and a luncheon party for members of the Executive Council. It was also considered politically expedient for Prince Philip to see some of the hurricane damage and visit the temporary town of Hattieville (14 miles west of Belize on the Western Highway), which had been constructed since 6 November to house about 3000 people whom the hurricane had made homeless. The problem was that HRH's plane was scheduled to arrive at 9.45 a.m. and to leave at 2.50 p.m., thus allowing only a few short minutes over five hours to complete such an ambitious programme. The analogy of getting a quart into a pint bottle sprang to mind.

The garrison commander undertook to make all the necessary arrangements involving the military and, as the junior member of the civil authority's triumvirate present, I was invited to plan in detail the main programme keeping the chief secretary and the governor informed of developments. This, as I saw it, bearing in mind the obvious difficulties over timing, was an invitation I would have willingly declined had such an option presented itself. I only hope that my lack of enthusiasm in accepting (as if I had had a choice!) did not appear too obvious.

Fortunately, there were several weeks in hand before the visit was due to take place, so we had time to work on the detail, which involved eliciting the cooperation of various ministries and a number of departments, which of course they freely gave. During that time we received details about the composition of the party accom-

panying HRH, as well as the usual personal and logistical information about such things as what food and drink to avoid and what
type and quantity of fuel was required should the royal aircraft need to
refuel at the airport. Also to arrive were the royal standards to be flown
on the vehicles in which HRH would be travelling when in the colony.

So, with the help of the chief secretary, a programme was worked
out and presented to the governor and other members of the
Executive Council for approval. My concern was that since a non-
stop sequence of events had been planned that involved each event
merging seamlessly into the next, any hitch would throw the whole
programme into disarray. And from my experience locally there was
always such a hitch waiting in the wings and ready to go on stage.
But we were now committed and in the circumstances the only thing
to do was to hope and pray – and to pray hard.

The 4 April dawned bright and clear. When I arrived at the airport
at around 8.30 a.m. local dignitaries were already assembling in the
lounge. Outside, on the apron, the guard of honour was forming up.
A red carpet was being rolled out from the terminal building towards
the apron and members of the public were beginning to crowd the
top of the whole building complex. Just before 9.30 a.m. the chief
secretary arrived in full uniform (one of the very few occasions I ever
saw him wear it) closely followed by the governor in full
gubernatorial gear, in white, complete with plumed hat. Within
minutes, air traffic control informed us that the royal aircraft was
approaching and, as we searched the sky, a small black dot was
discernable that quickly developed into the profile of the expected
aircraft. It came to rest exactly on time, at 9.45 a.m. precisely, with
Prince Philip at the controls.

After greeting His Royal Highness, Sir Peter presented the garrison
commander, Colonel G. T. Anderson, OBE, MC, who conducted
HRH to the dais for a royal salute followed by an inspection of the
guard of honour provided by Y Company, the first battalion of the
Royal Hampshire Regiment, together with the British Honduras
Volunteer Guard band.

With the welcoming ceremony completed, HRH, accompanied by
his personal staff and the governor, set off along the red carpet
towards the airport building, acknowledging the cheers of the

9. Visit of HRH the Duke of Edinburgh: arrival ceremony.

crowds on the roof as he did so. Inside the building the governor presented him to the chief secretary, the chief justice, all members of the legislative assembly (apart from the first minister who was in London and the Speaker who was also absent from the territory) and other important dignitaries. Before leaving the airport His Royal Highness, as previously arranged, broadcast to the people he would be unable to meet personally in his programme and included a message of good wishes to British Honduras from Her Majesty the Queen.

The opening phase of the visit thus completed, Prince Philip and the governor then drove off in the Government House car to the outskirts of Belize where the former then changed to a gleaming newly painted open Land Rover flying the royal standard, in which he stood while being driven through some of the hurricane-damaged areas of the city to the open space adjoining the northeast foreshore (opposite the MCC sports stadium) where about 10,000 school-children aged between 3 and 18 (including our daughters) were formed up in four columns making two avenues. As the Land Rover drove slowly along these avenues the children, caught up in an atmosphere of excitement at what for them was a most unusual and emotional event, gave him a truly royal welcome with the rousing cheers their teachers had orchestrated. The next part of the journey took him along a street riddled with potholes a few days earlier but now filled and the whole street resurfaced. No wonder the residents in the vicinity were there to give the royal visitor a special cheer. That it happened to be in the first minister's constituency was, I believe, coincidental. The drive in the open Land Rover took half an hour and finished at Government House. The governor, incidentally, did not accompany HRH on this part of the programme and therefore had the opportunity to change out of uniform into a light suit for the next stage of the visit.

Ten minutes later, at 11 a.m., His Royal Highness and the governor left for Hattieville. Many visitors from other towns had joined the 3000 inhabitants there and the large crowd was excited and enthusiastic. On arrival HRH was greeted with a royal salute performed by a group of volunteer musicians from the nearby Listowel Boy's Training School (an approved school the Salvation Army ran to provide training for delinquent boys who had failed to respond to probation or other methods of social readjustment) in the absence of the volunteer guard and police bands whose members were engaged on other duties at the time. Their commendable rendering was spirited and more or less recognizable.

The intention at this stage was to present a number of senior departmental officers who would normally have attended the Government House reception, the next item on the programme, but because of restrictions on numbers, had to give way to political representatives and a few of the local clergy. However, as the representatives of the latter had literally heeded the biblical exhortation to 'Be fruitful and multiply', the original limited list had become swollen with a vast array of 'dog collars' of every conceivable denomination. Consequently, though giving much satisfaction to the clergy and their respective congregations, these unforeseen additional presentations meant that it was impossible in the time remaining to secure proper recognition for those departmental officers who had contributed beyond the call of duty after the hurricane. None the less, HRH bore nobly with this profusion of presentations.

As Prince Philip was about to cross the road to commence his tour of the temporary town, the Listowel Boy's Training School band spotted him and, misinterpreting their brief, embarked on yet another royal salute, which delayed us still further. A police officer had to be deputed to tell them that their task had already been completed, thank you very much, and that no further contribution from them was necessary. Fortunately, they complied or we might have been there yet.

After inspecting the hospital, water supply, children's playroom and a so-called typical living quarter (which as the governor observed to the chief secretary later that day was in fact atypical because it was fly-screened and thoroughly clean and tidy) and the two schools, Prince Philip chatted to young members of Hattieville's various sporting teams. The inspection and visit over, the visitors left at 12.15 p.m. for a reception at Government House to which all legislators, career consuls, church leaders and other representatives had been invited – 70 people in all received this honour.

Florence and I were among this group and, as I was being presented, the governor introduced me to HRH as the one who had arranged his programme. While this was probably intended as a bouquet, it did occur to me at the time that should there have been royal displeasure at the crowded non-stop nature of the programme, or any real or perceived cockups, the perpetrator had been identified. In short, 'I had been fingered!' As it was, Prince Philip murmured, 'very good'. For the record I should mention that my cynicism was unworthy, for, in his dispatch to the Colonial Office covering the visit a few days later, Sir Peter was good enough to record that an important factor in securing the success of the visit was the result of my 'careful planning and hard work'. I mention this not to say, 'what a good boy am I', but to indicate my heartfelt relief that there had been no actual disaster or recriminations as I had feared there might have been. Now it was time for the ensuing lunch.

As I was not present at the lunch itself (as explained below I was invited to be present at the coffee stage) I cannot disclose the topics of conversation, what was on the menu and what wines were served.

10. HRH in relaxed mood in Hattieville.

What I can do is provide some further background that might be seen as a story within a story.

Government House had been severely damaged in the hurricane. Its wooden structure had been badly affected and the floor of the main reception room now sloped down alarmingly at one end. Other rooms were uninhabitable. A tide mark about 15 feet high on the walls was evident in all downstairs rooms where the sea had swept in and then receded. This was the situation when Sir Peter Stallard arrived to take up duty, but if he was dismayed by this he did not show it. He took it in his stride. Indeed, he made it clear from the word go that all other reconstruction work should be given priority over repairs to Government House. In the ensuing reorganization of the building the old dining room was turned into the main office. Consequently, the entrance hall offered the only large space where the dining table could be set up and it was here that the luncheon was held. But space was still tight and numbers had to be restricted. In these circumstances the governor limited invitations to members of the Executive Council and their wives, and the chief justice.

Before sending out these invitations he called me in to say that, as I was clerk to the council, he would normally have included me and

Florence in the luncheon party, but since out of necessity numbers had to be restricted he was sure that I would understand if we were not included. He went on to say, however, that he would like me to join the group after the main courses when coffee was being served and that I was to be included in the proposed photograph of HRH and members of the Executive Council. He added 'although it may be of small consolation to you "the dog" is not being invited to this particular function'. This was a sobriquet he had attached to our permanent secretary of finance following a recent incident that had incurred his displeasure.

Permanent Secretary Quantrill was a competent officer, a churchgoer and generally pleasant company. However, he exuded social pretentiousness and was acutely aware of his status, which, before the redesignation of his post from that of financial secretary the previous year, had given him the right to attend Executive Council as an *ex officio* member. Under the new constitutional arrangements he continued to hold that right but not as a member. None the less, he tended to act as though he was. He had previously served in Malaya where the distinction between rulers and natives was marked, as indeed it was between the senior expatriate and local junior strands of the civil service there. He, therefore, found it difficult to come to terms with the more relaxed approach to work and less concern with status that existed in British Honduras. He also had difficulty accepting the policy of giving more and more responsibility in government to local politicians and local staff. In particular, he found it difficult to get on with the first minister (who was also minister of finance) whom, I believe, he thought to be too 'interfering' in matters of finance and too progressive in the pursuit of easing out expatriate officers in an attempt to localize the civil service. Likewise, he found the new governor, Sir Peter Stallard, less easy to get on with than his predecessor with whom he and his wife had enjoyed inclusion in his bridge circle. Moreover, the informality of the former contrasted sharply with the more traditional older type of governor the latter had represented and with whom he, the permanent secretary of finance, felt more at home. His wife, though a gentle soul, presented a mirror reflection in the striking of social attitudes. At functions she was always easily identifiable by the fluttering of a Chinese fan in front of her face, which could have been attributable either to her reaction to the heat or to affectation.

As far as I was aware they had no children. They did, however, have a dog, Danny, a small, short legged, shaggy haired Lhasa Apso well into his dotage and on whom they both doted. Not only could they be observed most evenings taking Danny for his constitutional or, on other occasions, bringing him along to coffee parties and the like, but invariably his name would come up in conversation as though he were their child. So once Quantrill had got on the wrong side of Sir Peter, the latter thereafter dubbed him in private as 'the dog'. Now what was the incident from which all this stemmed?

At an Executive Council meeting earlier in the year, the first minister mentioned that, in looking forward to the future, specifically independence, he and his colleagues felt they must prepare the country for a national anthem of its own. What they, the ruling political party, wished to adopt in this context was a patriotic song, 'Land of the Gods', which two British Hondurans living in the United States, Samuel Haynes and Dr Selwyn Young, had written and composed. Would the governor, therefore, be good enough to forward the music to the Royal Military School of Music at Kneller Hall with the request that they orchestrate it? The governor agreed.

Shortly before the royal visit the duly orchestrated music was returned with a cassette containing a recorded version played by the army school's band. This was brought into a subsequent meeting of Executive Council by the governor who disclosed that the cost was in the region of £100. He then asked Quantrill to arrange the necessary payment. The latter replied that there was no appropriate vote from which it could be met. 'Surely,' said the governor, 'there must be some miscellaneous pocket from which this comparatively small amount can be found?' Again the reply was in the negative. The governor tried once more, but once again he refused to budge. Recalling an analogous situation when the disciple Peter also denied his master three times, I waited with bated breath fully expecting to hear the sound of a cock crowing or perhaps the clinking of thirty pieces of silver being pocketed somewhere around the table. But if there were such sounds, my hearing was insufficiently acute to pick them up.

There is no doubt that this was a legitimate charge on government funds that could easily have been met. But Quantrill, aware that the opposition political party objected to the proposed national anthem, decided to throw a spanner in the works, as it were, to frustrate the first minister. Having thus far exhausted his attempts to obtain government financing and unwilling to draw the first minister in his capacity of minister of finance into this impasse, the governor, now placed in an embarrassing position and his face red with suppressed anger, turned to the first minister and said 'Well, in that case, I will meet the cost from my own pocket.' As the former and his political colleagues expressed their thanks, Quantrill sat there with a sheepish grin on his face not fully realizing at that moment that he had 'crossed' someone who was not by nature of the forgiving kind. He was soon to find out.

After the governor had spoken to me about my attendance (or rather non-attendance) at the luncheon, he called Quantrill to Government House and explained that for logistical reasons it was necessary to limit the number of guests he could invite to attend this particular function. He added that obviously all the elected and *ex officio* members of Executive Council and their wives, together with the chief justice, would have to be invited and that, unfortunately, this meant that non-members of council and any others had to be excluded. In the circumstances he was very sorry to have to let him know that, because of the limitations on space, he and his wife would not be receiving invitations to the lunch. This news would not have gone down well with someone to whom social standing and 'loss of face' assumed disproportionate importance, but when he subsequently learnt that I had been invited to join the group at the coffee stage and was to be included in the official photograph, the full impact of the snub finally dawned on him.

Although incidental, I should perhaps mention for the record that after the meeting of Executive Council mentioned above, the first minister asked me to take the cassette to Rudy Castillo at Radio Belize with instructions for it to be played as the prelude to the 12.30 p.m. news bulletin. This was done without explanation and the novelty and length of the recording was to bewilder local listeners who might have been forgiven had they thought that the Guatemalans had taken over the radio station. But as I said, this is an incidental point.

While I have been recounting this, we may assume that the main courses of lunch were eaten and, when coffee was served, I joined the group. Shortly afterwards Prince Philip and all members of Executive Council who were present, including myself, appeared on the front porch of Government House for a group photograph of which a copy was subsequently given to each of us. If 'the dog' ever saw it I, am sure that he would have recognized it as a very public recording of the snub and would have howled bitterly and mournfully long into the night. But now let us get back to the narrative.

The general public had been informed over the radio of the time HRH was due to leave Government House and the route he was to take. He drove in the open Land Rover through crowded streets. There was an especially enthusiastic crowd at the city boundary where he changed to the Government House car for the drive, with the governor, to the army camp at Pinecrest near the airport. However, some disappointment was expressed that he appeared in a lounge suit and not the naval uniform in which he was depicted in various photographs in the colony. Colonel Anderson met His Royal Highness at Pinecrest and together they walked around the camp to see the troops enjoying various forms of recreation. Then they proceeded on to the airport.

There the governor presented the chief civil aviation officer, the airport manager and a trade unionist who was attending the Duke of Edinburgh's conference in Canada the following month. Then it was time for HRH to walk along the red carpet to the aircraft bidding farewell to members of Executive Council and the chief justice and accepting a souvenir collection of especially mounted British Honduras postage stamps as he did so. He embarked at 2.50 p.m. and the royal aircraft was airborne at 2.55 p.m. It had, indeed been a whirlwind visit.

As the royal aircraft disappeared from view, the governor sent a radio message to the plane thanking HRH for his visit, which he said would have the effect of encouraging local efforts to overcome the

11. HRH with members of Executive Council at Government House.

present difficulties facing the territory. He went on to wish him a safe journey and to request that an assurance of British Honduras's fervent loyalty be conveyed to Her Majesty the Queen. In reply, HRH thanked the governor for his kind message adding that he had enjoyed his short visit and that he wished the people of British Honduras every success in the reconstruction work that lay ahead.

And so ended a five-hour whirlwind visit that had seemed to me to last five days – but all's well that ends well. The visit had been a success and there were no apparent mishaps. Well ... er ... let's not be too hasty, for later that afternoon the commissioner of police recounted to me an incident that had occurred while members of his force were guarding the royal aircraft during HRH's absence. It appears that two armed policemen were assigned to this duty and they took turns to patrol the vicinity of the aircraft. A simple and straightforward task, surely. But this was British Honduras and gremlins were always lurking.

To my cynical mind, even before the advantage of hindsight, I would have thought that if there was concern about the security of the royal aircraft, the last people to be allowed near it would have been the appropriately armed local constabulary. There was always the danger that this type of assignment, which fell outside their normal range of duties, would induce boredom and lack of concentration. But let me recite the events as I recall them, events pregnant with biblical undertones.

Now it came to pass that one of the constables deputed for this task was PC Cain, a name calculated to instill in all those readers of the Bible familiar with Genesis IV a feeling of apprehension. For, as they will know, Adam and Eve's first born, Cain, is forever associated with fratricide and for his disingenuous reply (when asked about his slain brother's whereabouts) 'Am I my brother's keeper?' On his stint of duty, PC Cain, undoubtedly a chip off the original block, was patrolling round the aircraft with a loaded rifle over his shoulder and, for some unaccountable reason, on impulse, pulled the trigger just as he was passing the nearside wing. Now I forget whether I was told that the bullet actually passed through the wing of the plane or merely grazed it, but apparently there was great consternation among technical staff at the airport lest serious damage had ensued. That it had not did not detract from the seriousness with which the incident was viewed. When the commissioner of police learnt of what had happened, PC Cain was, as they used to say, 'hauled over the coals' and the inevitable punishment considered. The proposed punishment, details of which have long since escaped my memory, probably took the form of a fine or a severe reprimand (perhaps both) and, in accordance with procedure relating to serious misdemeanours by members of the force, the relevant file setting this out was submitted to the governor for approval. I happened to glance at it in his 'out' tray on its way back to police headquarters.

Now Sir Peter Stallard had a nice sense of humour and, as befitting the son of a clergyman, more than a passing acquaintance with the Bible. Under the commissioner of police's recommendation he had minuted with gubernatorial trademark red ink in his neat handwriting: 'I agree. But let us be thankful that PC Abel was not under the other wing.' To this, I added my own silent prayer of thanks. Here endeth this tale of a royal visit. Amen!

Chapter 18
Scorpio Club

L IKE A METEOR colliding with the earth's atmosphere, the Scorpio Club created a brief incandescent trace as it streaked momentarily across the November sky before fading into oblivion. Conceived in an alcoholic haze, its demise was similarly shrouded. Because of its strictly ephemeral nature no constitution was ever framed, no rules promulgated, no committee formed and no minutes taken. But as the subject may be of interest to the astrological as well as the colonial world, albeit marginally, I feel it incumbent upon me to disclose the hitherto unrevealed story of the club's meteoric rise and fall. In so doing, I trust that others involved in its genesis will not accuse me of indecently lifting the veil.

It all began, like so many bright expatriate ideas, at the bar of the Belize Club. The occasion was the second Saturday of November 1962. That night the club was more crowded than usual because many of those present were required to attend the annual Armistice Day service the following day. This meant that the usual weekend exodus to the cayes or to Mountain Pine Ridge was not an available option. By about 10.00 p.m. the vociferous minority had imposed the ritual table thumping rugby-cum-service choruses on the gathering and groups were crowded around the bar doing what they did best – drinking, gossiping and generally maligning absent friends and colleagues. One more ritual remained to be observed, Bob Alleyn's party piece.

Bob was a 'Jekyll and Hyde' sort of character in the sense that he showed two contrasting faces to the outside world. Weekdays, he was a quiet and serious-minded accountant in the private business sector who went about his work in a sober and conscientious way. But on Saturday nights at the club he would undergo a personality transformation. He would log in to party mode and 'let his hair down', to coin a phrase. This particular night, fired by drink, as was

12. Picnic at Mountain Pine Ridge. Russell Waters, Lyndsie Lewis, Florence
and Glynne Lewis. In the foreground a lurking Heineken beer bottle
gets into the act.

usual at about this stage in the proceedings, he retrieved the tennis
trophy (a large two-handled silver cup) from the club's trophy shelf
situated behind the bar. Then with the cup upside down on his head
and looking from the neck upwards like a stereotype marauding
Viking warrior (and from the grin on his face possibly one who had
been posted to the squad assigned to raping, looting and pillaging),
he capered around the clubhouse with light mincing steps chanting
his own special incantation:

> There he goes
> On his toes
> Chasing arse
> I suppose.

Meanwhile, his wife, Barbara, a natural comedienne, had returned
to the clubroom having earlier accepted Doug Manning's offer of a
'spin' in his new Chevrolet. 'Did you enjoy the experience?' someone
asked. 'Oh, he's got a lovely clutch', she leered. As he was incredibly
shy without the courage supplied by a snifter or two and not
reckoned to be 'a ladies man', he was able to underline the joke by
putting his arm around her shoulders.

This short and not unprecedented interlude was accepted with amused tolerance as part of a normal Saturday night at the club, a spontaneous amateur night cabaret, if you like. When Bob's ritual was over and the cup restored to its normal place behind the bar, the hum of conversation resumed. For some reason, apropos nothing in particular, I happened to mention that my birthday was on the 19 November. Why? I cannot now imagine. It was obviously not in the expectation or hope of receiving a present. But mention it I did. The reaction was totally unexpected. Don Reading declared that his birthday was on the 18th and Dennis Malone, who had just come into the club, disclosed that he too was a Scorpio – a running flush, indeed. But it did not stop there. As word got around Norman Stalker revealed that his birthday was on the 15th and Doug Manning's a day or so earlier. So a cluster (or whatever the collective noun is) of Scorpios was foregathered together on that particular occasion as if presaging an unknown but possibly significant event. As someone remarked, with no great originality, that never before in the history of the Belize Club had so many people born under the same sign of the zodiac assembled under its roof on a Saturday in November and in a year ending with the figure two. Looking back, with all the advantage of hindsight, it now seems a typically alcoholic lark. But in the village atmosphere of British Honduras in those days, the expatriate community would seize upon anything novel and exploited it to the full.

The situation having prompted a celebratory round of drinks was to be given a further twist. 'Let's form a Scorpio Club' someone suggested; and in a mood of euphoria the idea was embraced with no one giving any thought to what it might entail other than an excuse for a party. Carried away in the prevailing heady atmosphere Dennis Malone insisted that the club's first meeting should take place the following morning at his house, which was in fact the house of the chief justice who was then on leave. He would, he said, prepare a special rum punch to mark the occasion and, of course, wives would be welcome – thus demonstrating that there was no discrimination in our society unless it was against teetotallers. A few special friends were also included in the invitation. So happily was all this received and endorsed that

Dennis began to entertain doubts about the wisdom of his invitation. With his warning antennae now flickering from green to red he hastily added a cautionary amber note by remembering that he had also invited some of his friends in the legal profession to an early lunch that day prior to their attendance at the Armistice Day service. That note was to the effect that he was not proposing a party as such but simply a modest get-together to signal the birth of the Scorpio Club. Also, that he expected everybody to leave well before his luncheon guests arrived. I doubt, however, that he was very reassured by the tacit acceptance of this condition for, with the whiff of a party in its nostrils, the group he had just addressed was a difficult one to dislodge once established.

In all this Dennis displayed the duality of his nature, impulsive yet cautious. This is perhaps explained by his background and status. He was born in St Kitts and was one of the sons of Chief Justice of the Windward and Leeward Islands Sir Clement Malone. He attended an English public school (and could still perform without too much persuasion or embarrassment his role as one of the three little maids in the school's production of The Mikado) and served as a flight lieutenant in the RAF bomber command during the Second World War. After subsequently studying law at Oxford University and being called to the Bar he joined the colonial legal service. He served with distinction as legal draftsman in Barbados where his obvious abilities marked him out for early promotion. It was no surprise, therefore, when in 1961 and still under the age of 40 he was appointed Puisne Judge in British Honduras. Shortly after his arrival the attorney-general went on leave and, in the absence of a locum, the ubiquitous Malone assumed the appointment in a temporary capacity. His short tenure in that office coincided with the advent of Hurricane Hattie and, in its immediate aftermath, he produced with commendable speed, skill and accuracy legislation for the imposition of the state of emergency that was deemed necessary. Thereafter, he reverted to his substantive post of puisne judge and it was in that capacity he was currently serving.

Inherent in all this was his dilemma. On the one hand, as a comparatively young man with a zest for life, his instinct was to let his hair (or wig) down whenever possible. On the other hand, he was conscious of his status both in society at large and in the judiciary in particular and with it the gravitas expected of him. That he succeeded in negotiating this tricky high wire of social and professional behaviour is manifest in his subsequent career where, while still enjoying life, he emulated his father by receiving a knighthood and becoming a chief justice – in his case both in British Honduras and subsequently the Cayman Islands.

The following morning, Sunday, we assembled at Dennis's temporary home on Cork Street. This overlooked Fort George Park where the Armistice Day service was to be held. The park, not much larger than a football pitch in length but perhaps wider, is simply an open stretch of grass running inland from the southern foreshore and bordered by Park and Cork Streets. It was here on Armistice Day 1925, that the then governor, Sir John Burdon, unveiled a red granite obelisk dedicated to the memory of the many men of the colony who volunteered to fight for Britain and the empire in the First World War, serving mainly in the Middle East campaigns. Close to the obelisk is a small covered bandstand of the type common to British parks and seafronts in the late nineteenth and early twentieth centuries and still in vogue in many such places today. It was around this that the traditional service was to be held.

At this, the inaugural meeting of the Scorpio Club, Dennis ladled out his special rum punch and proposed a toast to the founding and future of the club. This went down well; I mean the punch as well as the toast. Many other toasts were proposed as this involved the recharging of glasses. However, before long, the number of guests became swollen as gatecrashers from other astrological denominations claimed that their presence was in response to an invitation that had been written in the stars. Inevitably, the supply of rum punch dried up and attention turned to other tipples. Drink and conversation flowed. To the surprise of everyone and the relief of Dennis all left reasonably punctually when last orders were called and time was up.

But the impact of fresh air after the morning's bout of drinking was to create havoc as far as future plans were concerned. The effect of a well mixed rum punch is as potentially lethal as a hand grenade with its pin removed. It is so smooth to the palate that its alcoholic content is seldom recognized until too late. To put it another way, a little rum punch can be dangerous. By the same token, a lot can be devastating. So, in blissful state we departed, noting in so doing that soldiers from the garrison were setting up a 'Wombat' (a piece of anti-tank artillery) outside the Holden Memorial Hospital in readiness for the firing of a blank round to signal the start of the traditional two-minute silence. Members of the Public Works Department, presumably on overtime, were also observed putting up chairs in the enclosure around the bandstand marked off for invited guests. So an air of readiness for the service was already discernible.

However, with still some time to go before the service was due to begin, Florence and I decided to go home for a quick shower and light lunch before taking up our places. But once indoors and under the soporific influence of the rum punch we first opted for a short nap to reorient ourselves, as it were. In the event we both fell into a deep sleep.

At the appointed hour the 'Wombat' blasted off. In so doing the explosion blew in all the windows of the Holden Memorial Hospital and many others in the neighbourhood, thus rudely shattering the silence it was intended to introduce. It also awakened the two of us. In a panic we hastened back to Fort George Park where the service was already underway. Unfortunately, such was the size of the crowd around the perimeter of the invited guests' enclosure that it was impossible to get to our seats without causing a disturbance. I was aware that it would not go down well with the governor if he thought I had skipped the service – and governors always seem to notice such things – so the only strategy available was to get as close to the front of the enclosure as possible and sing 'Abide with Me' and other hymns loudly in the hope of being recognized. This was finally achieved though not without some odd looks in my direction from the governor and chief secretary.

But where were the other Scorpios? Dennis Malone was there in the enclosure, of course, attired in his scarlet judicial robe and wig. But whether as a result of an injudicious intake of his rum punch or not, his wig was so awry that his appearance was that of a dejected spaniel with lopsided ears. Don and Pat Reading came along later with their small son, Anthony, but there was no sign whatsoever of the other founder members. I subsequently learnt that they had wisely taken to their beds.

Thus the Scorpio Club failed to develop beyond the embryonic stage. It is now forgotten, except perhaps by those participants who witnessed its rise and fall. No attempt was ever made to resurrect it and, as far as I know, it was never referred to again in expatriate circles. It was a good idea and (with apologies to 'Saki' and his musing on 'good cooks') as good ideas go, this one came and went. And on that philosophical note it is perhaps time to lower the veil once again on this hitherto undisclosed piece of imperial and astrological history. But before leaving the subject, a few final words are needed to complete the story.

Scorpio(n)s are noted for the sting in their tail. It should, therefore, come as no surprise to learn that there was a sting (well, all right then, sequel or postscript might be more appropriate descriptions) in the tail of the above narrated tale. A few years ago I had reason to look up Sir Dennis Malone's reference in Who's Who and noticed that his date of birth was given as 24 November. With it came the realization that one of the most prominent founder members of the Scorpio Club was in fact 'not one of us' but one whose sign of the zodiac was Sagittarius. Although in his chosen profession ignorance of the law or recognized rules is considered as no excuse for transgression I, for one, am prepared to accept his claim that he too was a Scorpio was based on a genuine misunderstanding by assuming that the upper date for inclusion in the Scorpio classification extended beyond 21 November. And who can blame him for wishing to be associated with such illustrious company? But perhaps, in the light of this discovery with its embarrassing undertones of an intruder in our midst, it was just as well that the club never advanced beyond the embryonic stage. With that thought, the veil referred to in the previous paragraph can now finally be lowered.

Chapter 19
Toledo

FOR ADMINISTRATIVE purposes in the colonial era, British Honduras was divided into six districts: Corozal, Orange Walk, Cayo, Belize, Stann Creek and Toledo. Each district, for which a district officer was responsible, has its own distinctive geographical features, economic activities, points of interest and charm. What they all have in common is that each displays in varying degrees of magnitude traces of ancient Maya settlements.

Corozal District in the north, a gateway to southern Mexico, is the main sugar growing and refinery region. Much of the country is low lying with swamps and lagoons. Its immediate southern neighbour, Orange Walk, is the centre for intensive logging based on the Gallon Jug estate. It is rich in agricultural land and pastures. To the west is Cayo with its frontier post with Guatemala at Benque Viejo. It is noted for chicle (a form of latex that is the base for chewing gum), logging, cattle raising and agricultural produce. The archaeological site at Xunantunich, with its large monuments of the ancient Maya civilization, is a growing tourist attraction. As its name implies, Belize District takes in the capital and its environs. It is mostly swampy, interlaced with lagoons, rising slightly inland to the Manatee mountains. It also embraces many of the cayes. The main industries are agriculture and secondary wood sawmilling. Further south, along the coastal plain, is Stann Creek, populated chiefly by Caribs and Creoles. The Cockscomb range lies within this district. It is the citrus growing area and, in addition, produces bananas, cacao and cassava. The most southerly district, Toledo, is populated mainly by Maya and Ketchi Amerindians. Most of the Maya mountains fall within its boundaries. The main economic activities include logging and various forms of agriculture. It was once an important sugar growing area, for a number of migratory Americans from the southern United States of America established a thriving sugar industry there in 1867. Although the introduction of sugar beet into Europe subsequently crippled the industry, a small quantity of high quality brown sugar was produced there until the early years of the twentieth century.

Whenever an opportunity arose to visit the districts, I would take it, for only then could one get a true feeling for the colony as a whole with its diversity of peoples, scenery and economic activities. Sometimes I would accompany the chief secretary, district officers, attend army and British Honduras Volunteer Guard exercises or venture off on my own on some assignment decreed by the governor or chief secretary. Did I have a favourite district? Not really. As already mentioned, each had its own attractions. But if pressed really hard I am bound to declare a faint bias towards the Toledo District. This I suspect, without serious analysis, was probably induced by the frisson of excitement I felt at being in a part of the country that is to some extent unexplored and in the company of some of the less sophisticated and, in a way, more unusual of its peoples.

What do I remember of visits there? With the passage of time the purpose and details of most visits have gone beyond recall or remain as isolated incidents in an incoherent pattern that occasionally comes to mind. But two visits remain vivid for special reasons.

In 1963, when he was acting governor, Michael Porcher decided to show the flag, as it were, and organized an official visit to the Toledo District. His wife Mollie and I accompanied him. Once the dates had been agreed, early one morning we set off from Customs House Wharf on the government launch *Lolette* for Punta Gorda, a distance of about 80 miles. Our first port of call was Gales Point, a sand spit projecting into the sea 15 miles south of Belize. There we went ashore to meet the villagers and to listen to their inevitable complaints about the government's alleged failure to meet their needs.

Thereafter, back on board, we passed Mullins River and Stann Creek. Further along the coast we caught a glimpse of the Cockscombs in the hinterland as they towered darkly into a sullen looking sky. With time to spare we talked 'shop', gossiped and set out fishing lines for trawling. Sufficient sea mackerel obliged to provide a kedgeree supper that night for ourselves and an evening meal for the crew. And, in relaxed mood, we made inroads into a case of Heineken beer. As each squat green bottle was emptied it was tossed overboard for target practice for Michael who, for some reason, had brought a revolver with him. At first his aim was impressive. But with each successive emptied bottle his shooting became more and more erratic. As night began closing in, we arrived at Punta Gorda where the district officer, Tom Sabido, met us and took us to the government rest house where we discussed the programme that had been arranged. While this was taking place supper was being prepared. And so, after our meal and a nightcap it was time for bed in anticipation of an early start the next day.

The following morning, accompanied by Tom Sabido, we inspected the local police station (with its complement of 12 under the control of a sergeant) and had meetings with local dignitaries. We then embarked on the small motor launch *Anna*, which had been hired to take us along the Sarstoon River to Cadenas, a village on the southwestern boundary with Guatemala. Because of its shallow draught the *Anna* was one of the few available suitable vessels able to negotiate the sandbanks at the mouth of the river.

The Sarstoon also marks the southern boundary between British Honduras and Guatemala. As we proceeded we speculated on where the actual boundary lay. According to international law, this is determined by the 'thalweg', which the dictionary defines as the centre of the navigable part of the river. But although we wondered at times whether we were technically in Guatemalan waters, the skipper of our vessel, Austin, was in no way influenced by such academic thoughts and steered according to his inclination and experience.

On both sides of the river dense bush and forest seemed to hedge us in. Overhanging trees with heavy foliage were mirrored in the water giving it a dark green appearance. Shafts of sunlight filtering through the trees added to the colour and lush tropical setting. Parakeets and kingfishers abounded and, from the heavier boughs of some of the overhanging trees, iguanas looking like miniature dragons cast their baleful eyes on us. As our eyes adjusted to the scene we saw the occasional snake cleverly camouflaged as a branch of a tree ready to entrap some unsuspecting prey – and so on to Cadenas.

I do not really know what I expected but it turned out to be little more than a clearing in the bush by the side of the river on which stood a village store that a Mr Flynn owned and ran. A few Maya Indians were sitting around. Whether they were Guatemalan or British Honduran nationals was of no significance, for national boundaries have no real meaning for locals in that part of the country. We discussed with Flynn what life was like in the area, but to my regret I never asked him how he had come to live in such an outlandish place. For our part we had visited a piece of the country that very few people in the colony had seen and, thus enlightened yet not really much wiser, we took our leave.

Early the next day we set off for San Antonio, a Maya village 20 or so miles west of Punta Gorda. The road was surprisingly good, with the first half having a tarmac surface. The village was nestled under tall hills that were covered in mist when we arrived. The area was heavily forested. After discussions with the village elders we were taken along to the school, a large open-sided thatched barn-like building in the centre of a clearing. Directed by their teacher, a Carib, the children in a large class of mixed sexes and ages welcomed us with a song, which they sang heartily. The highlight, however, was when he asked the senior girl, who was in fact his teenage daughter, to recite us a poem. She chose one that was (and probably still is) familiar to generations of British schoolchildren – Hilaire Belloc's, 'Matilda', with its subtitle, 'Who Told Lies and was Burned to Death'. It tells the tale of a young girl who, one day, when her aunt goes to the theatre to see a current play, *The Second Mrs Tanqueray*, telephones the London Fire Brigade to report that her house is burning. This, of course, is a false alarm for which her aunt has to pay for the cost of the call out. A few weeks later the house actually does catch fire, but her shouts and screams fall on deaf ears. As the poem concludes: 'For every time she shouted "Fire!" They only answered "Little Liar! And therefore when her Aunt returned, Matilda and the House were Burned!' The moral of the poem, of course, is that children who lie or cry wolf are liable to get their comeuppance.

The pupil delivered the poem, which is a bit of a romp, with great zest and feeling. Our applause when she finished was both genuine and unreserved. It was a *tour de force*. However, I did wonder what the children made of it. The moral was clearly discernable but what did they make of British humour, London place names and British imagery? In a forest clearing in Central America it seemed so out of place.

There was one more duty that also turned out to be a pleasure. The ladies of the village, dressed in traditional Indian costume, entertained us to a display of colourful and lively dancing. Then it was time to leave and to return to Punta Gorda and the *Lolette*.

The return journey was uneventful until we had just passed Stann Creek when Michael turned to me and asked 'What day is Hennings due to arrive?' John Hennings was then the colonial attaché at the British embassy in Washington who had arranged to visit British Honduras on a 'familiarization' tour. In this connection it should be remembered that this was at a time when colonial issues were still alive and often raised in the United Nations Committee of 24, which dealt with such matters. Because of the Guatemalan claim, British Honduras was regarded as a 'disputed territory' and so was often the subject of the committee's attention. From time to time the colonial attaché was called upon to explain the British position.

Although I had played no part in drawing up the programme, which had been arranged through the governor's office, I remembered that he was due to arrive on the 16th, and this I relayed to Michael. 'What's the date today?' he asked. Looking at our programme for Toledo, I was able to tell him that it was the 16th. So there we were, three or four hours away from Belize with our visitor due to arrive at the airport within the hour. What were we to do? Fortunately, Michael was not the sort to dwell on how the situation had arisen but how to get out of it. It was this problem that he addressed. Soon we were anchored off Mullins River where there was access to a telephone. From there I put through a call to the permanent secretary of finance who was minding the shop, so to speak, while Michael was on tour and asked him to arrange through police headquarters for Hennings to be picked up from the airport and to be kept entertained until our return. He was to explain that the acting governor had unfortunately been delayed but was now on his way back to Belize and expected to be with him shortly. In the event, these arrangements worked smoothly and no one outside our circle was any the wiser. So once again it was a case of all's well that ends well. But the truth is that in the rush to fit in the Toledo tour while the substantive governor was away, the colonial attaché's visit had been overlooked. Had we spent another day in that district an embarrassing situation could have arisen. As it was, it was a close shave.

About a year later, just before I was due to leave the colony, I again visited the Toledo District, this time in company with the new Military Intelligence Liaison Officer (MILO) Major Mickey Brentford. There had been a bizarre shooting at Cadenas that had resulted in the death of a Guatemalan national. The local police report on the incident had been relayed to the Guatemalan authorities who had found it unconvincing. Consequently, the governor asked me to visit the site to see if the police report 'hung together'. I was accompanied by Mickey who, because he was attached to the British Honduras police force, was familiar with the background to the case as provided by the statements taken by the police officers stationed at Punta Gorda.

Aside from this, we had a secondary mission of our own. We had learnt that the Public Works Department and the Forestry Department, between them, had made a preliminary start on the proposed Southern Highway, which for the first time would provide a road link between Stann Creek and Punta Gorda. Still in embryonic form it was little more than a track through the bush, hacked out by a bulldozer and smoothed by a grader, just wide enough to allow a vehicle such as a Land Rover through. With several river crossings to negotiate, it was only possible to traverse its whole length in the dry season. And this was the dry season. I was keen to see this road link before my departure and Mickey, who was something of an adventurer, hit upon the idea of walking part of the wilder southern section.

We set off from Belize in the MILO's Land Rover driven by PC Baird. At Stann Creek, Mickey and I embarked upon the MV *Heron* bound for Punta Gorda after instructing Baird to meet us with the vehicle on the Southern Highway at the Golden Stream crossing in the late afternoon of the day after next. Our plan was to walk along the road until just before dusk, by which time we believed we would have reached the Golden Stream, and then be able to complete the rest of the journey by vehicle. Having reached Punta Gorda we met Tom Sabido who, in delivering us to the rest house, confirmed that the *Anna* had been chartered to take us along the Sarstoon to Cadenas as arranged.

At the vessel the following morning we found that the skipper, Austin, had been 'on the rum' and was not in the best condition. Fortunately, his crew member was sober and it was he who took the helm. And so their roles were reversed. We chugged gently along the Sarstoon, which I have already described as a green tropical waterway winding its way through the jungle. After a while, Austin, in an attempt to sober up or justify his presence decided to clean the *Anna*'s deck with river water. His method was to throw a bucket attached to a rope over the side and, when full, haul it aboard where he would sluice down the deck and then slowly repeat the action. This was repeated several times until the bucket caught fast under the keel. He jerked hard on the rope, but instead of releasing the bucket the force of his pull catapulted him into the river. A little earlier Mickey and I had been wondering whether the fierce and deadly pirhana fish were present in these waters. The fact that Austin was hauled back on board with all his limbs intact suggests, perhaps, that the Sarstoon is pirhana free. But I would not like to bet on it. As for Austin, for the remainder of the journey he lay on board drying out in the sun and slowly sobering up.

Flynn, who was at the centre of the incident we had come to investigate, met us at Cadenas. Other key witnesses had also been assembled. In this jungle clearing there was of all things an ancient steam-engine. What it was doing there in such an isolated spot, or how it had got there, were questions I dared not ask because I had been brought up to believe that if you ask a silly question you will get a silly answer. But this was British Honduras so I was not unduly surprised. Its significance was that the death took place on it.

Apparently, it was common practice to cover the steam-engine with a large tarpaulin, presumably to stop birds nesting there or to shield it from the heat of the sun or occasional torrential tropical storm. On the day of the incident, unbeknown to anyone, a Maya

Indian from the Guatemalan side of the border had crept under the tarpaulin and fallen asleep in the driving seat area. He was just awakening when Flynn came to the door of his store. Seeing movement under the tarpaulin and thinking it was a large animal he rushed back for his revolver and then fired several shots at the unseen target. In the event the shots killed the unfortunate Maya. At the inquest the verdict was death by misadventure.

On the surface, this seems an unlikely story, in fact so unlikely that it stretches the bounds of credibility. It was not surprising, therefore, that the Guatemalan authorities should find it unconvincing. However, it is necessary to recognize that the incident took place in the back of beyond where normal civilized behaviour, as most Western people would understand it, would not necessarily prevail. In other words, different standards seem to operate in settings where law enforcement is virtually non-existent. If my memory serves me correctly, that rollicking Canadian poet, Robert Service, in one of his poems about the Alaskan gold rush, opens with the words, 'There are strange things done in the midnight sun By the men who moil for gold.' Well, equally strange things are done in the tropical sun and the incident at Cadenas was a case in point. Our investigations revealed no antagonisms between the parties or any logical reason why Flynn should deliberately engineer the death of the unfortunate Maya. Our conclusion was that it was the result of a wild and reckless act, possibly induced by drink, or a temporary mental aberration brought about by the loneliness of living in such a remote area. Our task, however, was not to sit in judgement but simply to marshal the facts and report on the situation as we saw it. Visiting Guatemala City on my way back to Britain several weeks later I called in on the ministry of foreign affairs and shared these findings with officials there. With some reluctance they accepted that the shooting was an accident and not deliberate but found it hard to accept the circumstances as explained.

It was late afternoon when we returned to Punta Gorda. From there, Tom Sabido drove us to San Antonio where we were to spend the night. Before the evening meal, he entertained us with local anecdotes and spun several yarns based on Maya myth and legend. In the gathering darkness some of his stories were quite eerie. One story he told still lingers in my mind. It went something like this.

A young Maya mother was confounded because her newly born baby would still scream with hunger after being suckled hard for its nightly feed. To add to her concern, it was putting on very little weight. The village nurse was equally puzzled. One night when the baby was being fed (this was in the dark because there was no electricity in the village and one would not normally light an oil lamp to feed a baby) the husband thought he heard an unusual sound and lit the lamp to investigate. By its light he saw that a snake that had attached itself to the baby was sucking at the mother's breast and that the baby was sucking the 'tip' of the snake's tail – an apocryphal tale if ever I heard one! However, delivered at dusk in the manner of that spinner of dark tales on the radio, the late Valentine Dyall, it was creepy. Each noise after that had Mickey and me looking anxiously around wondering whether some intelligent serpent was in our midst and up to no good. Thereafter, we were relieved when the oil lamps in the rest house were lit but less happy when they were turned off when we finally went to bed. Needless to say, with each slight noise raising irrational but understandable fears, neither of us slept easily.

Next day, after an early lunch, we set off for the Southern Highway. At mile 12 on the Punta Gorda–San Antonio road (that is to say, 12 miles from the former) where the new highway joins it at a 'T' junction, we said goodbye to Tom Sabido and began our walk. As already mentioned, our destination was the Golden Stream about eight miles along the track. We each carried a small pack containing our personal effects, some chocolate and water. Mickey also carried a service revolver as an insurance against the unknown. A new track through the bush is always a source of interest, for it presents the possibility that strange animals or exotic birds will appear. But our early interest focused on the track itself. As the grader had levelled off the surface it had revealed below a myriad of small seashells, thus indicating, at least to our amateur geological minds, that this part of the country had once been under the sea. Rivers or their tributaries criss-crossed the track at various intervals, but they were all shallow at this time of the year and easily fordable. At the Rio Grande crossing we could see in the wet earth the pug marks of some large animal – a jaguar, perhaps? To heighten dramatic intent I would like to add at this point that Mickey nervously fingered his revolver, but I don't think he did. Shortly afterwards the animal revealed itself.

As we plodded on through the bush, no doubt wondering why on earth we had embarked on such an adventure in the name of interest and pleasure, we heard what appeared to be the sound of a loud human cough. Looking into the bush on our left we saw what at first sight seemed to be a small elephant, but on closer inspection we identified it as a tapir or, as they call it locally, a mountain cow. It was the first I had ever seen in the territory.

The journey thus far had taken us longer than anticipated, but at last we reached the Golden Stream crossing just as night was closing in. About half a mile ahead of us on the track the MILO's Land Rover was vaguely visible in the dusk, but to our dismay and consternation we suddenly saw its tail lights and realized that it had turned and was heading away from us, probably on its way back to Stann Creek. This brought the further realization that Baird had probably assumed that we would not be arriving that night and with it the prospect of our spending the night in the bush or plodding on in the dark to our destination. Neither option had any appeal.

In a last minute attempt to attract Baird's attention, Mickey fired two shots from his revolver into the air. Although to us the noise was deafening it was obviously inaudible to Baird over the noise of the Land Rover's engine. So we stumbled on cursing our driver and, among other thoughts and expressions, questioning his legitimacy. But our pessimism was unfounded thanks to Baird's Casanova streak. After about a mile we came across a hut in a clearing with the Land Rover parked outside. Inside was Baird in company with a buxom Indian wench and, no doubt to our suspicious minds, envisaging staying the night there if we failed to turn up. But turn up we did, thus demonstrating once again Robert Burns's wise words on the best laid schemes going awry. And if we had spiked his romantic plans – well too bad! If we had not tracked him down our own plans would have been in worse array.

Baird tried to assure us that he would have returned along the trail every hour to see if we had got through, but the way he was comfortably ensconced in the hut cast reasonable doubt on this. And so we drove off seeing nothing of the remainder of the new road except those parts of it illuminated in our headlights. An hour or so later we reached Melinda in the Stann Creek District where friends fed and accommodated us. That was my last visit to the Toledo District. It was a memorable one for sundry reasons, not least the daunting but fortunately unfulfilled prospect of walking all the way to Melinda in the dark thanks to Baird's impatience or romantic inclinations.

In the wider context of administrative life in British Honduras in those days it was just a normal visit. None the less, it was one like the other visit recorded above, the memory of which still lingers to this day and perhaps helps to explain whatever bias I may have towards the Toledo District – never a dull moment.

Chapter 20
Mennonites

THE BUZZ WORD in Belize when my family and I first arrived was 'Mennonites'. Farmers from that ascetic religious community had recently set up a shop in the city selling inexpensive farm produce. Its significance was that it was seen as a welcome challenge to the prevailing dependence on expensive imported frozen and canned goods. It also offered better quality. For example, fresh instead of tinned, condensed or evaporated milk. But mention of Mennonites begs several interconnected questions such as, who are they, why did they emigrate to British Honduras and what was (and still is) their impact on the local economy and society? Before attempting to answer these questions, however, it is necessary to emphasize the importance of agricultural development to the local economy and the perceived political problems of imported labour.

It was recognized as far back as the nineteenth century that if British Honduras was to develop its obvious agricultural potential it would have to attract immigrants. But in the parochial atmosphere of the colony this was never a popular option, other than on a very modest scale, as the reaction to the publication in 1948 of the *Evans Commission Report* made clear.[1] Evans and his team had investigated the possibility of settling some of the population from the overcrowded British West Indian islands and Europeans displaced during the Second World War in British Honduras and British Guiana, the other British colony on the central or southern American mainland. Consequently, they recommended several economic projects designed to realize the 'tremendous agricultural possibilities' in the two territories. This found little favour in British Honduras whose government and people feared that large-scale immigration of the sort proposed would swamp their culture.

The issue resurfaced in 1959 when an economist from HM

Treasury, Jack Downie, produced a report[2] in which he expressed, among other things, the opinion that the British Honduran economy would always remain underdeveloped unless the population was substantially increased to about 300,000 by 1975 (it was then estimated at between 60,000 and 90,000), which would not be achieved by natural increase at the then current annual rate of 3.7 per cent. Accordingly, he recommended an annual intake of primary agricultural settlers from whom new and concentrated peasant communities would be established. In so doing he acknowledged that this, in effect, was an echo of an old theme. As he put it, his report 'merely rehearsed the old tune of the Evans Commission of 1948 without the full orchestra' and this, too, found little favour locally.

Indeed, when the subject came up in London at the British Honduras constitutional conference of 1960, one of the delegates, Archdeacon Gilbert Rodwell Hulse, declared dramatically 'that the impact of, say, the immigration of a thousand Italians (no one incidentally had previously mentioned Italians so I have no idea what he held against them) would be like a dagger at the heart of the British Honduran people'. So the *Downie Report*, like its predecessor the *Evans Commission Report*, was quietly allowed to run into the sand where it soon became buried.

This is not to say, however, that immigration *per se* was necessarily discouraged. Indeed, in its time the country had seen a wide variety of immigrants. In particular, the transition from a slave system to a free society in 1834 led to a shortage of labour in forestry work. To meet this deficiency, the importation of indentured Chinese workers was tried in 1865. However, as an experiment, it failed. Many succumbed to various forms of disease and most found forestry work too hard. As a result, a large number drifted off to neighbouring Spanish Honduras in search of agricultural opportunities. Of the original 474 who landed, only 265 were left three years later.[3] Their entrepreneurial skills surfaced as the demand for their forestry and agricultural labour waned and, as a community, they now run profitable commercial businesses in Belize and some of the district towns. In fact, they have been so successful that they are now well and truly integrated into local society.

Earlier, in 1858, following the Indian Mutiny, the British government shipped to the territory 1000 sepoy mutineers and their families. But that was more to solve its own political dilemma than that of the settlement's economic problems. None the less, this source encouraged the hope that India would provide a regular supply of satisfactory labour as was the pattern for the West Indies. In the event, East Indians were imported from Calcutta in the early 1880s to work in the sugar estates throughout the country, especially in the Toledo District where, as mentioned earlier, a number of southerners from the United States had set up plantations after the American Civil War. Small numbers of the former's countrymen also drifted into the settlement from the West Indian islands in subsequent years.[4] But despite its agricultural potential, British Honduras was not an agricultural society. Furthermore, the importation of East Indian labour throughout the Caribbean declined towards the end of the nineteenth century. As a result of the short lived immigration, and lacking systematic contact with other similar ethnic communities in the West Indies, the local group lost most of its cultural characteristics. Nowadays, its members speak no East Indian languages and have long since abandoned their style of dress and religious and marriage customs in favour of the more common local social values and practices.

Other minority immigrant populations include Europeans, North Americans, Cubans, Lebanese and Syrians. But these are mostly the providers of capital or successful prominent businessmen.

Thus, insofar as British Honduras has a policy on the subject it is that mass immigration is unacceptable because of its perceived threat to local culture and employment; but in certain circumstances small numbers would be welcome to facilitate agricultural development. Indeed, it was against this background that, shortly before the *Downie Report* came out, the controversial experiment of admitting a body of immigrants from the Mennonite communities was approved. The words 'controversial experiment' are used advisedly in this context because it was recognized that the Mennonites are a cultural group intent on maintaining their own special distinctiveness and, as such, were bound to occupy the most marginal position on the fringe of the local political and social systems. So, who are they?

The Mennonites are members of a diverse nonconformist Protestant Church movement that has its roots in the sixteenth century. They take their name from one of the movement's early leaders, Menno Simons, a Dutch priest living in Germany. When the Reformation broke out, some German peasants took the Bible as their guide to life and interpreted it literally. This was to put them at odds with the various authorities. Persecuted for their religious beliefs they became scattered across Europe, though they were able to maintain flourishing large-scale communities in Germany. Beginning in 1663, under the pressure of continuing state and church persecution, many groups started to emigrate to the new colonies of North America to preserve the faith of their fathers, seek economic opportunities and escape from what to them was repressive European society. Retaining their Germanic language, although in a dialect that was becoming archaic, their main concern was to be left alone to worship according to their conscience and tradition. To a large extent they have prospered in the New World, but some friction with governments, coupled with a constant need for more agricultural land as population expands, has led them continually to seek pastures new.

The British Honduran group are mostly Canadians of Germanic extraction who left the Canadian prairies in batches during the interwar years (that is to say between the first and second world wars) when that government levied hefty taxes on them for refusing to send their children to state schools. These devoutly religious people prefer to educate their children themselves. In 1920, President Obrigon of Mexico invited them there; between 1920 and 1930 several thousand emigrated to the states of Chihuahua and Durango where they remained for 30 years. During that time their numbers multiplied considerably and, as a result, land inevitably became scarce for their cooperative farming activities. Consequently, British Honduras became the next logical staging post in a traverse from north to south.

Under the terms of an agreement reached with the British Honduras government in the late 1950s, they undertook to meet all the expenses of their removal and establishment and to bring with them capital amounting to about one million dollars for agricultural development. In consequence, they purchased about 150,000 acres of land that they have gradually put under cultivation or used for grazing. Their reputation for being excellent farmers and not getting involved in local politics were important factors in their acceptance. In return, to meet their religious beliefs, they were exempted from any potential military service and from participation in any compulsory insurance or social welfare schemes that might be introduced but were to pay all other taxes.

About 1000 members from two communities, the Reinland and Kleingeimeinde, emigrated in batches from Canada and Mexico from 1957 to 1959 and settled in remote parts of the Orange Walk and Cayo districts. The main communities are to be found at Blue Creek, Shipyard and Richmond Hill in the former and at Spanish Lookout in the latter. In the event, the impressively successful conversion of virgin lands into highly productive agricultural areas has made a significant contribution to a society in which hitherto subsistence farming based on traditional methods prevailed.

In my time in the colony between 1961 and 1964 the Mennonite shop in Belize was immensely popular. The produce sold there was not only fresh but, as already indicated, much cheaper than its imported equivalent that other retailers sold. Eggs, salads, milk, cheese and vegetables helped to improve people's diets and this was only the start. Both variety and volume of produce were to increase considerably over the years.

Although for the reasons already mentioned the Mennonites are not fully assimilated into British Honduras life, they have none the less been good neighbours and have made a real contribution to their new homeland. It was, therefore, with a sense of loss that in June 1973 some families from the Blue Creek and Shipyard communities began an organized withdrawal to a new settlement in Bolivia. But, despite this exodus, the settlements in those two places have remained firmly established.

Although the Mennonites have been good neighbours, the host government has not always found their presence and practices easy. Like other indigenous farmers they are allowed access to local credit union funds and their repayment record is good, but administering the loans has occasionally proved to be a nightmare. With so much shuffling of community elders on representative committees, those who signed the loan agreement were in some cases no longer in office when the time came around for repayment. As a result, there were sometimes arguments over who the recipients of the loans actually were and whose responsibility it was to repay them.

One problem that landed on my desk quite early in my service concerned the community at Shipyard where the elders had laid down a ruling prohibiting the use of rubber tyres on agricultural tractors. This was because they feared that the availability of such vehicles might encourage some of their flock, especially the younger members, to visit the towns and thus become exposed to the wicked outside world. As the nearest town, Orange Walk, was then little more than a so-called main street consisting largely of a police station, a general store and a bar, albeit one with a juke box that boomed out pop music to accompanying flashing lights, it was hardly a den of iniquity. No matter – that was their perception. This ruling, however, was to bring the Mennonites into conflict with the government because the spiked steel wheels on their tractors were damaging the surrounding roads, which were already in poor condition.

In June 1961 a group of elders from Shipyard called unannounced on the chief secretary to make representations about the govern-ment's insistence on rubber tyres. The latter, who had already experienced many difficult and tedious meetings of this sort, claimed, with regret of course, that because of prior commitments he was unable to see them that morning and referred them to me. Once the secretariat staff had produced sufficient chairs they sat around my desk in a semicircle. They were a dour and sombre lot. Shortly after they had embarked on their representations there was a strained silence and I was conscious of ten pairs of eyes staring at something on the right-hand side of my desk. It was an ashtray left by my predecessor, an occasional smoker, but it was not an ordinary ashtray. It was a small round glass dish enclosed in a miniature rubber tractor tyre with a ribbed tread, an advertising gimmick produced by one of the leading tractor tyre manufacturers of the day. I have no idea what my visitors made of it, but for a moment they seemed transfixed. On reflection, its presence could I suppose have been seen as deliberately provocative on my part had I been aware of the purpose of their visit or perhaps had received an omen from 'above'.

After this unrehearsed diversion they resumed their representations, though with less emphasis than before. I found their arguments convoluted and difficult to follow. At one point the main thrust, insofar as I understood it, was that as there was no reference to rubber tyres in the Bible they should not be allowed. Well, I ask you! Where is the reference to motorized tractors? However, stripping aside the subsidiary arguments it was evident that their reluctance to sanction rubber tyres for use on tractors was based on a fear that some of their number might consider sampling life outside the community and thus be exposed to unwelcome influences.

My visitors finally departed, but they were clearly unhappy that their arguments had fallen on unreceptive ears. Possibly they had interpreted the presence of the rubber-tyre ashtray (and this is why I referred to the problem landing on my desk) as a sign from 'above' of the way the meeting was likely to go. That said, they subsequently complied with the government's ruling and, so far as I know, it did not lead to any collapse of community discipline or outside impingement on the group's isolation.

One Blue Creek elder, Peter Liebe, was a regular visitor to the secretariat. He was unusually gregarious for a Mennonite and seemed free from any fear of contact with the outside world. Peter, who spoke good English with a North American accent, often acted as spokesman for his community and used to make a habit of calling on me for a chat on his regular visits to Belize. He was a short, slight, wiry, middle-aged man with sharp features and bad teeth. His dress followed the conventional Mennonite male fashion – dungarees, open-necked blue shirt and a wide-brimmed straw hat. My first impression of him was of a small town hick as portrayed in an American Midwest film set in the depression years of the 1930s. One day I was to find out that he was worldlier than I had ever envisaged.

Shortly before my departure from the colony in 1964, Peter called on me, but there was nothing unusual about that. However, on this occasion he looked shamefaced and was less outgoing than usual. I asked if anything was wrong and in response he muttered something to the effect that the Blue Creek community had taken action against him because of a moral lapse. More specifically, as I was to find out, he had been excommunicated, or whatever expression Mennonites use for expulsion or deprivation of religious privileges. I then asked how this had come about. 'A woman', he said. 'A woman?' I echoed. 'Yes' he said, 'I took her'. 'Took her where?' I responded innocently, not comprehending at that stage the full import of the meaning of his words. He gave me an embarrassed grin and from what he told me somewhat obliquely I gathered that the involvement was one of carnal knowledge – an expression, which, according to reports of cases brought before the Bow Street Magistrates' Court then regularly being featured in humorous sketch form in the old London *Evening News*, used to trip easily off the tongues of the 'beaks' addressing those in the dock charged with such sexual carryings on as soliciting and connected transgressions of the law. As for the details, lurid or otherwise, I thought it best not to enquire, but I must say that my imagination was set racing as I tried to imagine this slight, unimposing elderly hillbilly locked in a passionate embrace. Did he have the courtesy and good manners to remove his hat during the 'taking' process I idly wondered?

I saw Peter Liebe a few more times in Belize after that, but not to speak to, just a wave of recognition. I have often wondered what became of him. Although general disunity of thought exists between modern Mennonite communities, a literal interpretation of the Bible governs them all. Would the Blue Creek community regard any breach of the Ten Commandments or misdemeanours analogous to them as so serious as to be incapable of absolution? Or would they adopt a more conciliatory approach along the lines of the New Testament and practise forgiveness? The answer to these questions would have determined Peter's future in the community.

When I returned briefly to British Honduras at the beginning of 1976, at a time when the Guatemalans were perceived to be sabre-rattling on the border, I was stationed at Belmopan, the new capital city. While there I took the opportunity to visit the nearby Mennonite community at Spanish Lookout and was astounded at the transformation in the landscape. Forests and bush had been turned into lush rolling countryside filled with well-fed contented grazing cattle. New farmhouses and other farm buildings completed an idyllic scene. An atmosphere of tranquillity and simple efficiency prevailed.

At the agricultural research station at Central Farm, young and alert looking Mennonite farmers were seeking and receiving advice. And in Belmopan, as in Belize, there was a large Mennonite shop selling a whole range of farm produce supplemented by similar produce being sold in the streets from vans and stalls. I came away thoroughly impressed by the economic and social impact these unusual immigrants had made and were still making.

It also seemed to me that the children of the original settlers were more at ease than their parents with other locals. That is understandable, but neighbourliness is not assimilation. It remains to be seen whether the prevailing isolationism of the Mennonites in British Honduras, living in what is in effect a state within a state, can remain unaffected in the new millennium with all the tremendous changes now taking place in the world.

Looking back on my days in the colony, the Mennonite communities there, even after all these years, still loom large. In particular, I recall the astonishment and interest I felt at my first sight of a group of these farmers, colourfully dressed in hillbilly style, while their womenfolk looked pale and unhealthy by contrast with their wide brimmed hats and long dark dresses buttoned up to the neck. And, like my colleagues in government, I was greatly impressed with the way they set about their agricultural labours and the remarkable results that followed.

Of subsequent interest to me were the same communities a decade or so later, for they had grown more lively and confident as they became more established. Although there was still criticism locally of what some British Hondurans regarded as backward religious communities, it was none the less generally recognized that, as a people, the Mennonites had shown how hard work, determination and agricultural skills could transform virgin forest into fertile land. Consequently, their vegetable and dairy farming expertise not only had a marked effect on the local economy but it also introduced big changes to the eating habits of many of its people. I am sure that I am not alone in applauding their enterprise and endeavours. While, to the modern Western mind, their religious beliefs and practices are dark echoes of the pre-Enlightenment age, it could be argued that their simple way of life, coupled with the community work ethic that accompanies it, offers an attractive alternative to today's rat race geared to material success and the pursuit of self-interest.

I can still vividly recollect my old friend Peter Liebe standing before me and confessing his great sin. What a character, and such 'taking' ways!

Chapter 21
Among My Souvenirs

BROWSING THROUGH my souvenirs of British Honduras recently, I came across a black and white photograph taken at Chetumal in the southern Mexican state of Quintana Roo on 16 September 1962. It evoked a whole chain of memories. The photograph, set in the dining area of a restaurant, shows five people, three male (of whom I am one) and two female, sitting in a straight line on wooden chairs a foot or so apart. They appear to be in a privileged position for behind them can be seen other guests or diners still seated at their tables. Because of the angle at which the photograph was taken, the line of chairs appears diagonally upwards from left to right so that the five people dominate the whole picture. All are looking at someone or something immediately in front of them. Four show no particular emotion and are gazing ahead impassively, but the fifth, a male, is smiling and obviously amused. What was the occasion and the story behind the photograph? The memory cells are now beginning to stir.

About a fortnight earlier, as I entered my office to start the day's work, my secretary, Mrs Lillian Dakers, told me that the Mexican consul, Señor Almirez, had phoned a few minutes earlier to ask if I could see him urgently. I told her to ring back straightaway to say that I was on my way and would be with him shortly. I then drove to the corner of Gabourel Lane and Hutson Street where the consulate, which also served as the residence, was situated. The building, of wooden construction and painted white, was set back 50 yards from Gabourel Lane in a large garden full of tropical trees and shrubs and overlooked on the Hutson Street side by St Catherine's Convent school. In the humid atmosphere the colourful green, white and red Mexican flag drooped limply from the top of the flagpole in the centre of the garden. A straight path led from the house to the road and at the gate, waiting to meet me, was the consul, Señor Almirez.

As in other professions, any attempt to describe a stereotype diplomat is likely to conjure up an image well wide of the mark. Indeed, I doubt whether many people meeting Señor Almirez for the first time would have recognized him as the diplomat he most certainly was. He was a small, squat, corpulent man who usually wore baggy white trousers and a crumpled *guyabera* (Mexican style shirt – that is to say a loose shirt with many pleats and pockets worn outside the trousers). As such, he cut a sorry figure. His looks were also against him. He had a large domed head, almost bald save for a wisp of hair at the front, a heavily lined forehead and a cast in one eye that unfortunately gave him an undeserved shifty look. A visiting British journalist, so I understand, once described him as a character straight out of a Graham Greene novel in a Latin American setting. That, if true, summed him up beautifully, although it failed to acknowledge that he was an Anglophile, a highly cultured man and given to great personal kindnesses. In this cruel world, alas, appearances count for so much, even though they are often deceptive.

We exchanged courtesies and when Señor Almirez mentioned that he was looking forward to retiring shortly from the Mexican foreign service, I gallantly and tactfully protested that he was surely far too young to be contemplating such a move. He demurred and added that he had now become tired and was looking for a life outside public service. He then went on to say for no particular reason (unless it was to explain his tiredness) 'You know, Mr Godden, in Mexico we start f***ing before we are 13.' In fact, I did not know. Indeed, this was a piece of unsolicited information that had hitherto not come my way. But obviously the consul felt he should share it with me. Resisting the puerile rejoinders rooted in barrack-room days that flitted across my mind such as, 'lucky you're not superstitious', or, conversely, perhaps, the old Housey Housey (Bingo) cry whenever number 13 came out of the bag, 'unlucky for some', I tried to look serious and sympathetic while contemplating the sexual mores of precocious Mexican teenagers. In those long lost days of innocence it never occurred to me that within a decade or so the Mexican practice in this respect would become commonplace among teenagers throughout the world and would far exceed the Mexican wave in terms of practice and popularity.

This diversion aside, Señor Almirez came to the point of our meeting. 'The 16 September,' he said, 'was Mexico's national day and the governor of Quintana Roo had instructed him to invite the governor of British Honduras and senior officials to the celebrations to be held in Chetumal that day.' Aware that 15 and not 16 September was the common national day for neighbouring former Spanish states, I thought it necessary to query the date mentioned. I was told that Mexico was almost unique in the region by adopting the 16th, thus reminding me that a little knowledge openly displayed in trying to impress can be a dangerous thing. We then discussed relevant details. Having ascertained sufficient supplementary information about numbers, accommodation and programme, I undertook to inform the governor of the Mexican authorities' kind invitation and let him (the consul) have a response before the end of the day.

In accordance with procedure, I first referred the invitation to the chief secretary, Michael Porcher, who was enthusiastic about the idea of taking a weekend break in Mexico. He then arranged for the two of us to see the governor, who we knew would want us to respond positively because Mexico was a good and important neighbour. This the latter confirmed. He said, however, that because of prior commitments that day he would be unable to attend personally but that the chief secretary should represent him. He added that he was prepared to look after the shop alone, so to speak, and that he thought that the chief justice and I together with such heads of department as could be spared should attend. I suspect that his generous decision to allow the temporary absence from the colony of so many of his senior staff was possibly prompted by the prospect of a few days of peace and quiet with 'that lot' away. Accordingly, Michael took soundings and subsequently drew up a list of names, which I passed on to Señor Almirez. Formal invitations followed.

The programme that accompanied the invitation called on us to arrive at a specified hotel in Chetumal on the afternoon of Sunday 15, attend functions that evening and the national day celebrations the following day, allowing us to return to the colony on Tuesday 17 September. Here I should explain that Chetumal is just a few miles into Mexico from its southern border with British Honduras.

Shortly after lunch on the Sunday a small caravan of invitees (which incidentally included politicians, other dignitaries, and prominent businessmen and their wives) set off for Chetumal, a distance of about 96 miles. The first 11 miles north from Belize is along a narrow causeway built over mangrove swamp with the Belize River to its left and the Caribbean Sea to its right. At mile 11 there is a turnoff to the west leading to Stanley Field Airport, so named in honour of the then secretary of state, Oliver Stanley, who opened it in January 1945. Thereafter, the main road continued northwards in a winding fashion over a surface resembling the face of the moon, with potholes and craters more obvious than actual road surface. Traversing this was slow and difficult and did little to prolong the longevity of the cars' suspension. Once through Orange Walk we crossed New River by way of the Tower Hill ferry, a large raft winched across manually and capable of accommodating several vehicles along with their passengers. The road then ran another 28 miles to Corozal, the most northerly town in the colony, and then on for another eight miles towards the Mexican frontier where a ferry across the River Hondo connected with the road to and from Chetumal. For the record I should perhaps mention that shortly afterwards the Mexican authorities built a bridge to replace this ferry.

The journey northwards was through flat and generally uninspiring country, but not without points of interest. The rectangular thatched Maya adobe cottages at Orange Walk, for example, which follow centuries of conventional design, gave the area a distinctly Central American appearance and atmosphere. Their walls are made up of close vertical sticks covered, inside and out, with several inches of a mixture of whitewashed clay, lime and hair. The roof is thatched with fan-shaped juana or bay leaves. If invited inside, the visitor would probably be greeted by the bizarre sight in such a setting of posters depicting the royal family and British tourist attractions such as Parliament, Buckingham Palace, and Windsor, Edinburgh and Caernafon Castles serving as wallpaper. In an attempt to sustain the British connection, the Central Office of Information in London would have sent these to the local information department, which, at a loss to know where to display them, would have forwarded them to schools or rural communities always on the lookout for colourful posters with which to adorn their bare walls.

Near the Tower Hill ferry I saw a Mennonite preacher and his wife driving past briskly in a horse-drawn carriage. Dressed in black, like Puritans from another century as depicted in old oil paintings, they presented quite an unusual and archaic picture. In this connection I should mention that preachers in Mennonite communities have no pastoral duties but simply conduct services on a Sunday. For the other six days of the week they are farmers like everyone else and obliged to work for their living in exactly the same way. As this was a Sunday I had seen a rare sight.

Our rooms at the hotel in Chetumal had already been allocated. I had struck lucky, so I thought, for I alone had been provided with a large room to myself. All the others were placed two to a room. The designation of my post, Principal Secretary (External Affairs) as relayed by Señor Almirez had seemingly carried weight with my counterparts in the Mexican Ministry of Foreign Affairs (MFA). Very commendable, too, was my appreciative reaction.

The walls of the room were panelled in a dark wood and the furniture was equally dark and heavy looking – in effect, a bit gloomy. The focal point was a heavily quilted double bed. Was there any significance in this, I wondered? In a reverie of romantic fantasy I conjured up a picture of an alluring *señorita*, provided by the MFA, slinking into my room at the end of the day to round off the celebrations in what romantic fiction writers of old might have described as 'a time honoured way'. Mind you, even in my imagination, a douche of cold water was immediately directed at such thoughts. As an Englishman with a puritanical upbringing in which strict observance of the marriage vows had been emphasized (to say nothing of what the neighbours might think of such goings-on) there was never any shadow of doubt that I would reject this imaginary siren's eye-fluttering advances and that she would be sent packing forthwith. But I must confess that the train of thought thus engendered tended to linger longer in my imagination than such a summary rejection deemed necessary. Yet, even as I was engaged in this private fantasy, other forces were at work to dispel such romantic dreaming, for, given the way of the world, envy and status invariably raised their ugly heads to bring my fantasy firmly down to earth.

This manifested itself in the form of Michael Porcher who, on looking in to see how my room compared with his, had no doubt whatsoever that a mistake had been made in the matter of room allocation and that this would be rectified by our switching rooms. He reasoned that, as chief secretary and accordingly the most senior government officer present, he could not be expected to share with others while sole occupancy was possible, albeit at my expense. He had the grace to apologize for pulling rank and smiled as he did so, but I must say that I saw precious little of the sorrow he professed at this. However, just as he was no doubt congratulating himself at trumping my ace, as it were, he was beaten by a heavier card played by the chief justice. It was the usual judicial ploy, namely that it would be invidious for someone in his special position to share a room with a person, however respectable, who might appear before him in court one day either as the accused or as a witness. In such an event his judgement might be open to subsequent charges of favouritism or bias. It was a weak excuse, no doubt, but an effective one when deployed by so august a personage as the chief justice. Michael knew better than to resist and gave way gracefully, leaving me to contemplate, not for the first time, that colonial protocol moves less in mysterious ways its wonders to perform and more in relation to the pecking order and perceptions of status.

After we had settled in, showered and dressed for the evening (the highlight of which was to be a buffet supper at the home of a prominent local businessman) Michael Porcher, the commissioner of police, Bruce Taylor, the principal auditor, Norman Stalker, and I ventured on to the streets of Chetumal for a quiet drink before the evening's festivities got under way. We found a pleasant and respectable looking café and tried out our limited Spanish on the waiter, *Cuatro whisky por favor*, which he seemed to understand. While he was gone Bruce asked if we knew the Spanish word for lavatory, for he was, as he inelegantly put it, 'bursting'. In the absence of any response from the others I suggested he might try the word *caballeros* on the waiter on his return as it meant 'gentlemen', which in Britain, at least, carried a lavatorial connotation.

The waiter duly returned carrying a tray on which had been placed four glasses, a carafe of water, an ice bucket and a bottle of 'Black and White' whisky. As he was about to pour from the bottle,

Bruce barked at him, *caballeros*. The waiter looked puzzled. Bruce tried again, this time a bit louder. The waiter again looked nonplussed, but, after a few seconds, a glimmer of understanding lit up his face in a manner now reminiscent of Manuel in the old BBC television series *Fawlty Towers*. Responding with, *si*, he picked up the whisky bottle and made off to the bar. 'Bloody fool', said Bruce, 'what does he think he's up to?' We did not have to wait long to find out. The waiter returned with a triumphant smile on his face, this time carrying a bottle of 'White Horse' whisky. Then the *peso* dropped. Apart from meaning 'gentlemen', *caballeros* also means 'horsemen'. So, to be fair, the waiter had intelligently assumed that we were asking for a change in the brand of whisky. And what could be more appropriate in the circumstances than 'White Horse?' But none of this was any consolation to Bruce who by now was oozing sweat from his forehead as he tried to control the force of nature. However, a simple question, 'toilets?' brought a pointed direction, and a much relieved Bruce (both before and after) shot off like an arrow in the direction indicated. And so on to the rest of the evening's entertainment.

The supper party to which we had been invited had brought together a large assembly of guests who roamed the huge house and spacious gardens in good humour and animated conversation. The house blazed with light and the garden, with coloured lights strung out between the trees, looked like fairyland. A marimba band could occasionally be heard above the daunting hum of conversation and laughter. The evening was warm and pleasant outdoors; the food was plentiful and good and liquor flowed. Among the many guests to whom I spoke was an American, one of two bullfighters whom we were to see performing the following morning. I plied him with many questions about his calling, the most significant perhaps being 'What are your emotions when faced by a charging bull?' He replied laughingly, 'I'm shit scared.' This, as an Englishman, I attributed to the false modesty of a brave man deliberately underplaying obvious danger. He would no doubt show us his mettle in the arena. And so the evening agreeably and quickly passed into night and we returned to our hotel ready for a good night's rest in anticipation of the national day programme lined-up for the following day.

After breakfast we were transported to the municipal buildings where we were introduced to the governor of Quintana Roo and local dignitaries before being conducted to our seats. Courtesies thus observed we sat watching the parade go by – carnival floats, bands and all sorts of colourful pageantry. A march past of a detachment of the Mexican army signalled the release of a hundred or so doves, which were, I suppose, expected to fly off to some destination rather like homing pigeons. Yet, like humans, birds can be unpredictable. Very few rose much above head height and most of them were soon mixed up with the feet of the marching men. This was to give rise to the indignant squawking of the birds and the shuffling of soldiers' boots as they tried to avoid stepping on them. For a short time there was chaos. But in the carnival atmosphere such a minor mishap was easily brushed off as being part of the entertainment. The parade finally ended and soon champagne was flowing in our enclosure. It was then time to move off to the bullfight.

To the best of my knowledge there was no bullring as such in Chetumal. The venue we attended appeared to be the car park of the local football stadium, but it might have been an area of waste ground. Temporary metal scaffolding on the shady side of the ground facilitated elevated seating for the invited guests and perimeter fencing had been installed. At strategic intervals around the arena were *burladeros*, shields of wooden planks offering pro-tection to those inside the ring who might wish to escape the attention of a rampaging bull. Not having seen a bullfight before I had no idea of what to expect. It soon, however, became evident that what we were about to witness would bear little relationship to the activities at the Plaza de Toros in Mexico City where professionalism of a high standard is demanded by the bullfighting cognoscenti. Only young and inexperienced bulls were to perform and there was to be no killing. In other words the team assembled that day were amateur *torero*s and drawn from one of the lower divisions at that. This was soon to become apparent.

After the governor and his party arrived there was a parade of par-ticipants. It included picadors on horseback with their lances (looking like book illustrations of Don Quixote in one of his windmill tilting sorties), *banderillero*s and the matador I had met the previous night and his colleague, both looking colourful and resplendent in their silk suits of lights heavily encrusted with embroidery. They circled the ring to music relayed over a loud-speaker that even British Rail might have scrapped for its mangled sounds and distortions. On reaching the governor's box the matadors doffed their hats and gave a slight bow. Thereafter, the parade dispersed and the stage was set for the bullfighting to begin.

In due course a young bull was released into the arena. It was clearly bewildered. In an attempt to provoke it, the picadors prodded it with their lances but it showed no sign of animation. Others joined in the baiting without any obvious show of success. At last my matador friend made his appearance trailing the traditional red cape. By this time the bull was getting restless and irritable and beginning to charge at anyone who attracted its attention. Finally, enraged by the attention of the picadors and others, the bull set off in the direction of the matador who, with a less than enthusiastic flourish of his cape, allowed it to pass. This performance was repeated several more times with no great danger to either the bull or the matador. But now the bull was becoming increasingly enraged and beginning to charge with greater and greater belligerence. Once again he charged, this time his horns only just clearing the matador's ribcage and, before the latter could properly compose himself, the bull had turned and was thundering back towards him with the clear intention of doing him an injury. Demonstrating that discretion is better than valour, the matador took off like a rocket for the nearest of the *burladeros* and safety. The audience, stunned at first, began to whistle and hiss. To sounds of derisive laughter the reluctant matador was coaxed out only for his nerve to fail once again. At this point I realized that what he had told me the night before about being 'shit scared' in such a situation was a fact and not false modesty. Meanwhile, confused by the noise the crowd was making, the bull crashed through the perimeter fencing and the next thing I saw was it charging and rocking an ice-cream vendor's van with its horns while people in the vicinity scattered in all directions. For us official spectators lunch was now beckoning and we were expected to leave because the transport to collect us had arrived. Thus, I missed subsequent events. But if this was bullfighting, I was all for it.

Lunch and a siesta set us up for the final engagement, a dinner that evening at a nearby restaurant, which, set back from the road, had a large and spacious dining area. When we arrived, the tables were already set out and covered with colourful tablecloths enhanced by shining cutlery and sparkling glassware. Apart from a centerpiece of a vase of flowers, each table had been allocated a squat bottle of 'Old Parr' whisky, which, interestingly was not a familiar brand in British Honduras. In the event, we dined well and liquor flowed. In addition to the whisky already provided, wine, tequila and beer lubricated our tongues and contributed to a relaxed atmosphere. A band provided background music. After dinner came the cabaret, which consisted of a number of musical turns and at that point several of us were invited forward to be in a better position to see and hear. My companions in this move were Bruce Taylor, Eugene Robinson and two women from our table. We were the five in the photograph mentioned above, which must have been taken at that time. So what was attracting our attention? It was, in fact, the star of the show, a vivacious and popular female Mexican cabaret artiste with an agreeable personality and melodious singing voice. However, as the lyrics were in Spanish, only those familiar with the nuances of the language were able to understand what she was actually singing about. Eugene Robinson was such a person and he is the one in the photograph who is seen smiling.

After I had been given the photograph (by whom I can longer recall) I showed it to him and asked what had tickled his fancy. He explained that the lady to whom we were listening in the cabaret was at that time singing a particularly risqué song, which he had found most amusing.

After such a long story this explanation will no doubt come as an anti-climax to anyone expecting something more profound or exciting. But the purpose of this account is not to underline any moral or clear up any deep mystery. It is simply to point out that, as in this instance, looking at a photograph many years after it was taken often unlocks memories that have remained dormant for years. You should perhaps try it sometime.

Chapter 22
Cops and Robbers

NOWADAYS, MOST of us accept, with varying degrees of reluctance, the principle of redistribution of wealth through the tax system. Those who gain from this are, of course, more enthusiastic about its virtues than those who do not. Both groups, however, take a less philosophical view of those who enter their property uninvited and walk off with some of their valuables and other possessions in order to redress a perceived imbalance between 'haves' and 'have-nots'. It is not only the loss of possessions that rankles. The turning over of private papers and items of clothing by a total stranger or strangers gives rise to a sense of personal violation. Compound this with a feeling of frustration generated by the antics of the local constabulary, whose detectives seemed to have Peter Sellers as Inspector Clouseau as a role model, then you may have some idea of how we as a family felt when our house was burgled.

This particular story starts at a routine cocktail party given by His Excellency the Governor Sir Peter Stallard at Government House. The guest list followed the usual pattern: members of the Executive and Legislative Councils, prominent business people, senior civil servants, church leaders and other worthy and responsible citizens. It was my lot to attend most of these functions, almost as a duty, and so it was on this occasion. My specific role, devised by the governor, apart from that of a sort of glorified ADC, was to start the exodus of guests as the 8.00 p.m. deadline approached; otherwise they would linger on indefinitely as long as there was the prospect of another drink in the offing. In that role I would approach the governor ostentatiously at, say, ten minutes to eight, and in a loud voice say something to the effect of, 'I know you have other things to do after this, Your Excellency, so I will set an example by leaving now.' This was capable of many variations and generally worked. The governor's other engagement was, of course, none other than the prospect of a few hours of peace and quiet after his duty as host had been discharged. This procedure was followed on that particular evening.

On leaving Government House, Florence and I moved towards our car, which was parked in Regent Street near Wesley School. Just behind us was Sandy Hunter (subsequently Sir Alexander Hunter and Speaker of the National Assembly after independence) who was then minister of agriculture and natural resources. 'What about one for the road at the Fort George Hotel?' he suggested. We agreed and shortly afterwards were ensconced in the hotel lounge. Already busy with the usual weekend trade, it began to fill up as others leaving the Government House party began to drift in. Waiters plied between tables taking orders or delivering drinks. On a small dais in an area that served as a dance floor a large black musician sat at a grand piano entertaining the audience in what might be described as 'the Fats Waller style'. The songs he warbled, unlike those that pass as popular music now, were tuneful and the lyrics clearly discernable. But, then, I am now crotchety, long in the tooth and relate to popular music not later than the early 1960s!

It was while he was giving voice to a then popular number, 'Saturday Night' that I was surprised to see the chief secretary, Michael Porcher, enter the lounge and head towards our table and correctly assumed that I was the person he had come to see. Had the Guatemalans invaded, I wondered, or was I to be asked to decipher an urgent telegram from London? Neither seemed likely for it was not long since I had spoken to him at the cocktail party. So what was it? I was soon to learn. His message was unexpected. 'I am sorry to be the bearer of bad news,' he said, 'but your daughters have just phoned to say that your house has been broken into and that they have been unable to track you down to let you know.' He added that he had promised to find us and had informed the police who would send CID officers to the scene early the next morning.

As Florence and I digested this unwelcome information the singer at the piano was in full voice as he rendered an encore: the plaintive tale of some unfortunate chap who, having just got paid and facing another Saturday night in his own company, was in search of 'a honey to help me spend my money', presumably motivated by thoughts that were less than altruistic. As it was, I thought it rather a pity that the burglars had not called to relieve him of some instead of breaking into our home. Some people do not know when they are well off. So we finished our drinks, thanked Michael for taking the trouble to find us to break the news and Sandy for his commiserations, and then departed.

Obviously, we wanted to get home as quickly as possible to reassure our daughters and to assess the extent of the damage. On the way home I reflected that there were not many places in the world where one could be found within minutes. Yet Michael had found us straightaway even though the Fort George Hotel was not one of our regular haunts and, so far as I knew, no one had any idea that we were going there. But in Belize in those days nothing escaped local eyes. It seemed to be full of Miss Marples or their male equivalents watching every movement. More is the pity, therefore, that because of the Government House cocktail party the govern-ment quarters at Newtown Barracks were virtually deserted that evening. Obviously, the burglars were well aware of that.

On arrival home Jan and Sue were waiting for us at the top of the flight of stairs leading to the front door, which was open. From the lights inside the house we could see where the thieves had entered. They had removed a number of the glass louvre window sections and had then cut a large square in the metal mosquito netting below, allowing for someone to squeeze through. Inside the house the signs of entry were equally obvious. Drawers had been pulled out and clothes and papers rifled through. At first it seemed that nothing of value had been taken. But on closer inspection we discovered that a large store of liquor that had recently been delivered in preparation for a party we were to give a week later had been taken from the storeroom. Only one bottle remained and that was of sherry. Our cutlery had also been taken along with a few trinkets.

I phoned the police station, where it was confirmed that the break-in had been recorded and I was reminded to leave things as we found them until the CID detectives arrived. So we embarked on an uneasy night's sleep wondering what the morning would bring. In the event, my old friend Wellby, now a CID sergeant with a UK detective training course under his belt, was the officer in charge. While his colleague took statements, he roamed the house looking for clues. He paid particular attention to the sideboard from which the cutlery had been taken and also the sherry bottle. He said that both were a source of fingerprints. He then brought out the tools of the trade, dusted the sideboard with powder to show various blurred patches, which he confidently asserted were the culprit's fingerprints, took away the sherry bottle for closer examination (and evidence for the court should an arrest be made) and said not to touch the sideboard until he told us to do so.

Well, Saturday drifted into Sunday and Sunday into Monday and still there was no word from Wellby. On the Tuesday I called on him at his office at police headquarters. He was his usual pleasant and agreeable self. 'When are you coming to photograph the fingerprints?' I asked. He looked puzzled and then said that this was out of the question for the obvious reason that he had no photographic equipment for that purpose. I then asked what I thought was a reasonable question: 'Then why did you dust for fingerprints if you could take no follow-up action?' 'Because that was what I was taught on my course,' he replied triumphantly. What could I say to that? I now realized that there was little prospect of the cutlery being recovered (the drink would have been consumed by now and its recovery a lost cause) unless someone informed on the thieves. This was unlikely because locals would have regarded my family and me as affluent outsiders who could well afford to suffer financial loss. It so happened that the insurance did not cover the cutlery and, equally importantly, there was little hope of buying comparable replacements locally. That, however, was our problem.

From time to time I enquired about progress. Ever the optimist, Wellby was always following a promising lead with the prospect of an arrest in the offing. When no one had been brought to book he then switched tack by suggesting that the culprits had fled to Mexico and that accordingly the trail had gone cold. Moreover, he added, now they were aware that the British Honduras police knew who they were, it was unlikely they would return in the foreseeable future. As I inferred earlier, shades of Peter Sellers as 'Inspector Clouseau'. We never recovered the cutlery or liquor and Wellby was too tactful to raise the subject ever again. For my part, I knew it would be useless to do so. And so the story of our break-in comes to a close. Well, not quite; there was a sequel.

Some months later, after the burglary had all but been forgotten, Florence and I returned home one Sunday afternoon having been to a curry lunch with nearby friends. It was a particularly hot day and, with nothing special to do, a siesta beckoned. No sooner had I dropped off into a deep sleep than a loud hammering on the front door awakened me. Arousing myself with difficulty and reluctance I went to see who it was. It was Corporal Belisle of the British Honduras police force. He whipped up a smart salute with one hand and waved a bottle under my nose with the other. 'Returning the evidence, Sir,' he said, adding, 'you will have to sign for it.' With that he produced a tattered school exercise book and pointed to where my signature should be appended. I duly signed. By this time I realized that the bottle was the one that the burglars had kindly left behind and the one Welby had taken as evidence in the unlikely event of them being apprehended. I looked at it: it was empty. 'But it is empty', I said. 'Yes, Sir', said Belisle no doubt suitably impressed by my powers of observation. 'Not much point in returning it then', I added sarcastically. 'We always return such evidence when a case is closed', was his rejoinder. 'You don't suppose Sergeant Welby would be willing to investigate the mystery of who drank the sherry, do you?' I parried. Corporal Belisle grinned, gave another salute and roared off on his motorcycle. All that was missing, apart from the drink and cutlery, was the presence of 'Inspector Clouseau' himself. As it was, the element of farce was preserved to the last.

Chapter 23
The Cockscombs

'A DILIGENT SEARCH among the archives of the colony and a careful reading of most of the books that have either treated directly or indirectly of British Honduras, have not been productive of evidence that the Coxcomb (*sic*) Mountains have ever been explored.' Thus begins the *Report of the Expedition to the Unexplored Cockscomb Mountains of British Honduras* prepared by the then colonial secretary Mr Hubert Jerningham, and submitted to His Excellency the Governor Mr R. T. Goldsworthy, CMG, on 8 June 1888.[1]

In that account (hereafter referred to as the Goldsworthy Report or simply the report) it was claimed that the surveyor general, Mr Gordon Allen, and Mr J. Bellamy had ascended the highest point in the range, which they had named 'Victoria Peak' in honour of Her Majesty the reigning Queen. However, expeditions to the area in the 1920s pointed to confused descriptions and incorrect mapping, which suggested that the topography of the range had never been properly mastered and that the peak ascended and named 'Victoria' may not have been the highest. Herein lies a story and connected esoteric local mystery of minor proportions that was to fascinate me and a few friends during our service in the colony and evoke memories even to this day.

So where in the colony is the Cockscomb range located and what prompted the 1888 expedition? In the opening paragraph of Chapter 19, I present an outline of the topography of British Honduras. Within it, the Maya Mountains are situated mainly in the southernmost district, Toledo. The highest section of these is an independent range or spur known as the Cockscombs (just under 4000 feet), which stands out as a precipitous jagged ridge of quartzite with its steepest slopes thinly clothed in mosses. It runs from east to west for about 15 miles and falls within the Stann

Creek District. It is so named because part of the profile of the range resembles a cock's comb.

In 1888 the Maya Mountains and surrounding district were virtually unexplored. The primary reason for this was the poor system of communications to facilitate travel. The southern towns of Monkey River, Stann Creek and Punta Gorda could be reached by sea. Elsewhere, travel was by river, horse or on foot along village tracks or logging trails. Heavy bush and deep forest covered much of the area away from the coastal plain. Consequently, although the Cockscomb peaks were visible from the sea or from high points around Stann Creek, they were soon lost to sight as one moved towards them. Then again, the mountains had always been shrouded in a cloud of mystery. Local Amerindian and Carib people believed that evil spirits and mysterious creatures guarded the peaks and that the main peak (believed to be the location of a cavern full of gold) was surrounded by a lake and unapproachable. In short, for the local population at large, it was an area to avoid. But times were changing.

By the time Queen Victoria ascended the throne in 1837 the geography of the world had been fully revealed in outline. The next stage saw a more intensive exploration of the interior of continents and countries in search of scientific knowledge, or of mineral, agricultural or trading opportunities. The opening up of Africa was a classic example of this. Explorers' travels were translated into maps, and anthropological and zoological findings were widely disseminated in scientific journals around the world. So, as the end of the nineteenth century approached, only a few pockets in the world's jungles, deserts and polar regions remained completely unknown. In early 1888 the area around the Cockscomb Mountains was such a pocket.

At the same time, the European powers were still vying with each other for colonial possessions and the British were especially active in this respect. This was the heyday of the 'Pax Britannica'. One feature of that period was a tendency to name new geographical discoveries after the queen – hence Victoria Falls, Lake Victoria, the Australian state of Victoria and Victoria Land, to name but a few examples.

By the late nineteenth century the spirit of the age had pervaded

British Honduras. In 1872, in a survey of the western district, Messrs Mechling and Warner came in sight of the Cockscomb range from about 20 miles away and wrote 'that it presented much the appearance of a Cockscomb and at its highest point cannot be less than 5000 feet'.[2] The following year, 1873, Messrs Drake and Worth, while prospecting for gold up the Sittee River, also came in sight of the range bearing south and, according to their notes, subsequently explored an unspecified part of the mountains above 1000 feet before giving up any further attempt.[3] In 1876, while in the course of a survey of the Monkey River, a very competent independent local surveyor, Wilson, reached the range and ascended one of the peaks. In his terse but comprehensive notes he mentioned that he 'followed the trail between the 2nd and 3rd peak from the west' adding 'that the 2nd is inaccessible owing to the eastern face being precipitous'.[4]

Whether these reports influenced the decision to organize an official expedition to the region is now a matter of idle speculation. Certainly, they were studied. What we do know is that in 1888 a large expedition led by Governor Goldsworthy conducted the first serious exploration of the Cockscomb range. It is possible that this reflected the spirit of the age and a desire to explore a hitherto unexplored area that might reveal mineral or archaeological finds. A cynic, however, might suggest an alternative explanation. As explained earlier (Chapter 9), Goldsworthy left the colony in 1886 under a cloud and the Colonial Office's decision to send him back for another tour was greeted with dismay locally. It is, therefore, not unreasonable to suggest that he felt he was under an obligation to the British government for supporting him. What could be more appropriate than to return that confidence by conducting an expedition to a previously unexplored mountain range and then to name the highest peak after the monarch and another after the secretary of state for the colonies, which he did. These days it would be regarded as 'a brown nose job'. But let us be charitable and assume that the former explanation was the most likely one. And so the expedition was mounted under Goldsworthy's leadership.

The team consisted of the colonial secretary, Jerningham, surveyor general, Allen, and 'four other gentlemen' (Messrs Bellamy, Wickham, Gabb and Blockley, all of whom had surveying or other skills to contribute) supported by a party of 22 locals employed as cutters, cooks, doreymen, mule drivers and messengers. Nowadays, the size and composition of such a party would invite the analogy of sledgehammers and nuts, but it should be remembered that they were visiting a hitherto unexplored region and it was, after all, the imperial age when 'gentlemen' expected to have local labour available to cope with many of the chores.

The departure date was fixed for Thursday 5 April. The night before, the governor gave a ball at Government House for Major Caulfield and the officers of the second West Indian Regiment, the troops then providing the garrison, which was expected to depart from the colony before the expedition returned.

As the Goldsworthy Report records the expedition began in style:

> At 9 a.m., Dr Mumby photographed the Governor, the Colonial Secretary, the Surveyor General, Mr Wickham and Mr F. Blockley in a group on the steps of Government House. Variously dressed with machetes to which they were not accustomed, Soudan (sic) water bottles slung over the shoulder and a couple of rifles never to be used they presented an effective picture.[5]

Where, I wonder, is that photograph now? We also learn from the report that, by way of equipment, each was allowed a rug, two waterproof sheets, a mosquito net, a tin pannikin and a plate, a machete, a water bottle, a set of pyjamas, three flannel shirts and one change of clothes – the whole to be carried in one waterproof bag – no doubt by an accompanying porter.

The report follows the diary pattern: in other words, it is in chronological order with each day's events recorded in sequence. For the purpose of this chapter, however, I propose to summarize details of the events leading to the ascent of presumed 'Victoria' and then add comments based on other recorded details. One further point I wish to make is that the approach to the range was from the south and the intention was to reach the foothills and then progress from east to west along the line of the peaks comprising the cockscomb.

Outline of Cockscomb peaks bearing S70°W as seen from a hill 620 feet
high, three hours N40°W of Scorpion Bank.

Immediately after the group photograph was taken, the governor
and his party set off south on his barge *Experience* for All Pines on
the Sittee River and arrived there at 7.00 p.m. Messrs Gabb and
Bellamy had arrived earlier. Travelling variously by horse, mule, foot
and dory the whole party assembled at Lopez Bank on 8 April.
Moving on, they set up camp at Price's Bank, to be renamed
Scorpion Camp after the presence of a number of that particular
species of arachnids caused a degree of panic, especially after the
colonial secretary was stung by one of them. It was so painful that as
he recorded at the time it 'brought the notion of death immediately
to my mind'.[6] Later that day, Bellamy, after climbing a tree to a
height of 50 feet, caught a glimpse of the Cockscomb range bearing
southwest to northwest seemingly about ten miles away. Early the
following day Messrs Allen and Wickham ascended a hill south of
the camp that afforded a 'glorious view of the mountain range'.[7] This
was christened Observation Hill.

At this point in the narrative Jerningham refers to a sketch of the
view made by Wickham with the words: 'Among the numerous
drawings made by Mr Wickham during the expedition, not one has
the power or gives a more faithful rendering of a grand landscape
than the sketch he took from this point.'[8] Yet, the Goldsworthy
Report contains none of his illustrations. However, in Bellamy's own
account of the expedition, which he sent separately to the Royal

Geographical Society (see sketch above), several drawings are included. As one of Wickham's functions appears to have been that of official artist it seems reasonable to conclude that the drawings were his and not those of Bellamy. This seems to be confirmed by the caption under the sketch reproduced above, which coincides with the position of Observation Hill.

Even now, after all these years, it is possible to sense the excitement of the party at seeing this first close-up glimpse of the Cockscomb peaks rising tall above the forest ceiling.

The foothills of the range were reached on Tuesday 10 April and the first ridge (named 'Prior Ridge' after the governor's wife's maiden name) was reached at a height of 1240 feet from which the first or most easterly peak was clearly discernable. From here it was to take the next five days to explore the main peaks, a task that was to prove both difficult and hazardous. Because of bare and precipitous ridges it was invariably necessary to descend to lower levels and then reclimb in order to move from one peak to another. Here again, the terrain was unhelpful and involved crossing deep-sided ravines, gullies and streams as well as clambering over slippery rocks and boulders. However, these diversions gave an opportunity to study the geology of the range, indications of metals and minerals, trees, plants and mosses. There were occasions when it was possible to follow contours rather than ascend or descend, but this sometimes led to confusion when lateral and vertical tracks crossed.

On 11 April Bellamy and Allen, whose tracks the governor and Wickham followed, ascended the most easterly peak to a height of 1240 feet. The latter reached 1700 feet but had to descend when the governor experienced an attack of giddiness that prevented further progress. This peak was named 'Goldsworthy'. The following morning, 12 April, Allen and Bellamy skirted Goldsworthy Peak and explored the river bed below. Striking upwards they topped a ridge just below what they assumed to be the next peak. This they ascended to a height of 1800 feet. Pine trees and 'splendid' and varied orchids were seen towards the top of the peak which was named 'Bellamy' (see Wickham's illustration on p. 285).

Descending they formed a camp in a ravine at a height of 1000 feet. This was given the name of Reunion Camp. At this point an interesting omission should be mentioned. Two peaks, 'Goldsworthy' and 'Bellamy', had been partially climbed within two days. Yet the profile that accompanied the Goldsworthy Report drawn up by Allen (see Plate A, p. 293) shows a cluster of three peaks, 'Goldsworthy-Molar-Bellamy'. The mystery is why there is no mention of the 'Molar' in the narrative or, for that matter, in Bellamy's subsequent account. This was to be the subject of comment by later expeditions as indeed was the reference to pine trees.

On 13 April provisions were brought up to Reunion Camp in preparation for the climbing of the main peak. It was here that the main party was to assemble. The route westward was explored and it appeared from a brief reconnaissance that a long narrow saddle east of the main peak offered the best approach.

Next day, 14 April, Allen, Wickham and Jerningham followed this saddle (to be christened 'Blockley Saddle') where, after a dip in the terrain, they came across a peak covered with orchids and ferns. They scrambled to the top, not more than three feet square, and recorded the height as 2000 feet. This, the first on the expedition to be fully ascended, was dubbed 'Jerningham Peak'. Descending and working their way along the contours they found themselves on a gradient of 25 feet to 1 on the shoulder of a much larger peak that was to be called 'Holland' after the then secretary of state for the colonies, Sir Henry Holland (soon to be elevated to the peerage as Lord Knutsford under the Marquess of Salisbury's administration). As this was next to the assumed highest peak, it is not unreasonable, as already suggested, to attribute its naming to a sycophantic and ambitious governor who had already reserved the name 'Victoria' for the highest. The return journey back to Reunion Camp proved to be both tricky and perilous. However, despite numerous scares over its safety the party arrived back safely confident that the ascent of what they presumed to be 'Victoria' could be mounted the next day.

On Sunday 15 April Messrs Wickham and Blockley were sent out to look for an easy route by which to ascend the main peak. The latter remained on the saddle east of the peak at an elevation of 1800 feet to prepare a camp while Wickham continued the ascent, which he managed by climbing round the heads of spurs over many

Sketch of Cockscomb peaks

difficult and dangerous places and, finally, after a precipitous and arduous climb, especially over the last 500 feet, succeeded in reaching within a short distance of the summit. That afternoon the governor, Gabb and Bellamy, who were working their way westward along the saddle to meet Blockley, met Wickham who conveyed the good news that the peak was accessible. He was, however, exhausted by his efforts. He reported that the westward prong of the main peak was about a hundred feet lower in height than the summit and that the high perpendicular rock face was covered to a great thickness with a beautiful moss that afforded a means of ascent in places otherwise inaccessible. Before 7 a.m. on 16 April, Jerningham, who together with Allen had been occupying Reunion Camp, received the following letter brought to him by messenger:

Dear J,

Your man met us on the line of march upwards to 'Jerningham Peak' which we reached. Palpitations ruled supreme for a short time but some of the medicine and a little brandy did me good.

We shall all attack the 'Victoria' one today. Wickham says it is doubtful whether the fig roots will bear any weight: it is almost climbing sheer perpendicular rock for that distance.

& R.T.G.[9]

On receipt of this, Jerningham and Allen moved out of their camp and reached Saddle Camp within 45 minutes. The ascent began at 11.42 a.m. and here the narrative is taken up by Jerningham based on his own experience:

> We retreated before these noble walls of the royal peak, and in order to circumvent them had to go down some 200 feet so that at ¼ past 1, we were only 2270 feet high. At ¼ to 2, however, we had reached 2500. Then the rope had to be used. Mr Allen and I took the lead until we reached a narrow ledge from which a very extensive view could be obtained at a height of 3000 feet, when knowing the Governor's distressing illness and fearing his resolve if we all did, I waited for him while Mr Allen went on by himself. His Excellency arrived some ten minutes later in a condition that was almost alarming, and it was clear that any further ascent from him would have been madness, so we sat together on the lovely pink and white moss and beheld to the south a precipitous rock and to the north a boundless ocean of trees while to the E was a perpendicular rock some 20 feet [200?] in height which Mr Allen, Mr Bellamy, Mr Blockley and six Caribs successfully climbed.[10]

Thereafter, Allen's account is both graphic and relevant. 'The climbing was almost sheer up and the surface of the rock covered with the most exquisite moss from 2 to 3 feet deep affording very unreliable holding.' At 2.20 p.m. he reached what he took to be the highest point, but, while turning around in the limited space to take observations, he noticed through the stunted fig trees another summit. 'A very narrow ledge led to it. But the track along was difficult and dangerous as the moss was so thick that the precipitous edges were hidden by it and great care was necessary whilst picking out a path.' Bellamy and three Caribs joined him. 'And then the five upstanding gave three cheers for Her Majesty Queen Victoria and then three for His Excellency Governor Goldsworthy.'[11]

Observations from the summit were difficult. The weather was hazy and plantation clearing fires along the coast obscured all sight of the sea. None the less, a good panoramic view was had over densely wooded ridges and valleys. Strangely, however, there is no reference in the narrative to the neighbouring peak to the west, which they named, 'Allen', the second highest in the range. Jerningham then records:

> At ¼ to 4 they descended, and on reaching the ledge where the Governor, Mr Wickham and I had rested, lighted a bonfire which tho' it did not burn as well as anticipated was, we afterward heard, observed by sailors along the coast. We also left a bottle, inside which we put a paper commemorating our presence on the majestic peak, and leaving our narrow resting place at 4 p.m. continued by dint of much exertion to get passed (*sic*) all difficulties, as darkness set in. At 8 p.m. we walked into camp.[12]

Camp was broken at 7.30 a.m. on 17 April. Some of the party returned to Saddle Camp where a mark on a tree and an empty sardine can bearing the initial 'G' over the year, 1888, under which the initials 'JAGBWB' were recorded and stuck on a pole to mark the expedition and its principal members. Thereafter it was back to Reunion Camp before spending the night at Scorpion Bank. The governor and those returning to Belize left All Pines on the *Experience* at 10 p.m. on 18 April and the vessel dropped anchor in Belize harbour at 6.00 a.m. the following morning, the expedition having been successfully completed within a fortnight instead of the month originally anticipated. So what had been achieved?

The Cockscomb range had been widely explored for the first time and, although only two peaks had actually been ascended ('Jerningham' and 'Victoria') all the main ones had been named and their heights estimated. While the exploration of the mountain range assumed centre stage, the party in general had many other interests. They saw no signs of early Maya civilization in the area and were able to dispel the many legends and myths surrounding the mountains. Agricultural possibilities were noted and although Bellamy was unable to devote as much time as he would have wished to prospecting, he saw enough to convince himself that there was considerable mineral wealth in the district, although he made no reference to commercial opportunities.

As already indicated, the Goldsworthy Report was written in journal form. It is, in effect, an adventure story of 'Boy's Own' proportions and, as such, easy to read. In the main it displays all the Victorian attention to detail recording aneroid readings, compass bearings, temperatures and exact times. References are made to flora and fauna, trees, bird life, geological features and mineral traces. There are encounters with snakes, scorpions, vampire bats, botlass flies and other irritating or predatory insects with the noise of howling monkeys constantly in the background. At one stage we learn that 'Dr Gabb shot an iguana (huge lizard)with 63 eggs which filled the Caribs with delight, and two macaws which proved excellent eating.'[13] The narrative is not devoid of the lighter aspects of the expedition. Thus it is recorded on 7 April 'that the gay colours of Macaws and other birds of royal plumage, vied with the Governor's red pyjamas'. Also, after dinner on the same night 'that before turning in, three games of whist by the light of a candle stuck into an empty claret bottle ended the day'.[14] But whatever the scientific, land use and resource finding purposes of the expedition, the overriding consideration was undoubtedly, certainly so far as Goldsworthy was concerned, to identify the main peak in the Cockscomb range and to attach to it the name of 'Victoria'.

The weakness of the report is that Jerningham, an administrator in his first year of service in the colony with no specialist technical knowledge, compiled it mainly from what Allen, Bellamy and Wickham had told him or he had gleaned from their notes. Therefore, the narrative is not always as clear as it might have been had, say, Allen written it alone. For example, he mentions that Blockley was with Allen and Bellamy when the main peak was ascended. Yet, in his report, Bellamy makes no reference to him being present on that occasion. Also, Jerningham's account gives the impression that the climbing party's descent from the summit took 15 minutes to join the governor and the others resting below on the ledge. Bellamy, however, records that the latter had left for Saddle Camp before he and his party reached that ledge. It was due to such inconsistencies and confusion in the narrative, and lack of description and precision regarding the identification of peaks, that was to lead successive expeditions in the 1920s to question whether the 1880 expedition had fully mastered the topography. But to be fair to Jerningham, his task was to try and write a readable report based largely on the contributions of others whom one hopes would have been given an opportunity to comment on it and make appropriate amendments before publication.

✧ ✧ ✧

Bellamy wrote a separate, shorter, more succinct and sharper report. It includes three of Wickham's sketches (two of which appear above). Dated 6 October 1888 from his home at Mullins River it was published in *Proceedings, Royal Geographical Society* in 1889 under the heading 'Expedition to the Cockscomb Mountains, British Honduras'.[15] In general, it echoes the topographical findings of the Goldsworthy Report and is equally obscure about the identification and naming of the 'Molar' and the omission of any specific reference to 'Allen Peak'.

However, his observations of the view from the summit of the peak named 'Victoria' differ somewhat from Allen's and are, therefore, worth reproducing:

> The top of the peak is a thorough peak with but little room for moving about, and an extensive view is obtained on all sides. For some distance the prospect is nothing but alternate ridge and valley densely wooded. There are no higher points north of us, but to the south Montague and Omoa in Spanish Honduras were seen towering over the rest. No open Country was seen, nor any of the traditional lakes. I took observations for altitude and cross bearings to localize all the principal points. The barometer was a little under 4000 feet.
>
> The descent from the peak was even more dangerous than the ascent, and we could never have managed it without the rope, so it was late when we reached the shoulder of rock where we had left the rest of the party. They had already started for camp, so as to pass all the difficulties before

darkness overtook them. So we hastened on and reached the
camp on the saddle at 8 p.m.[16]

On other matters, which were perhaps nearer to his heart, he was
clearly impressed by what he perceived to be opportunities for
agricultural and mineral exploitation provided road communications
could be effected and immigration encouraged. Both the Evans
Commission and the treasury economist, Jack Downie subsequently
adopted this theme half a century or so later. But, in the Victorian
era, no serious follow-up action seems to have been taken. Not until
the second half of the twentieth century was any significant attempt
made to improve road communications; but, if I may be forgiven a
pun, it has to be recognized that for all its importance to the local
economy, agriculture has always been a hot potato in British
Honduras when coupled with immigration.

The puzzle is, why did Bellamy, who was not only an experienced
surveyor but also a geologist, and Allen, who was after all the
surveyor general, fail in their observations from the top of 'Victoria'
to mention the next peak to the west, the second highest in the
range, which the expedition named 'Allen'? As already intimated,
some 40 years later their successors were puzzled by and
commented on their failure to do so and their omission from the
narratives of any explanation about the 'Molar'.

With the publication of the Goldsworthy and Bellamy accounts,
another part of the colony's topographical jigsaw had seemingly been
fitted into place. In 1896 a geologist, Dr Carl Sapper, on a traverse
from El Cayo in the west to the coast in the east reached the western
limit of the Cockscomb range. So far as is known, he was the last
person to have reached the mountains until H. T. Grant (who is the
subject of the next chapter) did so in May 1927. The latter's account
is to be found in the December 1927 issue of the *Geographical
Journal*, under the heading 'The Cockscombs Revisited'.[17]

✿ ✿ ✿

On 10 May 1927 Grant, accompanied by two Maya Indians, set out
to reach the range. His purpose as an adventurer, entrepreneur and

prospector was to seek evidence, if any, of the remains of early Mayan civilization, to determine the height at which mahogany might be found and to look for any sign of precious metals. Not until his return did he have sight of the report of the 1888 expedition. Therefore, he had to rely on a route the surveyor general's department provided, which they admitted was 'not too accurate'. In the event, he was to follow initially the path of the Goldsworthy party but then, instead of arriving towards the eastern end of the range, he came up at the end of the second day under the higher peaks on the southern side. One of the accompanying Indians first sighted the mountains and Grant described the moment dramatically: 'crouching close to the ground and peering through the treetops, I saw a spectacle that filled me with awe. There, perhaps four miles away, the cone of a solid rock shot perpendicularly skywards seemingly to float on the very roof of the forest.'[18] Never one to resist a challenge, Grant, accompanied by the Mayans, had a dangerous climb over difficult terrain and in rainy conditions that brought them to a ridge 30–40 yards wide between two large peaks. As the western peak seemed the higher the group chose that one to climb. Using roots, twigs, rocks and the thick moss to give purchase they inched their way to the top of what Grant later supposed was the peak named 'Holland' in the Goldsworthy Report.

Looking eastward from the summit they saw that part of the range was open to view. To the west, however, seemingly within a stone's throw, was what Grant, after reference to the Goldsworthy Report, presumed to be Victoria peak 'revealed as two spires. The southerly perhaps 100 feet higher than its neighbour, set slightly back. The twain rising, sheer, slim and perpendicular 800 or 900 feet from forest shoulders on either side'.[19] He assumed this to be the most westerly point in the range because nothing else was visible in that direction and the twin spires obscured any further view. He judged that any attempt to scale this peak from the east was impossible. With time for the expedition running out he began the return journey; he had observed mahogany growing at 1800 feet and had seen evidence of slight traces of gold, but no archaeological sites.

✧✧✧

The then conservator of forests, J. N. Oliphant, and his deputy Duncan Stevenson mounted a further official expedition the following year. An account is given in the *Geographical Journal* under the heading 'An Expedition to the Cockscomb Mountains, British Honduras, in March 1928'[20] (hereafter referred to as the Forestry Report). The principal terms of reference were to study the region in which the Cockscombs lie and its potential for forestry, agricultural settlement and as a line of approach to the high level mahogany in the western territory. A secondary aim was to clear up doubts about the physiology of the range, and to collect as much information as possible in the space of a short trip on the vegetation, and soil and rock formation. Although the wish to reach the highest point was a natural one, it was made clear at the outset that the expedition was not meant to be a mountain climbing 'stunt'.

Starting on 12 March 1928, Oliphant and Stevenson were accompanied by Westly, whom the Tidewater Lumber Company loaned for the period of the tour along with three Ketchi Indian bearers. Survey of the route was made by prismatic oil compass and cyclometer wheel reading chains. Mapping was carried out by compass and pacing; and data derived from photographs taken *en route* helped materially in their completion. The topography westward of the first of the higher peaks was established mostly by intersections from known points. Surveyors' aneroids were used to determine heights. Binoculars helped locate long range landmarks not easily distinguishable to the naked eye. In short, the expedition was highly professional in its approach.

A preliminary reconnaissance by Stevenson had established the best route and method of approach to the mountains. This, coupled with the employment of animal transport, enabled the party to reach a starting point well up on the range at its eastern end on the afternoon of the second day, 14 March.

The following day they reached what they assumed to be the 'Hill of Pines' referred to in the Goldsworthy Report, from which a view could be had along the range. Like their Victorian predecessors they found that encircling the peaks was difficult and tedious. Therefore,

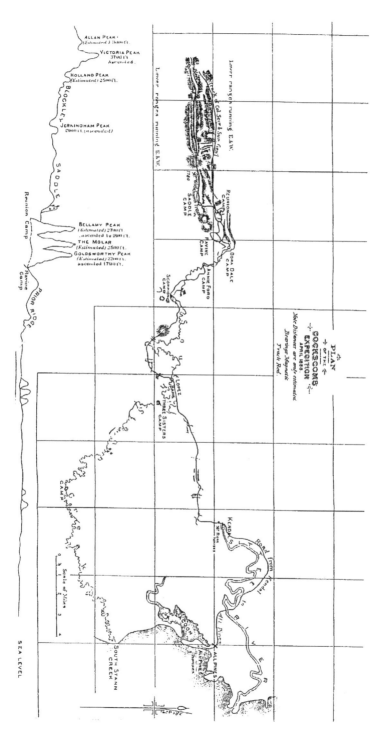

Figure A. Plan of the Cockscomb expedition

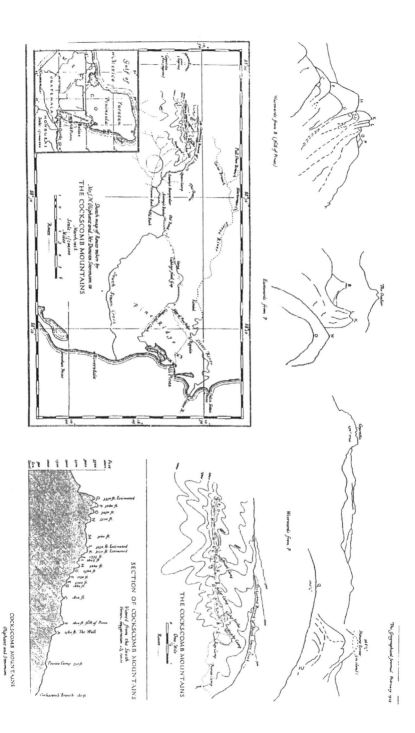

Figure B. The Cockscomb mountains

though recognizing that a certain amount of this was unavoidable, they learnt much earlier that easier progress could be made by keeping to the ridges, however steep they might be.

Moving westward and ascending all peaks as they proceeded (and assigning to them, in order of progression, letters of the alphabet instead of names) they became increasingly baffled as their findings could not be reconciled with those recorded in the Goldsworthy Report. The problem centred on the 'amazing error'[21] in the profile in the map accompanying the Goldsworthy report, which indicated an important cluster of peaks (Goldsworthy–Molar–Bellamy) to the east of the distinctly pictured 'Hill of Pines', which they believed to be the hill marked 'B' on their profile at the eastern end of the range. Looking westward along the main ridge from the 'Hill of Pines' the party concluded that this cluster must be behind them and that the rounded peak facing them and the sharp pinnacle behind it must be 'Holland' and 'Victoria' respectively. They assumed, correctly, that the former was the peak that Grant had ascended the previous year.

On 17 March they reached the summit of presumed 'Holland' and, on descending, climbed over three excrescences along the ridge leading to presumed 'Victoria'. The pinnacle of this presented a sheer rock face broken only by a rather sparsely vegetated gully on the northeast side. After reconnaissance a possible route was selected and climbed to a height of 2810 feet until a difficult rock face proved impassable. But the altitude reading suggested that something was not right. They were near the top of a peak that was supposed to be 3700 feet with an altitude reading well below this.

Next morning the party made another unsuccessful attempt to reach the summit, this time from the north face. Following this second failure they decided to explore the possibility of a route around the western face. After encircling the peak, they observed a hill lying a little north of west that they thought must be 'Allen', but is really a shoulder running northeast from the main ridge.

On reaching the shoulder and looking back slightly south of east, they observed a gash in the ridge apparently isolating a pinnacle slightly east of it. This they assumed to be one of the 'prongs of Victoria'. Thus, on crossing over southwards to the main ridge they expected to see that peak to the east. All that could be seen in that direction, however, was a continuation of the ridge on which they were standing without any marked rise in its elevation. But on turning westward they were confronted by a bold group of three peaks at the end of a long ascending saddle, all of which were considerably higher than the point of observation, 3060 feet – the farthest in all probability being the highest in the range.

Setting off along the saddle they surmounted the first of these peaks 'N' (mapped at 3320 feet) without much difficulty; and the second 'O' (3450 feet), after a tricky bit of climbing, at 12.50 p.m., over moss covered rock surfaces. They attempted the third at 1.25 p.m. and, apart from a rope being required to tackle the final 100 feet, they found it reasonably easy. They reached the top 'P' (3680 feet) at 2.35 p.m. Clearly, this was the highest peak in the range. By this time rain was falling and visibility poor, hampering to some extent observations, photography and sketching. But the party was able to obtain a fair view of the range over yet another peak to the west 'Q' (about 3550 feet), which was close by, and to 'Mount Escott' and 'Copetella' in the distance. With darkness falling they began the descent at 3.50 p.m. but not before leaving a small glass Vaseline jar containing the signatures of all the members of the ascent with a handkerchief tied to a bush at the highest point.[22]

Although identification of the peaks was not intended to be the central focus of the Forestry Report, the team spent more time on this than anticipated as they tried unsuccessfully to reconcile their findings with those contained in the Goldsworthy Report. Not surprising, therefore, photographs of the peaks and the sketches they made of them fully supported their account in the *Geographical Journal*. The latter are reproduced as Plate B.

So what were Oliphant and Stevenson's conclusions on the identification of the peaks *vis-à-vis* the Goldsworthy Report? Without wishing to decry the achievements of that expedition, and the disentanglement of the truth being the only motive, they suggested that the method of naming peaks that had neither been ascended nor accurately located had produced singularly unhappy results. From their analysis of the Goldsworthy findings they believed, for example, that one peak attempted from two different directions and ascended from a third was named after the three characters concerned in apparent ignorance of its single entity.[23] This confusion also appeared to them to have extended to the peak named 'Molar' of which there is no description but, more puzzlingly, no mention of it in the whole course of the narrative.

The Forestry Report also deals with the two peaks that were definitely to have been ascended, namely 'Jerningham' and 'Victoria'. Their preliminary conclusion was that the former, from its description, seems to coincide with the prominence marked 'E' on their profile; and that the peak named 'Victoria' that Allen and Bellamy climbed was not 'P' (the highest point in the range) but the twin pinnacle 'K–L', which, when viewed from the eastern end of the range, appears as undoubtedly its most prominent feature.[24]

Yet, despite these conclusions, Messrs Oliphant and Stevenson recognized that there were two main objections to their theory on the climbing of the highest peak. First, the recorded height of the peak climbed in 1888 was 3700 feet, which accords closely with their team's own aneroid reading for 'P'. Second, if the earlier party had been on the summit of 'K–L', its members would surely have observed the much higher mountain mass of 'N–O–P' to the west of them unless clouds obscured that series of peaks. Against that, however, they argued that it was remarkable that the account of the earlier expedition was completely silent on the subject of the view westwards. Not even 'Allen peak', which if 'Victoria' had been identified with 'P' would have been overlooked at such close quarters, is mentioned. And why were the peaks further to the west, 'Escott' and 'Copetella', which would have been seen under the moderate conditions that obtained at the time of descent, ignored completely in the report?

Messrs Oliphant and Stevenson also noted that 'Holland', described as immediately to the east of 'Victoria' with an estimated height of 2500 feet, shows a resemblance to 'H' (2600 feet) but none to 'N' (3320 feet) or 'O' (3450 feet). Furthermore, the altitude reading for the 'Victoria' of the Goldsworthy Report seems suspect. They pointed out that their own climb from the foot of the peak to the summit of 'P', a height of 500 feet, took them an hour and fifteen minutes going all out, whereas Messrs Allen and Bellamy made a climb of something in the neighbourhood of 1000 feet in 35 minutes. Perhaps the most telling point they made was that the highest peak in the range, 'P', has a flat elongated top possessing neither 'prongs' nor narrow ledges. In short, the description of 'Victoria' in the Goldsworthy Report seemed to tally with that of 'K–L'.[25]

On the wider purpose of the expedition, namely the prospects for economic development, the conclusions of the forestry team follow closely those their Victorian predecessors reached, although in much more detail – especially in respect of types of trees and how extracted timber might be transported to the coast. Of course, the account in the *Geographical Journal* was primarily concerned with a description of the topography of the Cockscomb range and with which peak was 'Victoria'.

✿ ✿ ✿

Not surprisingly, the intrepid H. T. Grant, who was already planning another trip to the region in 1928 to study its geology, expressed interest in the forestry team expedition's findings. Oliphant, whom he consulted, gave him a copy of the report; and Stevenson, through conversation, photographs and sketches, whetted his appetite to ascend the twin peaks of 'K–L' to see if that might throw any light on what peak named 'Victoria' the Goldsworthy expedition climbed and thus clear up the mystery. His account of the climb was published in the *Geographical Journal* later that year.[26]

On 17 April Grant, with two Indian companions, one Maya and one Ketchi, set off at dawn from All Pines travelling light and, on the morning of the second day, emerged on the saddle halfway between 'H' and 'K–L'. Following in the footsteps of the forestry team they made an attempt to climb the latter by way of the quartz rock face and, when that failed, by way of a chimney with an overhanging roof. That, too, was unsuccessful.

The party then worked its way westward around the pinnacle towards 'M'. There for the first time Grant saw the highest peaks 'N–O–P'. To the east, the pinnacle of 'L' now seemed insignificant whereas when viewed from the opposite direction the spires of 'K–L' appeared lofty and dominant. This was explained by the fact that they were now viewing the twin peaks from an elevation of around

3000 feet, almost in line with their summits. Believing that this now represented an easy way to those peaks, the party was dismayed to find that the saddle descended as they progressed eastward and was then transformed into a broken knife-edge ridge with sheer precipices on both sides. From that point the pinnacle 'L' appeared as an unbroken wall rising to about 150 feet above the party's elevation. From the south side of the saddle, it appeared as a cliff of some 2000 feet. The only route seemingly open was on the north side, but a previous attempt from that direction had been unsuccessful.

Deferring any decision on how to tackle the climb, the party turned westward. It ascended 'P' (the highest peak) and photographed the handkerchief and Vaseline jar the forestry expedition had left and to which they added a slip of paper with their own signatures. The altitude recorded was 3620 feet. Because a sea mist reduced visibility, neither 'Allen' nor 'Escott' was seen. Descending they climbed 'O' and 'N' on their return to the saddle when they made yet another unsuccessful attempt on 'K–L' via the chimney. However, on scrutinizing the ground yet again, they noticed a promising line of ascent. A short reconnaissance of this generated optimism for a final attempt the following morning.

In the event the climb was hair-raising. Indeed, it is doubtful whether the summit would have been reached without the skill and perseverance of the Mayan, Placido Tesceun. The hard quartz face afforded only the most meagre of holds and Grant admits that, nearing the summit his nerve was severely shaken. But working his way around a very narrow moss-carpeted ledge, about two feet wide and overhanging a straight drop, Placido succeeded in throwing a rope to the others and practically dragged them to a position from which the route to the top was open.

They emerged on the east end of 'K' from which they looked directly down on 'H'. From both east and west at lower levels the southeastern prong of 'K' seemed higher. But from the top a different impression was gained. Grant recorded:

We were taken back on the actual summit, therefore, to find the north western prong 'L' shows distinctly higher and that an inviting approach via the hummock discernable between the prongs separated us from it. This hummock is like a great moss covered mushroom exquisitely pink. My impression had been that the moss on the rock face was not so colourful as it had been in May 1927; but this hummock was gorgeously tinted. Descending about 50 feet and working around the south side of the hummock proved a simple matter. And Placido leading the way as usual, the ascent of one nasty little face brought us to 'L'. From here looking back 'K' showed higher. Actually these summits are of equal height – 3150 feet. The varying heights of the vegetation is partly responsible for this illusion. Between it and the moss in which one sinks it is not easy to say which is the highest point of any of these peaks.

We left on one of the more open places on the top, a cylindrical tin in which Placido carried matches with the date April 20, and our names, and on a twig beside it an empty metal film container. The peak K–L consists of two flat ridges in echelon, each about 150 yards long and much narrower than the summits of 'N, O and P'. In places the narrow parts of these tops are only 3 or 4 feet wide, but one can walk along them comfortably without risk. From every part of these peaks, 'N, O' and 'P' show up boldly a little more than a mile away, unmistakenly much loftier, as one would expect at this short distance, 'P' being 500 feet higher.[27]

Despite these new revelations, the question of which peak was climbed in 1880 and named 'Victoria' still remained obscure. Grant's conclusions chime generally with those of Oliphant and Stevenson. As he pointed out, if Allen and Bellamy climbed 'P', one could perhaps understand their silence regarding lower peaks to the west. Yet it was clear to him that the description the two of them gave of the summit did not fit 'P'. On the other hand, if 'K–L' had been scaled, he found it inconceivable that, from the joint summit, with 'N–O–P' showing up in the west, they could have believed it was the highest peak in the Cockscomb range.

His conclusion reads as follows 'Since it was the obvious intention of the Goldsworthy expedition to give the name 'Victoria' to the highest peak, it seems fitting that hereafter "P" be known by that name.' Summing up, he added: 'It will, to my mind, remain a mystery what they climbed and named Victoria.'[28] That, so far as I am aware, remains the position.

✿ ✿ ✿

Although this brings the story of exploration as such to its end, perhaps I might be allowed to add a personal footnote. My first glimpse of the Cockscomb Mountains was from the governor's launch *Patricia* in the summer of 1961 on its way south to Punta Gorda. Looking inland as we passed Stann Creek I could see the profile of the range as a sabre, smudgy mass silhouetted against a lowering sky. It looked dark and sinister. On the return journey the weather had improved but now the peaks were shrouded in mist, a not unusual situation to create in some local minds the illusion of a surrounding lake. The following spring I was to gain a totally different impression. From near to the forestry rest house at Melinda in the Stann Creek district, in company with my friends Glynne Lewis and Russell Waters, we were astonished to see in the distance a line of exceedingly narrow ridged peaks towering into the sky, the late afternoon sun glinting on the quartz and pink moss aspects. The impression gained was that of a gigantic fairy castle in the sky. This clinched our determination to visit the range – something we had been considering for some time.

Obviously we needed background information before making plans. The only person in the colony known to have been there was H. T. Grant. He was the oracle we consulted. Like the listeners in Millais's famous painting, 'The Boyhood of Raleigh', though much older and dressed in modern attire, we draped ourselves metaphorically around the feet of the master as we listened avidly to his account of the 1888 and 1920s expeditions. By way of consolidation he made available to us the relevant *Geographical Journals* giving details of his expeditions and that of the forestry team together with photographs he had taken of the peaks from various points along the range. This was accompanied by copious advice and warnings of various dangers. Unfortunately, we could not find anyone in the colony who had a copy of the Goldsworthy Report.

Armed with this information the next step was to get time off from our normal duties during the short dry seasons – usually March and April and perhaps August – when visibility along the range was likely to be better and rivers could be forded or their beds used as a route to the mountains. Ideally, we believed that we would need at least a week to explore the range; but had to accept that the most the administration would allow us to be away was four days, preferably over a holiday. As a result the two attempts we made were at times when we could be released from duties and not necessarily ideal times. But be that as it may.

The first attempt was made in April 1962. Our party consisted of Glynne, Russell and me plus two Mayan Indians. Our aim was to come up on the range from the southeast following in the footsteps of the Grant expeditions, but damage to the forest by the 1931 and 1961 hurricanes had created so many obstacles that we were constantly diverted and unable to follow our compass bearings. As a result, after two days of stumbling around the bush in the heat, we still had no sight of the mountains or any idea of how close we were to them. So we reluctantly gave up but not before recognizing some of the physical warnings given to us by Grant (such as, how easy it is to lose one's way in deep forest and how formidable the approach to the mountains could be) and just how irritating and painful was the attention of the botlass fly, one of the scourges of the 1888 expedition. My back resembled a pin cushion as a result of their bites, which left small black insertions, each the size of a pinhead.

Shortly afterwards we got wind of a track opened up by one of the forestry contractors that seemed to run close to the cluster of the main peaks. A quick reconnaissance of this by Russell suggested it offered the best approach for a glimpse of the range and a speedy climb of 'Victoria' within the short time we could spare for such an excursion. We mentioned this to Grant who thought it a reasonable proposition, but he warned us of the possibility of getting too far west of the range and finding ourselves 'in unexplored country'.

In the event, we did not get another opportunity until late August 1963. The omens were not good for it was dangerously near the rainy season. Indeed, as we set off along the Western Highway for Melinda where we were to spend the night prior to a dawn departure the following day, we could see lightning in the night sky over the Maya Mountains. But the rain held off and, accompanied by two Caribs, we set off, largely in optimistic mood, shortly after dawn the following morning. Early on the second day we caught a glimpse of a cluster of peaks seemingly only a few miles away; and that afternoon we found ourselves on a rise where, through peering upwards through gaps in the trees we could see a huge peak towering above us that we assumed to be 'L'. Pressing on until dusk in a westerly direction we camped overnight in a clearing not far from the saddle hoping to make the ascent of 'P' ('Victoria') the following morning and to have a general view of the topography of the range before starting back. Unfortunately, heavy rain fell during the night and persisted throughout the morning. Above us a heavy mist reduced visibility to just a few yards; and when we descended to the Cockscomb Branch we found that the river, which was shallow on the inward leg, was now rising significantly. As our return route required us to ford the rivers in places and wade through other stretches to avoid dense forest, the situation was becoming dangerous. Consequently, prudence dictated that we should abandon our attempt to reach the peaks otherwise we might be trapped in the area for several days – dangerous and unpleasant for us and a headache for those who would be called upon to mount a search party. So we cut our losses and made our way back to our starting point; Glynne and I recognizing sadly that this had been our last chance as we were both leaving the colony early in 1964. Disappointing as this was, we also recognized realistically that exploring and climbing the Cockscombs was not part of our official duties. It was just an obsession.

Going through the bush on the way back I was about three yards behind Glynne Lewis when suddenly a large snake, about ten feet long, slid seemingly from under his heels and crossed the trail in front of me. I yelled out 'snake' and instinctively struck it a blow behind the head with a stick I was carrying. This, on reflection, was not sensible for the serpent rose up on its tail in a manner reminiscent of a cobra rising out of a basket to the seductive sounds of a snake charmer's music although, in this case, in an alarmingly hostile way. Fortunately, after fixing me malevolently with its dark beady eyes (so it seemed to me) rather like a drill sergeant inspecting new recruits lined up on parade, it then dropped down and slithered off into the bush with a swishing sound and scything motion. This incident served to make us a bit jumpy on the rest of the return journey and to keep us on the *qui vive*. It was also a timely warning that there are many hazards in dense forest and bush and that constant vigilance and care are needed.

However, involvement in our obsession with the Cockscombs did not end with that last attempt. Shortly before our departure from the colony, Russell had a bright idea by way of consolation. 'Why not', he suggested, 'charter a light aircraft and fly around the mountains at peak height as the second best way of examining the range close up?' This Glynne and I thought was an admirable suggestion and we improved on it by insisting we take our mentor, H. T. Grant, along if he was interested. Not only was he interested but he jumped at the chance. No sooner the word: the deed. And so, one bright morning early in 1964 we took off from the Haulover Bridge private airstrip.

Approaching the range from the east we could see the Cockscombs rising high and proud above a thick green blanket of forest. Following the route taken by the 1888 expedition we flew alongside the peaks on the southern side and close to them. We were able to see how the twin peaks 'K–L' dominated the range from the eastern end creating the illusion it was the highest point; but as we came up to it we could also see that the ridge sloped upwards and that the peaks forming the cluster 'N—O—P—Q', were higher, with 'P' being the highest and 'Q' running it close. Turning back beyond 'Escott' we examined the range from the northern side noting that the bare cliff-like sides of 'K–L' made it formidable to ascend from all directions and, having been round once, we persuaded the pilot at Grant's suggestion to go round again. Although obviously less satisfying than exploring the range on foot, it was the next best thing, and one that helped our understanding of all we had read and heard about the earlier explorations. As for Grant, he was absolutely delighted to have had this opportunity to see the peaks once again at close quarters and, on this occasion, without the physical effort expended on previous encounters.

✧ ✧ ✧

Locally, the events of 1888 are described in little detail. A single sentence in *A Brief Sketch of British Honduras* records that 'Victoria' was climbed that year 'by Mr Gordon Allen, Surveyor General, and Mr J. Bellamy, members of an exploring party led by Governor Goldsworthy who himself reached a point 700 feet from the top'. This is more expansive than most other references. So it may be said that the foregoing adds colour and detail to the event besides introducing accounts of the explorations in the 1920s of which most present-day Belizeans are probably unaware. Disappointedly, perhaps, it provides no fresh insight into the mystery of the peak climbed in 1888 and named 'Victoria'.

Do I have any thoughts on this mystery? I must admit straight-away that I am reluctant to venture any theory in this matter as, to do so, involves entering a labyrinth of tangled and conflicting information into which one can easily get lost and wander around without making progress. Sir Arthur Galsworthy, head of the Colonial Office before its absorption into the Commonwealth Office used to describe such academic exercises as, 'juggling with smoke': and that just about sums it up. But if, despite this, I were to 'put in my two-pennyworth' (based largely on a rereading of the relevant papers with special reference to the various connected illustrations) it would be that I believe a *prima facie* case could be made out to establish that the peak the Goldsworthy expedition ascended and named 'Victoria' was, in fact, the highest in the range.

However, having said that, I recognize that, in so doing, I have put up in parallel an Aunt Sally that can be knocked down by strong counter arguments drawn from the same source. So in the end, I fall back on, and take refuge in, Grant's sensible observation that, because of the confused accounts and the time lapse between 1888 and the expeditions of the 1920s, we are never likely to know exactly what peak they actually climbed and named 'Victoria'. On that note, surely, there can be no dispute.

But to that I add a rider. It may be that some day an intrepid climber will come across the bottle containing the signatures the Goldsworthy expedition left or perhaps the sardine tin that would

13. Foothills of the Cockscomb Mountains seen through deep rainforest.

identify Saddle Camp. Or, perhaps, that a photograph known to have been taken by Bellamy and a sketch made by Wickham of that part of the range on the morning of 17 April 1888, before leaving for Reunion Camp, will some day come to light even after all these years.[29] In either event, it is possible that this minor mystery will eventually be resolved.

Although the foregoing attempt to reconstruct the proceedings of the Goldsworthy party by piecing together scraps of confusing evidence well after the event is not without interest to a few, it takes no great perception to accept that it is an esoteric subject of limited interest. But once interested as Glynne, Russell and I were, it became a fascinating if unproductive pastime – almost an obsession.

Grant's departure from British Honduras in 1964 to retire to his native Scotland, broke the last local link between the 1888 and 1928 expeditions. Should anyone now be interested in his findings they will have to research the annals of the now ageing *Geographical Journals*. But what is there in these stories to interest present and future generations? After all, the topography of the Cockscomb range is no longer in dispute and the question of which peak the Goldsworthy party actually climbed and named 'Victoria' is now academic. And with tourism opening up new vistas of the mountains, current interest is likely to remain with the present and future rather than the past. In short, the world has moved on since my secondment there in the early 1960s.

Those familiar with high mountain peaks such as to be found in, say, the Himalayas, Andes or Alps, may well regard the recording of these expeditions to the Cockscombs with its peaks of under 4000 feet as the making of mountains out of molehills. But that is to miss the point. The stories are about exploration, discovery, adventure and a minor mystery of what was actually achieved in 1888, not mountaineering as such. Above all they are part of the history of British Honduras/Belize – admittedly marginally so – but none the less a history worth recording. And, who knows, as I have already said, it may even be helpful background should the bottle containing the signatures of the Goldsworthy party or the sardine tin be found, or if relevant photographs or further sketches by Wickham ever come to light.

Chapter 24
'HT'

T HEY DON'T MAKE 'EM any more like Herbert Thomson Grant or 'HT' as he was generally addressed or referred to in the colony, even by his wife, Sil. The late Victorian/ Edwardian mould in which he had been cast has long since been discarded and consigned to its chronological niche in imperial history. He was a product of his time: a disciple of the Samuel Smiles school of self-reliance, intensely patriotic and filled with a sense of adventure. In short, he typified the countless Britons who over the ages established, developed and sustained the empire. As such, his passing should not, in my view, be allowed to fade unsung. He deserves to be remembered both for himself and for the age through which he lived.

I only came to know HT in his latter years, so there are surely others who knew him more intimately and, therefore, would have been better qualified to attempt his eulogy. But, in the comparatively short time that I knew him, we became close friends and he talked to me in some detail about certain aspects of his life. So, in the absence of others coming forward to do the honours, as it were, here goes.

From what I gathered in our conversations HT was born in Edinburgh in the 1890s – as the-class conscious would have it, of humble origin. He acquired a sound secondary education and was widely read, although Scottish authors like Sir Walter Scott and Robert Louis Stevenson were clearly his favourites. It was likewise in poetry; although he could, and often did, quote from the works of Robert Burns he was better acquainted with the verses of William McGonagall whose public performances in the mid-nineteenth century in reciting his poems (which critics dismissed as naive, banal in content and fringed with rhymes that were invariably painful) earned him the doubtful but perhaps well-deserved reputation as Scotland's worst poet. Yet, despite the ridicule he attracted, his name still appears in serious literary compendiums and, in Scotland, he has entered immortality. Certainly, HT thought his verses a hoot and was ever ready to draw on those he remembered. And he remembered snatches from many.

It is a blinding glimpse of the obvious to say that the world into which he was born was vastly different from the one we know today. Queen Victoria was still on the throne and Britannia ruled the waves. British economic, diplomatic and naval hegemony seemed unassailable, despite growing challenges from the United States of America and Germany. The imperial dream lingered on and new territories, especially in Africa, were still being added to a far-flung empire on which the sun never set. Dominion over palm and pine prevailed. Not surprising, therefore, many young Britons saw the world as their oyster and were tempted to seek a future beyond their native shores. HT was one such young person. After leaving school he worked in the accounts departments of a number of firms, but he was ambitious and restless. Recognizing that there was little hope of a fulfilled and rewarding life in his native Scotland, he decided to seek his destiny elsewhere. Unpersuaded by Samuel Johnson's oft quoted remark 'Sir, the noblest prospect which a Scotchman ever sees is the high road that leads him to England,' he ventured forth to the United States to seek his fortune in the gold fields of California. In the event, hope and realization failed to mesh, though his optimism remained undimmed.

At the outbreak of war in 1914 he returned voluntarily to Britain to join the armed forces. He enlisted as a private in the Royal Scots ('Pontius Pilate's Bodyguard' as he would proudly inform me) and, among other action, saw bitter fighting in the Gallipoli campaign. Surviving the war he returned to the United States and from there, in due course, drifted down into Mexico – always in search of a fortune. In the early 1920s he crossed the border into British Honduras and it was there that he settled.

None of the foregoing was known to me when I embarked *en route* for the colony in 1961 on the SS *Camito*. However, while serving in the West Indian Department of the Colonial Office and dealing with the affairs of British Honduras for the previous three years, I became aware that HT was the local British Council representative and, in that capacity, had been awarded the MBE in 1960. I also learnt that he was honorary consul for Norway, so, officially at least, our paths were bound to cross.

By coincidence, one of his daughters, Rita, was also a passenger on that vessel and Florence and I became acquainted with her. She and her husband had been travelling to Trinidad where the latter was due to take up an appointment with Barclays International Bank in Port of Spain. On becoming aware of our destination she asked us to convey her love to her parents and to say that she hoped to visit them there in the not too distant future.

After a few days spent settling in, I was sitting on the veranda of the Belize Club in the late afternoon enjoying a cold beer with new acquaintances when I spotted an elderly white man bearing down on the club with some purpose. He was of slight build, about five-foot six inches tall and striding along at a light infantry pace that belied his age, which I took to be late sixties. As he climbed the stairs to the entrance I noticed his severe features and a hearing aid attached to his left ear. Under one arm he carried a sheaf of papers, which I subsequently learnt were the club's accounts that he had audited. After nodding curtly to the members of the group with whom I was sitting he advanced into the snooker room where his cronies, the senior members of the club, were gathered as was their wont. Immediately a loud cry went up directed to the elderly bar tender, Milton – 'whisky/water for HT'. Thus, the identity of the elderly newcomer, which I had already ascertained from my drinking companions, was confirmed.

After allowing a short interval to elapse, I ventured forward to introduce myself and to relay Rita's message. He thanked me for the latter and said he looked forward to meeting me informally as well as officially, adding that he had enjoyed an excellent rapport with my predecessor, Ken Osborne. All the time I sensed that he was weighing me up carefully and probably cataloguing me as another Colonial Office 'liberal' busily selling the empire down the river with the prevailing decolonization policies. For my part, I quickly summed him up as an old reactionary very much at home in an all-white club that still operated the blackball system to preserve the ethnic and social attitudes of the 'old school'. Despite these conceivably hasty and ill-informed impressions, a strong bond of friendship soon grew up between us.

We enjoyed each other's company and had shared interests in history, especially local history. He had been a member of a committee the then governor, Sir John Burdon, formed in the late 1920s with a view to collecting historical sources for inclusion in the colony's archives, which were being compiled for the first time in a comprehensive form. He had a detailed knowledge of local history and the fact that British Honduras was one of the main settlements of the mysterious Maya civilization and still unexplored in places added spice to our musings. Perhaps, too, our friendship may have contained a hint of a father–son relationship in the sense that he was of the generation that fought in the 1914–18 war, while I represented their sons who served during the 1939–45 conflict. But this introduces an unnecessary diversion invoking thoughts of the *Psychiatrist's Chair*, which are far too deep for a simple person like me. The essential point is that we got on well together and it was from our meetings and conversations that I was able to glean some idea of his life and experiences and what made him tick.

In addition to his British Council and honorary consul duties, he was the accountant for the Belize Estate and Produce Company, which the Hoare family established in 1875. Its main business was to extract timber for export, mostly to Britain. An incidental point of interest was that one of its directors in the 1920s was Sir Samuel Hoare who later became British foreign secretary and, in that capacity in 1935, he entered into unauthorized negotiations with his French counterpart in the infamous Hoare–Laval pact, which proposed 'selling out' Abyssinian interests in exchange for a friendly settlement of the then current Italian–Ethiopian dispute. This act, which caused turmoil in Westminster and the country, led to his resignation in humiliating circumstances. But I digress.

Glickstein & Sons of London acquired the company in 1942. HT's appointment with them, however, was comparatively recent. In earlier years his business ventures included, among other things, growing and harvesting sponges, cultivating bananas, speculating in land, and prospecting for gold or other minerals. He told me on many occasions that he had made several fortunes and had lost them all bar one. He did not elaborate on his one success and it would have been intrusive, insensitive and probably unproductive to press him on it. But on occasions when we were together and his consumption of whisky exceeded the norm, he would turn to me and demand 'Do you know what BH stands for?' To my standard reply of 'You mean British Honduras?' he would thunder 'No,' banging the table to add emphasis, 'Busted Hopes, Busted Hopes.' This little charade was played out at intervals with its well-rehearsed identical dialogue. To me it was his sad summing up of the hopes he had entertained and his frustration at not having achieved them.

But it was his role of adventurer and explorer that fascinated me most. Although he was not in the same league as, say, Livingstone, Stanley, Burton or Speke, he shared their spirit and determination and always kept detailed records of his travels, which if appropriate he would send to the Royal Geographical Society. When I could draw him out, he would describe his journeys into the rainforests in search of archaeological objects and minerals of commercial value, especially gold. It was on such travels that he became familiar with the Cockscomb range and the puzzle over whether the 1880 team led by Governor Goldsworthy had actually ascended the highest peak.

When he learnt that Glynne Lewis, Russell Waters and I were contemplating climbing the range he was encouraging and generous with his advice and practical help. In particular, he made available to us photographs and back numbers of the *National Geographical Journals* in which accounts of the various 1920s' expeditions were recorded. Among other things, he emphasized that as the approach was through dense forest it was simply not possible to follow a direct compass bearing to a specific point in the range because the nature of the terrain would determine whether progress would be forward or sideways. By way of illustration he showed us an old magazine (*Blackwoods* I believe) containing an article he had written in the 1920s called 'The Lizard'. It was an account of how he had become lost in an area at the foot of the Cockscomb range and had wandered around for several days with no clear sense of direction and unable to escape from the jungle maze in which he found himself. Just as he was beginning to despair he saw a lizard. The significance of this was that in his wife's country, Mexico, there is a superstition that the close sighting of this small reptile is a sign of good luck, much as some people in England might regard a black cat crossing their path. Thus encouraged he climbed a tree and, on this occasion, spotted a familiar landmark and was able to plot an escape route. He was in no doubt that, until then, his chance of survival was slight. This little tale was intended to warn us of the ease of getting lost in deep forest and the consequences. It was one we were to respect and appreciate when we came to experience the problem for ourselves on the ground. This concern for our safety was also an insight into the considerate side of his character.

As I mentioned in the previous chapter, we made two serious attempts to reach the Cockscombs and only on the last did we actually climb towards the main peaks. Unfortunately, the climb had to be abandoned through adverse weather conditions. For me and Glynne Lewis, it was our last chance because we were leaving the colony shortly afterwards. HT was sympathetic and genuinely shared our disappointment, but he would have been less than human if he had not enjoyed at least a whiff of *Schadenfreude* at our failure to emulate his achievements. And who could blame him? Not only had we failed to do what he had done thirty or so years earlier but he was still the last known person to have ascended Victoria peak. And he was justly proud of that achievement.

Our amateur status as adventurers was put even more in the shade when we invited HT to join us on an aerial flight around the Cockscomb range to see the peaks close up, the easy way. Having chartered a light aircraft for this purpose we arranged to meet at a small private airfield near Haulover Bridge at 8.00 a.m. on a specified morning. All three of us arrived early and, while awaiting his arrival, we nervously eyed our pilot, an American wearing dark glasses, whom we were reliably informed had been seen staggering out of the Caribbean Club only a few hours earlier looking the worse for wear. But British Honduras in those days was no place for the faint hearted and, stoically accepting destiny, we hoped that by now he had sobered up sufficiently to control the aircraft safely. That aside, I now need to explain the above reference to amateur status.

Stepping out of a PWD Land Rover whose driver had given him a lift, HT put our generation to shame with his foresight and attention to detail. It was evident that he clearly embraced the motto Baden-Powell had bequeathed to the Boy Scouts' movement, 'be prepared'. On his back was a small haversack containing emergency rations. Around his waist was a cord to which was attached a water bottle and compass. He also carried a machete. When we teased him about his Christmas tree appearance, he reminded us that someone ought to be prepared if we were unfortunate enough to crash-land in the forest. We had given no thought to such an eventuality, but he had. The fact is that although we would not have given long odds on our survival in the event of crashing into the forest, we had to admit that HT had none the less shown the same sense of self reliance that was the badge of his generation.

At the completion of my secondment in spring 1964 my family and I left British Honduras. HT and his wife, Sil, followed a few weeks later. Now in his seventies he was anxious to return to his native Scotland where he cherished the notion that he would enjoy a well-deserved retirement away from the parochial colonial life in British Honduras of which he had now tired. That July he wrote to me saying that he had bought a house near the Murrayfield rugby ground (it had always been his dream to settle on the south side of Edinburgh; he particularly liked Morningside but had constantly been outbid for property there) and issuing an invitation to visit him at any time.

He ended that letter with the last two lines from Robert Louis Stevenson's short but moving poem 'Requiem'. To put those lines in context and to give an insight to HT's feelings at that time, I reproduce the poem in its entirety:

> Under the wide and starry sky,
> Dig the grave and let me lie,
> Glad did I live and gladly die,
> And I laid me down with a will.
> This be the verse you grave for me:
> 'Here he lies where he longed to be;
> Home is the sailor, home from the sea,
> And the hunter home from the hill.'

In short, HT believed he would settle down and end his days in his native Scotland as he had always dreamt he would. His main concern was that Sil, who had always lived in hot countries, would react adversely to a startling change in climate and environment. But, of course, life never works out as expected. Sil, a short plump, practical, hard-working woman with a keen sense of humour and an infectious laugh, took to these changes like the proverbial duck to water. Geographically, she was close to some of her daughters and grandchildren for the first time since they had grown up, and the variety and novelty of the numerous high-quality stores and shops in Princess Street and other parts of Edinburgh compared with those available in Belize were both a revelation and stimulus to her. As for the Scottish weather, a fur coat, electric blanket and bottles of brandy (clandestinely hidden from HT) were more than a match for bitter east winds.

Perversely, her husband was now less at home in this environment. Like many expatriates returning home after long years abroad, he had underestimated how many changes had taken place since he had left. The Scotland in which he now lived was no longer the mythical country of his dreams. After so many years spent abroad he had little in common with the neighbours and other compatriots whom he met. Thus, his hopes of making new acquaintances, if not friends, were unrealized and, unlike British Honduras where he had been a familiar character and greeted accordingly, he was now an anonymous figure in a sea of bustling people going about their lives in Scotland's capital city. Indeed, he told me that the only person who had greeted him with any warmth in the early days of his return was Owen Phillips who had retired from the British Honduras forestry service a few years earlier and whom he had met by chance in Princess Street. Apart from missing companionship and recognition he found the contrast in climate too much for his thinning blood. He therefore took to following the sun each winter – to the Canary Islands, other Mediterranean venues and the Middle East.

We met on several occasions in London, Sussex and Edinburgh and shared many happy reminiscences. On one visit to Edinburgh I took him to the site of the battle of Bannockburn in the nearby countryside, which he had never before visited (probably because he did not drive). Tears welled in his eyes as the sense of history affected him. This was where the Jocks had defeated the English and he thanked me profusely for giving him the opportunity to visit the scene of Scotland's glory in the fourteenth century. The thing we English do for our friends! Being of a diplomatic nature I refrained from offering to take him up to Culloden the next time we met.

We remained in touch through correspondence and occasional visits on both sides; then I received a letter from him giving the sad news of Sil's death. This affected him deeply and, as he put it at the time, he was 'badly cut up' by her passing. Shortly afterwards, when home on leave from my then appointment at the British embassy in Helsinki, a strange coincidence with psychic undertones occurred.

One day, when Florence and I were staying at a rented cottage near Bognor Regis, I felt a compelling urge to phone HT, from whom I had not heard for some months. There was no telephone in the cottage, so, armed with a pocketful of coins, I set off to find a public call box. Having found one I dialled his number in Edinburgh and, bearing in mind that he was hard of hearing, allowed the ringing to continue for a long time. Just as I was about to ring off he answered. After the usual preliminaries he explained that he could no longer cope in the house on his own, so had sold it and was going to live with one of his daughters and that this was moving day. Before handing in the keys to the estate agent he was standing at the living room door having a last look round and drinking in old memories when he realized that the telephone was ringing. It was my call. Had I not rung at that moment I would have missed him. That was our last conversation together. We spoke for as long as my mountain of coins lasted and before closing he undertook to write to me after he had settled in at his new address. I returned to Finland shortly afterwards but never heard from him again. He was a conscientious correspondent and in the absence of news and with no idea of where he had gone to live, I had to assume (with apologies to Shakespeare and Hamlet) that he had 'shuffled off this mortal coil'.

To me, HT was a friend who personified a generation that, compared with its successors, had to work extremely hard for very little material gain or comforts. But work hard he and they did without complaint and accepting that this was their lot in life. I was sorry that our last contact was over the telephone, but I am glad we had that conversation.

When the great book-keeper in the sky came to audit HT's life's ledger I am sure he found him in credit and, therefore, allocated him a place in the heavenly establishment. But how has the latter reacted to eternal peace and tranquillity? My guess is that in a passive environment without any challenges he would soon become restless and disillusioned. I can just imagine the following conversation recurring between him and the celestial gate-keeper with whom he enjoyed the occasional noggin of nectar: 'BH, you know what that stands for?' 'Blessed Heaven?' answers St Peter innocently. 'No', thunders HT banging his harp on a nearby cloud for added emphasis, thus causing a much needed rainstorm over Belize during the dry season, 'Busted Hopes, Busted Hopes'.

In short, HT with his various characteristics and qualities was a child of his times – a product of an age when Britain ruled the waves and with it the roost. Those days are now gone and so, alas, is the subject of this chapter. As I said at the outset, 'they don't make 'em like that any more', although no doubt different times will call for different types and different qualities as the next pages of British history come to be written. Meanwhile, let us salute an ordinary man who, like so many of his generation, led an extraordinary life without fuss through all manner of hardships and, in so doing, personified the courage and determination of his many contemporaries and earlier Britons who over the years built and sustained the empire without ever making a drama out of their contribution.

Chapter 25
A Soldier's Tale

A S THE FOLLOWING story illustrates, the interaction between such concepts as justice, honour, special interest, indulgence and compassion can produce unforeseen situations and evoke conflicting attitudes and emotions. It concerns Private Jones (that for obvious reasons was not his real name), an army driver stationed at Airport Camp.

The colony with its coastline, swamps, dense forests, mountains and rivers offered great scope for training soldiers in a wide variety of military situations. But to the modern serviceman used to the sophisticated environments of, say, West Germany and Hong Kong (it should be remembered that this story is set in the early 1960s) it offered little by way of social interest or attraction. That is not to say that the army neglected this aspect of life, far from it. Provision was made in the camp for a wide range of sporting activities including a large open-air swimming pool; also a cinema and a NAAFI. In addition, the Nuffield Trust had provided a small motor launch that was used for taking small parties of soldiers and their families to the cayes where they could swim, picnic and generally relax. To facilitate social contact with the local population, each weekend army trucks would bring troops in civilian clothes into Belize. Some would disappear into local homes where they had, in their own words, 'their feet under the table'. The majority, however, would invariably end up in the many bars and so-called night clubs. Thereafter, in various states of inebriation, they would be poured back onto their vehicles and returned to camp. In general, they were well behaved for virile and boisterous young men and there were very few incidents to turn the public against them. Indeed, their presence and the trade they generated was welcomed.

It was against this background that Private Jones became acquainted in one of the city's bars with a small group of locals. The latter, once they felt able to talk freely in front of him, disclosed that they had plans to break into a nearby local factory where jeans were manufactured. There was little risk of being caught, they said, and the stolen articles would attract a good price on the black market. All they needed was a vehicle in which to transport the stolen goods from the factory. They knew that Jones had access to such a vehicle and wondered if he would be interested in joining them. He was indeed swayed, not by any pressing need for additional wherewithal, but probably by a sense of adventure or relief from boredom. So he and his vehicle became involved. But the romantic aspect was an illusion. The truth was that, like the parable in the Gospel of St Luke about a certain man who travelled from Jericho to Jerusalem, he had fallen among thieves, although wittingly so in this case, and not very smart ones at that. Alas, when their plans went awry there was no Good Samaritan to come to his rescue.

The raid on the factory went according to plan but the thieves were so pleased with their success that they boasted about it. Therefore, it was not long before telltale gossip reached the ears of the local constabulary and then only a matter of time before the ringleader was arrested when he tried to dispose of the jeans. Shortly afterwards, the others, including Jones, were also arrested and held in custody.

Three times their case was brought before the magistrates' court and on each occasion it was adjourned on some technical point or another. The governor, having previously served in Nigeria and familiar with court practice there, was cynical about such deferments and said to me, 'Don't these people realize that such delays are designed to enable them to grease the magistrate's palm and so obtain an acquittal?' But in fairness to the magistrate concerned, any suggestion that he was open to corruption was wide of the mark because when he was a boy his father had been found guilty of murder and had been executed. This had left an indelible mark on his character and, as a magistrate and to redeem his family's honour, he regarded it as his duty to be tough on crime rather than on the causes of crime. So, when the accused were finally arraigned before him and their guilt established without doubt, they were each given the maximum custodial sentence.

Now, the idea of a British soldier being incarcerated in Belize prison, not the most salubrious of establishments, where among other things he could not expect to receive the sort of diet to which he was accustomed, caused the army authorities some concern. Perhaps, more to the point, however, was the fact that a soldier serving a sentence in company with local criminals was seen in some quarters as a blot on the army's escutcheon. In short, as the military hierarchy perceived it, a question of honour was involved, but very little in life in British Honduras in those days was straightforward. While the army authorities were deliberating on what to do about Private Jones, concepts other than honour were simmering away beneath the main issue.

In addition to his driving skills, Jones was also a motor mechanic – a trade in which good artisans were in short supply in the colony. It so happened that on its books the prison had two lorries for conveying prisoners to and from places of outdoor work and a Land Rover for the chief prison officer to use. These vehicles suffered from lack of proper maintenance and were always breaking down. Jones, eager to do something useful, offered to take a look at them and before long they were in good working condition.

As his reputation as a mechanic grew he also began to maintain the vehicles of the prison staff and then, in some cases, of their families and friends. This sometimes involved visits outside the prison walls and, as a prisoner, he was on a very loose rein, in fact so loose that he was often seen in local bars, with his warder chaperon, drinking tea, coffee or beer. On occasions, so I was told, some of his old pals from the garrison on duty visits to the city would join him and news of all this inevitably trickled back to senior officers.

None of this went down well with the garrison commander who presumably now felt that the situation had become farcical. Accordingly, after consulting the governor, who discussed the matter with the attorney general, he found that Jones could be repatriated to Britain under the provisions of a late Victorian piece of legislation, the 'Colonial Prisoners Removal Act'. The necessary arrangements were put in hand and Jones was told what to expect once the formalities had been completed.

On learning the news the chief prison officer, backed by some local opinion, protested on the grounds that as the crime had been committed in the territory the sentence should be served there. But it did not take a cynic to recognize this as special pleading. In truth, he was anxious not to lose a star prisoner who had brought the prison vehicles up to scratch and one who was also providing a service to the wider community, however unorthodox. The latter, perhaps, was not a good selling point so far as the army was concerned. In the event this protest, admittedly *sotto voce*, got nowhere.

About that time I had reason to call on the chief prison officer and, while there, was told that Jones had asked to see me. He told me that his appeal to the army authorities at the local garrison to be allowed to complete his sentence locally had been dismissed and wondered whether the governor could override that decision. Could I, therefore, put his case to him? His case, put simply, was that he recognized he had to be punished for committing a stupid criminal act, but that if he were returned to Britain as proposed his family would be stigmatized for his misdeeds. At present, when asked, they could truthfully say that he was still serving in British Honduras and did not need to disclose in what capacity. When released and then discharged from the army he could then return looking bronzed and friends and neighbours would be none the wiser. If, however, he was to return to finish his sentence in a British prison, family visits to see him coupled with inevitable disclosures through gossip or unguarded moments would soon give the game away. This would bring shame on his wife, children and parents, all innocent parties. And from a local point of view, was he not serving his time in a constructive manner? As for his visits outside the prison, which were always supervised, was this greatly different from the latitude given to inmates held in open prisons in Britain?

I listened attentively and said that I fully appreciated his dilemma. For what it was worth, he had my personal sympathy. I said that I was prepared to relay our conversation to the governor but that, in my view, there could be no question of any reversal of the decision already taken. If for no other reason the governor, as nominal commander in chief, had approved it and would certainly not go against a considered decision that had involved so many different authorities, including him. In short, he would be unwise to hold out any hope of a last minute reprieve.

When I reported to the governor he too expressed sympathy for Jones's dilemma, but confirmed that he had to support the garrison commander in this matter, especially since he fully agreed with the decision, to which he had contributed, that had been reached. So Jones went back to Britain to complete his sentence and the prison vehicles lapsed again into disrepair. I hope that since then fate has been kind to him.

This, to my mind, is a sad little story that moved towards an inevitable conclusion. Although it is possible to feel sympathy for Jones in trying to protect his family from shame (and in Britain what the neighbours think is not unimportant) and to understand the background to the chief prison officer's representations to allow him to complete his sentence locally, it has to be recognized that he was a serving soldier and, as such, always subject to military codes. As a disciplined force in which morale, honour and public standing are inextricably entwined, the army was clearly embarrassed that one of its numbers should be tried in a civilian court, convicted and then imprisoned in the same territory he was there to defend. As I have already inferred, the outcome was inevitable.

If there is a moral to this story then I leave it for others to identify. I am merely the narrator. The only point I wish to make appears in the opening sentence of this chapter, namely that in the crucible of life a compound of such concepts as justice, honour, special interest, indulgence and compassion can produce unforeseen situations and evoke conflicting attitudes and emotions. Put that in the context of British Honduras in the early 1960s and you have the story of Private Jones and his impact on the local society. But if his tale arouses your sympathy, if nothing else, I for one would understand.

Chapter 26
I, Too, Have Nothing to Say

A LTHOUGH THE SAME department in the Colonial Office, the West Indian Department, dealt with the affairs of both British Honduras and the British island colonies in the Caribbean, it should be recognized that despite similarities based on British history and culture, the two areas differ from one another in many respects. Situated as it is on the Central American mainland, British Honduran culture contains Amerindian and Hispanic influences that arise from its own particular history and geographical location and, unlike most island colonies in the Eastern Caribbean dollar area, it has its own currency. Moreover, like its counterpart further south on the American continent, British Guiana, it opted out of the proposal in the 1950s to group all the British colonies in the region into one homogeneous body, the West Indies Federation. Although ethnic considerations played a part in this decision, there was also the fear that such a grouping could lead locally to unemployment arising out of a perceived influx of workers from the islands creating labour competition.

This is not to suggest, however, that British Honduras was isolated from its island neighbours. Indeed, it had good commercial and other relations with Jamaica and actively participated in the joint common services available in the region, particularly the educational and training facilities the University of the West Indies and the School of Tropical Agriculture offered. As a result, there was an outflow of students and government officers to Jamaica, Trinidad and Barbados and an inflow of academics and experts in a variety of fields in the reverse direction who contributed to the affairs of government, economic development or business. Also, several 'islanders' held positions in the local civil service.

During my service in the colony there were two visits from the islands that remain in my memory because they bear upon the federation issue, both directly and indirectly, and illustrate West Indian humour at its best in relation to political situations. The visits concern Arthur (I think that was his forename, but memory can play tricks) Sealy from Jamaica and Sir Hugh Wooding from Trinidad.

One morning, a few weeks after Hurricane Hattie had left its visiting card, I was at home doing some clearing up when I heard voices in the front garden. Peering through the mosquito mesh I saw Dennis Malone and a few other government officers heading towards the steps leading to my front door in company with a stranger. As they entered the house the stranger was introduced to me as Sealy, editor of the *Daily Gleaner*, Jamaica's main daily newspaper that had launched an appeal fund for our hurricane victims. He had come to British Honduras to see the damage and to find out what reconstruction and rehabilitation measures were being contemplated. These were discussed around my dining table. At this point I should furnish a description of the table as it features in the subsequent narrative.

Like most furniture provided for government quarters, it had been made by the local Public Works Department. Its appeal was functional rather than aesthetic, though it did have the advantage of being made from solid mahogany (even our coat hangers were made from that splendid timber). The top consisted of four large boards about eight feet long by one foot wide glued together in butt joints. Nicely stained and polished it was quite presentable. This was the setting for the discussion.

Physically, Sealy, then in his late fifties or early sixties, was a powerfully built man, short in stature, broad and corpulent. A full and flowing mane of greyish hair set off his large face. Mentally he was a giant holding strong views he was not afraid to advance. He disclosed that, although he had lived much of his life in Jamaica, he had actually been born in British Honduras in the Corozal District. He questioned us closely on the impact of the hurricane and how we saw the future with particular reference to whether we thought the population of Belize would be moved to a new capital inland and what its reaction to that might be. Then, for some unaccountable reason, the conversation veered towards West Indian politics in general and in particular the Jamaican referendum that summer rejecting the federal concept.

It was during the conversation about the referendum that someone around the table blamed Jamaica for the break-up of the West Indies Federation. This angered Sealy. 'That is a lie', he thundered thumping his right fist down on the table top with all the force of a sledge hammer. The power of the blow caused all the joints to part leaving four separate planks – some splintered around the edges. For a moment there was a deathly silence. Then I found myself saying 'I don't know who was responsible for the break up of the federation, but I know who was responsible for the break up of my dining table.' At this Sealy roared with laughter, all temper evaporated and good humour was restored. It was like the sun coming out after a severe storm.

Some weeks later the table was repaired and restored to its original state, but I remembered the incident for three reasons. First, it reminded me that in the British Caribbean, politics is always simmering beneath the surface and is easily brought to the boil. Second, it was to me yet another demonstration of how, in the region, humour so often turns anger to laughter, whether intentional or otherwise. Third, it reminded me of a story a friend and colleague in the Colonial Office, John Malarkey (yes that was his real name) told me more than half a century ago.

John, who was parliamentary, protocol and conference officer during part of the 1950s and 1960s, was a Yorkshireman originally from Bradford. In his early career he had been a sales representative with a textile firm and had travelled widely in South America. During the Second World War he joined the civil service and, after the cessation of hostilities, served with the control commission in Berlin before joining the Colonial Office. With his presence, wide experience, maturity, confidence, humour, ability to get on with high and low and with no racial hang-ups, he was a round peg in a round hole in the post he was filling. Not surprisingly, by the nature of his duties, he was often privy to what went on in the inner sanctums of the office. A born storyteller he was only too happy to share accounts of non-confidential goings on, sometimes highly embellished, with those of us in the West Indian Department to whose floor he often gravitated. This particular story, which underlines the two other reasons I mention above, concerned a larger than life Jamaican trade unionist and politician who became the country's first prime minister after independence, Sir Alexander Bustamante.

Bustamante, a tall powerfully built man, was a flamboyant character given to dramatic gestures and passionate rhetoric. Of mixed European and African blood with family links to the old plantocracy, he was born in Jamaica and christened William Alexander Clarke. On reaching adulthood he left the island to seek his fortune elsewhere and, if we accept his account (and in this regard he was the only source and the only authority) for the next 29 years he spent much of his time in Cuba, the United States, Canada and Spain. According to legend (which he instigated) he made a fortune on the New York stock exchange but this, like so many aspects of his life during that period, relied on whatever personal disclosures he was willing to impart and most of his accounts were inconsistent in the subsequent retelling. What is known is that he turned up in New York in 1932 calling himself Alejando Bustamante, a cultivated white gentleman of Spanish birth. In reality, he appears at the time to have been a hospital attendant at one of New York's better known private hospitals.

On returning to Jamaica in 1935, now aged fifty, he found that the political and social environment was changing. Criticism of crown colony status was becoming widespread and poor pay and unemployment, accentuated by the Great Depression, was widening the gap between the haves and have-nots – the latter being predominantly the black labouring classes. Into this locale he set himself up as a person of independent means. More specifically, he went into business as a money lender. But before long this failed to sustain his interest and energies and he began to write letters to the local press on a number of public issues with particular reference to the plight of the poor. As his reputation grew he began to appear on public platforms echoing the same themes. From there he was only a short step away from setting up a trade union. The authorities deemed him an agitator and, like many other union and political leaders in the colonial pre-independence era, he was charged with sedition and subsequently imprisoned. After this tutelage, his movement into the political arena proper became inevitable.

The story of the life he reinvented after his return to Jamaica in

1935 worked more to his advantage than disadvantage. Amazingly, he claimed that a Spanish mariner named Bustamante had adopted him at the age of five and taken him to Spain where he was brought up; he also claimed that as a young man he became involved in military escapades in Spanish Morocco. In the light of the foregoing this can be seen as a colourful and imaginative story, but to preserve consistency and to ensure there was no reason to delete him from the electoral roll, he formally changed his name from Clarke to Bustamante by deed poll in 1944.[1]

Every bit the showman, his excessive rhetoric and eccentricities were the very things to appeal to the labouring masses, especially in the rural areas where he was acclaimed a Messiah. When stories circulated, as they often did in so hothouse a political atmosphere, suggesting he had 'his fingers in the till', the working-class reaction was 'so what?' – he had helped them far more than he had helped himself. The following story, which I was assured was true though it could well be apocryphal, illustrates this point well. Following a whispering campaign to the effect that he was the recipient of a large bribe, while addressing a worker's rally he began: 'It is being said that I have accepted a bribe of $20,000. That is a downright lie. To suggest that I would sell my integrity for such an amount is nothing short of libellous. It was, in fact, $50,000!' His audience knew, of course, that he was teasing them with a joke, but such was his command over them that he could get away with things for which other politicians would have been crucified. It takes no stretch of the imagination to predict what the current British media would make of such remarks.

Once in the political arena he became leader of the Jamaica Labour Party and majority leader in the legislature in 1952. He lost power in the 1955 general election and for the next seven years was leader of the opposition. During that period his views on Jamaica's participation in the West Indies Federation were ambivalent. He began as a sceptic maintaining that it was a device the British engineered to push onto the larger islands responsibility for the future of the smaller ones on economic assumptions that were not sustainable. Later he mellowed and became more cooperative, but in the late 1950s, looking for a cause on which to fight the next general election, he again became anti-federalist.

This then is the background to the story John Malarkey told me. It goes as follows. At a West Indian constitutional conference in London the secretary of state for the colonies, Iain Macleod, held a private meeting with Bustamante, at which the former rehearsed the arguments in favour of federation. Bustamante, however, argued that not only would federation involve Jamaica subsidizing the economies of most of the other islands but that it would also expose Jamaican sovereignty to the whims of the smaller Eastern Caribbean states. Resorting to his gift of rhetoric, he turned angrily on the secretary of state and said 'How would you like it, Mr Macleod, if England were run by Scotland?' To this Macleod (a Scot as was his minister of state, Lord Perth, and his permanent under secretary, Sir John McPherson), having been appointed by the prime minister, Harold Macmillian, the son of a Scottish crofter, replied, 'It is, and I like it very much.' Once Bustamante saw the joke, tension eased and, as in the case of Sealy above, the anger turned to laughter.

In elaborating this story I have taken the opportunity, albeit obliquely, to remind current generations of the type of leaders being thrown up in the West Indian colonies and elsewhere in the postwar period leading up to independence. Jamaica was fortunate at that time to have two natural leaders in Alexander Bustamante and his cousin Norman Manley, though of the two Manley was the more intellectual and Bustamante undoubtedly the more charismatic. By the same token, British Honduras was fortunate in having George Price as leader, for he was also capable of creating enough national spirit to give the country confidence to take the plunge into independence. But, interesting as this aspect may be, it is perhaps straying a bit too far from the subject in hand.

The other visit I remember because of the link with the federation was of Sir Hugh Wooding, chief justice of Trinidad and Tobago. A charming and urbane man with a puckish sense of humour, he was a gifted raconteur. It was around my dining table, the very one Sealy had thumped so hard and decisively, that he recounted the following story about a debate in the federal parliament some months before its demise. One of the ministers was on his feet in the chamber delivering a lengthy and turgid speech, which was little more than a boring monologue of dull and conceivably inconsequential material.

Several times during this discourse a member from the benches opposite rose to his feet to interrupt only to be waved down by the Speaker when the minister refused to give way. When he finally sat down at the end of this long and tedious recital the Speaker invited the would-be interrupter to say his piece. This he did briefly and with devastating effect, 'Mr Speaker', he said, 'I, too, have nothing to say.' With that, he resumed his seat with the house convulsed in laughter. They don't make politicians with wit like that nowadays except, perhaps, in the former British West Indian colonies.

But, reverting to my opening remarks, it was meeting people like Sealy and Wooding that led me to ponder over the similarities and differences in the approach to politics and its social implications between British Honduras and its neighbouring island colonies. Most obviously, both have similar social attitudes and are wedded to parliamentary democracy, freedom of expression and upholding justice. Any shade of difference between them is possibly attributable to style: the British Honduras approach to politics is perhaps more sober and restrained in comparison with its flamboyant island neighbours. In this, its geographic location and unique history coupled with its racial and cultural mix undoubtedly play a part. But, admittedly, this is a simplistic overview.

In *The Making of Modern Belize*, Grant provides a deeper analysis in which he cites three specific similarities. First, both share a colonial heritage, which encourages authoritarianism on the part of leaders *vis-à-vis* followers, resulting in little mass participation in decisions that affect the interests of society at large. Second, both are subject to the singular political and social characteristics of smaller territories and here he draws on the studies of Burton Benedict and P. J. Wood. In *Problems of Smaller Territories*[2] Benedict explores kinship, friendship and political relationships within such territories to see how tribal loyalties induce, intrude or impinge adversely on wider impersonal and even-handed allegiances demanded by modern democratic societies. This is manifested in many ways. For example, personal antagonisms can poison public affairs and disagreements over policy can estrange private lives. Third (linked to the second) the economies of small territories are generally unable to provide and sustain an acceptable level of employment, thus increasing the role of government in the field of employment and patronage and, with it, the likelihood of rewards to kin and political supporters at the expense of opposition counterparts.

But notwithstanding the similarities, there were during the colonial period (and still are) significant differences. Overshadowing all else was the complication over sovereignty. Although British Honduras shared with the larger islands the goal of early political independence, the long-running Guatemalan claim to sovereignty put a brake on moves in that direction. Conscious of the vital British military commitment to its defence it was, in consequence, compared with the larger islands, less impatient to sever the imperial connection while that dispute remained unresolved. But with independence finally achieved this, of course, is a difference that has long since been overtaken by events.

The most fundamental difference, and one of some significance that Grant as well as Waddell[3] highlighted, has its roots in the two quite different and distinct cultural complexes thrown up in British Honduras by the many and diverse racial groups such as Africans, Caribs, Chinese, East Indians, Europeans (including Mennonites), Lebanese, Syrians, Ketchi, Mayan and other Amerindians. These are identified as white–Creole–Carib as opposed to Spanish–Mestizo–Indian complexes. Drawing on this, Grant goes on to assert that these complexes give the country 'a racial, linguistic and cultural heterogeneity that is unusual in either the West Indies or Central America'. A reflection of this diversity, for example, is that five different languages are spoken (English, Spanish, Maya, Carib and a form of German peculiar to the Mennonite community) as well as Creole, a local dialect in widespread use.[4]

From all this it is possible to conclude that, although history and the colonial connection have given rise to many similarities between British Honduras (now Belize) and the former British West Indian islands, its racial/cultural mix and contiguity to its Central American neighbours has given it the unique position of having a foot in both worlds. How this might develop in the future is a matter for conjecture. But in introducing this subject and linking it to the now defunct federation issue I have managed to impart a few anecdotes that in my view, at least, are worth preserving for posterity.

Chapter 27
BH Revisited

I T IS OFTEN SAID by those who assume knowledge in such matters, that you should never go back after a long absence to any place with romantic or other agreeable associations that linger in the memory in idealized form because significant changes would undoubtedly have taken place in the interim, leading inevitably to disappointment in the new scenario. Obviously, as this great big world keeps on turning, new situations and other aspects such as changing tastes are continually arising to destroy old dreams or illusions. Yet, although I find no quarrel with this observation as a generalization, I can honestly say that on the three occasions I revisited British Honduras after my secondment there in 1961–64, I was in no way disappointed in what I found. Certainly, changes, not always for the better, had taken place and many old friends and colleagues no longer graced the local scene. Also, new political, economic and social conditions prevailed. None the less, whether it was because of the familiar atmosphere, other sights or smells or the friendliness of the people, the 'old magic' seemed to affect me and I felt at home straightaway.

The first of these visits took place in 1969 and the second in 1975–76. These I touch upon briefly below. The third was in connection with the independence celebrations that took place in 1981 and is the subject of a separate later chapter.

In 1969 I was serving as private secretary to Lord Shepherd, the minister of state at the Foreign and Commonwealth Office whose ministerial responsibilities at that time included the interests of the dependent territories. In that capacity arrangements had been made for him that year to pay a familiarization visit to British Honduras and to discuss with local politicians there the independence issue that the continuing complications arising out of the Guatemalan territorial claim had bogged down. When he set off Assistant Under

14. George Price and author exchange warm greetings at Stanley Field
Airport 1969. Lord Shepherd extreme right of picture.

Secretary James Morgan, the head of the West Indian Department
Michael Atkinson and I accompanied him.

We were met on arrival at Stanley Field Airport by Premier (as he
was now styled) Mr George Price, and after courtesies and preliminary discussions, we were driven to Government House where
we were to be accommodated by the governor, Sir John Paul and his
wife, Lady Audrey. So far as I was concerned I was back in a familiar
setting. At talks later that day I was pleased to renew my
acquaintance with those members of Executive Council who were
still serving since the time I was clerk to the council. As for the
outcome of our discussions, well, that is now academic: for although
it was to take several more years, independence was finally achieved.

As our visit was scheduled to last only a few days there was little
chance to see anything of the country outside Belize, though
arrangements were made for us to pay a brief visit to St George's
Caye with the governor to 'talk shop' and bathe at the same time.
Apart from that, I also managed to slip the leash on a few occasions
just to get a feel of the city and to visit a few old haunts, friends and
colleagues.

Such was the village atmosphere in those days that once, on walking along Regent Street on my way back to Government House, an elderly local who knew me during my earlier secondment stopped me and said 'Hello, Mr Godden, I haven't seen you for some time.' Whether this was his way of saying, 'Nice to see you again after all these years' or he had not realized that I had left the colony several years earlier is something I still ponder over. For my part, I neither explained my long absence nor was asked anything about it. But this was the British Honduras with which I was familiar – a sort of *Alice in Wonderland* setting.

The day before we left we were joined at Government House by Frank Trew, our consul in Guatemala City and the sole British diplomat there at that time. It was considered important for him to be aware of the discussions that had taken place so he was in the picture, as it were, and to assure the Guatemalans should they enquire that the minister of state's visit was simply routine and of no special significance.

That night after dinner at Government House Frank rose to return to the Fort George Hotel where he was staying. Sir John apologized for being unable to lay on transport to get him there because, as he explained, his driver was not available at that late hour. It was also not possible to obtain a taxi. In the circumstances I volunteered to do the honours by driving the governor's car. This was readily accepted and, with instructions to put the car away and lock up when I got back, I set off and drove Frank to his hotel. On my way back I approached the Caribbean Club and, on impulse, stopped and went in. I came upon a familiar scene, for as usual at that time of night the club was pulsating with life and music. After one drink and a few words with old acquaintances I left well within the hour to return to Government House with, on reflection, a troubled conscience.

As I lay in bed that night, the possible consequences of my visit to the Caribbean Club hit me. With the governor's car parked outside in a prominent position, any passer-by could assume that he was inside enjoying a night on the town and many people in the community regarded the club, if not as a den of iniquity at least unsavoury. Would accusing eyes be turned on him at church the following Sunday to the accompaniment of, say, a sermon featuring

the lesson of Sodom and Gomorrah? (For those of modern generations unfamiliar with the Old Testament I should explain that these
were biblical towns and not a local firm of solicitors or accountants.)
In all this I was reminded of a radio monologue delivered in the late
1940s or early 1950s by that splendid character actor, Bernard Miles,
in which he assumed the role of a country yokel accused by a 'sour
widow lady' prominent in the village of indulging in the 'demon
drink' because she spotted his bicycle propped against the wall of the
local pub. So incensed was he about this that, in revenge, he left his
bicycle propped up against the hedge in front of her house all
through the following night, leaving her in the morning to worry
about what conclusions neighbours and other villagers would have
drawn from that. One needs to be discreet in a village because of
prying eyes and gossip; and although Belize was the country's capital
it was to all extents and purposes, in those days, little more than a
village, certainly when it came to prying eyes and gossip.

When we said goodbye the following morning I thought it
prudent not to mention the incident to Sir John Paul, though I am
sure he would have been amused had I done so. If there were
repercussions he never mentioned them to me. Indeed, that year he
sent me a Christmas card (which I still have) of a sketch he had
made of Punta Negra in the Toledo District – he was a splendid and
competent artist. And so concluded my first revisit; the next would
be about seven or so years later.

After almost five years as private secretary to four ministers (three
with dependent territory responsibilities) I was appointed as a first
secretary at the British embassy in Helsinki, Finland in September
1971. There I served until December 1975. Shortly before my tour
ended I was given a broad hint that, after due leave, I would be off
on another overseas assignment. Yet, within a week or so of
departure, I had no confirmation of this and began to feel anxious.
Then the ambassador, Sir James Cable, called me into his office to
say that the personnel department had asked him to sound me out
about taking up an urgent temporary post as first secretary in British
Honduras (now called Belize) where the substantive holder of the
post, Ken Oldfield, had badly injured a leg and was back in the
United Kingdom for medical treatment. The urgency was because

the Guatemalans on the border had apparently been engaging in so much sabre rattling that an emergency situation was arising and it had been considered necessary to strengthen the military garrison *inter alia* by the dispatch of 12 Harrier aircraft of the RAF. Even under normal conditions, the only support the governor had on the civilian side of his staff was a first secretary, archivist and communications officer (one post) and a personal assistant, so a replacement first secretary was clearly needed. As I had previous experience of the colony and was readily available I was seen as an obvious candidate. In the circumstances I said that I would be willing to be considered provided I could spend Christmas (then only a little over a week away) with my family in the United Kingdom. This was considered reasonable after a long tour in Finland and arrangements were made for me to arrive on the last day of the year, 31 December 1975.

Waiting to meet me at Stanley Field Airport was the archivist, Michael Holmes, who was to drive me to Belmopan, the country's new capital situated at the junction of Roaring Creek (40 miles along the Western Highway) and Hummingbird Highway. It was here that the new Government House was sited. This was the first of several changes I was to experience since my previous visits. The second and more significant one was that because of constitutional changes, the governor now spent most of his time on external affairs and defence, leaving ministries more or less to run their own show within the limits of good government. With the prevailing emergency, this was now patently obvious.

The governor Dick Posnett (later Sir Richard) and his wife Shirley had kindly offered to accommodate me at Government House over the New Year holiday – an offer I was only too happy to accept – to give me time to adjust to my new surroundings. It was evening when I arrived and, after an exchange of greetings, they explained they were on their way to a New Year's party, but that a meal was ready for me and that they were sure, given my previous service in the country, I would find something to keep me amused.

So, it was New Year's Eve and what was I to do? A quick reconnaissance of the area, with its new housing estates and government buildings, indicated that it was at that stage in its development little more than the nucleus of an administrative city. Most of its inhabitants, civil servants, had left for their old homes in Belize City and the attraction of 'bright lights' and all that entails. This I was to discover later was the pattern that was followed at weekends. As government offices closed late on Friday afternoons there would be an exodus of staff in their cars in the direction of the old capital and a procession back early on Monday mornings. Notwithstanding this, I managed to find a bar from which light and noise emanated. Among the crowd were several soldiers from the Royal Irish Rangers regiment who, at that time were part of the local garrison. As I discovered then, and subsequently, they were a splendid body and, as usual, were doing an arduous and sensitive job in difficult circumstances with the minimum of fuss. But that night they were in sombre mood. One of them had died that day from, if I remember rightly, a heart attack. So at midnight, instead of 'Auld Lang Syne', a regimental piper stood on a table and played a lament while a senior sergeant asked his colleagues to remember their comrade. It was a touching and moving occasion.

After the holiday I moved into Ken Oldfield's house. As far as my official duties were concerned, the perceived Guatemalan threat was dictating events. Therefore, the governor (nominally commander-in-chief) was largely involved locally with the garrison commander on military matters and London in regard to the wider defence and foreign affairs dimensions. It was in these areas that I assisted him, mostly in liaison with the military staff and keeping an eye on inward telegrams on which action might be required. Fortunately, Dick Posnett was a decisive governor, as well as being considerate, so I experienced no problems.

As tension on the military front eased, I was able to venture outside the immediate environs of Belmopan, especially at weekends. With Michael Holmes I visited old haunts at Pine Ridge, Maya ruins at Xunantunich and Altun Ha, Stann Creek and El Cayo. Only the discreet presence of troops at strategic points reminded me that the situation was different from 1961–64. Socially, too, I was well looked after. Dennis Malone was now the chief justice in Belize City and his predecessor, Sir Clifford de Lisle Innis, was living in Belmopan, and I was able to enjoy their company and hospitality on several occasions. There were other old friends (notably Tommy Searle, the Raes and Spooners) who invited me out, but the main social contact was with the company commander, officers and senior NCOs of the Royal Irish Rangers based around the new capital.

Two unusual events during my time there are perhaps worth recording. First, Dick Posnett's tour was almost at an end and his successor, Peter McEntee, had been selected, though his appointment had not been announced. It was felt that before he actually took up his duties it would be useful for him to visit the colony to get a feel for it. So it was arranged for a Foreign and Commonwealth Office official (none other than Peter McEntee) to come out, seemingly on a routine visit. When he arrived, I had the task of introducing him to government ministers and others without disclosing that he was their next governor designate – though no doubt they guessed this was so.

Second, there was a devastating earthquake in and around Guatemala City, with its effect felt 200 miles away in Belmopan. I was fast asleep at night when it struck and the resultant earth tremor was considerable. Speaking personally, it was as though a large animal had got under my bed and was trying to push it over. For a few seconds I wondered what on earth was happening, but then I realized. For a few days afterwards, Belmopan was the only link between our consul in Guatemala City and the Foreign and Commonwealth Office in London. So, despite the sophistication of modern communications, contact was maintained initially along telephone lines resting on poles (sometimes standing drunkenly at odd angles in relation to the ground) between the two capitals.

Time was now passing quickly. Ken Oldfield would be returning shortly, so enabling me to return home to finish my leave and prepare for my next assignment, wherever that might be. Would I be able to visit the Maya ruins at Tikal some 40 miles across the border in the Peten district of Guatemala? This was something I had hoped to do during my earlier secondment, but for a variety of reasons it had not happened. With relations with Guatemala strained the prospect looked dim, although tensions had seemingly eased at that stage. I answer that question in the next chapter.

Ken Oldfield returned and after a day or so of handing over Dick

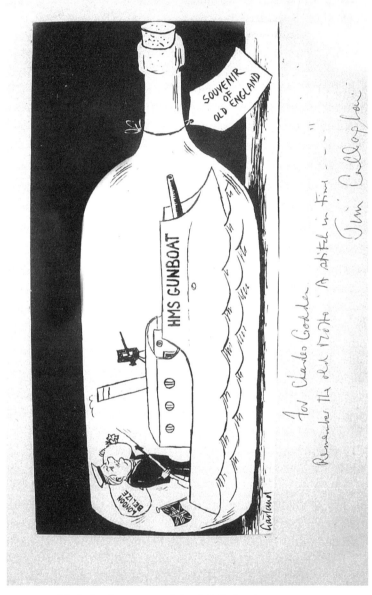

15. Garland cartoon with Lord Callaghan's inscription.

and Shirley Posnett gave me a farewell party. Before leaving the territory the garrison commander's staff, with whom I had worked closely, handed me a souvenir. It was a photocopy of a cartoon by Garland that had appeared in the *Daily Telegraph* when the current emergency situation first arose. It depicted a corked bottle lying horizontally towards the right with a tag around the neck bearing the words 'Souvenir of old England'. Inside the bottle was a small motor vessel with the words 'HMS *Gunboat*' painted on the side with a cannon protruding from the bow and the Union Jack flying from the stern. A gun is sited on top of the cabin and at deck level between the cabin and the flag stands the familiar figure of the then foreign and commonwealth secretary, James Callaghan, in a naval rating's uniform with a full kitbag over his left shoulder and a rifle at the 'at ease' position in his right hand. On the kitbag were the words 'London/Belize'. There was no caption but the message was clear: in response to the perceived Guatemalan threat to the colony, Britain, in the form of the foreign and commonwealth secretary, who had himself served in the Royal Navy during the Second World War, had sent the modern equivalent of the old fashioned gunboat in the form of 12 Harrier aircraft as a deterrent. It was a souvenir that I kept among my papers.

Some years later, when our elder daughter, Janet, was working as personal assistant to the former prime minister (now Lord Callaghan) he invited our whole family over for tea one Sunday afternoon at his home in nearby Ringmer. During our conversation I happened to mention the cartoon, which he remembered. It was, he said, essential to act decisively and quickly in such situations and that Belize in 1975 was a case in point. He went on to say *vis-à-vis* the 1980 Falklands War than when he faced an earlier perceived threat to the colony from Argentina in 1977, the situation was defused by the immediate dispatch of a frigate to reinforce the presence of HMS *Endurance* followed by a naval task force including a nuclear submarine. Contrasting this with the events of 1980, he went on to suggest that, although the perceived threat to the islands had not receded, the government had taken its eye off the ball and failed to make clear to the Argentineans its readiness to defend the colony with appropriate force until it was too late for the latter to pull back. He was particularly critical of the decision to withdraw HMS *Endurance*, which he believed encouraged the Argentine armed forces to conclude that they could embark on an invasion without a serious British military response.

I interpreted this as an implied criticism of the Thatcher government's handling of the situation leading up to the Falklands' War. In other words, if only it had taken early decisive action to signal to the Argentineans that any attempt to invade the islands would lead to serious reprisals, that conflict might have been averted by such 'preventative diplomacy'. This appears to have been confirmed in his memoirs[1] where he discusses the comparison and makes these points in greater detail. And, as for the reinforcement of the local garrison in British Honduras by the Harrier aircraft via Canada in 1975 to signal a warning to the Guatemalans, his contention that decisive and early action was a necessary deterrent is underlined by the following sequel.

On my next birthday Janet took the photocopy of the cartoon to Lord Callaghan and explained to him that she proposed to have it framed and given to me as a birthday present. She then went on to say that as I had spoken to him about it she wondered whether he would be prepared to sign it. This he did with the words, 'For Charles Godden. Remember the old motto "A stitch in time" ... Jim Callaghan.' This axiom was certainly observed in the context of Belize in 1975–76 then facing a perceived military threat from Guatemala. The significance of the reinforced British military presence was fully recognized and appreciated at the time locally.

The Garland cartoon hangs in the hallway of my home and is a constant reminder of the second of my revisits; and one that took place at an important and interesting time in the colony's progression towards full self-determination. It is also a reminder that, without the British military commitment to the defence of colonial people generally, and Belize in particular, the destinies of several of those territories might have taken a different course than that of the ultimate emergence of independent statehood. Sadly, this is seldom recognized by the critics of colonialism.

Chapter 28
Tikal

I N THE CONTEXT of empire, the history of British Honduras begins in the seventeenth century with the establishment of the logwood settlements. But there is a much earlier history. The earliest inhabitants of whom anything was known were the Maya, perhaps the most significant of the Meso-American Indian tribes who at one time dominated the region. But what is actually known about them? As I am ill qualified to answer this question from any original historical or archaeological research I can only present the following outline, gleaned from a wide variety of secondary sources, with special reference to Tikal (the greatest of all the Maya cities) and drawing the connection with British Honduras wherever relevant.

Early in the nineteenth century stories began to circulate in North America and Europe about ancient stone ruins of archaeological interest that were supposed to exist in the jungles of Central America. Descriptions uncovered in earlier Mexican literature appeared to confirm that some form of high culture had once existed in the region. Yet, in the West, this excited little public interest. The notion that primitive American Indians, generally thought of in those days as savages, could be responsible for creating a form of civilization as advanced as, say, Egypt or Greece, was generally pooh-poohed by so-called expert opinion of the day. None the less, sufficient interest was aroused to attract the attention of a few foreign adventurers and explorers who then visited the area to investigate these stories. What they were to uncover was to take everyone by surprise. Thus, just over 170 or so years ago, the outside world learnt for the first time of the existence of the mysterious Maya civilization. I use the word 'mysterious' because the question of what prompted the rise and fall of that civilization, even now after all this time, has only been partly answered.

Historians and anthropologists inform us that the people

categorized as Amerindians originated in central Asia and migrated to the American continent via the Baring Straits in a series of waves spread over thousands of years. In the drive southwards, several groups reached the waist of the continent that divides North America from the south (nowadays generally described as Central America geographically, but in 1823 coined as a political term to describe a republic intended to follow the Spanish withdrawal from the region comprising Mexico, Guatemala, Salvador, Honduras, Nicaragua and Costa Rica) so that, around 2000 BC, there existed in an area centred on the Yucatán Peninsula embracing parts of what became known as Mexico, Guatemala, British Honduras and northern Honduras, a group of tribes that generally followed a homogeneous culture and religion.

From this mosaic sprang one dominant tribe, the Maya. Whether they were late migrants or simply emerged from the pack as the dominant force is now largely academic. What is evident is that they were to create what might arguably be described as the greatest civilization of ancient America and, certainly, one to stand comparison with others elsewhere.

Among their achievements they plotted the movements of the sun, moon and planets; they also evolved a complicated but accurate calendar, glyptic writing and processional mathematics using the concept of zero possibly centuries before it appeared in the Old World. Their language was recorded in wood and stone carvings and is found today in monuments, on painted walls and in pottery. Some writings were also painted on *codices* made of deer hide or paper produced from the inner bark of fig trees, bleached, then covered by a thin layer of plaster and folded like an accordion. A few of these *codices*, books in effect, still exist although many were destroyed during the Spanish occupation on the grounds that their contents were heretical. Evidence suggests that the Maya were possibly the original producers of maize. They were skilled potters and weavers, worked gold and silver and in other ways too were expert craftsmen. They developed an elaborate and beautiful tradition of sculpture and built fabulous pyramid temples from immense quantities of quarried stone and, without recourse to iron or any other metal tools, covered them as already intimated with intricate carvings of hieroglyphic words (now largely deciphered) and art representations. They began to build ceremonial centres and by AD 200 these had developed into cities containing temples, pyramids and palaces. The political system was hierarchical and its elite, in a society of slaves, commoners, scribes, priests and aristocrats, wore cloaks of feathers and plumes adorned with jade jewellery. Torture and sacrifice were fundamental parts of their religious rituals, presumably to assure favourable harvests and otherwise demonstrate piety to the gods. At its peak, the Maya population is believed to have reached about two or three million, mostly settled in Guatemala.

This civilization flourished and its heyday appears to have been the period between AD 200 and 900, known to archaeologists as the classic period of Mayan culture. After that came its decline and fall. All records of civilizing activity ceased; buildings remained half finished and the once great cities were abandoned, soon to become overgrown by jungle and thus hidden from view for almost a thousand years. The cause of this decline is uncertain. Some scholars suggest it was due to the failure of agriculture to keep pace with an increasing population while others favour the theory that there was a revolt by the masses against the dominant priestly class. Other theories include external wars, pandemic disease or a devastating ecological disaster, such as a long and persistent drought leading to famine and a subsequent breakdown in the fabric of society resulting in a massive upheaval and widespread slaughter of the people. But at present, so far as I am aware, there is no conclusive evidence to support any one of these suggestions.

Whatever the cause, the people abandoned their major ceremonial centres to the ever waiting jungle. Some apparently migrated to northern Yucatán, where the civilization enjoyed a minor renaissance until the Spaniards invaded the country and finally destroyed it. Their descendants still live in the region in the same thatch-roofed clay-sided adobe huts their forebears once occupied and they are still following the same agricultural practices with the production of maize, beans and squash remaining prominent. But inevitably their culture is becoming more and more Westernized. Almost all are nominally Roman Catholic but their inherited pagan religion generally overlays their Christianity.

It is puzzling that while the Maya still people the region the intellectual driving force behind their advanced civilization seems to have evaporated without trace. What happened to the ruling group whose intellectual impetus provided the dominant ideology? Were they all eliminated leaving only the commoners and tribal memories? Or was it simply a case, to parody an old saying, of rags to riches and back again to rags over the span of three millennia? Answers on a postcard, please!

Systematic and recorded explorations of Maya sites are said to have begun in the 1830s. Prominent among the early explorers were the Anglo-American duo, John Lloyd Stephens and Frederick Catherwood, who between them found 44 archaeological sites in the Central American region between the years 1839 and 1843; they produced detailed and colourful accounts of their findings in what reviewers described as a well-written two-volume illustrated book called *Incidents of Travel in Central America, Chiapas and Yucatán*.[1] Oddly, they never visited Tikal, the greatest Mayan city of all because, apparently they had not heard it existed.

By chance I first became aware of their explorations shortly before I left Finland for British Honduras (now designated Belize) in 1975. I had received through my book club, Book Club Associates, a copy of *Search for the Maya*[2] by Victor von Hagen, which, among other things, tells the story of this duo. On Wednesday 3 October 1839 Stephens, an American lawyer, traveller and amateur archaeologist, embarked from New York on the British brig *Mary Ann* for the Bay of Honduras. His companion, Catherwood, was a British artist and architect. Although enthralled by their adventures and findings, I was intrigued to learn that their starting point in Central America in the last weeks of 1839 was British Honduras (at the time the most convenient postern for access to the newly formed republics of Central America) and fascinated by the remarkable picture it presented at that stage in its history – especially in respect of racial relationships.

The opening paragraphs of von Hagen's Chapter 8 appears to have been distilled from Stephens's description of the colony as recorded in the two-part volume relating to their travels mentioned above. From that we learn that the duo were enchanted by the vision the town presented as they were rowed ashore from the *Mary Ann* in a government dory fashioned from the trunk of a mahogany tree. Apparently, it conjured up memories of Venice and Alexandria, scenes of some of their earlier explorations. As Stephens described it:

> A range of white houses extended about a mile along the shore, terminated at one end by the Government House, and at the other by the barracks, and intersected by the river Balise (*sic*), the bridge across which formed a picturesque object, while the fort at a little island at the mouth of the river, the spire of a Gothic church[3] behind the Government House, and groves of coconut trees which at that distance reminded us of the palm trees of Egypt, gave it an appearance of actual beauty.

But so much for appearances, for the illusion faded on landing. Entering the town, the streets of which were flooded through heavy rain, they found accommodation and then went on a walkabout. Sinking to their boot tops in the muddy streets and painfully aware of the 'heavy odour of human sewage', Belize exhibited its true character; it was a shabby, tropical port with serious sanitation problems. Wandering around, they noted that the settlement, which the river intersected, contained most of its principal buildings on its western side. There were two avenues, Front and Back Streets, along which, scavenger hogs were taking mud baths in water-filled holes. All the houses were raised on stilts, airily balconied, carefully planted with tropical flowers, scarlet hibiscus and flaming crotons offsetting to some extent the depressing influence of the mud and stench of the port. At the extreme end of Front Street were Government House, the barracks, parade ground, church and rectory, school and cemetery. Behind this was an area of tall, toughly succulent savanna grass on which the town cattle browsed against a background of deep impenetrable jungle. This led Stephens to observe that 'With no land communication with the interior, Belize hung on the jagged littoral, a brief oasis in the chaos of disorder that was then Central America.'[4]

Of the settlement's 6000 population, listed in the then current

Honduras Almanac, 4000 were black, the preponderance of whom on
the streets, according to Stephens, gave the town the impression of a
Negro republic. He recorded:

> They were a fine looking race, tall, straight and athletic,
> with skins black, smooth and glossy as velvet, and well
> dressed, the men in white cotton shirts and trousers, with
> straw hats, and the women in white frocks with short
> sleeves and broad red borders; and I could not help
> remarking that the frock was their only article of dress, and
> that it was the fashion of these sable ladies to drop this
> considerably from the right shoulder, and to carry the skirt
> in the left hand, and raise it to any height necessary for
> crossing puddles.[5]

Coming from a country where women in those days, were tightly
corseted and swathed in petticoats, thus making the ankle the most
exciting feature, it is not surprising that his observations on the local
females should have been so detailed. That aside, it was the relationship between the different ethnic groups that was to intrigue him the
most.

Breakfast at a merchant's house found the explorers seated with
an assortment of people and colours – a white British officer in
brilliant red coat and 'neatly dressed mulattoes'. As for Stephens, he
was sandwiched between two 'coloured gentlemen'. He was to
observe and comment in this connection that 'Some of my
countrymen would perhaps have hesitated about taking it, but I did
not; both were well dressed, well educated and polite. They talked of
their mahogany works, of England, hunting, horses, ladies and
wine.'[6]

Over the meal Stephens was to learn that locally there was no
rigid demarcation between white and black as in the United States.
He was informed 'that the great work of practical amalgamation, the
subject of so much angry controversy at home [here it will be
remembered that he was writing in 1839] had been going on quietly
for generations, colour was considered a mere matter of taste'. Citing
a practical illustration of this unusually early liberal approach on the

subject, he noted that some of the most respectable inhabitants had black wives and 'mongrel' children, whom they educated with as much care, and made money for with as much zeal, as if their skins were perfectly white, adding 'I hardly knew whether to be shocked or amused at this condition of society.'[7] For the record it is perhaps interesting to note that on 31 August 1839, shortly before Stephens's arrival, the nominal yoke of slavery (although in this particular settlement slavery was by then only casually practised) was removed by the general act of abolition.

The outline of these early impressions was still discernable when my family and I first arrived in 1961. Of course, the motor launch had long since superseded the mahogany dugouts that once carried passengers from ship to shore; and no longer did scavenger hogs wallow in muddy streets, though many of the streets remained potholed. But houses, in general, continued to be built on stilts and the two main avenues still existed under the names of Regent and Albert Streets. But, of course, more significant changes had taken place. For example, the straits surrounding the little Fort George Island had been filled and its area incorporated in the capital, while the steeple that originally formed part of the cathedral had been removed for structural reasons. Also, the road programme introduced after the Second World War had opened up the hinterland and linked up with the road networks of Guatemala and Mexico. Alas, the stench from the human detritus deposited in the city's canals continued to offend the nostrils although, after a time, this was to become acceptable as part of the environment and thus bearable.

Above all, the racial tolerance that so impressed Stephens 120 years earlier still existed during my service in the colony. This is not to say that there were no cases of discrimination between the various ethnic groups that made up the population. In the Belize Club, for instance, there was a 'whites only' policy, though many of the locals who strongly supported it were of mixed blood. I suspect that this discrimination had more to do with class than colour. By 1962 even that policy had become an anachronism. But in my service there I found that most local people, whatever their ethnic origin or colour, treated each other as fellow citizens and coexisted in comparative harmony.

These impressions of Belize in the 1830s will no doubt be of particular interest to those who served there in the twentieth century. More importantly, they describe the place from which Stephens and Catherwood set out in search of the Maya. From this starting point they were to travel by sea to the Rio Dulce in Nicaragua, then into Lake Isabel to the Port of Isabel where they disembarked to take the mountain trail to Copan in Spanish Honduras and other Maya cities in the region.

Before departing Stephens, whom the United States government had accredited with diplomatic status on his travels, paid an official call on the settlement's superintendent, Colonel Macdonald, a professional soldier whose enterprising – if not always authorized – imperialistic excursions in the area I touched upon in Chapter 5. He received full honours and his status was formally acknowledged by a 13-gun salute as he left *en route* to the Rio Dulce on the wood-burning vessel *Vera Paz*.[8] But, it is with that echo of diplomatic niceties that I recognize I am now straying well away from the main subject, Tikal. Though I plead justification by way of background as well as interest in respect of the British Honduran connection, I should get back to the subject.

About 200 miles north of Guatemala City and about 40 miles west of Benque Viejo del Carmen on the British Honduras border lies the lake Peten Itza and the inland island city of Flores in the department of El Peten. It was here that the greatest of all the Maya cities, Tikal, was built. And it was to endure the longest. Its great stone temples, mounted on massive pyramid pedestals, some over 200 feet high, still rise out of the forest surrounded by time markers and the ruins of palaces.

The discovery of this long abandoned city goes back to the early nineteenth century, though its presence was undoubtedly known locally much earlier. In 1845 Medesto Mendez and Ambrosio Tut, respectively commissioner and governor of the department of El Peten, mounted an official Guatemalan expedition to the site and Mendez is reputed to have returned there four years later. The Swiss explorer Dr Gustav Bernoulli visited the site in 1877 and took away some carvings, which are still in the Basle museum. The first systematic exploration and recording, however, was begun by Alfred

Maudsley, a pioneering Englishman and one of the first to bring so many Maya ruins to the attention of science. He travelled to the site in 1881 and again the following year and made a map and plan of its major architectural features. His hired local workers cut trees and cleared jungle to reveal some of the temples and other features of archaeological interest. His accounts of these findings with accompanying photographs of temples and monuments were published in archaeological journals of the day where they attracted wide interest. A German, Teobert Maler, performed subsequent important investigations at the site under the auspices of Harvard University's Peabody Museum. Thereafter the pace of exploration, excavation, consolidation and preservation continued steadily into the twentieth century and will no doubt continue for many more years to come. Each year as this research continues new facts and new artefacts come to light to stimulate speculation and lead to further insights into Maya culture.

Tikal's main ruins are concentrated at the centre of the Tikal National Park, which embraces an area of about 220 square miles. A handbook in my possession produced by the Museum of the University of Pennsylvania, Philadelphia, reprinted in 1975,[9] poses the question: 'What actually is Tikal?' and then goes on to answer by listing in considerable detail the findings to that time. It explains that about six square miles of central Tikal had been mapped, revealing more than 3000 separate constructions – temples, palaces, shrines, ceremonial platforms, small to middling residences, ball courts, terraces, causeways, small and large plazas, even a structure built for some sauna type of bathing. Concentrated in and around the city's ceremonial precincts are more than 200 stone monuments in the form of sculptured and plain stelae and altars. These are vertically set shafts of stone and round, drum shaped stones, usually paired. Burials and ritually cached offerings have been found in their hundreds. As many as 10,000 earlier platforms and buildings lying sealed beneath the surface were mapped in 1957 and 1960. Excavations have revealed at least 1100 years of apparently ceaseless construction. Stone monuments erected at the site have been in place for 900 to 1000 years. More than 100,000 tools, ceremonial objects, personal ornaments and other items have been unearthed. A million odd potsherds, so important for establishing sequence and relative dating, have also been collected during the course of the excavation work.[10]

The handbook then goes on to make the valid point that such statistics only hint at the enormity and richness of Tikal when it is realized that only a small percentage of the site has actually been excavated. In short, it is rather like the proverbial iceberg: although its tip is showing, the bulk is invisible beneath what is seen on the surface. It will take many more years yet before a fuller picture emerges.

I only became aware of the relevance to the colony of the Mayan people through my involvement in the affairs of British Honduras while with the West Indian Department of the Colonial Office. All was revealed, as they say, when I read the chapter on archaeology in the then current annual report, *British Honduras 1958*.[11] Hitherto, I had been only vaguely aware that they were its original inhabitants and knew little of the extent of the Maya civilization. However, once in the colony I paid early visits to Xunantunich, Altun Ha and other local excavated sites. This increased my interest in the Maya, as indeed did the presence all around the country of literally hundreds of mounds, which I was reliably informed contained Maya ruins of one sort or another. Information gleaned from the archaeological commissioner Hamilton Anderson, my old explorer friend H. T. Grant and visiting archaeologists stimulated this interest further. It was they who advised me to find time if I could before leaving the region to visit the greatest of all the Mayan sites, Tikal, which was comparatively few miles into Guatemala across the western border.

Unfortunately, I found neither the time nor opportunity to act on this advice during my 1961–64 secondment. I contemplated a visit at the conclusion of my tour, but decided instead to visit Guatemala City, Antigua, Lake Aticlan and Huehuetenango with my family on a route through Guatemala, Mexico, the United States and Canada before joining the *Queen Mary* at New York for the voyage home. Of course, life is about choices, but I vowed that if the chance occurred again I would take it.

Would that opportunity arise during my short service in British Honduras (now Belize) in 1975–76? Initially the omens were far from ideal. Tension with Guatemala made it a bad time to apply for a visa to visit that country even if the governor was agreeable to my going. But gradually the perceived military threat receded and the prospect looked brighter.

Shortly before Ken Oldfield's date of return was confirmed, I mentioned my ambition to visit Tikal to Dick Posnett. I had always found him helpful and sympathetic on personal matters and so he was on this occasion. My plan, if he approved, was to take advantage of a weekend by leaving by road on a Saturday morning and returning late afternoon the next day, Sunday. The governor said that provided the Guatemalans were prepared to issue the necessary visa, he would raise no objection and that if Michael Holmes wished to accompany me (and he had so indicated) that was all right by him. He added for good measure that I could take the Government House Land Rover provided I arranged private insurance for the journey. The Guatemalan consulate issued the visas and I insured the Land Rover. And the following weekend we set off.

From Belmopan to the Guatemalan border is about 30 or so miles along a winding road, the Western Highway, which, like the proverbial curate's egg, was only good in parts. With few signs of human activity and familiar scenery of bush and forest, the main interest was avoiding bone shattering potholes. It was late morning when we crossed the Hawksworth Bridge into San Ignacio del Cayo (formerly El Cayo, as I had known it from my earlier days in the colony – El Cayo, meaning 'the Caye', was so named because the town in effect formed an island between two branches of the Belize River, the Macal and Mopan). Then we proceeded on to the border post at Benque Viejo del Carmen (formerly Benque Viejo) where, once the Belizean immigration authorities had cleared us, we went across the short neutral zone to the Guatemalan border post.

Not surprisingly, the questioning of what we intended to do in Guatemala and the time scale involved was quite searching, but we were allowed through. Just as we were leaving the border town of Melchor de Menchos five Guatemalan soldiers armed with rifles stepped out in the road in front of us and waved the vehicle down. Were we, I thought, now going to be involved in an embarrassing diplomatic incident? I was pleasantly surprised, therefore, when the sergeant in charge asked for a 'lift' to Flores, our primary destination close to Tikal. Without waiting for a reply, though I think I may have nodded assent in my relieved state, they were in the back of the Land Rover with a noisy clatter of boots and weapons on the metal chassis.

The more I thought about this incident the more I believed it was no coincidence. As we and our unexpected passengers drove along that potholed road to Flores, with the latter rolling around in the back of the vehicle like dice being shaken in a receptacle, it occurred to me that they were there to ensure that we were not on a spying trip. Although this may sound dramatic, the fact was that the Guatemalan army barracks at Poptun was not far away and obviously any sniffing around there would have been unwelcome, especially while the military on both sides of the border were at some state of alert. Against that I recognized that it was a Saturday and what could be more natural than for a group of squaddies to spend the evening sampling the delights, whatever they might be, of a larger town away from their barracks, but the cynical side of my mind prevailed and I opted for the conspiracy theory.

Just before entering Flores we were amazed to see on the verge at the right-hand side of the road a crashed light aircraft, nose downwards, balanced at an angle of about 45 degrees and surrounded by offerings of flowers. From subsequent enquiries we learnt that the aircraft had crashed some months earlier killing all its occupants and that it had been decided to leave it there as a memorial and a shrine.

In Flores we dropped off our 'escort', who seemed unaffected by their roller-coaster experience at the back of our vehicle, and looked for a café in which to have lunch. We found a pleasant establishment by the lake with a miniature aviary containing a number of exotic birds, which added interest to our meal. Lunch over, we arrived next at Tikal airstrip and then went on to seek out the adjacent 'Jungle Inn' where we hoped to find accommodation for the night.

The 'Jungle Inn' turned out to be quite basic. For a few US dollars we were accommodated in a large native style hut with a thatched roof and reed sides with a gap between the roof and sides that was open to the elements. If this was primitive, the so-called beds were even more so – just low wooden frames covered by thin mattresses with rough blankets and one pillow in a small pile on top. There were no other facilities in the hut other than an oil lamp we were to share with two others, members of a group of male students from Mexico. Washing and toilet facilities were outside in a separate hut and communal, but it was adequate for our purpose and our stay was only overnight: and it provided atmosphere.

After establishing ourselves in the hut, Michael and I went on a reconnaissance of the area while daylight held. We found the small museum where some of the material archaeologists had unearthed was on display and spent time examining it. We also purchased a handbook, which, among other things, listed the major attractions and a suggested sequence of how they might be visited. By the time we had found the route into the site, darkness was closing in and it was time to return to the 'Jungle Inn'.

The only meal available at the establishment that evening was a large plate of rice and beans, which if nothing else could be described as filling. That and a few beers concluded the local entertainment. As we proposed to make an early start for our sightseeing the next morning, we chose to have an early night. The hut was home to swarms of mosquitoes, but fortunately we had been warned of this likelihood and were well prepared with repellent and mosquito coils. Outside, after other guests at the inn had settled down for the night, the sounds of various animals in the surrounding forest could be heard in the distance – or was this my imagination? And so we drifted off to sleep.

Next morning we were awake early and after a hasty wash were ready to start. According to the handbook it would take about 20 minutes to reach the Great Plaza from the Jungle Inn via the Mendez Causeway. It was a misty morning and walking along the gentle upward gradient of the tree-lined causeway in its forest setting was an eerie experience. Then, about three-quarters of the way along we saw close by, soaring above the high trees, a tall narrow pyramid surmounted by a structure we took to be a temple. Shrouded in mist it looked awesome and impressive. It was possible to imagine the thrill and excitement the pioneer explorers would have experienced on catching a glimpse of this as they hacked their way through the jungle.

Reaching the plaza we were able to see it in the context of the other buildings spread out over a wide area in which stone monuments and fallen masonry were strewn, seemingly at random. Beautifully proportioned, it was a breathtaking sight. Although a visit to the pyramids and the sphinx at Giza during my Second World War military service in the Middle East had impressed me greatly, despite having the romantic illusion shattered by getting to the site by tram rather than camel, this was a more awe inspiring spectacle. The extent of the ruins, the sheer size of the pyramids (from about 150 to 200 feet above the various plazas) and the inscriptions and other art representations on the numerous monuments were clear testimony to a most remarkable civilization that had remained unknown to the outside world for so long.

We spent the morning visiting and photographing as many structures as we had time to see and examining the various inscriptions on lintels and stones. But by now, the sun was revealing its strength and it was becoming unpleasantly hot. We had seen much but it was clear that it was only a fraction of what was on offer. Only one personal ambition was left to be realized, to climb one of the four excavated main temple pyramids. Since I had clambered to the top of the King Cheops pyramid at Giza it was, to my way of thinking, only appropriate to follow suit on this occasion. And here the route to the top was by a stairway. It could not be easier. Or could it? One thing was certain. There would be no elderly and persistent Egyptian guide lurking around on top this time offering, in exchange for a few piastres, to show me the very spot from where in the 1920s HRH Edward, Prince of Wales, had allegedly driven a golf ball into what might be described as the massive sand bunker of the desert below. Or, to take loan of his penknife for a similar fee to carve my initials into the surrounding stone – neither offer, I hasten to add, being taken up.

The choice of climb was between temples 1 and 4, the latter slightly higher but otherwise similar. In the event we opted for the former, which is the one often prominently displayed on tourist posters or picture postcards.

However, the climb was less easy than I had envisaged. What in theory had seemed an advantage, that is to say the prospect of an ascent by staircase rather than a clamber over large stone cubes, proved less so in practice. The treads and risers were narrow and the angle of ascent steep – seemingly well short of 45 degrees on a climb of something in the region of about 150 feet. A rope handrail provided some comfort but, connected loosely as it was between iron stanchions driven into the side of the staircase, it failed to inspire confidence in its holding capacity. But the top was reached and we examined the temple there. Fortunately, there was no equivalent of the elderly Egyptian guide to distract us.

The view from the top was stunning. Looking down on the vast extent of the excavated structures and monuments gave one some idea of how ambitious the original concept had been and how incredible it was that such a vast project could have been accomplished by labour alone aided by what, in comparative terms, were primitive tools and technology.

Looking across from where we were standing, the tops of the temples rose from above a blanket of forest, and I had a distinct feeling of *déjà vu* that I could not place in spite of echoes of some past recollection. Not until I reread Victor von Hagen's *Search for the Maya* did the connection occur to me, for he refers to a conversation between Stephens and a Spanish priest in which the latter said that, in his younger days, he had climbed the highest peak of the Cordillera, 12,000 feet, and there as the clouds parted he could see the flat plains of Yucatán and the undulating blue of the Caribbean. Below him, he avowed, he had seen 'the white towers of a great city rising from the vivid green jungle, glittering white in the sun'. The author suggests in a footnote, with justification I venture to think, that 'he had probably seen the ruined tall towering temples of Tikal'.[12] It therefore occurred to me that the sight of the temple tops rising from the jungle on my visit to Tikal had subconsciously reminded me of the time I had flown around the Cockscomb range in a light aircraft and seen the eponymous peaks rising like the pyramid temples out of the forest ceiling. Certainly, with that image now in mind, I could now see why I felt that I had witnessed the scene before. But perhaps I was simply putting two and two together and coming up with five.

If the ascent caused a few palpitations the descent was even more nerve wracking. Stepping onto the first narrow step on a staircase that seemed to descend almost perpendicularly towards the ground,

16. Author at Tikal at the foot of a temple pyramid.

which appeared to be a frighteningly long way below, was not for the faint hearted. The first few tentative steps grasping the shaky rope handrail, and seemingly launching ourselves into space, confirmed that Michael and I were among those in such a category. But where there is a will there is a way. The practical solution was to come down slowly backwards facing the steps and without looking down. This we did – not elegant, but effective. I wondered how the Maya coped without even such a shaky handrail.

Returning to the 'Jungle Inn' and our vehicle, we set off on the return leg of the journey. After a quick lunch at Flores we were to give the springs of the Land Rover a further testing on what passed as the road to Melchor de Menchos and the border, this time without a military escort. It was late afternoon when we cleared the border posts on both the Guatemalan and Belizean sides and we were back at Belmopan on schedule before dusk, a day older but a little more enlightened about the Maya civilization, as well as stirred and impressed by all we had seen. And then I mused on how the present generations of Maya whom we dealt with locally in everyday matters would have reacted had they, too, seen what their forebears had built at Tikal. Would they have been equally awed and impressed as we were and, if so, would such a glimpse of their past have imbued them with a sense of pride?

My guess is that their preoccupation with everyday living, with all its hardships and difficulties in the region, would override any historical curiosity. But it is something over which I still occasionally brood. For my part, I subsequently looked at the Mayan people in a different light and with a new respect after my visit to the site. Talk about live and learn!

Chapter 29
Ya Da Fu We Belize
(This is Our Belize)

A T MIDNIGHT, in that split second between Sunday 20 and Monday 21 September 1981, the Union Jack was slowly lowered from the top of the flagpost on the lawn behind Government House and passed by the new Belizean flag travelling in the opposite direction, thus signifying the emergence of a newcomer into the family of independent nations, Belize, as it was once and is now again called. So, some 320 years after British buccaneers had used the coast for shelter and later settled at the mouth of the Belize River to cut and export logwood, and through various forms of administration by Britain, their descendants – and the descendants of slaves, later immigrants and indigenous Amerindians – were now charged with the responsibility for determining their own destiny within the usual constraints imposed by the wider global framework. This was to give great satisfaction to those in the country and in Britain who had worked hard to see that goal finally achieved.

Among the essays written 100 years earlier in 1881 by the Scottish master storyteller, Robert Louis Stevenson, and subsequently published in a slim volume under the title *Virginibus Puerisque*,[1] is one headed 'El Dorado', the concluding words of which have echoed down over the years and still reverberate today: 'to travel hopefully is a better thing than to arrive, and the true success is to labour.'[2]

The general point he was making was that a sense of personal achievement hinges on how we begin rather than how we end and what we want rather than what we have, the emphasis falling on the journey and not the destination. In other words, it is the aspiration coupled with the effort involved and not necessarily the achievement that provides the dynamic of human existence. By way of illustration he cites the examples of Alexander the Great, who wept bitterly when he realized he had no more worlds to subdue, and Gibbon, who when he had finished writing *The History of the Decline and Fall of the Roman Empire* had only a few moments of joy before being overtaken by 'a sober and melancholy feeling' at being parted from his labours.[3] Stevenson also recognized that we live in a world in which one thing leads to another in an endless series so that, on reaching a particular goal, new challenges and aspirations will inevitably arise to set up the next.

A different interpretation of Stevenson's words is that, very often, the expectancy of what one hopes to find on arrival at one's destination might easily end in disillusionment. Expectancy and reality are seldom natural bedfellows. Carrying this line of thought into the colonial theatre, many local politicians on the road to independence found the journey more hopeful than the reality of arrival when they were required to assume the reins of government and grapple with the inevitable problems with no one to blame but themselves when things went wrong, as they inevitably do. This is not to suggest, however, that the status quo was an option in an age of decolonization. Here I must emphasize that, in the British Honduras case, because of the international complications arising from the Guatemalan territorial claim, the road to independence was longer than that traversed by most other British colonies at the same stage of political development, as amplified in the five succeeding paragraphs. Yet its people travelled always in hope and were sustained by it. Now having arrived at their destination, independence, one prays that the journey was thought worthwhile while recognizing that new aspirations and challenges will provide new travels as their future unfolds.

When I arrived in the colony in 1961 the changes negotiated at the London conference the previous year had just been introduced. The main feature was a full ministerial system with a majority of elected members on the Executive Council at the expense of the hitherto nominated ones and a reduced number of *ex officio* members. With the new governor Sir Peter Stallard providing the impetus later that year, the pace of further constitutional advance quickened. In July 1963 a further constitutional conference was held in London that resulted in the colony being granted full internal self-government: in other words, as from January 1964 local politicians would be virtually running their own show. In practice, this was to add Cabinet responsibility to their ministerial functions, with the governor's responsibilities limited to external affairs, defence, internal security and some financial control. For the uninitiated in colonial affairs, this in effect was the final constitutional stage before independence. Indeed, local expectations at the time were that independence would be achieved shortly thereafter and bring in its wake large-scale investment from the United States and trade opportunities and development aid from Central America, where it was assumed in government circles that the country's future lay. But the reality was different. It soon became apparent to the People's United Party (PUP) led by George Price that the country's relationships with both the United States and Central America were not developing in the progressive manner anticipated.

On the economic front, optimism about the scale and nature of potential United States investment proved to be unjustified. Disenchantment also set in when closer economic ties with Central America failed to develop significantly. Progress on the external political front was equally disappointing. The new constitutional situation was to give rise to a challenge to local aspirations in this connection by Guatemala, which voiced yet again its claim to the territory. This was to result in a political log jam, difficult to free, despite patience and increased diplomatic activity, including an attempt in 1968 by a United States mediator, Bethuel Webster, to resolve the dispute by drawing up a draft treaty, which in the event the British Honduras (also referred to as Belize at that time but not formally until 1973) government found totally unacceptable. By this time their prevailing economic and political orientation was moving away from Central America and back towards the Commonwealth and Commonwealth Caribbean in particular.

Anglo–Guatemalan negotiations, which subsequently expanded into tripartite talks by including local ministers, failed to make significant progress. At these talks (which I occasionally attended when Lord Shepherd led Foreign and Commonwealth Office teams) the Guatemalan negotiating tactic was to demand a large area of the southern part of the country as a *quid pro quo* for dropping its claim, a price that predictably the Belizean representatives were not prepared to pay. However, as time went on, the latter's case began to attract wide international support. In 1975, for example, the first United Nations resolution on the subject was passed with 110 in favour and 9 against. Although this was satisfactory, it showed up a serious weakness. No Spanish-speaking Latin American country had voted in favour, including the colony's Central American neighbours with economic and historic ties with Guatemala. It was shortly thereafter, following sabre rattling on the border by the Guatemalan army, that the perceived military threat arose.

Undeterred by this setback, diplomatic activity, which included intensive lobbying on the part of the Belizeans in their quest for further converts, continued to good effect and, by November 1980, international support for an independent Belize was almost unanimous. A UN resolution called for independence without strings attached and with security by the end of 1981. This time the United States, which had previously abstained on all the Belize resolutions since 1975, voted in favour with no country voting against. Significantly, the last bastion to fall was when the Organization of American States (OAS), which had traditionally sided with Guatemala in the controversy, endorsed by an overwhelming majority the UN resolution.

Notwithstanding this welcome change of events, especially the solid mounting support, attempts were still made to carry the Guatemalans along with the spirit if not the letter of the unanimously agreed UN resolution. But far from showing a favourable response to these efforts to find a peaceful negotiated settlement in everyone's interest, they still insisted on land concessions as the price for dropping their claim. So could an independent Belize face a secure future with an avowed predatory nation on its border? Against this background a decision was taken with the consent of the British government and the blessing of the international community, for the country to proceed to independence as proposed and thereafter to develop friendly relations with the government and people of Guatemala. To ensure that such a tender new plant, the newly emerged country of Belize, would survive and develop firm roots, the British government agreed to continue to defend the country and to station troops there for this purpose with the consent of the Belizean government. And so, with the long road to independence having been traversed, always with hope, and the destination virtually reached, all that remained was to name the date. This was settled as 21 September.

When I left the territory after my short stint in 1976 I had only a rough idea of many of the subsequent events recorded above. But serving as I did in both Jamaica and Anguilla in the Leeward Islands I was able to learn a little through the Caribbean grapevine as well as the odd snippet or two from Foreign and Commonwealth Office sources, the British press and the overseas service of the BBC. Little did I imagine, however, that I would have the good fortune to attend the Belize independence celebrations: I say 'good fortune' because, having been part of the colonial administration that brought in the penultimate constitution changes leading to independence, it would naturally be rewarding to be present when that objective was actually achieved. So how did it come about?

On 17 August 1981 Ronald Webster, the chief minister of Anguilla, received a telegram from the Belizean premier (shortly to be restyled prime minister), George Price, inviting him and one other to attend the independence celebrations. This was followed by a confirmatory letter that went on to say that, if prior commitments prevented this, perhaps the chief minister would be good enough to nominate a personal representative to lead the island's delegation, which, because of restraints on accommodation in Belize at that time, would have to be limited to two.

On receipt of these communications, Ronald Webster came to me to suggest that I should represent the island. He had only just returned from an overseas visit and felt that there would be some local criticism if he went off again so soon. In the hothouse climate of a small West Indian island this was a valid point. But, as we enjoyed good personal relations, I suspect that because of his awareness of my past service and continuing interest in Belize he assumed that I would like to attend. Notwithstanding this personal consideration I said that, as chief minister, he was the most appropriate representative at an independence celebration and that he should attend. He countered by maintaining that as Her Majesty's commissioner for the island I would be an acceptable alternative. In that event, he added, I could perhaps take with me his last appointed ministerial colleague, Osborne Fleming, to give him some experience in the world of foreign affairs. As he would not budge from this line I agreed to put the proposal to the Foreign and Commonwealth Office suggesting that as I was well known to the premier of Belize it was unlikely that there would be any objection from that quarter. This received official concurrence on the usual understanding that none of the cost would fall on Her Majesty's government. Accordingly, a telegram was sent off to the Belize independence secretariat confirming that Osborne and I would be arriving on Thursday 17 September on Flight TA311 from Miami.

I now take up the story from notes I made at the time and amplified shortly afterwards out of interest.

17 September

Arrived at Miami shortly after noon; airport crowded; heavy Spanish atmosphere with that language more noticeable than English. How times have changed since I was first here twenty or so years ago. Found we were only waitlisted on TAN flight leaving at 15.30. This gave rise to anxiety as this was the last flight to Belize today and no hope of getting away tomorrow as all flights fully booked; much special pleading on our part. In the event we were accommodated. The flight was a bit tense for there was considerable air turbulence and, to my mind at least, the engines sounded strained. Soon the cayes, Airport Camp and the Belize River came into sight (so familiar) and shortly afterwards we landed at what is now designated Belize International Airport. To my surprise we were asked to alight before the other passengers.

Coming down the steps of the aircraft, an old friend Louis Sylvestre, now minister of communications and works, welcomed me; when he directed me to the ranks of the newly formed Belize army drawn up nearby I then realized that a guard of honour had been provided. So, with the other passengers on our flight no doubt wondering who I was, I took the salute and inspected the guard – a smart and professional body consisting, so it seemed to me, of members of most of the diverse ethnic groups that make up the Belizean nation.

I was deeply moved by this unexpected reception and honour, though the courtesy was undoubtedly accorded to other heads of governments or delegations. As they say in Jamaica, 'water come to de eye'. With that over, I noticed another old friend, Rudy Castillo, who later was to become 'Sir Rudy' during a subsequent distinguished diplomatic career at ambassadorial level. After greeting each other and exchanging news it was into the airport building where Osborne and I were briefed on the programme ahead of us.

We were told that we were to be accommodated in a newly built house at Belmopan, the country's new capital, where a cook would come in each morning to provide breakfast and a maid to tidy up. We were also allocated a driver, who was to be with us during our stay, and introduced to a charming young lady we learnt was our liaison officer (must check with the dictionary to see if 'liaison' means what I think it does). To be serious, these liaison officers were senior girls from local schools, allocated to each delegation, whose task was to ensure that drivers got us to the various functions on time and to iron out any local difficulties that might arise. Ours was Michelle Longsworth, who immediately conveyed to me her father's regards: we had been colleagues in the administration during my 1961–64 secondment. She is intelligent, conscientious and as bright as a button and, from what I have seen already, a typical example of the new generation of Belizeans.

Leaving the airport, we passed garrison headquarters and an obvious military presence and were soon on the road to Belize City with mangrove swamp and the Caribbean Sea to the left and the Belize River on the right. The section of road near Haulover Bridge evoked memories of the night John Hall, returning from a darts evening in the sergeants' mess at Airport Camp, drove into an unlit steamroller parked on the road. Not only did he smash his hip but he gave the driver, who was asleep on top, a nasty shock. Between miles one and two there is frantic activity as PWD workers try to complete the building of a group of houses to be used initially to accommodate some of the delegations arriving tomorrow. Here we stopped for a brief inspection of the site. Thereafter, a word with Michelle, and she arranged for the driver to give us a circular tour of Belize City before setting off for Belmopan – a trip down memory lane.

17. Ya Da Fu We Belize ('This is our Belize'). Michelle, with Osborne in attendance, make the point.

The journey took us past Pallotti Convent, Donald Fairweather's house (he is still going strong, I hear: must call on him and his wife before I leave), clock tower, the swing bridge and into the one-way system that branches into Regent Street where we passed the market, Scots Kirk, Courthouse Wharf, Bliss Institute, the supreme court, the old secretariat and Government House (now restored to its former glory for it is to be the residence of the incoming governor-general, Mrs Minita Gordon), Wesley School and St John's Cathedral. Swinging round the cathedral into Albert Street we passed the main shopping centre and stores (for example Brodie's, Quan's and Estafan's), Barclays Bank and then back over the swing bridge. With the post office and Paslow Building on our left and the fire station on our right we then proceeded along North Front Street, Marketing Board, customs sheds, former Volunteer Guard headquarters (now Price Barracks), Baron Bliss tomb, Holden Memorial Hospital, Memorial Park (where schoolchildren were seen rehearsing for celebrations) the chief justice's house, Belize Hospital, Lover's Point, Belize Club, which now embraces members of the old Pickwick Club, Newtown Barracks, Princess Margaret Drive and then back to our starting point.

Michelle explained that there was now no need to cross the swing bridge and go out via Yarborough cemetery to reach the Western Highway. The new bridge over the Belize River, near the Pallotti Convent offered not only an alternative but also a quicker route. This was the one we took. Once on the highway we passed Gracie Rock, Hattieville, Churchyard, Never Delay (these village names sound like those given to racehorses) and so on until we reached Roaring Creek and the turnoff to Hummingbird Highway. A short distance along the latter brought us to Belmopan where we were soon installed in our quarters for the short duration of our visit. Michelle told us that there had been a buzz of excitement there earlier in the day when the prime minister designate, George Price, personally led a group of schoolchildren in a civic drive to rid the streets of any litter to ensure that visitors to the celebrations would not form a superficially unfavourable impression of the new capital. This was so typical of George Price with his attention to detail and pride in his country. We had dinner that night (rice, beans and meat balls) at the 'Bull Frog', a small but extremely pleasant restaurant not too far away from the house; so we went to bed after a long and tiring day.

18 September

We were awakened early by the arrival of the cook and maid who prepared breakfast and thereafter tidied up. Osborne and I decided to reconnoitre the area on foot as our vehicle and driver were at that time in Belize City. First we went to the shopping centre, which had expanded considerably since I was here last. There was a considerable Mennonite presence. I bumped into the former chief justice, Sir Clifford de Lisle Innis, who was shopping for food. What a charming and dignified old man he is, although now looking his years. We undertook to meet socially if an opportunity arose.

Passing the government buildings I saw George Price speaking on the telephone in his office on the upper floor. He spotted me and waved me into the building. He came out to greet me warmly and Osborne and I joined him in his room, passing several of his constituents waiting to see him as we did so. Although he has aged a little since I last saw him (no doubt he would have made the same observation about me) he had lost none of his energy and vigour. In

18. Author on top of Gracie Rock.

19. Independence programme for visiting delegations begins. Michelle
Longsworth and Osborne Fleming at the Bull Frog restaurant, Belmopan.

conversation it was evident he was still the dynamic and dedicated
politician he had been since I first met him in the 1950s.

When we harped back to the 1960s he surprised me by recalling
I had trodden on a nail in the immediate post-Hattie period but
that this did not prevent me 'humping rice sacks at the Marketing
Board'. I should not have been surprised, for his attention to detail
was remarkable and he was always appreciative of anyone whom
he believed to be a friend of his country. He spoke highly of Sir
Peter Stallard with great warmth describing him as the governor
and architect of independence and was good enough to say a few
kind words about me, adding that he was pleased that I was able to
attend the independence celebrations. He then touched upon the
future of Belize in optimistic tones although he was not unaware
that a difficult road still lay ahead. Altogether we spent over half
an hour with him at a time when he was obviously very busy
considering the heavy programme with which he was involved. It
was a tribute to his usual unfailing courtesy and ability to make
visitors feel at home, as it were.

Back at the house Alan Jenkins (police adviser) called to invite me and Osborne for drinks and a meal with Mr and Mrs Eric King. Eric was chief agricultural officer during my early service in the colony and he and his family had decided to settle there after his contract expired. The other guests were Dick Posnett (now Sir Richard) governor of Bermuda, who was governor of Belize when I arrived in 1975, and Sir Clifford de Lisle Innis. There was much talking and reminiscing and it was an agreeable and enjoyable get-together – another trip down memory lane!

I had left a note in the house for Michelle saying we had gone to the Kings and would be back before 7.30 p.m. in time for our next engagement. She arrived shortly after our return to remind us that we were expected at the community centre for a buffet supper to meet some other delegates who had arrived that day and some of the local citizens. The centre is a large, modern building that looked more spacious than it is because it was far from crowded. I saw some familiar faces (Fuller's, Espat's and Rosaldo's) and exchanged pleas-antries and news. We also met other delegates. Records provided background music until a family atmosphere was generated when Mrs Lopez, whom I had known only as a shop owner in Belize City in the early 1960s, began playing the piano. She played beautifully and this encouraged some singing and then dancing. Having been on soft drinks only all evening my participation was restrained, but when it came to tripping the light fantastic, Osborne danced for Anguilla in typical West Indian style. A suggestion by the latter that we might look for unspecified night-life in San Ignacio del Cayo fortunately came to nothing because of lack of available transport.

19 September

Today is the first in the official programme of events to mark the celebrations. Four excursions have been arranged for the visiting delegations – a tour of the Maya ruins at Xunantunich, a visit to Ambergris Caye, a Belize River cruise or a visit to a livestock exhibition. The first mentioned was the nearest to Belmopan and I was happy to be included in that party.

En route we passed through countryside that was once very familiar and which now evoked many memories. Roaring Creek, the forestry road leading to Mountain Pine Ridge, Begonia Bank, the

Hawksworth Bridge, San Ignacio del Cayo (formerly El Cayo) and Succotz. At Succotz, we crossed the green waters of the Mopan River by the hand-operated ferry where, on landing, vehicles were waiting to take us the short distance to the site of the ruins.

A free translation of the name, Xunantunich, is 'Stone Lady'. Possibly the lady referred in question was similar to one of the female priest rulers depicted on some of the site's monuments. Many years ago, according to local legend, a villager hunting in the area was startled to see, as he was passing one of the ruined temples, a vision of a Mayan maiden who stood gazing fixedly to the west. Fleeing in panic at the sight of this ghostly apparition he rushed back to his village where he spilled out his story to priests who returned with him to the scene. But no trace of the 'lady' was seen then or later. Obviously, the story appealed to the superstitious Maya for it was to become incorporated into their folklore. Accordingly, from that day to this, the site became generally known as Xunantunich although it has also been called Mt Maloney and Benque Viejo.

It would appear that originally Xunantunich was a ceremonial centre made up of three adjoining plazas, several temples and ball courts among other structures including altars and carved stelae. By contrast with, say, Tikal, it is small beer, but it should be recognized that most of the site remains to be excavated.

The first published account of a visit to the ruins was that of Thomas Gann, a British doctor who lived and journeyed extensively in the colony. In the late nineteenth century, travelling by river, the only direct way of reaching the interior of the country at that time, he came to the site and subsequently published his findings in 1894–95. He returned again in 1924 and, after excavations in which beautiful jade ear ornaments were found, he carried back to England with him an altar carving that he donated to the British Museum. Further excavations by amateur archaeologists followed including many undertaken by locally appointed archaeological commissioners. The site has also attracted the interest of numerous archaeologists of international renown, but until more financial resources can be found for fuller excavations at the site, its full significance to Maya history will not be known. Some of the foregoing information, provided by our guides, was previously unknown to me.

As I gazed at the various structures, particularly the carved symbols on the stucco decorated frieze that once graced part of the lower temple and the diverse carvings of rulers in ornate headdress and jaguar head masks on monuments, I could not help but wonder yet again at the rise and fall of the Maya civilization. And as I took in the view from the highest mound across the sea of trees to the Guatemalan border town of Melchor de Menchos to the west and back to San Ignacio del Cayo to the east, I also tried to imagine Dr Gann's emotions on his first sight of these overgrown ruins in their jungle setting – perhaps a tinge of awe mixed with excitement. So there was much to talk about when we returned to Succotz and sat down to a lunch prepared and cooked by the descendants of those who built and worshipped at Xunantunich.

Back to Belmopan and, after a short rest, we set off again to Belize City where at 6.00 p.m. we were to attend a 'cultural night' at the Bliss Institute. This turned out to be a programme of music, dancing and poetry reflecting the various ethnic strains that make up Belizean society. It was not as highbrow as some might imagine, but it was in fact good entertainment.

After the programme ended there was still an hour or so before the next engagement, a barbeque at Price Barracks, so I wandered around the streets taking in the atmosphere. Traditionally, Saturday night is shopping night so stores and shops were open and streets crowded. I looked into Brodie's store and then crossed the swing bridge into Queens Street and Geggs store. There was a tourist shop opposite the police headquarters where I bought some black coral bracelets. Then North Front Street, Price Barracks, barbeque and back to Belmopan – a tiring day but one full of interest.

20 September

At 9.00 a.m., together with other delegates, I attended a service of dedication and thanksgiving at the Ecumenical Centre, Belmopan, to mark the imminent independence of Belize. There were familiar hymns. It was gratifying to hear, among the prayers of Thanksgiving and Intercession 'Today also we give thanks for Her Majesty Queen Elizabeth, and the government of the United Kingdom that has aided and assisted our Belizean people and has prepared us to achieve the glory and the responsibility of our Nationhood.' Also, there was a well deserved tribute to the prime minister. 'We pray for our Prime Minister, the Honourable George Price, who has carried the burden of public office, and now brings us to our nationhood: may the Lord continue to bless him, and give him wisdom and strength.' To these prayers I added my own heartfelt Amen.

At 1.00 p.m. we attended a government-hosted official lunch, buffet style, at the SJC gymnasium. The afternoon was spent resting prior to the functions we were to attend in Belize City that night.

It is 10.00 p.m. Just like old times – state reception at Government House but hosted, not by the governor but by the prime minister. To combat possible gate-crashers Royal Navy ratings examined our invitation cards at the gate before we could gain admission. There was much animated conversation and barely concealed excitement as the minutes ticked away towards midnight. The flag-raising ceremony was due to begin at 11.45 p.m. at the rear of Government House between the house and the sea. Meanwhile, a fireworks display attracted attention. Shortly afterwards there was a heavy downfall of rain that precipitated a stampede into the large marquee at the east of the house where drinks were being served. Thereafter the scene was reminiscent of a crowded London underground train in the rush hour. Pressed tightly together, and with the sides of the marquee bulging, we listened unenthusiastically to those who opined that the rain was a good omen for the country's future while we waited for it to stop hoping and praying that it would do so before the ceremony was due to begin. Despite the discomfort of little body and air space I was able to strike up a conversation with Barry Bowen whose father, Eric, I knew from my earlier days in the country and whose family lineage had been traced back to the eighteenth century. The latter was then the owner of the soft drinks factory that had the franchise for Coca Cola. The business had since expanded with Barry now at the helm to include a brewery at which the local beer, 'Belican', was brewed and bottled. This I found interesting because I had suspected for some time that the son had inherited the father's entrepreneurial skills.

Fortunately, just before the scheduled time for the flag raising ceremony, the rain stopped and we were able to join the crowd assembling around the flagpole with a searchlight fixed on the Union Jack at its top. The back door to Government House then opened and out stepped HRH Prince Michael of Kent and HRH Princess Michael who were representing Her Majesty the Queen; the Prime Minister as he was now titled, George Price; the Governor, Sir James Hennesey and Lady Hennesey; Nicholas and Mrs Ridley representing Her Majesty's Government and a few others comprising the Royal Party.

The sequence of events that now followed became somewhat blurred in the ensuing feelings of emotion. The band and a trumpeter struck up several chords and tunes, including a well known snatch from Sibelius's 'Finlandia' to which I attached some superstitiously psychic emphasis (having gone from that country to the colony in 1975) and, at the appropriate stage, the national anthems of the departing and inheriting countries. Then at midnight, the Union Jack was slowly lowered and the Belizean flag (blue with a white centre depicting the country's coat of arms and a red horizontal edge bordering the top and bottom) was raised. This gave rise to a spontaneous round of applause. A salute of 21 guns from the British frigate in the harbour was heard and more fireworks were set off.

Standing next to me as the Union Jack was lowered and Belizean flag raised was Colonel Donald Fairweather whom I had known as commandant of the local Volunteer Guard and now very much a senior citizen. He was a Belizean patriot, a descendant of one of the early settlers, and proud of the British connection. Tears were streaming down his face as he wept openly and copiously. Was it because of his pride that his country had finally achieved independence or because the British were leaving after three centuries or so? Caught up in the swirl of emotion I, too, felt a few tears glisten at being present at the birth of a nation and witnessing my own country's graceful withdrawal and the style in which it was done. Both tear stained we shook hands and he asked me to call on him and his wife before returning to Anguilla.

In my time I had been present at several independence celebrations but, because of past personal connections and memories, none was as moving as this. And so I set off on the forty or so mile journey back to Belmopan in the early hours of the morning with plenty to occupy my thoughts *en route*.

21 September
Independence Day and a morning of ceremony and pageantry: I
arrived by car outside the National Assembly buildings just before
10.30 a.m. Michelle was waiting and handed the relevant invitation
card to an officer of the Belize Defence Force who then escorted me
to a seat on the special pavilion platform reserved for HRH Princess
Michael of Kent and heads of governments or states. My past
connection with the country must have been recognized for Osborne
was allowed to join me. While waiting for the ceremonies to begin I
murmured in a loud aside, 'please turn round your Royal Highness
so that I can get a picture of you.' To my surprise she did so and that
photograph is now in my collection.

At 10.40 a.m. the Prime Minister arrived and was escorted to the
ceremonial platform to the accompaniment of a fanfare played by the
band. This was followed by the Belizean national anthem and a
march on of troops on parade. At 10.58 a.m. the Speaker of the
House of Representatives and President of the Senate met His Royal
Highness Prince Michael of Kent and escorted him to the platform.
Thereafter there was a royal salute, followed by the playing of God
Save the Queen and prayers.

The Speaker then invited HRH to present the constitutional
instruments, which he did after delivering a message from Her
Majesty the Queen. These the Prime Minister accepted. There
followed a presentation from the British government by Nicholas
Ridley, minister of state at the Foreign and Commonwealth Office.
The Speaker then called upon the Chief Justice to administer the
Oath of Allegiance to the Governor-General Designate, Dr Gordon.

That having been done, she proceeded, together with HRH and
the Prime Minister, to the site of the proposed independence
memorial where the foundation stone was laid. The party returned to
the platform in time to witness a fly-past by the Royal Air Force. The
Belizean national anthem was then played and, after a royal salute,
the royal party departed. All this took about fifty minutes. The
troops then marched off parade to the accompaniment of familiar
British martial music, which, as a resident of east Sussex, I was
pleased to note included 'Sussex by the Sea' – shades of agreeable
summer Sunday afternoons on the promenade at Eastbourne with

20. HRH Princess Michael of Kent smiles for the camera while waiting for the independence celebrations to begin.

Florence listening to the music of military bands and a sharp contrast with the Central American setting of Belmopan.

The main celebrations over, we attended a state luncheon at the civic centre, hosted by the newly installed governor-general. There were a few short speeches and the inevitable toasts. The cuisine was Belizean insofar as the produce was local, with lobster and home reared beef featuring on the menu. There was one further function to attend to wind up the celebrations. This was a festival of peace and cooperation held at Independence Hill, Belmopan, between the hours of 3.00 and 6.00 p.m. The programme indicated that there were to be 'speeches and entertainment'. My only clear recollection of this event was that just before dark, as I was leaving the area, I witnessed a swirling and gyrating mass of people swaying rhythmically to the emphasized beat of one of the popular tunes of the day, 'Ire Tempo', performed by the Trinidadian calypsonian, Lord Laro. It was colourful, graceful, lively and harmonious, a happy omen for the future.

22 September
Awake early and packed ready and at about 7.00 a.m. received a

message that we were booked on a chartered aircraft leaving around
9.00 a.m. and that, if we missed it, we might not get away today. So
we were soon speeding along the Western Highway towards Belize
City. Although time was extremely short, I was determined to pay
my respects to Colonel and Mrs Fairweather before leaving. It was
indeed a brief meeting but it was achieved. Now at the airport, we
said goodbye to Michelle after thanking her for the considerable help
and guidance she had delivered with such charming courtesy and
efficiency. Louis Sylvestre was there to see us off and then we were
on board the aircraft and *en route* to Miami within minutes, or so it
seemed. The onward flight brought us in to Queen Wilhemena
Airport, St Maarten after dark, too late for a flight to Anguilla that
night. So we spent a night in a hotel and were back home early the
following morning.

✿ ✿ ✿

The foregoing is a record of the Belize independence celebrations as
seen through the eyes of an expatriate. But it should be recognized
that this is only one snapshot in time and from a particular
perspective. Others, especially Belizeans, will undoubtedly have
recorded their own accounts with different accents of emphasis.

As I explain in other references in earlier pages (and here at the
risk of being branded tedious I recite them again to present a
coherent picture) my own interest in the independence of Belize was
because, not least, it was the culmination of my association with the
country that began in the mid to late 1950s when the drive towards
political self determination began to gather pace. I was at that time
serving in the section of the West Indian Department of the Colonial
Office that dealt, among other subjects and territories, with its
affairs. As such I was one of the secretaries to the British Honduras
constitutional conference in 1960 at which the advance to a
ministerial form of government was agreed. The following year I was
seconded to the colony where I served with the chief secretary on
the governor's staff for three years. It was during that time that the
way was paved for a further constitutional change to be introduced.
At the constitutional conference held in London in 1963, full

internal self-government was granted to take effect from 1 January 1964. The Guatemalan territorial complication held up the final step, independence; and it was during that period, back at the Foreign and Commonwealth Office, that I again visited Belize and was involved as a minor player in some of the talks with the various parties. And, at the end of 1975 until early 1976, I was back in the colony on a short assignment. So to be present when independence was finally achieved was, as I say, the culmination of my association with the territory and its people. And for this I give my thanks to luck or destiny, whichever was responsible. But I am bound to say that I was truly sorry that those colonial service officers under whom I served during my secondment, notably Sir Peter Stallard and Michael Porcher, were unable for various reasons to be present when the final curtain of the colonial play, as it were, came down. They both played a significant part in the move towards independence and were otherwise good friends of Belize.

Now as I come to recall the event after all these years, which memories remain most vivid? First, is my pleasure at being present at such a significant occasion and meeting so many 'old' Belizean colleagues and friends. Second, the intensely emotionally charged moment when the Union Jack was lowered and the Belizean flag raised as a new national symbol. Third, and last but not least, the recollection of how moved I was when, at the service of dedication and thanksgiving on 20 September, mentioned above, a prayer of thanks was offered to 'Her Majesty Queen Elizabeth, and the government of the United Kingdom that has aided and assisted our Belizean people and has prepared us to receive this glory and the responsibility of our nationhood.'

A generous recognition, indeed, and an echo of Sir Gawain Bell's words about the rich tapestry of empire, following its various stages, recorded in the Prologue above. In interpreting these words I concluded that in Belize, at least, the colonial trespassers in the form of the old British administrating power had now been forgiven.

Notes

Prologue
1 Transferred from the Foreign and India Offices in 1921.
2 Angus Wilson, *The Strange Ride of Rudyard Kipling: His Life and Works* (London: Granada, 1979) p. 23.
3 Ibid., pp 23–5.
4 Ibid., p. 274.
5 Ibid., pp. 273, 274.
6 Edward Grierson, *The Imperial Dream: British Commonwealth and Empire 1775–1969* (London: Collins, 1972) p. 126.
7 Sir Gawain Bell, *An Imperial Twilight* (London: Lester Crook, 1989).
8 Sir Charles Jeffries, *Whitehall and the Colonial Service: An Administrative Memoir, 1939–1956* (London: The Athlone Press, 1972).
9 Sir Roy Porter, *Enlightenment: Britain and the Creation of the Modern World* (London: Penguin, 2000) p. 239.
10 Sir John Alder Burdon (ed.) *Archives of British Honduras* (London: Sifton Praed, 1931–35), vol. 1, p. 106 signatories to Admiral Burnaby's code of laws. See also n. 9 above.
11 Burdon, *Archives of British Honduras*, Introduction, pp xii–xv.

Chapter 1: En Route
1 Pat Reading.
2 L. W. Cowie, *Eighteenth Century Europe* (London: G. Bell & Sons, 1966) p. 74.
3 Joseph Sturge and Thomas Harvey, *The West Indies in 1837* (reprinted New York: Augustus M. Kelley, 1969) p. 152.
4 Anthony Trollope, *The West Indies and the Spanish Main* (reprinted London: Dawsons, Pall Mall, 1968) p. 205.
5 Charles Kingsley, *Westward Ho!* (London: Macmillan, 1888) p. 320.
6 Richard Hughes, *A High Wind in Jamaica* (London: Grafton Books, 1976).
7 Lady Maria Nugent, *Lady Nugent's Journal* (Kingston: Institute of Jamaica, 1966) edited by Philip Knight.

Chapter 3: Baron Bliss
1 More commonly known as Haulover Creek.

Chapter 5: The Mosquito Shore and Other Imperial Links
1 Sir John Alder Burdon (ed.) *Archives of British Honduras* (London: Sifton Praed, 1931–35) vol. 1, p. 48 cites 'Long Papers Book 1, Chapter 12.'

2 Keith Feiling, *A History of England* (London: Macmillan, 1966) pp. 592, 611.

3 Ibid., p. 611. Further background is provided by Stephen L. Caiger, *British Honduras Past and Present* (London: Allen & Unwin, 1959) p. 232. His research suggests that while Admiral Benbow was commander-in-chief of the West Indies station during 1697–98, he sailed to Cartagena and was able to prevent the Spanish fleet assembled there from its projected attack on Darien. But he subsequently received orders from the admiralty not to get involved in further assistance.

4 John Kenneth Galbraith, *The Age of Uncertainty* (London: BBC Publications, 1977) p. 176.

5 Burdon, *Archives of British Honduras*, vol. 1, p. 64.

6 Ibid., pp. 53 and 64.

7 Cowie, *Eighteenth Century Europe*, p. 74. Also, Feiling, *A History of England*, p. 635.

8 Burdon, *Archives of British Honduras*, vol. 1, p. 64.

9 J. H. Parry, *Trade and Dominion* (London: Cardinal, 1974) p. 150.

10 The word 'jingoism' was not coined until the late nineteenth century, but, in this context, it depicts the self-interest lurking behind the highly emotional banner of patriotism.

11 Fred Anderson, *Crucible of War* (London: Faber & Faber, 2000) pp. 485–8.

12 Burdon, *Archives of British Honduras*, vol. 2, opposite title page.

13 Caiger, *British Honturis Past and Present*, p. 110.

14 Ibid., pp. 27–8.

15 *The South American Handbook*, 1963, p. 634.

16 Nugent, *Lady Nugent's Journal*, p. 279.

17 Burdon, *Archives of British Honduras*, vol. 2, p. 282.

18 W. S. Gilbert, *The Babs Ballads* (London: Macmillan, 1919) p. 86.

19 Galbraith, *Age of Uncertainty*, p. 178.

20 Feiling, *History of England*, p. 651.

21 Galbraith, *Age of Uncertainty*, p. 178.

22 Burdon, *Archives of British Honduras*, vol. 2, p. 275.

23 Ibid., p. 274.

24 Ibid., p. 282.

25 Ibid., p. 276.

26 Ibid., p. 276.

27 Ibid., p. 276.

28 Ibid., p. 281.

29 Ibid., p. 282.

30 Ibid., p. 286.

31 Carl N. Degler, *Out of our Past* (New York: Harper & Row, 1984) p. 496. See also, Jasper Ridley, *Lord Palmerston* (London: Panther, 1972) p. 359.

32 R. A. Humphreys, *The Diplomatic History of British Honduras, 1638–1901* (Oxford: Oxford University Press, 1961) p. 36.

33 Ibid., p. 36.

34 Ibid., p. 36.

35 Ridley, *Lord Palmerston*, pp. 615–17. Patrick Walker should not be con-

fused with his namesake William Walker, the American filibuster active in Nicaragua around that time who, in 1856, with the help of American privateers, seized Greytown – thus straining relations between Britain and the United States.

36   Humphreys, *Diplomatic History*, p. 37.
37   Ibid., p. 37.
38   *South American Handbook 1963*, p. 735.
39   Trollope, *West Indies and the Spanish Main*, pp 324–44.
40   Humphreys, *Diplomatic History*, p. 37.
41   Victor von Hagen, *Search for the Maya* (London: Book Club Associates, 1973) p. 349.
42   Humphreys, *Diplomatic History*, p. 38.
43   Ibid., p. 39.
44   Bradford Perkins, *The Great Rapprochment* (London: Victor Gollancz, 1969) p. 178.
45   *South American Handbook 1963*, p. 735.
46   Perkins, *The Great Rapprochment*, pp. 178–85.
47   *South American Handbook 1963*, p. 735.
48   This is a credible theory. Coincidentally, the small French territory in the Pacific, Wallis Islands, was named after Captain Samuel Wallis of HMS *Dolphin* who discovered the group in 1767.

Chapter 7: 1931 Hurricane
1   A. H. Anderson, *A Brief Sketch of British Honduras* (Belize: Belize Printing Department, reprinted 1954) pp. 33–4. Inevitably, the worldwide economic depression of the late 1920s and early 1930s badly affected the British Honduran economy. Hardest hit were the hundreds of labourers normally employed in the forestry industry. As work dried up, they poured into the capital hoping for alternative employment, which was seldom available. Driven by poverty they were living in over-crowded small shacks or condemned housing and were thus particularly exposed to the impact of the hurricane.
2   Ibid., p. 3.
3   Aldous Huxley, *Beyond the Mexique Bay* (reprinted London: Triad Paladin Books, 1984) p. 18.

Chapter 9: Eighteenth- and Nineteenth-century Characters
1   Burdon, *Archives of British Honduras*, vol. 1, pp. 124–5.
2   Ibid., p. 142.
3   Ibid., p. 156.
4   Ibid., p. 411.
5   Ibid., p. 157.
6   Ibid., p. 157.
7   Ibid., p. 158.
8   Ibid., p. 158.

9 Ibid., p. 162–3.
10 Ibid., Introduction, p. 22.
11 Ibid., p. 158.
12 Ibid., p. 168–9.
13 Ibid.
14 Ibid.
15 Ibid., p. 173.
16 Ibid., p. 174.
17 Ibid., p. 177.
18 Ibid., p. 178.
19 Ibid., p. 193.
20 Ibid.
21 Ibid., p. 179.
22 Ibid., p. 195.
23 Feiling, *A History of England*, p. 756.
24 Tom Pocock, *The Terror before Trafalgar* (London: John Morris, 2003) pp. 75–7.
25 M Jay, *The Unfortunate Colonel Despard* (London: Bantam Press, 2004) pp. 301–2.
26 Ibid., p. 302.
27 Ibid., p. 302.
28 Burdon, *Archives of British Honduras*, vol. 1, p. 35.
29 Peter Ashdown, 'Race, Class and the Unofficial Majority in British Honduras, 1890–1949', updated Ph.D. thesis, University of Sussex, 1979, p. 71.
30 This story is covered, among others, by Ashdown, 'Race, Class and the Unofficial Majority', pp. 53–72; Caiger, *British Honduras Past and Present*; Wayne M. Clegern, *British Honduras: Colonial Dead End, 1859–1900* (Baton Rouge: Louisiana State University Press, 1967); and Byron Foster, *The Baymen's Legacy* (Belize: Cubola Productions, 1987) pp. 45–7.
31 *Colonial Guardian*, 1 March 1890, cited by Ashdown, 'Race, Class and the Unofficial Majority', p. 54.
32 Clegern, *British Honduras*, p. 80.
33 Ibid., p. 77. Also *Colonial Guardian*, 1 October 1890, cited by Ashdown, 'Race, Class and the Unofficial Majority', p. 72.
34 CO123/195 (28 February 1890) cited by Ashdown, 'Race, Class and the Unofficial Majority', p. 56.
35 Ibid., p. 57.
36 Ibid., p. 58.
37 Ibid., p. 65.
38 Ibid., p. 64.
39 Ibid., p. 65.
40 Ibid., p. 64. However, according to C. H. Grant, *The Making of Modern Belize: Politics, Society, and British Colonialism in Central America* (Cambridge: Cambridge University Press, 1976) p. 56, the colony did not have direct access to the judicial court of the Privy Council until 1911;

prior to that the Jamaican Supreme Court was the recognized appellate court.

41 Ibid., p. 66.

42 FO 15/22 cited by Humphreys, *The Diplomatic History of British Honduras*, p. 95.

43 FO 15/242 cited by Humphreys, *The Diplomatic History of British Honduras*, p. 96.

44 A. R. Gregg, *British Honduras* (London: Her Majesty's Stationery Office, 1968) p. 121. Despard was the youngest of seven brothers (six surviving) of whom the eldest inherited the family estate in Mountrath, Ireland. All the others enlisted in the army: two, one attaining the rank of general and the other of major, served with distinction in the American War of Independence. The Goldsworthy family would appear to have held an influential position in society in Victorian times. According to *Who was Who 1897–1915*, a Major General Walter Tuckfield Goldsworthy, CB (1837–1909) served in India during the Mutiny and also was a member of the Abyssinian Expedition. He was subsequently elected MP. His father, Tuckfield Goldsworthy, appears to have been prominent in Calcutta. It seems reasonable to conclude from this that Sir Roger Tuckfield Goldsworthy was in some way related.

Chapter 12: Hurricane Hattie (1)

1 *Obeah* was strictly prohibited in the Belize settlement under a regulation introduced on 11 October 1791.

Chapter 16: Incursion

1 Sir Arthur Bryant, *Triumph in the West* (London: The Reprint Society, 1966) p. 356.

Chapter 20: Mennonites

1 Report of the British Guiana and British Honduras Settlement Commission (London: HMSO, 1948) Cmd 7533.

2 Jack Downie, *An Economic Policy for British Honduras* (Belize City: Government Printer, 1959)

3 Grant, *The Making of Modern Belize*, p. 50.

4 D. A. G. Waddell, *British Honduras: A Historical and Contemporary Survey* (London: Oxford University Press, 1961) p. 18.

Chapter 23: The Cockscombs

1 Hubert Jerningham, *Report of the Expedition to the Unexplored Cockscomb Mountains in British Honduras* (Belize: Government Printer, 1888, Goldsworthy report).

2 Ibid., p. 2.

3 Ibid.

4 Ibid.

5   Ibid., p. 6.
6   Ibid., p. 13.
7   Ibid., p. 14.
8   Ibid.
9   Ibid., p. 26.
10 Ibid., pp. 26–7.
11 Ibid., p. 27.
12 Ibid.
13 Ibid., p. 14.
14 Ibid., p. 12.
15 R. J. Bellamy, 'Expedition to the Cockscomb Mountains, British Honduras', *Proceedings Royal Geographical Society* (London, 1889) vol. xi.
16 Ibid., p. 550.
17 Herbert T. Grant, 'The Cockscombs Revisited', *Geographical Journal* (London, December 1927).
18 Ibid., p. 567.
19 Ibid., p. 569.
20 J. N. Oliphant and D. Stevenson, 'An Expedition to the Cockscomb Mountains, British Honduras in March 1928', *Geographical, Journal* (London, 1928).
21 Ibid., p. 125.
22 Ibid., p. 130.
23 Ibid., p. 135.
24 Ibid.
25 Ibid., p. 136.
26 Herbert T. Grant, 'A Second Cockscomb Expedition in 1928', *Geographical Journal* (London, 1928).
27 Ibid., pp. 140–2.
28 Ibid., p. 144.
29 Jerningham, *Goldsworthy Expedition*, p. 28.

Chapter 26: I, Too, Have Nothing to Say

1   Dr George Eaton, *Alexander Bustamente and Modern Jamaica* (Kingston: Kingston Publishers, 1975). Many stories of Bustamente, a larger than life character, abounded during the colonial period, and thereafter. But the definitive story of his life was written by Dr Eaton, a distinguished Jamaican professor of economics and political science (among other public service roles) in the book cited above. I have drawn on this source as appropriate to provide accuracy on some of the detail of Bustamante's life outlined in this chapter.
2   Burton Benedict, *Problems of Smaller Territories* (London: Athlone Press, 1967) Chpters 4 and 5.
3   Waddell, *British Honduras*.
4   Ibid., Chapter 5, 'Case Study: British Honduras', pp. 61–4.

Chapter 27: BH Revisited

1 Lord (James) Callaghan, *Time and Chance* (London: Collins, 1987) pp. 37–77.

Chapter 28: Tikal

1 John L. Stephens, *Incidents of Travel in Central America, Chiapas and Yucatán*, vol 1 (reprinted New York: Harper & Brothers, 1969).
2 von Hagen, *Search for the Maya*.
3 The 'little fort' was clearly Fort George and the Gothic spire (removed in 1862 for structural reasons) relates to St John's Cathedral.
4 Stephens, cited by Foster, *The Baymen's Legacy*, pp. 32–4.
5 Ibid.
6 Ibid.
7 Ibid.
8 von Hagen, *Search for the Maya*, p. 122.
9 William R. Coe, *Tikal* (Philadelphia: University of Pennsylvania Museum, 1975) 7th edn.
10 Ibid., p. 21.
11 *British Honduras 1958* (London: HMSO, 1960) Annual Report, Part 2, Chapter 14.
12 von Hagen, *Search for the Maya*, p. 175.

Chapter 29: Ya Da Fu We Belize (This is Our Belize)

1 Robert Louis Stevenson, *Virginibus Puerisque and Other Papers* (London: Chatto & Windus, 1903) pp. 117–20.
2 Ibid., p. 120.
3 Ibid., p. 118. A modern version of this sentiment is provided by the radio and TV political commentator, John Sergeant, in his autobiography *Give Me Ten Seconds* (London: Pan Books, 2001) p. 201. 'When you have contributed to a news programme the satisfaction is immediate, but after nine months of work on these programmes, watching them at home with Mary didn't give me much of a thrill.'

Bibliography

Anderson, A. H., *Brief Sketch of British Honduras,* Belize: Belize Printing Department, reprinted 1954

Anderson, Fred, *Crucible of War,* London: Faber & Faber, 2000

Ashdown, Peter, 'Race, Class and the Unofficial Majority in British Honduras, 1890–1949', unpublished Ph.D. thesis, University of Sussex, 1979

Bell, Sir Gawain, *An Imperial Twilight,* London: Lester Crook, 1989

Bellamy, R. J., 'Expedition to the Cockscomb Mountains, British Honduras', *Proceedings, Royal Geographical Society,* London: 1889

Benedict, Burton, *Problems of Smaller Territories,* London: Athlone Press, 1967

British Honduras 1958, London: HMSO, 1960

Brogan, H., *Longman History of the United States of America,* Longman, 1985

Bryant, Sir Arthur, *Triumph in the West,* London: The Reprint Society, 1960

Burdon, Sir John Alder (ed.) *Archives of British Honduras,* 3 vols, London: Sifton Praed, 1931–35.

Caiger, Stephen L, *British Honduras Past and Present,* London: Allen & Unwin 1959

Callaghan, (James) Lord, *Time and Chance,* London: Collins, 1987

Clegern, Wayne M., *British Honduras: Colonial Dead End, 1859–1900,* Baton Rouge: Louisiana State University Press, 1967

Coe, William R, *Tikal,* Philadelphia: University of Pennsylvania Museum, 1975 (7th edn)

Cole, T., *Nelson,* London: Bloomsbury, 2002

Cowie, L. W., *Eighteenth Century Europe,* London: G. Bell & Sons, 1966

Cross, Colin, *The Fall of the British Empire 1918–68,* London: Paladin, 1968

Degler, Carl N., *Out of our Past,* third edition, New York: Harper & Row, 1984

Downie, Jack, *An Economic Policy for British Honduras,* Belize City: Government Printer, 1959

Eaton, George E, *Alexander Bustamente and Modern Jamaica,* Kingston Publishers, 1975

Encyclopaedia Britannica

Feiling, Keith, *A History of England,* London: Macmillan, 1966

Fisher, H. A. L., *A History of Europe,* London: Edward Arnold, 1936

Foster, Byron, *The Baymen's Legacy,* Belize: Cubola Productions, 1987

Galbraith, John Kenneth, *The Age of Uncertainty,* London: BBC Publications, 1977

Gilbert, W. S., *The Babs Ballads,* London: Macmillan, 1919

Grant, C. H., *The Making of Modern Belize: Politics, Society, and British Colonialism in Central America,* Cambridge: Cambridge University Press, 1976

Grant, Herbert T., 'The Cockscombs Revisited', *Geographical Journal,* London, December 1927

Grant, Herbert T. 'A Second Cockscombs Expedition in 1928', *Geographical Journal*, London, 1928

Gregg, A. R., *British Honduras*, London: Her Majesty's Stationery Office, 1968

Grierson, Edward, *The Imperial Dream: British Commonwealth and Empire 1775–1969*, London: Collins 1972

Hughes, Richard, *A High Wind in Jamaica*, London: Grafton Books, 1976

Humphreys, R. A., *The Diplomatic History of British Honduras, 1638–1901*, Oxford: Oxford University Press, 1961

Huxley, Aldous, *Beyond The Mexique Bay*, London: Triad Paladin Books, 1984

Jay, Mike, *The Unfortunate Colonel Despard*, London: Bantam Press, 2004

Jeffries, Sir Charles, *Whitehall and the Colonial Service: An Administrative Memoir, 1939–1956*, London: The Athlone Press, 1972

Jerningham, Hubert, *Report of the Expedition to the Unexplored Cockscomb Mountains in British Honduras*, Belize: Government Printer, 1888 (Goldsworthy report)

Kingsley, Charles, *Westward Ho!* London: Macmillan, reprinted 1888

Nugent, Lady Maria, *Lady Nugent's Journal*, edited by Philip Knight, Kingston: Institute of Jamaica, 1966

Oliphant, J. N. and Duncan Stevenson, 'An Expedition to the Cockscomb Mountains, British Honduras in March 1928', *Royal Geographical Journal*, London, 1928

Parry, J. H., *Trade and Dominion*, London: Cardinal, 1974

Perkins, Bradford, *The Great Rapprochment*, London: Victor Gollancz, 1969

Pocock, Tom, *The Terror before Trafalgar*, London: John Morris, 2003

Porter, Sir Roy, *Enlightenment: Britain and the Creation of the Modern World*, London: Penguin, 2000

Report of the British Guiana and British Honduras Settlement Commission, Cmd 7533, 1948

Report of the British Honduras Land use Survey Team, London: HMSO, 1959

Ridley, Jasper, *Lord Palmerston*, London: Panther, 1972

Sergeant, John, *Give Me Ten Seconds*, London: Pan Books, 2001

Stephens, John L., *Incidents of Travel in Central America, Chiapas and Yucatán*, reprinted New York: Harper & Brothers, 1969

Stevenson, Robert Louis, *Virginibus Puerisque and Other Papers*, London: Chatto & Windus, 1903

Sturge, Joseph and Thomas Harvey, *The West Indies in 1837*, reprinted New York: Augustus M. Kelley, 1969

The South American Handbook, 1963, 39th annual edition

Trollope, Anthony, *The West Indies and the Spanish Main*, London 1859, reprinted London: Dawsons, Pall Mall, 1968

von Hagen, Victor, *Search for the Maya*, London: Book Club Associates, 1973

Waddell, D. A. G., *British Honduras: A Historical and Contemporary Survey*, London: Oxford University Press, 1961

Warner, Oliver, *A Portrait of Lord Nelson*, London: The Reprint Society, 1958

Wilson, Angus, *The Strange Ride of Rudyard Kipling: His Life and Works*, London: Grenada, 1979

Index